Turns in the Road

Turns in the Road

Narrative Studies of Lives in Transition

Edited by
Dan P. McAdams,
Ruthellen Josselson,
and Amia Lieblich

American Psychological Association
Washington, DC

First Printing, May 2001
Second Printing, April 2002
Third Printing, December 2005

Published by
American Psychological Association
750 First Street, NE
Washington, DC 20002
www.apa.org

To order
APA Order Department
P.O. Box 92984
Washington, DC 20090-2984
Tel: (800) 374-2721,
    Direct: (202) 336-5510
Fax: (202) 336-5502,
    TDD/TTY: (202) 336-6123
Online: www.apa.org/books/
Email: order@apa.org

In the U.K., Europe, Africa, and the
    Middle East, copies may be ordered from
American Psychological Association
3 Henrietta Street
Covent Garden, London
WC2E 8LU England

Typeset in Goudy by World Composition Services, Inc., Sterling, VA

Printer: Edwards Brothers, Inc., Ann Arbor, MI
Cover designer: Naylor Design, Washington, DC
Production Editor: Catherine Hudson
Project Manager/Editor: Debbie Hardin, New Page Publishing, Charlottesville, VA

The opinions and statements published are the responsibility of the authors, and such opinions and statements do not necessarily represent the policies of the American Psychological Association.

Library of Congress Cataloging-in-Publication Data
Turns in the road : narrative studies of lives in transition / edited by Dan P. McAdams, Ruthellen Josselson, Amia Lieblich.—1st ed.
    p.cm.
    Includes bibliographical references and index.
    ISBN 1-55798-773-4
    1. Life change events—Psychological aspects. 2. Change (Psychology) 3. Narration Rhetoric) 4. Autobiography.   I. McAdams, Dan P.   II. Josselson, Ruthellen.
    III. Lieblich, Amia, 1939–

BF637.L53 T87 2001
155.2'4—dc21

2001022342

British Library Cataloguing-in-Publication Data
A CIP record is available from the British Library.

Printed in the United States of America

CONTENTS

ACKNOWLEDGMENTS

The editors would like to thank the many people who reviewed manuscripts and provided substantive input for this volume. In particular, we offer our thanks to James Anderson, David Bearison, Ed de St. Aubin, Harold Grotevant, Ravenna Helson, Barton Hirsch, John Kotre, Morton Lieberman, Elliot Mishler, Richard Ochberg, Haim Omer, Catherine Kohler Riessman, Tod Sloan, John Shotter, Mark Tappan, George Vaillant, and Ann Finkbeiner for their hard work in reviewing manuscripts. We also extend a special thanks to Chris Rector, who served as our editorial assistant for this first volume. Finally, we wish to thank Jeanne M. Foley and the Foley Family Foundation for their generous support of our book series and for establishing the Foley Center for the Study of Lives at Northwestern University.

THE NARRATIVE STUDY OF LIVES ADVISORY BOARD

Gil Herdt, Anthropology, *San Francisco State University*
Hubert Hermans, Psychology, *University of Nijmegen, The Netherlands*
James E. Marcia, Psychology, *Simon Fraser University*
Jean Baker Miller, Psychoanalysis, *Stone Center, Wellesley College*
Elliot Mishler, Psychiatry, *Cambridge Hospital*
Richard L. Ochberg, Boston, MA
June H. Price, Nursing, *Farleigh Dickinson University*
Gabriele Rosenthal, Sociology, *Gesamthochschule Kassel, Germany*
George C. Rosenwald, Psychology, *University of Michigan*
William McKinley Runyan, School of Social Service, *University of California at Berkeley*
Abigail J. Stewart, Psychology and Women's Studies, *University of Michigan*
George E. Vaillant, Psychiatry, *Dartmouth Medical Center*
Guy Widdershoven, Philosophy, *University of Limburg, The Netherlands*

CONTRIBUTORS

Mary Louise Arnold, Ontario Institute for Studies in Education,
   University of Toronto, Canada
Philip J. Bowman, Institute for Research on Race and Public Policy,
   University of Illinois, Chicago
Michele L. Crossley, University Dental Hospital of Manchester,
   University of Manchester, UK
William Comeau, University of Massachusetts at Boston
Janet Landman, Babson College, Wellesley, MA
Varpu Löyttyniemi, School of Public Health, University of Tampere,
   Finland
Kathleen Mackey, Wilfrid Laurier University, Waterloo, Ontario,
   Canada
Dan P. McAdams, Northwestern University, Evanston, IL
Kathi Miner-Rubino, University of Michigan, Ann Arbor
Richard L. Ochberg, Boston, MA
Marcy Plunkett, Center for the Education of Women, University of
   Michigan, Ann Arbor
Michael W. Pratt, Wilfrid Laurier University, Waterloo, Ontario,
   Canada
J. Scott Roberts, VA Boston Healthcare System and Harvard Medical
   School, Boston
George C. Rosenwald, University of Michigan, Ann Arbor
William Todd Schultz, Pacific University, Forest Grove, OR
Jefferson A. Singer, Connecticut College, New London
Abigail J. Stewart, University of Michigan, Ann Arbor
Amy M. Young, University of Michigan, Ann Arbor

THE NARRATIVE STUDY OF LIVES: INTRODUCTION TO THE SERIES

DAN P. McADAMS, RUTHELLEN JOSSELSON, AND AMIA LIEBLICH,
SERIES EDITORS

This book is the first in a series showcasing research and scholarship using a "narrative study of lives." Each volume in the series will examine how psychologists, sociologists, anthropologists, historians, and other scholars examine and conceptualize human lives in narrative terms. The term *narrative* suggests matters that are both epistemological and conceptual. Under the wide umbrella of narrative epistemologies, we include case studies, autobiographical approaches, psychobiography, life histories, content analysis of life narrative accounts, discourse analysis, ethnographies, and other related approaches and traditions of study that emphasize qualitative over quantitative research, hermeneutic over logical–positivistic frames, idiographic over nomothetic points of view, and inductive over hypothetico–deductive strategies of inquiry. Narrative inquiry rests on the assumption of the storied nature of human experience, a standpoint that has been receiving increasing attention within psychology and related fields.

Even before the recent proliferation of theories, research programs, and psychological applications centered on stories, scripts, myths, autobiographical recollections, and the like, Theodore Sarbin (1986) suggested that the concept of narrative provides a new "root metaphor" for the field of psychology as a whole. Psychologists of many different persuasions have turned their attention toward what Sarbin first called "the storied nature of human conduct" (e.g., Birren, Kenyon, Ruth, Schroots, & Svennson, 1996; McAdams, 1999; McCabe & Peterson, 1991; Schank & Abelson, 1995). Included within this trend are the many different approaches to "narrative therapy" that have sprung up over the past decade (e.g., White & Epston, 1990). According to Jerome Bruner (1986, 1990), narrative modes of knowing privilege the particulars of lived experience rather than constructs about variables and classes. Meaning is not inherent in an act or experience but is constructed through social discourse. Meaning is generated by the linkages the participant makes between aspects of the life he or she is living and his or her understandings of these aspects. The role of the researcher is then to connect this understanding with some form of conceptual interpretation, which is meaning constructed at another level of analysis.

Although narrative approaches and concepts have come to have a significant influence in the field of psychology, it is clear to us that the narrative study of lives requires an interdisciplinary forum. Outside of psychology, many scholars have remarked on a turn toward narrative in the social sciences and the humanities (Gergen, 1992; Holstein & Gubrium, 2000). For example, life-history research methods are enjoying a renaissance in sociology (Denzin & Lincoln, 1994) and in research in education (Casey, 1996). Many historians now view historiography as, in part, the construction of convincing narratives about the past in light of current cultural concerns. Narrative theology has become an extremely influential movement in many Protestant and Catholic seminaries (Hauerwas & Jones, 1989), and in moral philosophy, MacIntyre (1981) has argued that human virtue has its essential meaning within the narrative quest that defines an individual life. In an applied vein, religious and moral educators underscore the importance of storytelling in the socialization of virtue and the enhancement of moral development (Coles, 1989; Vitz, 1990). Scholars of many persuasions speak of contemporary social life in the postindustrial West as akin to a storied text to be interpreted as if it were a literary product, as they debate a wide variety of hermeneutical problems pertaining to authorship, power, and identity in the construction of social texts (Shotter & Gergen, 1989; Widdershoven, 1993). Josselson and Lieblich (1993) wrote that the narrative study of lives is a wide-ranging and loosely coordinated interdisciplinary effort to write, interpret, and disseminate people's life stories, with special attention paid to the accounts of women, people of color, and representatives of other groups whose lives and whose stories have historically been squelched, marginalized, or ignored (Franz & Stewart, 1994; Heilbrun, 1988; Rosenwald & Ochberg, 1992). Furthermore, the upsurge of scholarly interest in narrative inside and outside of psychology is truly an international endeavor, with some of the most sophisticated and advanced thinking and research coming from Europe and other centers of scholarship outside of North America.

The purpose of the book series that we are launching with this volume is to publish the best work being done today on the narrative study of lives. We wish to provide a forum for first-class research and theorizing on narrative studies, life histories, psychobiography, and other qualitative approaches to psychological inquiry and to draw on a wide range of disciplines and an international authorship. We believe that such a forum is a great need today. Although many scholars are engaged in narrative research, very few publication outlets for the narrative study of lives currently exist.

Each volume in the series will be organized around a theme. To date, plans for three volumes have already been laid. The second volume in the series will focus on "Teaching and Learning Narrative Methods in Psychological and Social Research." The third volume will take up the broad topic of "Narrative and Psychotherapy." We look forward to more.

REFERENCES

Birren, J., Kenyon, G., Ruth, J. E., Shroots, J. J. F., & Svennson, J. (Eds.). (1996). *Aging and biography: Explorations in adult development.* New York: Springer.

Bruner, J. (1986). *Actual minds, possible worlds.* Cambridge, MA: Harvard University Press.

Bruner, J. (1990). *Acts of mind.* Cambridge, MA: Harvard University Press.

Casey, K. (1996). The new narrative research in education. In M. W. Apple (Ed.), *Review of research in education* (Vol. 21, pp. 211–253). Washington, DC: American Educational Research Association.

Coles, R. (1989). *The call of stories.* Boston: Houghton-Mifflin.

Denzin, N. K., & Lincoln, Y. S. (Eds.). (1994). *Handbook of qualitative research.* Thousand Oaks, CA: Sage.

Franz, C., & Stewart, A. J. (Eds.). (1994). *Women creating lives: Identities, resilience, and resistance.* Boulder, CO: Westview.

Gergen, K. J. (1992). *The saturated self: Dilemmas of identity in contemporary life.* New York: Basic Books.

Hauerwas, S., & Jones, G. (Eds.). (1989). *Why narrative? Readings in narrative theology.* Grand Rapids, MI: Eerdmans.

Heilbrun, C. G. (1988). *Writing a woman's life.* New York: Norton.

Holstein, J. A., & Gubrium, J. F. (2000). *The self we live by: Narrative identity in a postmodern world.* New York: Oxford University Press.

Josselson, R., & Lieblich, A. (Eds.). (1993). *The narrative study of lives* (Vol. 1). Thousand Oaks, CA: Sage.

MacIntyre, A. (1981). *After virtue.* Notre Dame, IN: University of Notre Dame Press.

McAdams, D. P. (1999). Personal narratives and the life story. In L. Pervin & O. John (Eds.), *Handbook of personality theory and research* (2nd ed., pp. 478–500). New York: Guilford Press.

McCabe, A., & Peterson, C. (Eds.). (1991). *Developing narrative structure.* Hillsdale, NJ: Erlbaum.

Rosenwald, G. C., & Ochberg, R. L. (Eds.). (1992). *Storied lives: The cultural politics of self-understanding.* New Haven, CT: Yale University Press.

Schank, R. C., & Abelson, R. P. (1995). Knowledge and memory: The real story. In R. S. Wyer, Jr. (Ed.), *Advances in social cognition* (Vol. 8, pp. 1–86). Hillsdale, NJ: Erlbaum.

Shotter, J., & Gergen, K. J. (Eds.). (1989). *Texts of identity*. London: Sage.

Vitz, P. C. (1990). The use of stories in moral development: New psychological reasons for an old educational method. *American Psychologist, 45,* 709–720.

White, M., & Epston, D. (1990). *Narrative means to therapeutic ends*. New York: Norton.

Widdershoven, G. A. M. (1993). The story of life: Hermeneutic perspectives on the relationship between narrative and life history. In R. Josselson & A. Lieblich (Eds.), *The narrative study of lives* (Vol. 1, pp. 1–20). Newbury Park, CA: Sage.

TURNS IN THE ROAD:
INTRODUCTION TO THE VOLUME

It has become a cliche in the modern world to say that the only thing that remains the same in human life is change. Whether we are talking about technology or fashion, medical knowledge or social norms, we cannot help but be struck by how things continue to change, how rapid and unpredictable change can be, how exhilarating it can be to witness change, how ill-prepared we may be for change, how we welcome change and how we dread it. As much as we cherish stability and predictability in our relationships and our routines, we expect our lives to change, too. Until death stops it all, human lives are always in transition. But some transitions, some periods of change, stand out as especially significant in the life course. We may see them as turns in the road, changes in the direction or the trajectory of our lives.

Even in the absence of dramatic external events, people construe and reconstrue their experiences to point to (or to foreclose) possibility in the future. Living involves continually constructing and reconstructing stories of our lives, without knowing their outcome, revising the plot as new events are added. The self, then, consists of a configuring of "personal events into a historical unity which includes not only what one has been but also anticipations of what one will be" (Polkinghorne, 1988, p. 150). Thus meaning-making lies at the heart of those turns in the road that people think of as life transitions. This is the central question of this book: How do people make meaning out of the transitions in their lives? We believe that such meaning-making centrally involves storytelling—the construction and the sharing of stories of the self. The stories we make and tell about the major transitions in our own lives contribute to our identities, help us cope with challenges and stress, shape how we see the future, and help to determine the nature of our interpersonal relationships and our unique positionings in the social and cultural world.

Since the 1970s, psychologists and other social scientists have recognized that developmentally consequential transitions can and do occur in the adult years. A central message of life-span theorists such as Bernice

Neugarten (1968), George Vaillant (1977), and Daniel Levinson (1978) was that psychological and social development does not end with adolescence. The interdisciplinary study of adult development and aging assumes that human lives continue to change up to the very end. Life stage theorists map out predictable sequences of transitions, passages, or seasons in life (Erikson, 1963; Gould, 1980; Levinson, 1978), whereas theorists who favor a life course perspective emphasize social context and roles, social timing, and the socially contingent nature of adult development (Cohler, Hostetler, & Boxer, 1998; Elder, 1995). Whether they talk in terms of stages or contexts, however, life-span theorists and researchers focus their attention both on the on-time and generally socially scripted transitions of life, such as getting married in young adulthood or retiring around age 65, and on the off-time, often unexpected turns in the psychosocial road—from divorce and personal trauma to winning the lottery to experiencing a religious conversion at age 55. To study these phenomena, researchers have developed and refined a wide range of methodologies and techniques. The research literature on life transitions is replete with well-designed survey studies, questionnaire assessments, psychological experiments, and other approaches that place a premium on quantification and hypothesis testing. But this literature leaves us without much sense of the phenomenology or meaning-making that accompanies life's changes. Such a silence hinders our efforts to devise theories that seek to understand complex developmental milestones.

The experience of life transition is one that is narratively constructed rather than imposed by social reality. People choose to make changes in their lives, or they make changes in their experience of their lives in response to external events. Sometimes there is awareness of a state of being in transition. At other times, people are unaware of having undergone a time of change until they look back and see that they and their lives are inexorably changed. They may wonder, "How did I get here?" Such a question invokes a need to restory their life—to make sense of events so that they form some coherent narrative that ends in the psychological place where they now find (construct) themselves.

People choose from among a vast array of events, thoughts, wishes, and interactions to form a unique and ever-changing life story. In studying these life stories, or narrations, we come to understand better the ways in which meanings of transitions are constructed. It is these meanings that guide the person through the next phase of their existence, only (usually) to have the meanings change once again as life moves on.

Each of the 11 chapters that make up this book uses the analysis of narratives to understand significant transitions and turning points in the human life course. The authors use a broad range of narrative modes of inquiry—from psychobiography to discourse analysis—and draw on a wide assortment of theories—from Erikson to Labov to Bakhtin—to make sense of lives in transition. Among the particular transitions they examine, we find adolescent identity struggles; the move from school to work; divorce; turning points in moral development; setbacks in professional careers; the onset of illness; recovery from addiction; and dramatic epiphanies and conversions in life involving crime, confession, and redemption.

Life transitions may be experienced as changes for better or for worse—depending on how they are viewed and storied. Sometimes what is experienced initially as tragedy or loss is later emplotted as epiphany or insight leading to growth. In chapter 1, Dan P. McAdams and Philip J. Bowman consider differences in people whose life stories contain sequences of redemption or contamination—that is, good following bad or bad following good. Redemption and contamination are ancient story forms, but they are appropriated into contemporary life narratives in ways that reflect culturally anchored hopes and fears, developmental issues, and the psychosocial ethos surrounding a single life. Blending qualitative and quantitative research strategies, McAdams and Bowman document important relationships between redemption and contamination forms in life narrative on the one hand and objective indices of psychological well-being and generativity on the other.

The theme of redemption is central to chapters 2 and 3 as well. In chapter 2, Janet Landman compares and contrasts two celebrated instances of crime and punishment—Dostoevsky's story of Raskolnikov and the real-life account of Katherine Ann Power, a former honors student at Brandeis University who was involved in a murder in 1970, lived underground for 23 years, and finally turned herself in to the authorities to begin serving a prison sentence in 1993. These remarkably parallel narrative accounts—one fictionalized in a classic novel and the other pieced together from journalistic accounts and Landman's own interviews of Power—explore the power of guilt and repentance in human life and the narrative links that people forge between suffering and personal salvation. Yet the two stories are very different as well, and on this score Power's life narrative may even improve on Dostoevsky, Landman claims, because it offers a fuller and more satisfying account of a transformation in moral commitment.

The ways in which guilt, suffering, and physical imprisonment combine to transform a person's ethical stance in the world are at the center of William Todd Schultz's examination of Oscar Wilde's life turning point in chapter 3. Schultz's psychobiographical study begins with what Wilde himself identified as the "tragically critical moment of all my life." Sentenced to serve two years in prison for "gross indecency" (sodomy), the famous playwright lost everything—his family, his money, his reputation. When he emerged from prison, he was a broken man. Yet Wilde claimed he underwent a conversion experience in prison, and he wrote about the transition in a posthumously published letter, titled *De Profundis*. Schultz examines the letter and Wilde's life with great care. Was Wilde really redeemed? Were his insights in prison more rhetorical than real? Does it matter? Schultz raises a host of fascinating questions about the relationships between life stories of transition and life transitions as actually lived.

Chapters 4 through 8 examine opportunities and complications that arise from the developmental challenges of going to college, choosing a career, and getting divorced. In chapter 4, J. Scott Roberts and George C. Rosenwald reveal the complexities of upward mobility in American society. What looks on the surface to be a progressive life transition, a positive movement from working-class origins to the comforts and prestige of the professional classes, brings with it considerable costs in interpersonal relationships and self-esteem. The compelling first-person accounts provided by Roberts and Rosenwald remind us of how well-suited qualitative research is for bringing abstract ideas to vivid life. In chapter 5, Richard L. Ochberg and William Comeau pick up where Roberts and Rosenwald leave off. Analyzing survey data and qualitative reports from working-class college seniors looking forward to graduate school, Ochberg and Comeau examine the conflicting moral agendas expressed by upwardly mobile children and their parents. Although the students may invest moral capital in self-fulfillment, their working-class parents often deeply resent the sense of entitlement they believe their children feel. Self-fulfillment looks like self-indulgence to them. Their worlds have different moral contours; their life plots are situated within different ideological settings.

Choice of career is similarly more multilayered and internally contradictory than univariate studies of vocational choice would suggest. In chapter 6, Marcy Plunkett explores themes of serendipity and agency in young women's stories of career change. Plunkett draws on Erikson, Levinson, and other theorists to discuss the ways in which young women fashion stories to account for their movement through careers. Plunkett's nuanced analysis reveals a complex interplay between two very different narrative voices—one depicting the protagonist in control of her choices and another suggesting that the plot is driven by chance encounters, unforeseen circumstances, lucky and unlucky breaks. Narratives of serendipity may be very valuable in the construction of identity, Plunkett maintains, because they create a space of uncertainty to accommodate the competing demands of careers and personal relationships.

Career strivings are also at the center of Varpu Löyttyniemi's explication of a setback of a doctor's career in chapter 7. Bringing together theoretical perspectives and methodological conventions from linguistic studies and communications, Löyttyniemi provides a richly layered, line-by-line analysis of a young doctor's description of a negative turn in his career—a turn that might have seemed only a minor bump in the road until both the narrator and the chapter's author recognize its import in the life story. As part of her analysis, Löyttyniemi addresses some of the same critical questions raised by Schultz in his study of Oscar Wilde: What features of a life episode qualify it as an important transition? Are transitions lived as real events or reconstructed as narrative accounts? What is the role of audience in life-story construction? For whom, to whom, and for what purposes are life transitions made, told, and lived?

Although divorce is usually understood as a marker of marriage in dissolution, its larger meaning may vary enormously across the life course. Amy M. Young, Abigail J. Stewart, and Kathi Miner-Rubino (chapter 8) examine how women talk about their own divorces. Their readings of longitudinal data from 51 women in midlife suggest that the meanings women invoke in accounting for their divorces are partly a function of the developmental demands they faced at the time of the divorce. Erikson's stages of identity, intimacy, and generativity provide a theoretical framework out of which the authors generate provocative hypotheses that could be tested in future studies.

Relationships with others have no independent existence outside of their narrative construction by the individuals involved. Research on adolescent development has tended to investigate the perception of parents by adolescents, but we know little about how young people story their parents into their sense of themselves. Developmental psychologists Michael W. Pratt, Mary Louise Arnold, and Kathleen Mackey in chapter 9 consider adolescents' accounts of moral turning points in terms of their representations of their parents' voices. To what extent is the adolescent responsive to the voice? To what extent does he or she appropriate the voice as his or her own? The study illustrates the use of qualitative, narrative data to build general theory. The authors arrive at a five-step stage model for representations of parental voice that proves to be useful for testing hypotheses drawn from sociocultural theories concerning the nature of moral development in the teenage years.

Although Pratt and his colleagues use qualitative data to build theory, Jefferson A. Singer takes the opposite approach in chapter 10. Returning to themes of suffering and (attempted) redemption, Singer uses concepts from existing life-narrative theories to analyze the struggles of one Richard Markham, a heroin addict in his early 40s. Though he has yet to achieve a lasting recovery, what we learn from Markham's account and Singer's interpretations is how an internalized narrative of the self continues to play a pivotal role in the choices Markham makes and the ways in which he moves through life transitions. Of particular interest are the narrative's competing protagonists—the "imagoes" of Richard-the-derelict and Richard-the-magician. Singer is not talking about dissociative states but rather narrative devices that people use to emplot contrasting tendencies they perceive in their own lives. Singer suggests that growth and healing for Markham should involve a creative recasting of the main characters in his life story.

Michele L. Crossley continues with the theme of sickness and suffering in chapter 11. Crossley interviewed 38 HIV-positive adults, all of whom had been living with the diagnosis for at least five years. Crossley finds in these narratives a factor largely neglected in psychological theories—the sense of place. The settings in which life is lived, like Markham's imagoes, may come in contrasting pairs, because, as Crossley puts it, "We all live with culturally saturated images of places of Paradise and places of Hell." Stories of lives in transition portray protagonists who move from place to place, from safe havens to risky spaces, for example, from the Garden of Eden to the perilous wilderness and back again. Like life transitions themselves, the places we go—and how we experience them—may be overdetermined symbols of complex psychological and cultural issues. Crossley's insightful readings of these life texts bring to light unexpected and important meanings in the stories we live by.

In conclusion, each chapter in this volume adopts a unique conceptual lens and narrative approach to understanding how people make sense of the most important transitions in their own lives. People convey change through stories. As social scientists, humanists, mental health professionals, and human beings, we need to tune in to the stories of change we hear all around us, the stories each of us tells ourselves about who we were, who we are now, and who we may be in the future.

REFERENCES

Cohler, B. J., Hostetler, A. J., & Boxer, A. M. (1998). Generativity, social context, and lived experience: Narratives of gay men in middle adulthood. In D. P. McAdams & E. de St. Aubin (Eds.), *Generativity and adult development: How and why we care for the next generation* (pp. 265–310). Washington, DC: American Psychological Association.

Elder, G. H., Jr. (1995). The life course paradigm: Social change and individual development. In P. Moen, G. H. Elder, Jr., & K. Luscher (Eds.), *Examining lives in context: Perspectives on the ecology of human development* (pp. 101–139). Washington, DC: American Psychological Association.

Erikson, E. H. (1963). *Childhood and society* (2nd ed.). New York: Norton.

Gould, R. L. (1980). Transformations during early and middle adult years. In N. J. Smelser & E. H. Erikson (Eds.), *Themes of love and work in adulthood* (pp. 213–237). Cambridge, MA: Harvard University Press.

Levinson, D. J. (1978). *The seasons of a man's life*. New York: Knopf.

Neugarten, B. J. (Ed.). (1968). *Middle age and aging*. Chicago: University of Chicago Press.

Polkinghorne, D. (1988). *Narrative knowing and the human sciences*. Albany, NY: SUNY Press.

Vaillant, G. E. (1977). *Adaptation to life*. Boston: Little, Brown.

Turns in the Road

1

NARRATING LIFE'S TURNING POINTS: REDEMPTION AND CONTAMINATION

DAN P. McADAMS AND PHILIP J. BOWMAN

A year or two before he was assassinated, the Rev. Martin Luther King Jr. came to a small city in midwestern United States to speak to civic and religious leaders and to rally citizens, Black and White, for civil rights. A Black police officer in his early 30s, Jerome Johnson,[1] was assigned to work as King's bodyguard. Johnson was struggling through an especially frustrating period in his life. He had been a sports star in high school and had also completed a tour of duty in the U.S. Air Force. Johnson was an ambitious man who dreamed someday of being police chief. But up to that time no Black police officer had ever even been promoted to sergeant in that city. Johnson's fellow officers counseled against taking the promotional exam. His friends told him he should be satisfied with what he had. In a life-story interview conducted 30 years later, Johnson described King's visit as the turning point in his life:

> [The turning point] was back during that time that I had mentioned earlier about my thoughts and feelings about not taking the promotional exam the department had. Even thinking about leaving the police department because I felt it was a hopeless thing that a black could ever be a police chief and the structure and, I mentioned before about quitting the basketball team [in college] and I have to say I had given

The research described in this chapter was supported by grants to Dan P. McAdams from the Spencer Foundation and from the Foley Family Foundation to establish the Foley Center for the Study of Lives. The authors would like to thank the following people who were involved in data collection, data analysis, and discussion of the case studies: Jay Azarow, Manini Bhakti, Reginald Blount, Irene Carvalho, Elizabeth Cole, Jennifer Goldberg, Holly Hart, Sandy Hermele, Amy Kegley, Erin Kennedy, Kenya Key, Martha Lewis, David McConville, Derek McNeil, Nathania Montes, Kelly Moore, Allison Patten, Elizabeth Reyes, and Jeff Reynolds. Special thanks are also extended to Amy Himsel and Jane Maring, who transcribed interviews.
[1] Jerome Johnson is a pseudonym.

strong thoughts to leaving the police force because of what I saw was happening to minorities there, you know, about [bad] assignments and all that stuff that happened. And then it was at the time I was assigned to be the bodyguard for Dr. Martin Luther King. And he was here, I think maybe two, three days. And so I spent some time with him. You know, when he was at the hotel and places where he went to speak and all, and escorting him, along with my wife. . . . It was a day that, it was the last time I ever saw him, a day that he was getting ready to leave, and he was standing in front of the hotel and waiting for transportation to take him to the airport. And we started talking, and I told him how frustrated I was about the fact that no black had ever been promoted and I was still frustrated until then. Maybe it's time to move on, because I didn't see there was anything that was gonna change at all. And he just said a couple of things, just very briefly he said, you know, he said, "Never give up." And that was basically the end of the conversation, and I thought about that before, but when he said it to me, and the way he said, "Keep the faith," you know, and "Never give up," you know, and "Never stop dreaming the dream," you know. And I held on to that, and I went on, and things changed. . . . He turned me around from walkin' out the door.

Johnson eventually took the exam and was promoted to sergeant. A few years later, the police department funded his return to school. He enrolled in the Academy of the Federal Bureau of Investigation (FBI), and graduated with distinction. Johnson's mother, wife, and two children accompanied him to the graduation dinner. The evening's speaker was FBI chief J. Edgar Hoover:

J. Edgar Hoover was the head of the FBI at the time. And ah, I mean he was the pinnacle of law enforcement. At that time, he was *the* man. . . . Hoover came in and stood in line to greet people. His body guards were gone. So he came into the reception area. And my youngest son I remember said, "Dad, I want to get something more to eat." [Johnson took his son back to the buffet to get more food.] So by the time I took him over there and was getting back, Hoover had already been in [and gone]. All the parents and the family members were shaking hands with him and taking pictures and now he was gone, and we didn't get to see him. So the guy, who [was in charge of Hoover's schedule arranged a private meeting between Hoover and Johnson's family.] So we go to the back room there, with the family, and we shake hands. And I'll never forget, my youngest son, he was about 6, 7, or 8 years old. He gave Hoover a black handshake. (Laugh). Oh, God, I'll never forget that, but ah, they ended up taking a picture of my family, which had myself in it. And the following month after graduation and everything, the picture came out on the FBI magazine that goes all over the world.

And we were on the front cover of that magazine, in color. And it was beautiful, and ah, I even framed that picture.

In the years following, Johnson continued to rise through the ranks in the police department. He eventually realized his dream and became the first African American police chief in that midwestern city. After serving as chief, he took an early retirement. Today, Johnson spends more time with his wife and adult children. He plans to write a book about his experiences on the police force. He hopes to become a grandfather soon. He invests a great deal of energy, furthermore, in volunteer community work with Black youth.

The two public figures who make cameo appearances in Johnson's life story were mortal antagonists in real life. Indeed, Hoover amassed a substantial FBI file on King and plotted to undermine his mission through blackmail and deceit. Johnson is aware of the ironies involved in featuring the icon of the American civil rights movement on the one hand and a paragon of White American authoritarianism on the other as two of the protagonist's best allies in the same life story. Yet the two larger-than-life figures symbolize some of the contradictions inherent in one Black man's struggle to become a leader in law enforcement in late-twentieth-century America. The King and Hoover scenes, furthermore, hint at a recurrent thematic trend in the stories that Johnson now tells to make sense of his life, as he reconstructs the past and looks ahead into his retirement years. In both scenes an emotionally negative situation is transformed into a positive outcome. In what Johnson himself identifies as the turning point in the story, a frustrating situation gives way to hope, which ultimately leads to success, by virtue of a brief conversation with Martin Luther King Jr. In the second scene, the mild disappointment of a missed opportunity gives way to a second chance to meet J. Edgar Hoover, which results in a very happy moment and a wonderful, if rather ironic, memory. Both scenes suggest a narrative sequence of *redemption*. A bad scene is redeemed by a positive outcome.

A redemption sequence is a movement in life storytelling from an emotionally negative or bad scene to an emotionally positive or good outcome. By contrast, a *contamination* sequence encodes the reverse movement—from good to bad. In a contamination sequence, an emotionally positive or good experience is spoiled, ruined, sullied, or contaminated by an emotionally negative or bad outcome. Patterns of redemption and contamination can be seen in many different life-narrative accounts, and they are especially prevalent in accounting for life transitions or life-narrative turning points. As narrative devices for charting upward movement from bad to good, redemption sequences can be used to convey a progressive understanding of self—the self as growing, moving forward, making progress over time (Gergen & Gergen, 1986). In sharp contrast, contamination sequences may express decline or stagnation in the plot, as characters fall backward, lose ground, or circle over the same ground again and again.

REDEMPTION SEQUENCES AND THE PROGRESSIVE NARRATIVE OF SELF IN THE LIFE STORY OF A POLICE CHIEF

If there is to be redemption, there must first be pain. Johnson's story begins by situating the protagonist in one of the most painful periods in American history—the Great Depression of the 1930s. "I was a Depression baby," Johnson begins, "So, we went through some very difficult times, when there was, you know, no food and there was no money available. . . . I do remember the struggles and things we had to overcome, and I really remember the hungry stomach and I remember Christmases when there was nothing under the tree, and that kind of thing." Johnson begins his life story interview with an explicit reference to a threatening situation, to danger. In beginning this way, Johnson's story resembles many we have collected in the past five years from African American adults between the ages of about 35 and 65 years. Rather than a golden age of innocence, life stories we have collected from Black, middle-aged adults are more likely to begin with death, illness, injury, abandonment, poverty, or enslavement (McAdams, Bowman, Lewis, Hart, & Cole, 1999). In Johnson's case, the protagonist begins life amid an economic catastrophe. At another point in the interview, Johnson is asked to describe his "earliest memory." He tells of finding his grandfather "asleep" upstairs and, after trying unsuccessfully to rouse him, falling asleep in the bed at his side. The boy learned later that his grandfather was dead.

In Johnson's account of his early years, these negative beginnings are eventually redeemed. In the case of his grandfather's death, Johnson recalls feeling a sense of peace and security as he lay at his grandfather's side, and even when he woke up and learned from his parents that his grandfather had passed, he recalls his time in bed with his grandfather's body as a very positive moment, and still thinks of it as positive today. Like many American adults, Black and White, who went through the Great Depression, Johnson underscores the positive lessons learned and the simple family virtues that characterized that time in his life. People were hungry, yes. But people helped each other out:

> I think about how growing up that things were like a real community. I mean, even though we were young and we were struggling and people all around you were all struggling, we all, people contributed to each other, you know. If we didn't have enough food, someone would bring us something. Vice versa, my dad would bring something in, and we'd be able to share that with somebody else, and just kind of a commonality

of responsibility that was there and I think has always made an impact upon me, that people reached out and helped each other then.

The community support that Johnson recalls extended even to the realm of discipline. It was not unusual, as Johnson remembers it, for adults in the community to take responsibility for many different children, not only their own. If a child in the neighborhood was out of line, any adult in the neighborhood might offer helpful discipline. Johnson recalls a time when he was disciplined:

> A friend of mine and me, we got in a fight, and on the way home got stopped by two, three adults, who ah, had heard about the fight even before I got [home], and chastised me and chastised my friend for fighting and then getting home and having to go pull the switch off the tree and ah, and getting a whippin' from mom about, you know, acting that way. And then getting back to school the next day and having a teacher, a black teacher, ah, who bounced the ball off my head and hit [punished] the other kid, too, 'cause we got involved in the fight. You know, and it just, just those kind of things made an impact upon me. . . . There was a type of network you don't see anymore. I think the discipline we saw in those days was much stronger. Even in the classroom in the fourth and fifth grade and having the teacher pop you on the side of the head, you know, when you acted out and those kinds of things. It all had a *good* impact upon my life.

In this scene, what is arguably a bad event—being punished (at least three times for the same fight)—takes on a redemptive meaning in the story, as the author insists that the punishment had a "good impact upon my life." In the King and Hoover scenes, a bad scene is rather suddenly transformed into something positive. In the accounts of growing up in the Great Depression, however, the good that follows the bad may take many years to manifest itself, Johnson suggests. It is now from the standpoint of retirement age that he reconstructs these events in redemptive terms. We have no way of knowing how the events were experienced at the time, nor how he might have reconstructed them, say, during the years Johnson struggled to become chief of police.

Johnson tells a life story in which the protagonist must continually struggle to overcome obstacles that society throws in his way. The subtle racism that Johnson occasionally experiences in grade school becomes much more overt and toxic in high school as Johnson begins to distinguish himself in athletics. His mother runs home in tears after attending a basketball game in which the opposing team taunts Jerome by calling him a "nigger." Some White teachers seem to discriminate against the Black students. Black parents who were involved in their children's grade schools feel alienated in this larger high school environment. As a high school student, Johnson begins to see that "the system" is working against him and his Black peers:

The racism and prejudice didn't really hit me till I got to high school. This high school right here [the local high school]. And it was like walking in the door and being slapped in the face. You know, getting teachers that really didn't care for you, and ah, having the experience of the history of trying to deal with teachers who traditionally never passed blacks, you know, through school. And, ah, dealing with a system where parents felt intimidated about coming into a system like this and questioning things that would happen to you, but it really, it really, it really slapped me hard.

Nonetheless, Johnson provides a redemptive meaning for much of what happened during these years. Some of the White teachers were very helpful, he points out. He makes much of a scene in which he was failing in a course and the teacher gave him extra help so that he could eventually pass. He makes much of the steady support he received from his mother and father. Certain coaches also provided sustenance and guidance. Overall, he concludes that the high school "environment was very difficult to deal with," but "I think that the things I faced here helped me to be stronger in my lifetime."

But not all negative scenes can be redeemed, even in the relentlessly upbeat, progressive narrative that Johnson constructs. In response to the request to describe a life story "low point," Johnson tells of an incident from his senior year in high school. He was the captain of the football team, the first Black student ever to achieve that status. According to tradition, the football captain and the homecoming queen are to walk out on stage together and lead the homecoming pep rally before the school's biggest game of the year. But he is Black, and the homecoming queen is White. The image of a beautiful White woman and strong Black man standing together on stage and jointly whipping the crowd into a frenzy is just too jarring for some teachers, students, or parents to take in this small American city in the early 1950s. The authorities tell Johnson that he cannot go out there:

> One experience I had here at the high school really stands out, the one that really hurt. And it's difficult for me to overcome. . . . It was just really devastating to me. First of all, to achieve being the first black captain of the football team. And to be the winner of the science award, the first black to do that. And then to be all pepped up and worked up to celebrate all this in front of all the student body and coplayers and all that stuff and lined up to walk out with the homecoming queen so that you could wave at everybody and then, then they cheer you and all that kind of stuff and have your name introduced and all that, and then to be told that you can't do that. That was devastating to me. You know, that was devastating. And, ah, I cried. I cried. I cried at home over that. And that was a real, real tough situation, was so emotional, to have that slap in the face at that particular time.

Johnson is describing a vintage contamination sequence. There is no redemptive message here: "It's difficult [still, even today] for me to overcome." Nothing good ever came out of this humiliating experience. The homecoming scene stands out as the only contamination sequence in Johnson's entire interview. But it is a poignant and powerful scene, and it shows that even the most tightly drawn life narrative can suggest thematic lines that run counter to the story's dominant thrust (Gregg, 1991; Wiersma, 1988).

Johnson experiences a mix of successes and setbacks as he moves through college and the Air Force. He is modestly successful in college football, but he quits the basketball team after the coach refuses to play him more. Johnson regrets that he quit. He blames himself for a lapse in discipline. His tour of duty in the Air Force is remembered fondly, for the most part. Some of the White authorities gave him a little trouble, and the Japanese seemed especially prejudiced during his time in Japan. But this period is viewed as a time of growth and building confidence. Returning to his home town, Johnson takes on a series of jobs but makes no progress until he joins the police force. In his mid 20s, he begins to make long-term plans for his life. He will marry and have a family. He will rise through the ranks, eventually to become police chief. He will do volunteer work in his community. He will build up a reputation as a good family man, solid citizen, upstanding representative of the Black middle-class. He will be a leader. When asked to describe the high point scene in his life story, Johnson gives a detailed account of how he planned assiduously and worked so hard to become police chief, the strategic relationships he cultivated along the path, the vision he articulated for the future of the police force. In a nutshell, the protagonist in Johnson's life story works hard to overcome obstacles and accomplish his goals. In his spare time, he reads books about slave life and the history of Blacks, "What they had to go through and overcome. ... I guess I'm kind of one-dimensional on this," Johnson admits. His favorite stories from childhood were his grandfather's tales of overcoming adversity.

Johnson's story is one of steady progress, fueled by repeated redemptive events in which bad things turn good, usually as a result of Johnson's perseverance and discipline. Nothing flashy in this story. No sudden epiphanies. The scene with King stands out as the only dramatic turning point. The story is mainly about doing good work for others, as a police officer and, secondarily, as a community volunteer. Family life seems positive, but Johnson provides little detail about his relationships with his children and his wife. There are surely other stories to tell, but Johnson appears to see them as tangential to the main, progressive plot that defines who he was, is, and will be. His fifth-grade teacher challenged the class one day when he said, "You're either on the destruction team or you're on the construction team in life; and you gotta make a choice now. Which of the teams are you gonna be on?" Johnson chose the construction team. Personal failures and frustrations get turned into good materials for the plot he continues to build. Redemptive sequences energize and direct the story's movement, resulting in a progressive narration of self. Johnson titles the current chapter of his life story "give-back time." Even after a life of public service, he will now increase his community involvements and redouble his efforts to help local Black youth. The construction continues.

THE LIFE STORIES OF HIGHLY GENERATIVE ADULTS

Johnson was asked to participate in our life-story research because he scored high on self-report measures of *generativity* that we had previously administered to a sample of more than 260 adults between the ages of 35 and 65 years, about half of whom were Black and half of whom were White and half of whom were male and half of whom were female (Hart, McAdams, Hirsch, & Bauer, in press). Generativity, introduced into the social sciences literature by Erik H. Erikson (1963), is an adult's concern for and commitment to promoting the well-being of later generations. In Erikson's well-known model for psychosocial development, generativity versus stagnation is the seventh of eight stages in the life cycle, identified mainly with midlife. According to the conventional Eriksonian scenario, once a person establishes a psychosocial sense of who he or she is (Stage 5: identity versus role confusion; late adolescence) and establishes long-term romantic and friendship bonds with others (Stage 6: intimacy versus isolation; young adulthood), he or she is psychosocially ready to engage in life projects that are aimed at benefiting generations to come. Through parenting most obviously, but also through teaching, mentoring, counseling, community service, leadership, and a wide range of constructive activities, adults seek to be generative and to generate positive legacies that will outlive the self (Kotre, 1984, 1999; McAdams & de St. Aubin, 1998). Although Erikson situated generativity as a midlife stage, he also argued that midlife adults differ from each other in their characteristic levels of generativity. Following Erikson, life-course perspectives on generativity have emphasized the ways in which generativity is shaped by culture and context, the sometimes unpredictable waxing and waning of generative strivings over the adult life course, the presence of generative inclinations among young adults and old adults as well, and the wide individual differences in generativity that can be observed in any sample of adults (Cohler, Hostetler, & Boxer, 1998; McAdams, in press).

If our self-report scales are any indication, Johnson is, at age 62, a highly generative adult. He scored at the very high end of the Loyola Generativity Scale (LGS; McAdams & de St. Aubin, 1992), a 20-item questionnaire that asks the respondent to rate, for example, the extent to which "I try to pass along knowledge I have gained through my experience" and "I have a responsibility to improve the neighborhood in which I live." Johnson also scored high on a measure of generative behaviors, which asks the respondent to report how many times he or she has engaged in each of 40 actions indicative of generativity over the previous two-month period (e.g., "read a story to a child," "taught somebody about right and wrong.") Finally, Johnson scored very high on a measure of generative goals. Modeled after Emmons (1986), the respondent provides short, open-ended descriptions of 10 "personal strivings" that he or she is currently engaged in. These daily goals can range from "losing 10 pounds before the start of the swimsuit season" to "figuring out the meaning of life." The responses are coded for generative imagery based on a system developed by McAdams, de St. Aubin, and Logan (1993).

Research has shown that adults who score high on self-report measures of generativity differ from their counterparts scoring low in many readily assessed ways. For example, parents scoring high in generativity use more authoritative, child-centered parenting styles (Peterson, Smirles, & Wentworth, 1997; Pratt, Danso, Arnold, & Norris, in press), emphasize the value of passing on wisdom to their children (Hart et al., in press), and are more involved in their children's schooling (Nakagawa, 1991), compared to parents scoring low on scales assessing generativity. Highly generative adults report greater levels of participation in religious institutions (Hart et al., in press) and more involvement in political activities, including voting, working for political campaigns and movements, and agitating for social reform (Cole & Stewart, 1996; Hart et al., in press; Peterson et al., 1997; Peterson & Klohnen, 1995). With respect to mental health, highly generative adults report lower levels of depression and higher levels of life satisfaction, happiness, self-esteem, and sense of life coherence, compared to adults low in generativity (Ackerman, Zuroff, & Moscowitz, in press; de St. Aubin & McAdams, 1995; Keyes & Ryff, 1998; McAdams, Hart, & Maruna, 1998).

Johnson's participation in our research came about because of a research question that focuses less on quantitative behaviors and mental health outcomes, however, and more on the narrative meanings of lives. Namely, what kinds of life stories do highly generative American adults construct? McAdams (1985, 1993, 1999) and others have argued that modern adults tend to provide their lives with some semblance of unity and purpose by constructing and internalizing self-defining life stories, complete with settings, scenes, characters, plots, and themes (see also Cohler, 1982; Giddens, 1991; Hermans & Hermans-Jansen, 1995; Josselson, 1995; Kenyon, 1996; MacIntyre, 1981; Randall, 1995; Rosenwald, 1992; Singer & Salovey, 1993; Widdershoven, 1993). According to McAdams's life-story theory, adult identity is an evolving and implicit narrative of the self that reconstructs the past and anticipates the future in such a way as to confer on the chaos of (post)modern life a modicum of direction, vitality, and followability. Although there are many different ways to study the process and product of life storytelling (e.g., Holstein & Gubrium, 2000), McAdams and colleagues have focused on the content and the structure of the life-story protocols themselves. Using a standardized life-narrative interview and often using reliable and objective content analysis procedures, the approach treats each life-narrative account as an interpretable text, comparing and contrasting different life narrative accounts obtained from different respondents coming out of different psychologically, sociologically, or demographically defined groups.

Johnson, then, was one of 35 men and women interviewed for a study comparing and contrasting the life stories told by highly generative and especially nongenerative African American adults (McAdams et al., 1999). Each of the 35 respondents was interviewed by an African American researcher, matched on gender. The life-story interview (Table 1-1) asks each respondent to begin by providing an overview of the main "chapters" in

TABLE 1-1
The Life Story Interview

I. **Life chapters.** Participant divides his or her life into its main "chapters" and provides a plot summary for each chapter.

II. **Significant scenes.** For each of the 8 scenes below, the participant describes exactly what happened, who was there, what he or she was thinking and feeling in the scene, and what he or she thinks the scene says about who he or she is, was, or might be.

    High point. A scene of great joy, happiness, positive affect. The best scene in the story.

    Low point. A scene of misery, fear, negative affect. The worst scene in the story.

    Turning point. A scene in which the participant experienced a significant life change.

    Earliest memory.

    Important childhood scene.

    Important adolescent scene.

    Important adult scene.

    Any **other important scene.**

III. **Life challenge.** Participant describes single greatest challenge in life.

IV. **Characters.**

    Most important **positive influence:** Describe the person or institution who has had the most positive impact on the story.

    Most important **negative influence:** Describe the person or institution who has had the most negative impact on the story.

V. **Favorite stories.** Describe favorite stories seen, read, or heard.

VI. **Future plot.** Where is the story going? What happens next? Goals for future.

VII. **Personal ideology.** A series of questions on fundamental values, religious and political beliefs, and how values have changed over time.

VIII. **Life theme.** Identify single integrative theme in the life story.

---

his or her life story, providing a title and plot summary for each. Then the respondent describes in detail each of 8 particular "scenes" in the story, including a life-story high point, low point, and turning point. For each scene, the respondent describes what happened, who was involved, what he or she was thinking and feeling in the scene, and what the scene may mean in the context of the overall life story. Following the accounts of important scenes, the respondent describes one important life challenge, positive and negative characters in the story, and where the story is going (future chapters). The interviewer also asks the respondent to identify and describe some of his or her favorite stories (from books, television, and so on) and to provide some details about his or her personal ideology, including religious and political beliefs and values. The interview ends by asking the respondent to look back over the story told and identify a central theme or message. Requiring between two and three hours of time to complete, the interview is eventually transcribed, the typed pages of which are then examined with various content-analysis procedures.

The main goal of the study in which Johnson participated was to distinguish between the life stories told by highly generative and nongenerative Black adults. A central finding in the study, mirrored in Johnson's account, was the prevalence of progressive narratives of the self among the highly generative Black adults. Like Johnson, a majority of the 21 highly generative adults told life stories in which steady goal-directed progress was set against a backdrop of danger and threat. Compared to their less generative counterparts, highly generative Black adults narrated the self as a growing, moving, developing construction, struggling not only to survive but to improve.

Like Johnson's, furthermore, these stories contained many redemption sequences. As reported in McAdams et al. (1999), for example, 13 of the 21 high-generativity adults (61%) described their single most important turning-point scene in redemptive terms, whereas only 2 of the 13 turning-point scenes described by low-generativity adults (15%) could be coded as redemption sequences. The theme of redemption was so pervasive in the life stories of highly generative African American adults that it occasionally served as something of a life credo. One highly generative Black woman—a 45-year-old divorced mother of one, employed as a marketing research manager—concluded her interview by stating, "The negativeness and the badness of the things I had to overcome emotionally, you know, dealing with the lies [of men] and the different things that he [her husband] said, um, it made me a better person, a stronger person; um, it sort of toughened me up." In her story, redemption came through hard-won struggles and considerable pain at the hands of abusive antagonists in her life. "That's not the way I would have chosen to get here, but it did force a lot of growth," she remarked. Her religious faith has promoted her movement forward: "Salvation is what helps me grow and to rise above." Another highly generative woman—61-years-old, divorced, employed by the telephone company—concluded that "any person with a little knowledge can turn their life around." For a 62-year-old accountant, married with one grown child, life began (literally) as a kind of redemption scene: His birth was the result of his mother's rape. What follows from childhood through midlife is one harrowing scene after another, culminating in the protagonist's recovery from a nearly fatal stab wound. "I was dead but the doctors brought me back alive"—the ultimate redemption sequence. "My philosophy of life," he said, "has always been to be positive instead of negative on any circumstances you deal with. . . . If you go with positive ideas, you'll progress; if you get involved in the negative, you'll drown."

The prevalence of redemption imagery in the life stories of highly generative adults was also a central finding in a study conducted by McAdams, Diamond, de St. Aubin, and Mansfield (1997). We interviewed 40 adults (mainly Anglo American) chosen as generativity exemplars by virtue of (a) their extremely high scores on self-report measures of generativity and (b) their demonstrated accomplishments in the teaching profession or in volunteer work aimed at benefiting children and families. We also interviewed a matched sample of 30 adults scoring relatively low on generativity and not involved in teaching or volunteer work. Again, the goal of the study was to discern thematic differences between the narrative identities constructed by highly generative and less generative American adults. We used rigorously defined content-analysis systems to code the interviews, blind to all identifying information on the 70 participants. This hypothesis-testing study used quantitative coding indexes and conventional statistical tests to evaluate a set of theoretically drawn hypotheses about generativity and identity.

The results showed that the highly generative adults were significantly more likely than their less generative counterparts to reconstruct the past and anticipate the future as variations on a prototypical *commitment story*. In a commitment story, the protagonist (a) enjoys an early family blessing or advantage, (b) is sensitized to others' suffering at an early age, (c) is guided by a clear and compelling personal ideology that remains relatively stable over time, (d) transforms or redeems bad scenes into good outcomes, and (e) sets goals for the future to benefit society. Although every life narrative account collected in this study had its own unique features, the five themes identified as the core of a commitment story consistently differentiated between stories told by the two groups of participants. The themes that made up the commitment story, furthermore, strongly resemble those identified by Colby and Damon (1992) in their exploratory study of the lives of 23 men and women identified by their peers as moral exemplars for their life commitments to social justice and serving poor individuals.

In McAdams et al. (1997), the life-story account that may have most closely approximated the prototypical commitment story was that told by Diana Collins.[2] Collins is a 49-year-old fourth-grade teacher and mother of three grown children. Diana's life story is one of the 18 out of 40 from the highly generative adults that begins with a kind of family blessing. Born in Iowa to a Methodist minister and his wife, she "was the first baby ever born in this Methodist parsonage" and therefore a favorite among the adults in that tiny community. People marvelled at the toddler's precocious ability to remember everybody's name. Collins remarked that families of church ministers rarely accumulate material wealth, but they still often enjoy an exalted social status by virtue of the respect accorded them by parishioners, some of whom themselves may be wealthy, famous, or especially accomplished. When Collins's family moved to Chicago, her father became associated with a wealthier congregation and with a seminary. As a result, "Many famous people I know are my friends and that gave me a different feeling about who I was and who I could be in life." Shortly after the move to Chicago, however, tragedy struck. When she was 8 years old, Diana was watching her younger brother one summer afternoon as her mother worked in the kitchen. The boy darted into the street and was run over by a car. The driver scooped the child up and drove him to the hospital even before Collins's mother could come running out of the house. The boy died shortly thereafter. At the same time, Collins was enduring a very difficult second-grade year. Her teacher was emotionally unstable, and at the end of the school year the teacher was "institutionalized." Collins remarked, "I think we were both [the teacher and Diana] having a very bad year, and the combination was horrible. *But after that things picked up.*"

In ending her account of these two negative incidents by suggesting an eventually positive turn, Collins appears on the verge of constructing a redemption sequence. She came back twice to the death of her brother later in the interview, and in both instances she concluded the account with a positive outcome. In one instance, she remarked that her college education was financed by the insurance money that came from her brother's death. In a second, she described again the day her brother died as the nadir experience, or low point, in her life, couching it as a classic contamination sequence in which a beautiful summer day suddenly turns horrific. But then Collins goes on to tell how she tried for years to be the son her father lost, to make amends for the guilt she felt after her brother was killed. She took up sports and thought she would grow up to be a doctor, as "good sons" might, she reasoned. Although these efforts failed, she ultimately experienced a

---

[2] Diana Collins is a pseudonym. She appears as Diana C. in McAdams et al. (1997).

redemptive success in marrying her high school sweetheart, who came to be treated by her father as his own son.

Collins's goals for the future include becoming a grandmother, moving to Kentucky to be near her daughter when she retires, doing some writing, incorporating more drama and storytelling into her teaching methods, and working for the betterment of the educational system, because "I'd like to give something back" to society. Invoking the most generative rhetoric in her interview, she said that the most important value in her life was "to grow and help others grow." Her interview is filled with metaphors of growth, development, and progress.

Like Collins, many of the highly generative adults interviewed in McAdams et al. (1997) described high points, low points, and turning points in their life stories in explicitly redemptive terms. Table 1-2 provides condensed examples of a number of redemption sequences found in this study. The table breaks the examples down into five categories—sacrifice, recovery, growth, learning, and improvement. But these groupings are somewhat arbitrary, and there would appear to be a plethora of contemporary discourses that people routinely draw on to get across the idea of redemption.

TABLE 1-2
Redemption Sequences: Condensed Examples

Sacrifice
Pain of delivery → birth of beautiful baby
Protagonist leaves husband because he wants her to have an abortion because of poverty → experiences the joy of loving her son
Recovery
Bout of severe depression → regained positive mood for good
Severe anorexia → therapist saves her life
Growth
Father's death → family becomes closer
Loneliness of childhood → protagonist becomes a resilient adult
Episode of anger and crying after father's death → protagonist no longer stutters, decreased anxiety
Protagonist is fired from job → comes to see himself as a whole person
Divorce → protagonist develops better relationship with her son
Drugs, dereliction → protagonist moves to new place, changes name, gets life organized
Learning
Exhausting workload → protagonist realizes life needs more balance
Severe criticism from coworker → protagonist becomes a better employee
Mother-in-law hates participant → protagonist learns how to be a good mother-in-law herself
Improvement
Bad year of teaching → protagonist moves to new school where she finds success, affirmation
Traffic accident → "all of a sudden it started to become a cool experience"

Source: Adapted from McAdams et al., 1997, p. 694.

In the discourse of medicine, for example, people speak of healing, recovery, and achieving wellness. In the legal system, terms such as rehabilitation and restitution are invoked. Educators speak of learning, growth, development, and socialization. Contemporary American society is suffused with the rhetoric of psychotherapy, and today many laypeople speak knowingly of personal transformation and personal growth, fulfillment and self-actualization, individuation and reintegration, and the improvement, enlargement, perfection, and full expression of the self (Cushman, 1995), all variations on redemption sequences. The burgeoning popular literature on self-help offers a cornucopia of redemption stories, as do contemporary television talk shows and human interest stories in the media. Of course the many discourses that may be grouped under the general category of religion and spirituality invoke concepts such as sacrifice, atonement, enlightenment, transcendence, conversion, and so on—all ideas that find their way readily into personal stories that people tell to account for their own lives.

Redemption sequences capture much of the central meaning in what Tomkins (1987) called a *limitation-remediation script*. These kinds of life scripts "address those aspects of the human condition perceived to be imperfect, to which some enduring, long-term response must be made and which it is believed can be remedied, with varying degrees of success, risk, effort, costs, and benefits" (Tomkins, 1987, p. 166). According to Tomkins, a limitation–remediation script begins with an "imperfect" state of affairs—a negative-affect situation in which the protagonist of the story must suffer in some way. Over time, the protagonist seeks to undo the suffering, improve or redeem the situation, and move forward to a positive-affect state. On the road to redemption, the protagonist may absorb a great deal of negative affect, but the hope and anticipation of an ultimate reward keep the protagonist going.

The limitation–remediation script, with its promise of eventual redemption, is an ancient story type (Miller & C'deBaca, 1994). May (1980) identified one variation on it in the ancient Greek myth of Demeter and Persephone, wherein bleak winter, occasioned by Persephone's imprisonment in the underworld, turns to spring when mother and daughter are reunited. "Demeter's suffering is followed by intense joy—a joy stronger than she would have felt had the sorrow and separation not preceded it" (May, 1980, p. 13). May argued that this sequence of deprivation followed by enhancement is ubiquitous in cultural myth and folklore and that its presence in personal fantasies holds significant psychological meaning. Von Franz (1980) discussed a redemption motif in fairy tales from around the world. The same sequence is variously scripted in major world religions. In *The Varieties of Religious Experience*, William James (1902/1958) wrote that most all religions converge on "a certain uniform deliverance" that involves an initial "sense that there is *something wrong about us* as we naturally stand"

and a subsequent "solution" whereby "*we are saved from the wrongness* by making proper connection with the higher powers" (p. 383).

Examples of stories that encode the sequence of early suffering followed by a (promised or actual) deliverance to a positive-affect state are legion in the Judaeo–Christian traditions: Abraham and Sarah suffer infertility into old age until God provides them with Isaac, their son; the Israelites suffer through Egyptian captivity and 40 years of wandering until God delivers them to the Promised Land; Christ is crucified but raised up on the third day. Today, personal stories of conversion—moving suddenly from a bad and sinful state to a good and Godly one—are a staple of many Christian communities, a traditional paragon for which is the New Testament story of Paul's conversion on the road to Damascus. Redemption sequences are also prevalent in Islam; indeed the Arabic term "Islam" means "surrender," as in surrendering to the ultimate will of Allah to be purified and redeemed. In Hinduism and Buddhism, redemption sequences take the form of the liberation from perpetual transmigration. The first and second of the Four Noble Truths of the Buddha explain how it is that human existence is *dukkha*—full of conflict, dissatisfaction, sorrow, and suffering. The third and fourth speak of the emancipation, liberation, and freedom for human beings that come from following the Noble Eightfold Path on the way to Nirvana.

In sum, the ancient story motif of redemption translates into a wide range of contemporary narrative forms, some of which eventually appear in people's life stories. Our research suggests that adults who are strongly committed to providing care for and making significant contributions to future generations—highly generative adults, in Erikson's terms—tend to construct life stories that feature many redemption sequences compared to less generative adults. A narrative identity that celebrates redemption may provide a solid platform from which to launch generative projects and endeavors. Perceiving one's own life in terms of redemption sequences may provide the hope that hard work today will yield positive dividends for the future, a hope that may sustain generative efforts as private as raising one's own child (Snarey, 1993) and as public as committing one's self to the advancement of one's own society or one's own people (Erikson, 1969).

CONTAMINATION SEQUENCES

Tanya Williams,[3] a mother of four whose husband is in prison and who herself has battled abusive men, drugs, alcohol, and the police her

---

[3] Tanya Williams is a pseudonym.

entire adult life, states, "I'm 41 years old, but I still feel kind of lost. I know what to do when I get up every day, but do I really know where I am going?" Tanya recalls happy years in early childhood. Her mother loved her; her sister and she stayed up late at night telling ghost stories; she learned to ride a bike. In Tanya's story, contamination begins with puberty. In junior high school, she discovers that she has a "mischievous streak," a trait she associates with her father. "They tended to tell me that I was like my father, which caused me a lot of problem." The legacy she received from her father is a love of "the streets." Like him, she embarked on a very rough and dangerous life, as if the protagonist in her story had no choice but to live out the trait that her father had given her. Around the time of puberty, she begins to drink. Soon she is using other drugs. By the time she is 15 years old, she has experimented with heroin.

Williams begins her life narrative account with an extended contamination sequence. The happiness and innocence of her childhood years give way to the troubles of adolescence. Puberty spoils what had been a happy tale to tell. In a contamination sequence, a very good or affectively positive life-narrative scene (or series of scenes) is followed by a very bad, affectively negative outcome. The bad ruins, spoils, sullies, or contaminates the good that precedes it. Contamination sequences are not as common in life narrative accounts as are redemption sequences. Nonetheless, most midlife adults we have interviewed included at least one explicit contamination sequence in their accounts. We have found that contamination sequences are significantly more prevalent in the life stories of adults scoring low on measures of generativity compared to those scoring high (McAdams et al., 1997; McAdams et al., 1999). In a sample of midlife African American adults, Williams was chosen for an interview because she scored at the very low end of our self-report generativity measures.

Out of the eight key scenes we asked Williams to narrate as part of the life-story interview, she constructed four of them as contamination sequences. It is interesting (and sad) to note that she imposed a contamination frame even on her account of the high-point scene in her life story. The high point is the birth of her first child, when she was 21 years old. In our research, we have found that the birth of a child is the single most common example provided by midlife adults as a life-story high point. Like many people, Williams recalls the birth as an experience of joy, wonder, and love. But unlike most people we have interviewed, Williams juxtaposes this happy scene with a very negative event. After describing the birth, she goes on to say that years later the child's father was found dead in a motel room, stabbed five times in the back. In real time, the father's death did not immediately follow the child's birth. But Williams tells the story so that death immediately follows birth in the narrative. The contamination sequence reinforces the belief that "in general good things do not happen to me." Perhaps more accurately, good things *do* happen, but they are often eventually ruined by bad things.

Williams's second contamination scene is her account of a low-point event in her life. The account begins positively with her marriage to a man who, she thinks, loves her. But once her husband proves sexually unfaithful, life deteriorates rapidly. Williams becomes depressed and angry. She drinks more and becomes more heavily involved in drugs. Soon she is selling drugs to support her habit. Her anxieties mount as she now fears she will be arrested. Thieves break into her apartment and steal money. With the pressure building, she becomes distraught one evening and calls a "stress line." She tells the person on the phone, "Please, someone come and help me with my daughter before I kill her." As Williams tells it, the authorities arrived shortly thereafter and took her daughter away. She expresses surprise today that the authorities believed her daughter was in danger. Her threat to kill her daughter was "simply a manner of speaking," she maintains. She did not mean to be taken literally. Williams does not tell what happened after that, but apparently her daughter was eventually returned to her care.

The contamination form of storytelling is equally apparent, if less dramatic, in Williams's account of an important scene from adolescence. She describes her triumphant graduation from eighth grade. "That was something I achieved on my own, and I felt very proud." Still, what follows immediately in her account is failure. "That was the last time I walked across the stage," she remarked. After graduating, Tanya became "the black sheep in the family." In the fourth contamination sequence, Tanya returns to her problems with men. In describing "one other important scene that stands out in your life story," Tanya tells of the happiness she felt when, in her mid-30s, she took up romantically with a much younger man. Trapped in an abusive marriage, she found comfort and excitement in the affair. Her lover, Frank, sold drugs. But as Williams tells it, he had finally decided to quit selling and take on a responsible job. Things were looking up until he was shot at a party:

> He [Frank] was a good friend to me. Matter of fact, I loved him. I find that when I care a lot about someone that they leave me, or they die, or someone else takes them. So I try not to love people too much. Even my kids. I love them to death, but I try to remember that something can happen to them. You know what I'm saying? We had just started back speaking [after a previous argument]. He had lung problems, okay? He had been sewed up real bad. They had to do an operation. He couldn't work or anything, so he went to selling drugs. Well, his mother had asked him, everybody was asking him to stop, because he had made a lot of money. He had a lot of money at 17, and this was back about

7 or 8 years ago. So you can imagine because kids then weren't doing what they're doing now. We were trying to tell him not to do this and not to do that, because he'll get in trouble with the police. Well, his brother had gotten arrested . . . [so he] picked this particular night to be the last night that he sold drugs or did anything like that. He even promised his mother. So he went to the party that night, told me to call around 3 o'clock. We had just gotten back together. Matter of fact, he was there dressed like L.L. Cool J. I think that was the thing that was going on back then. One of his friends went through the door and stepped on this girl's foot. He [Frank] didn't step on the girl's foot, but this other boy did. The girl turned around and saw him standing there and went to get her boyfriend. Her boyfriend came back with a gun, grabbed him around his neck, was putting the gun to his head. Everybody was like, "No, no!" They were trying to tell him that's not how it went, but about 10 of his [the gunman's] friends were there. . . . The gun went off and it shot somewhere back here [points to the back of her neck] and severed the spinal cord. He stayed in a coma for about two or three weeks. During this time was when everybody started finding out we were messing around. They called me to the hospital because I wouldn't go. They were like, "Tanya, maybe if Frank can hear your voice, maybe that'll bring him out of it." I was like, "How am I going to do this?" But I thought inside myself, "Man, if I could save a person like that, I'm going." So when I went, he was just laying there. His mother was in the room. He had some pictures he had taken in my bed, satin sheets, and she got them blown up about as big as his window. And when I went inside and seen those pictures of my bedroom, can you imagine how I felt stripped?! In my mind, I was like, "I don't want anybody to know." And then his mother like, "Do you see anything that's familiar to you?" And I said, "No." And then she calls me out of the room and told me that he had told her all about me, showed her the pictures and everything. . . . That was the night he was going to stop everything [selling drugs], you know. I miss him terribly. I loved him. He was the best friend I ever had. He was younger than me, too. But I think he was the best one I ever had, and I'll never get that back again.

The story Williams tells is filled with bloody and violent images and scenes of loss and betrayal. After this happened, soon before her interview, Williams's neighbor was murdered. Williams found her body, throat slit, lying in a pool of blood. Her cousin has been accused of a different murder. Williams took a swing at her husband and put her hand through a window. She needed more than 100 stitches to close the wound, she says. In her earliest memory, her sister is struck in the mouth by a moving swing—"meat and blood everywhere." In another bizarre scene from childhood, she recalls seeing lightning strike an apple tree and split the tree in half. Before the storm, there were frogs near the tree. But the lightning "turned the frogs into slime." After relating this event in the interview, she moves directly into an account of how the White kids in her neighborhood "used to tease us and call us crispy critters," presumably for the dark color of her and her siblings' skin. Like the frogs, Williams has been burned to a crisp. She is Black, but more importantly she is the black sheep of the family. Puberty was like the lightning that burned her soul and made her bad. She cannot undo what fiery nature has wrought. Instead, she is doomed to repeat the contamination sequence again and again. As a result of the repetition of violence, neglect, and betrayal, Williams feels empty and heartless at her core. In a chilling self-commentary, she admits,

> I know of some of the events to make me come to this point. But I really think there's something else deep inside, that maybe I don't even know myself, that really makes me feel that I don't care. When I say I don't care, I'm talking about I don't care. I really don't care about things. I'm only doing what I have to do. I'm alive, so I have to live.

Like redemption sequences, contamination stories have ancient sources (Kaplan & Schwartz, 1993). Greek mythology and drama are filled with tales of good things turning suddenly and irrevocably bad, typically because of the whims of fate (and the gods) or the hubris of protagonists. May (1980) wrote of the mythic sequence of enhancement followed by deprivation, as in the story of Icarus. Icarus fashions wings to fly to the sun, but as he ascends to his goal the heat melts the wax in the wings, and he plummets to the sea below. Murray (1955/1981) argued that this ancient story is a prototype of an Icarus Complex in some young American men, an autobiographical type that scripts steep ascent in life to be followed by precipitous falls. The idea of a fall from grace finds its way into many ancient stories about the beginning of the world. In the West, the most well-known examples are when Adam and Eve are expelled from the Garden of Eden and when Satan is cast out of heaven for insubordination. Sin becomes the ultimate contamination, and ancient texts include a plethora of accounts in which human actors repeat their contamination again and again, never able to undo the bad and get back to the good. Therefore, although redemption sequences sustain hope and commitment in narrative, contamination sequences suggest despair, hopelessness, and the endless repetition of a negative past.

The negative message of the contamination sequence suggests a fatalistic approach to life in which good events are doomed to end in failure and actors can never summon forth the confidence that one's best intentions will generate fruitful outcomes. This kind of confidence may undergird what Erikson (1963, p. 267) called a "belief in the species"—a faith in the worthwhileness of the human enterprise. Adults cannot be generative without a belief in the species, Erikson maintained. Like Williams, they find that they cannot effectively channel their energies into productive work aimed at securing a better future if they believe that bad outcomes will invariably occur. People who see the past as the inevitable evolution of good into bad may be less optimistic about the present and the future for their own lives and less able to commit themselves to improving the lives of others in the present and future. Although redemption sequences help to produce a progressive narrative of self, contamination sequences suggest that progress will not occur, resulting in stagnated or fixated life plots. The protagonist cannot move forward, cannot develop. Old problems are never overcome but instead recycle through the narrative again and again. In what Tomkins (1987) called *contamination scripts*, the protagonist may seek to undo the damage and reexperience an early state of goodness, but such efforts are doomed to failure—or at best half-successes. Tomkins wrote that in a contamination script, though the protagonist "may win battles she loses the war, though she may see the promised land she may never live in it. Her great benefits are paid for with great suffering and at great risk, which she has no choice but to accept for the benefits she can neither permanently possess nor renounce" (1987, p. 168).

Like redemption sequences, contamination sequences come in a wide range of contemporary variations. Table 1-3 lists a number of condensed examples from recent research. In each, the protagonist experiences an initial state of goodness, happiness, satisfaction, joy, excitement, peace, closeness, intimacy, pride, status, or the like—marriage is wonderful, a woman is promoted in her job, a young boy stands up to a bully, a mother gives birth to a beautiful child. But things turn bad—the marriage fails; the new job brings more headaches than the old one did; the bully's (even meaner) friends terrorize the boy; the baby dies.

Most people can recall contamination events in their lives, increasingly so as they move into and through midlife. But for some people, like Williams, contamination sequences are so numerous and so salient that they become the signature of the life-story plot. In stories dominated by contamination, protagonists seem unable to grow, to progress. At age 41, Williams sets goals for the future that are virtually identical to the goals she had 20 years ago: to graduate from high school, to get a good job, to find a friend, to be "better able to take care of myself." She also hopes "to stop hating my husband so much." Williams wants to grow; she wants to move ahead, but a complex set of forces and factors, both within her and in the threatening and abusive environment wherein she struggles, repeatedly block her attempts. "I am desperately seeking myself," she says. Scaling back her hopes by the end of the interview, Williams says she is looking for a "stepping

TABLE 1-3
Contamination Sequences: Condensed Examples

Protagonist believes marriage is wonderful → partner states he wants a divorce

Protagonist is proud at graduation → father comments on how fat she looked crossing the stage

New house is a joy → repairs and bills become a nightmare

Mother-in-law helps protagonist with children → mother-in-law criticizes her for needing help

Protagonist enjoys schoolwork and likes teacher → teacher publicly scolds her for an error

Playing happily in a park, enjoying freedom → protagonist is injured and cannot find parents

Protagonist enjoys senior class party → class breaks up, protagonist loses contact with good friends

Protagonist gets a desired promotion → the new job brings many frustrations and hassles

Joy at birth of first child → protagonist learns that child has a serious disorder

Looking forward to class trip → protagonist is horrified by the poverty observed on the trip

Protagonist finally establishes intimate relationship with partner → the two of them become homeless

Protagonist relocates so that son can have contact with grandfather → grandfather soon dies

Protagonist receives a gift → gift is stolen

Protagonist enjoys kissing friend on front porch → father shines flashlight and humiliates him

Protagonist enjoys sex → but then feels guilty

Protagonist marries man she loves → husband soon has affairs

Protagonist accomplishes long-sought goal → coworker criticizes her work

Father trusts protagonist to drive family car on business when he is underage → protagonist is arrested and jailed

Protagonist builds model airplane, is proud, takes it to school → schoolmate breaks the plane

---

stone"—a lucky break, a turn of events, a piece of advice that might provide her with the first step along a path that will take her to a better place. She holds out hope for redemption.[4]

NARRATIVE FORM AND THE QUALITY OF LIFE

Our ideas on redemption and contamination sequences were drawn originally from life-narrative research on highly generative and relatively

---

[4]Although we routinely screen out participants in our life-narrative studies who have a history of mental illness or extreme psychological distress, it is clear that Williams was a depressed and anxious woman. Toward the end of her interview, Williams seemed to be asking the interviewer, who was a trained PhD student in counseling psychology, for psychological assistance. Ethical standards for this research preclude our providing such assistance. In the rare instance that a research participant is in psychological distress, interviewers may suggest that the person seek help by consulting a therapist or counselor.

nongenerative adults (McAdams et al., 1997). As the case of Williams indicates, however, a preponderance of contamination sequences in life narratives may be associated with more than merely low levels of generativity. Williams appears to be a depressed and beleaguered woman whose problems extend well beyond issues of caring for the next generation. Indeed, there is no reason to believe that contamination and redemption in life narrative should be associated *only* with an adult's relative standing on the Eriksonian dimension of generativity, no matter how psychosocially significant that dimension might be. The characteristic ways that people narrate important turns in the perceived course of their lives may indeed speak more broadly to the overall quality of their lives.

Outside the literature on the narrative study of lives, psychologists of many stripes have argued that the kinds of meanings people draw from significant turning points have profound implications for their overall adaptation and mental health (e.g., Taylor, 1983; Tedeschi & Calhoun, 1995; Vaillant, 1977). In one particularly important line of research, investigators have examined how people cope with naturally occurring negative events, including how people sometimes interpret negative events as leading to personal benefits (Affleck & Tennen, 1996; Tedeschi & Calhoun, 1995; Tedeschi, Park, & Calhoun, 1998). Anecdotal evidence and empirical research suggest that people frequently find silver linings in the dark clouds of illness, bereavement, and trauma. Although the negative turn of events may bring considerable pain and misfortune, many people will conclude that something good came or will come from the adversity. Like Johnson, they may conclude that as a result of the adversity, they have developed greater courage, wisdom, patience, tolerance, empathy, or some other virtue. They may believe that their relationships with family and friends have improved. This kind of benefit-finding may prove to be useful in coping successfully with uncontrollable negative events (Aldwin, Sutton, & Lachman, 1996; Park, Cohen, & Murch, 1996), enabling the suffering person to exert a form of *interpretive control* over daunting personal challenges (Rothbaum, Weisz, & Snyder, 1982).

The message from the literature on benefit-finding is that people who perceive benefits in adversity tend to show better recovery from and adjustment to the negative events that brought them the adversity in the first place. Positive adaptational outcomes of benefit-finding are evident in many self-report indicators of psychological well-being. Empirical evidence suggests that benefit-finding relates to less negative affect in cancer patients (Wollman & Felton, 1983), superior psychological adjustment in women with breast cancer (Taylor, Lichtman, & Wood, 1984), and less mood disturbance and intrusive thoughts in mothers of acutely ill newborns (Affleck, Tennen, & Gershman, 1985). Affleck, Tennen, Croog, and Levine (1987) found that 58% of men in one cohort of heart attack victims reported benefits from their heart attacks after seven weeks of recovery. Eight years later, those who construed benefits were in significantly better cardiac health and were less likely to have suffered a subsequent heart attack. The predictive relation between early benefit-finding and subsequent cardiac health remained significant even after controlling for the patient's age, socioeconomic status, and severity of the initial attack.

Survivors of illness and trauma often report increased self-reliance and broader self-understanding, enhanced self-disclosure and emotional expressiveness in relationships, and a changed philosophy of life (Tedeschi & Calhoun, 1995). Major setbacks in life can challenge a person's assumptive world, but benefit-finding can help to reconstitute that world by specifying an anticipated redemption sequence in which bad events are expected to give way to good outcomes. According to Tedeschi and Calhoun (1995), those good outcomes often manifest themselves in three different areas: (a) changes in self, (b) changes in relationships with others, and (c) changes in philosophy of life and spiritual–existential beliefs. Janoff-Bulman (1992) wrote, "By engaging in interpretations and evaluations that focus on the benefits and lessons learned, survivors emphasize benevolence over malevolence, meaningfulness over randomness, and self-worth over self-abatement" (p. 133). Therefore, like the limitation–remediation script identified by Tomkins (1987), construals of benefits in the wake of adversity provide hope and sustain anticipations of a positive future. These kinds of adaptive construals bear striking similarity to narratives of personal redemption. As a consequence, we would predict that authors of life stories emphasizing redemption themes should show better psychosocial adaptation and mental health overall, compared to individuals whose stories are less redemptive. Conversely, contamination sequences in the life narrative accounts should be negatively associated with overall well-being.

To test these hypotheses, we recently collected life-narrative data and self-report measures of psychological well-being from two different samples of participants (McAdams, Reynolds, Lewis, Patten, & Bowman, 2001). The first sample consisted of 74 midlife adults, approximately half of whom were African American and half of whom were White, and equally divided between males and females. Each participant was interviewed according to the life story method we have already described. For this study, we focused on the eight key life-story scenes that make up the second section of the interview (Table 1-1). Each of the adults also completed self-report measures of life satisfaction, self-esteem, depression, and sense of life coherence, as well as assessments of generativity. The second sample consisted of 125 college students, each of whom provided detailed written accounts of 10 key life-story scenes: (a) high point, (b) low point, (c) turning point, (d) earliest memory, (e) important childhood scene, (f) important adolescent scene, (g) episode of personal continuity, (h) morality scene, (i) decision-making scene, and (j) a scene of setting or realizing a goal. The students completed self-report measures of life satisfaction and Ryff's (1989) six-scale self-report measure of psychological well-being, providing scores for autonomy, environmental mastery, personal growth, positive interpersonal relationships, purpose in life, and self-acceptance.

The eight scenes described by the midlife adults who were interviewed and the 10 scenes described in writing by each of the students were content-analyzed for redemption imagery according to a 4-point scheme. The scene received a quantitative score of +1 if the author explicitly described a turn from a clearly negative situation to a positive one. Following the research of Tedeschi and Calhoun (1995), furthermore, all scenes that initially received the score of +1 were further analyzed for three additional themes: (a) enhanced agency (feelings of self-confidence, power, autonomy, and so on), (b) enhanced communion (feelings of heightened interpersonal closeness, love, intimacy, and so on), and (c) enhanced religious or spiritual insight. As a consequence, a maximum score of +4 was possible—for a scene with an explicit redemptive turn from negative to positive that in turn led to enhanced personal agency, enhanced friendship or love, and enhanced religious or spiritual insight. For contamination sequences, a simpler yes–no coding scheme was used. The scene received a score of +1 if the author described an explicit turn from a positive to a negative situation in the account. Otherwise, the account received a score of 0 for contamination.[5]

The results from the midlife sample replicated findings we have obtained previously with respect to generativity. Highly generative adults constructed life-story scenes containing more redemptive and less contamination imagery than did adults scoring low on measures of generativity. In addition, redemption and contamination were significantly associated with well-being. The incidence of redemptive imagery in the eight scenes was significantly positively associated with independent, questionnaire measures of life satisfaction, self-esteem, and life coherence, and negatively correlated with depression. By contrast, contamination sequences were very strongly and positively associated with depression and negatively correlated with life satisfaction, self-esteem, and sense of coherence in life.

In reading the students' written accounts of significant scenes, we found very few examples of contamination sequences. The paucity of contamination sequences among the students may have been because of their relative youth or the written method we used, which does not appear to produce narrative accounts that are as rich and personally revealing as those obtained in the interview (Baerger & McAdams, 1999). As a consequence, we coded the students' scenes for redemption sequences only. Mirroring

---

[5] Coding manuals may be obtained from the first author.

findings with midlife adults, nonetheless, redemption scores from written scenes were significantly associated with life satisfaction and with five of the six scales developed by Ryff (1989) for assessing psychological well-being.

Do the findings on redemption sequences and well-being simply indicate that happy people write happy stories about their lives? Not exactly. We also coded the 10 scenes provided by the students for their overall emotional tone. Emotionally positive scenes received a high score; emotionally negative scenes received a low score. Our coding of emotional tone turned out to be only moderately positively correlated with redemption scores. More important, a multiple regression statistical procedure showed that the index of redemptive imagery was a much more powerful predictor of well-being than were the ratings of emotional tone. It is not the case, then, that happy, upbeat life narratives are strongly associated with psychological well-being. Rather, it is narratives in which negative scenes are transformed into positive outcomes that are strongly linked to feeling satisfied and fulfilled in life.

In conclusion, we view redemption and contamination sequences as narrative strategies for making sense of perceived transitions in life. This sense-making contributes to the construction of identity in adolescence and adulthood, as people attempt to integrate disparate elements of their lives into life stories (McAdams, 1985, 1993). Because we conceive of identity as a life story, identity exists as a product of the imagination. But life stories are not imagined out of thin air. Instead, they are based on reality as both personally known and consensually validated. There exists, therefore, a complex relationship between what "really happens" in a person's life and how the person chooses to remember and understand it. In depicting redemption and contamination sequences as narrative forms or strategies for making sense of life transitions, the emphasis is on how the person chooses to construct his or her reality. But it should also be emphasized that each person's reality is different in both subjective and objective senses. In this regard, one may also argue that a person chooses, say, to narrate particular events in his or her past in a redemptive manner because that is indeed how the events transpired: Bad things led to good things at the time. Following this line of reasoning, one may submit that our results show not so much the contemporaneous correlation between particular strategies for making sense of the past on the one hand and psychosocial adaptation on the other but rather how real events from the past come to shape a person's adaptation in the present. Following this line of reasoning, then, some participants are depressed and less satisfied with life because in the past many good events in their lives ultimately led to bad outcomes.

We cannot rule out either of the interpretations. Indeed, it is likely that both hold some truth. Psychosocial adjustment may be associated with both the use of particular narrative strategies for making sense of the past and the fact of having experienced certain kinds of events in the past. The first explanation emphasizes the sense in which life narration is a psychologically meaningful reconstruction of the past, whereas the second underscores the fact that real events in the past may have long-term influences on such things as adult generativity and psychological well-being. We view life stories as *psychosocial constructions* that are jointly authored by the individual whose life is being told and the culture within which the individual lives, from which he or she gathers the narrative resources and frameworks that shape storytelling itself. Different cultures provide different rules for how to tell a story about a life (Rosenwald & Ochberg, 1992). Western societies hold certain expectations about the veridicality of the past—about what counts as having really happened and what else may be pure fabrication or myth. The current controversy over the veridicality of repressed memories demonstrates just how much can be at stake when such cultural assumptions are challenged.

Our research into redemption and contamination sequences is based on the assumption that the participants told stories about the past that they believed to be more or less veridical. But it also assumes that a great deal of personal choice is usually involved in the telling of any autobiographical episode, especially when people are confronted with the task of choosing only a few events from the past that signify especially important happenings and developments in their lives. Choice is implicated not only in the selection of what particular scene to narrate but also in how to narrate the scene, how to frame its antecedents and consequences, and what conclusions to draw from it. In a redemption sequence, the individual narrates a sequence in which a very bad scene eventually results in some kind of positive outcome. In many instances, there are likely to be multiple outcomes of any particular event in a person's life. Yet the person telling the story in a redemptive manner manages, as Johnson did repeatedly, to elaborate on a particularly positive outcome. By contrast, the person who tells a contamination sequence manages to find the negative consequence of a particularly positive scene, and some people, like Williams, are especially wont to reconstruct their lives in this manner. In both cases, the consequences may have really occurred, but there are likely to have been other consequences as well, some of which the individual has chosen not to narrate.

Therefore, it is likely that individual differences in the ways in which people narrate life transitions and turning points reflect both differences in the objective past and differences in the styles and manners in which people choose to make narrative sense of life. The individual styles used, furthermore, are likely to be both the causes and the consequences of different levels of psychosocial adaptation. Thus depressed and nongenerative people may be especially prone to narrating life in contamination terms, and the tendency to narrate life via contamination sequences may exacerbate depression itself and undermine the adult's efforts to make positive contributions to the next generation. Similarly, people who feel relatively satisfied with their lives and feel that they are making important contributions to others may be especially prone to narrating their lives in redemptive terms, which in turn may enhance further their generative efforts and their sense of well-being.

REFERENCES

Ackerman, S., Zuroff, D., & Moscowitz, D. S. (in press). Generativity in midlife and young adults: Links to agency, communion, and well-being. *International Journal of Aging and Human Development.*

Affleck, G., & Tennen, H. (1996). Construing benefits from adversity: Adaptational significance and dispositional underpinnings. *Journal of Personality, 64,* 899–922.

Affleck, G., Tennen, H., Croog, S., & Levine, S. (1987). Causal attribution, perceived benefits, and morbidity following a heart attack: An eight-year study. *Journal of Consulting and Clinical Psychology, 55,* 29–35.

Affleck, G., Tennen, H., & Gershman, K. (1985). Cognitive adaptations to high risk infants: The search for meaning, mastery, and protection from future harm. *American Journal of Mental Deficiency, 89,* 653–656.

Aldwin, C. M., Sutton, K. J., & Lachman, M. (1996). The development of coping resources in adulthood. *Journal of Personality, 64,* 837–871.

Baerger, D., & McAdams, D. P. (1999). Life story coherence and its relation to psychological well-being. *Narrative Inquiry, 9,* 69–96.

Cohler, B. J. (1982). Personal narrative and the life course. In P. Baltes & O. G. Brim (Eds.), *Life span development and behavior* (Vol. 4, pp. 205–241). New York: Academic Press.

Cohler, B. J., Hostetler, A. J., & Boxer, A. M. (1998). Generativity, social context, and lived experience: Narratives of gay men in middle adulthood. In D. P. McAdams & E. de St. Aubin (Eds.), *Generativity and adult development: How and why we care for the next generation* (pp. 265–310). Washington, DC: American Psychological Association.

Colby, A., & Damon, W. (1992). *Some do care: Contemporary lives of moral commitment.* New York: Free Press.

Cole, E., & Stewart, A. J. (1996). Meanings of political participation among Black and White women: Political identity and social responsibility. *Journal of Personality and Social Psychology, 71,* 130–140.

Cushman, P. (1995). *Constructing the self, constructing America: A cultural history of psychotherapy.* Reading, MA: Addison-Wesley.

de St. Aubin, E., & McAdams, D. P. (1995). The relations of generative concern and generative action to personality traits, satisfaction/happiness with life, and ego development. *Journal of Adult Development, 2,* 99–112.

Emmons, R. A. (1986). Personal strivings: An approach to personality and subjective well-being. *Journal of Personality and Social Psychology, 51*, 1058–1068.

Erikson, E. H. (1963). *Childhood and society* (2nd ed.). New York: Norton.

Erikson, E. H. (1969). *Gandhi's truth: On the origins of militant nonviolence*. New York: Norton.

Gergen, K. J., & Gergen, M. (1986). Narrative form and the construction of psychological science. In T. R. Sarbin (Ed.), *Narrative psychology: The storied nature of human conduct* (pp. 22–44). New York: Praeger.

Giddens, A. (1991). *Modernity and self-identity: Self and society in the late modern age*. Stanford, CA: Stanford University Press.

Gregg, G. (1991). *Self-representation: Life narrative studies in identity and ideology*. New York: Greenwood Press.

Hart, H. M., McAdams, D. P., Hirsch, B. J., & Bauer, J. (in press). Generativity and social involvements among African-American and among white adults. *Journal of Research in Personality*.

Hermans, H. J. M., & Hermans-Jansen, E. (1995). *Self-narratives: The construction of meaning in psychotherapy*. New York: Guilford Press.

Holstein, J. A., & Gubrium, J. F. (2000). *The self we live by: Narrative identity in a postmodern world*. New York: Oxford University Press.

James, W. (1902/1958). *The varieties of religious experience*. New York: New American Library.

Janoff-Bulman, R. (1992). *Shattered assumptions: Toward a new psychology of trauma*. New York: Free Press.

Josselson, R. (1995). Narrative and psychological understanding. *Psychiatry, 58*, 330–343.

Kaplan, K. J., & Schwartz, M. B. (1993). *A psychology of hope: An antidote to the suicidal pathology of Western civilization*. New York: Praeger.

Kenyon, G. M. (1996). The meaning/value of personal storytelling. In J. E. Birren, G. M. Kenyon, J-E Ruth, J. J. F. Schroots, & T. Svennson (Eds.), *Aging and biography: Explorations in adult development* (pp. 21–38). New York: Springer.

Keyes, C. L. M., & Ryff, C. D. (1998). Generativity in adult lives: Social structural contours and the quality of life consequences. In D. P. McAdams & E. de St. Aubin (Eds.), *Generativity and adult development: How and why we care for the next generation* (pp. 227–264). Washington, DC: American Psychological Association.

Kotre, J. (1984). *Outliving the self: Generativity and the interpretation of lives*. Baltimore: Johns Hopkins University Press.

Kotre, J. (1999). *Make it count*. New York: Free Press.

MacIntyre, A. (1981). *After virtue*. Notre Dame, IN: University of Notre Dame Press.

May, R. (1980). *Sex and fantasy: Patterns of male and female development*. New York: Norton.

McAdams, D. P. (1985). *Power, intimacy, and the life story: Personological inquiries into identity*. New York: Guilford Press.

McAdams, D. P. (1993). *The stories we live by: Personal myths and the making of the self*. New York: Morrow.

McAdams, D. P. (1999). Personal narratives and the life story. In L. Pervin & O. John (Eds.), *Handbook of personality theory and research* (2nd ed.; pp. 478–500). New York: Guilford Press.

McAdams, D. P. (in press). Generativity in midlife. In M. Lachman (Ed.), *Handbook of midlife development*. New York: Oxford University Press.

McAdams, D. P., Bowman, P. J., Lewis, M., Hart, H. M., & Cole, E. (1999). *Generativity and the construction of life stories among African-American adults: A qualitative study*. Unpublished manuscript, Northwestern University.

McAdams, D. P., Diamond, A., de St. Aubin, E., & Mansfield, E. (1997). Stories of commitment: The psychosocial construction of generative lives. *Journal of Personality and Social Psychology, 72*, 678–694.

McAdams, D. P., & de St. Aubin, E. (1992). A theory of generativity and its assessment through self-report, behavioral acts, and narrative themes in autobiography. *Journal of Personality and Social Psychology, 62*, 1003–1015.

McAdams, D. P., & de St. Aubin, E. (Eds.). (1998). *Generativity and adult development: How and why we care for the next generation*. Washington, DC: American Psychological Association.

McAdams, D. P., de St. Aubin, E., & Logan, R. L. (1993). Generativity among young, midlife, and older adults. *Psychology and Aging, 8*, 221–230.

McAdams, D. P., Hart, H., & Maruna, S. (1998). The anatomy of generativity. In D. P. McAdams & E. de St. Aubin (Eds.), *Generativity and adult development: How and why we care for the next generation* (pp. 7–43). Washington, DC: American Psychological Association.

McAdams, D. P., Reynolds, J., Lewis, M., Patten, A. H., & Bowman, P. J. (2001). When bad things turn good and good things turn bad: Sequences of redemption and contamination in life narrative and their relation to psychosocial adaptation in midlife adults and in students. *Personality and Social Psychology Bulletin, 27*, 472–483.

Miller, W. R., & C'deBaca, J. (1994). Quantum change: Toward a psychology of transformation. In T. Heatherton & J. Weinberger (Eds.), *Can personality change?* (pp. 253–280). Washington, DC: American Psychological Association.

Murray, H. A. (1955/1981). American Icarus. In E. S. Shneidman (Ed.), *Endeavors in psychology: Selections from the personology of Henry A. Murray* (pp. 535–556). New York: Harper & Row.

Nakagawa, K. (1991). *Explorations into the correlates of public school reform and parental involvement*. Unpublished doctoral dissertation, Human Development and Social Policy, Northwestern University.

Park, C. L., Cohen, L. H., & Murch, R. L. (1996). Assessment and prediction of stress-related growth. *Journal of Personality, 64*, 71–105.

Peterson, B. E., & Klohnen, E. C. (1995). Realization of generativity in two samples of women at midlife. *Psychology and Aging, 10,* 20–29.

Peterson, B. E., Smirles, K. A., & Wentworth, P. A. (1997). Generativity and authoritarianism: Implications for personality, political involvement, and parenting. *Journal of Personality and Social Psychology, 72,* 1202–1216.

Pratt, M., Danso, H. A., Arnold, M. L., & Norris, J. (in press). Adults' generativity and the socialization of adolescents: Relations to mothers' and fathers' parenting beliefs, styles, and practices. *Journal of Personality.*

Randall, J. (1995). *The stories we are: An essay on self-creation.* Toronto: University of Toronto Press.

Rosenwald, G. C. (1992). Conclusion: Reflections on narrative self-understanding. In G. C. Rosenwald & R. L. Ochberg (Eds.), *Storied lives: The cultural politics of self-understanding* (pp. 265–289). New Haven, CT: Yale University Press.

Rosenwald, G. C., & Ochberg, R. L. (1992). (Eds.). *Storied lives: The cultural politics of self-understanding.* New Haven, CT: Yale University Press.

Rothbaum, F., Weisz, J. R., & Snyder, S. S. (1982). Changing the world and changing the self: A two-process model of perceived control. *Journal of Personality and Social Psychology, 42,* 5–37.

Ryff, C. D. (1989). Happiness is everything, or is it? Explorations on the meaning of psychological well-being. *Journal of Personality and Social Psychology, 57,* 1069–1081.

Singer, J. A., & Salovey, P. (1993). *The remembered self: Emotion and memory in personality.* New York: Free Press.

Snarey, J. (1993). *How fathers care for the next generation: A four-decade study.* Cambridge, MA: Harvard University Press.

Taylor, S. E. (1983). Adjustment to threatening events: A theory of cognitive adaptation. *American Psychologist, 38,* 624–630.

Taylor, S. E., Lichtman, R. R., & Wood, J. V. (1984). Attributions, beliefs about control, and adjustment to breast cancer. *Journal of Personality and Social Psychology, 46,* 489–502.

Tedeschi, R. G., & Calhoun, L. G. (1995). *Trauma and transformation: Growing in the aftermath of suffering.* Thousand Oaks, CA: Sage.

Tedeschi, R. G., Park, C. L., & Calhoun, L. G. (Eds.). (1998). *Posttraumatic growth: Positive changes in the aftermath of crisis.* Mahwah, NJ: Erlbaum.

Tomkins, S. S. (1987). Script theory. In J. Aronoff, A. I. Rabin, & R. A. Zucker (Eds.), *The emergence of personality* (pp. 147–216). New York: Springer.

Vaillant, G. E. (1977). *Adaptation to life.* Boston: Little, Brown.

von Franz, M.-L. (1980). *The psychological meaning of redemption motifs in fairytales.* Toronto: Inner City Books.

Widdershoven, G. A. M. (1993). The story of life: Hermeneutic perspectives on the relationship between narrative and life history. In R. Josselson & A.

Lieblich (Eds.), *The narrative study of lives* (Vol. 1, pp. 1–20). Thousand Oaks, CA: Sage.

Wiersma, J. (1988). The press release: Symbolic communication in life history interviewing. *Journal of Personality, 56,* 205–238.

Wollman, C., & Felton, B. (1983). Social supports as stress buffers for adult cancer patients. *Psychosomatic Medicine, 45,* 322–331.

2

THE CRIME, PUNISHMENT, AND ETHICAL TRANSFORMATION OF TWO RADICALS: OR HOW KATHERINE POWER IMPROVES ON DOSTOEVSKY

JANET LANDMAN

Crime and Punishment, Dostoevsky's 1866 novel, centers on the fictional character of Rodion Romanych Raskolnikov, an impoverished 23-year-old ex-student. Raskolnikov is portrayed as acting out two strands of radical sociopolitical thought of his day: nihilism and utilitarianism. He construed these theories in such a way as to convince himself that he was the kind of "extraordinary man" who is justified in committing murder. In the belief (or hope) that he is an extraordinary man, Raskolnikov ax-murders and robs an elderly female pawnbroker. In the process of committing this murder, he ends up killing the good-hearted, simple-minded sister of the pawnbroker as well. This—the Crime—transpires in Book I, fewer than 100 pages into the 630-page 1991 British Penguin paperback edition of *Crime and Punishment* (Dostoevsky, 1991, hereinafter referred to as "C&P"). Books II through VI detail in 484 pages the excruciating twistings and turnings of Raskolnikov's psychological state during the month or so that he evades capture. A 17-page epilogue sketches Raskolnikov's surrender, trial, and imprisonment.

On September 23, 1970, Katherine Ann Power was a 20-year-old honors student at Brandeis, a good Catholic girl—and a member of a group

Preparation of this article was facilitated by a course release granted by the Babson College Board of Research. I thank Steve Collins, Laura Godtfredson, Jim Hoopes, Miriam Landman, and David Winter for critical readings of earlier versions of this manuscript. I am most grateful for Katherine Power's openness and willingness to engage herself with this project—and even more for the great good gift of her friendship. She has read and accepted this analysis as probative. As required by the Special Condition of Probation imposed in Suffolk Superior Court on October 6, 1993, Ms. Power will receive no profit or benefit from this work.

of five who were robbing the State Street Bank & Trust Company in Brighton, Massachusetts, near Boston. In the parlance of the day, the group was "liberating funds" from a collaborationist "establishment" to support the movement against the Vietnam War. Power, who was driving the getaway switch car, did not know it until later, but one of the group, ex-convict William Gilday, had stayed behind at the bank and shot and killed Boston police officer and father of nine Walter Schroeder. Under Massachusetts's felony murder law, because all five group members were engaged in a felony when someone was killed, all five were chargeable with murder.

Power went underground. For 23 years her family heard nothing from her, as she changed her name and moved from place to place to elude capture. She remained on the FBI's Ten Most Wanted list longer than any other woman in history. Finally, in September of 1993, she gave herself up, waived her right to a trial, pleaded guilty to manslaughter, and began serving an 8- to 12-year prison sentence in the Massachusetts Correctional Institution in Framingham.

There are a number of rather striking biographical parallels between these two characters, one fictional and the other not. Both Raskolnikov and Power could be called Sixties radicals—the 1860s for Raskolnikov and the 1960s for Power. Both were ex-college students in their early 20s when they engaged in criminal acts that resulted in murder. Both tried to elude capture for some time, eventually turned themselves in to a law enforcement system that had no tangible evidence of their guilt, confessed, and pleaded guilty. Both received prison sentences of eight years or more.

More significant, though, are the psychological and ethical parallels. For both Raskolnikov and Power, the crime was inspired in part by the sociopolitical thought of the times. For both, an excruciating sense of shame sent them fleeing from the law; thereafter, the physical isolation required of a fugitive produced in both an extremely painful sense of alienation from family and community. Both suffered psychological punishments in addition to shame, including regret and despair. Both sought to escape these feelings by throwing themselves into frantic activity. Both had powerful impulses to atone, confess, and be apprehended even while fleeing. In the end, both Raskolnikov and Power found that prison and its concomitant "cure through community" offered the only way to resolve their emotional and ethical afflictions.

REGRET AND ITS CURE

Lillian Hellman articulated the essence of the American attitude toward regret when she observed, "It is considered unhealthy in America to remember mistakes, neurotic to think about them, psychotic to dwell upon them." Though Hellman was playing rather fast and loose with the concepts of neuroticism and psychoticism, her social observation strikes me as right on target. Regret presents a direct affront to the militant optimism and future orientation of American culture—as expressed in a plethora of regret-averse maxims of ours like, "That was then, this is now"; "Oh, that's history"; "Don't dwell on the past"; and for goodness' sake, "Never cry over spilled milk." The fact remains that at some time in any adult life, *then* will bleed into *now*, we will find ourselves thinking about—maybe even dwelling on—mistakes, and tears will fall with the spilled milk (for elaboration, see Landman, 1993).

Fortunately, most people's regrets concern mistakes of a lesser magnitude than those of Katherine Power and her fictional counterpart, Raskolnikov. Yet because of the richness and nuance of their narratives, there is much to be learned from them of potential benefit to anyone with regrets—particularly regrets for having harmed someone else.

For one thing, these stories offer converging evidence of *ineffective* approaches to dealing with regret and similar emotions. In accord with an expanding body of psychological research, Raskolnikov's and Power's narratives demonstrate that efforts to suppress, deny, or otherwise circumvent unwanted emotions simply do not work (e.g., Pennebaker, 1993, 1997; Roemer & Borkovec, 1994; Wegner, 1994a, 1994b; Wegner, Schneider, Carter, & White, 1987). Or not for long. And not unless you are a sociopath. More important, the life stories of Power and Raskolnikov shed considerable light on the question of what *can* be done ethically to transform one's regret, guilt, and despair after having done serious harm to others.

According to sociologist Philip Rieff (1966), our Sixties radicals faced two possible avenues—one private, the other communal—to the transformation of the regret that followed from their crimes. The private, or in Rieff's formulation, the *analytic*, path leads inward to what Ryle refers to as the "secret grotto in the head" (Ryle, quoted in Geertz, 1973, p. 362); there the goal is a return to private well-being. In their respective secret grottoes these protagonists did much of the necessary work of feeling and self-reflection—especially feeling. These stories provide converging evidence of *emotion* as the basis of morality.

Alternatively, these protagonists could seek a communal cure through reconnection with others and with the world in which they had committed their crimes. *Or*, to de-dichotomize Rieff's analysis, they could do *both*—which is what I argue they did. In this chapter, I demonstrate how Raskolnikov and Power played out both trajectories, one inward to the secret grotto and the other outward toward community—complementary and intertwined paths to ethical development.

The present analysis relies focally on the field of narrative psychology, and more broadly, narratology, the "theory of narratives, narrative texts . . .

events, cultural artifacts that 'tell a story' " (Bal, 1997, p. 3). Central to the narrative perspective is the idea that "identity is a life story [told] . . . in order to provide [the individual's] life with unity or purpose and in order to articulate a meaningful niche in the psychosocial world" (McAdams, 1997, p. 5). Explications of narrative form reveal both of these stories as tragic in form—up to the point of their epilogues, which relate the stories of their imprisonment. At that point, both stories take on a romantic form (Frye, 1957; Gergen & Gergen, 1986; Landman, 1993, 1995). Despite this shared overall narrative arc, however, as I argue later, Raskolnikov's story exemplifies a more private, personal restitution story, and Power's a more relational and communal quest story (A. Frank, 1995).

Besides substantive contributions, I hope with this chapter to make methodological contributions by exploring the procedure of juxtaposing two different types of narrative data: fictional and nonfictional. I have culled the fictional data from several close readings (and teachings) of *Crime and Punishment*. The nonfiction narrative data on Katherine Power come from two sources: interviews or stories conducted or written by others and the story as Power has told it to me over the years from 1995 to the present. Preeminent in the former category is Lucinda Franks's perceptive 1994 *New Yorker* article, "Return of the Fugitive," based on postsurrender interviews with Power, her family, friends, former teachers, and others. The person-to-person narrative that Power has related to me began with a four-hour audiotape-recorded interview that I conducted with Power in prison in August 1995, and has continued to the present in the form of mailed correspondence, many prison visits, and postvisit notes that I took immediately after these prison visits.

Power possesses an unusually self-aware, articulate, and convincing ability to express her inner life. Still, she can hardly be expected to surpass what the master novelist, Dostoevsky, does in his 660-page *Crime and Punishment*. A fictional narrative like *Crime and Punishment* gives us the riches of novelistic truth, thickly described (Morson, 1994). Moreover, the novel condenses the action into a span of days and months, compared with the slow-motion 29-year span of time at issue for Power.

The primary goal of my analysis, however, is to uncover the specifics of the *transformational process*. Unfortunately for this project, Raskolnikov changes very little until the portion of the epilogue depicting his imprisonment. Even there, Dostoevsky outlines Raskolnikov's surrender, trial, and about nine months of his prison sentence in only 17 pages of the 630-page edition I have used in this analysis. In fact, a number of literary critics have viewed this sketchy epilogue as a blemish on an otherwise magnificent work. This is where the *nonfiction* narrative adds significantly to the analysis. Power, I argue, improves on Dostoevsky's epilogue. She writes a fuller, more coherent, more convincing, and more dramatic epilogue for her own life narrative. Power's epilogue fills in the gaps in Dostoevsky's narrative, contributing enormously to the understanding of what turning points make up the ethical transition from criminal fugitive to tribal elder.

ELEMENTS OF THE NARRATIVES

From this point on, I organize the analysis using prevalent elements of narrative identified by McAdams (1997) and Robinson and Hawpe (1986). These narrative elements, some slightly revised by me, include protagonist-in-context/protagonist-in-ideological setting, the predicament, the struggle with the predicament/consequences, and outcome/denouement. In addition, I add another narrative element to my knowledge not previously identified in the narrative literature—the epilogue.

Protagonist-in-Context/Protagonist-in-Ideological-Setting

Neither Raskolnikov nor Power thought up their crimes in a vacuum. For this reason, Robinson and Hawpe's (1986) idea of protagonist-in-context is especially apt. The concept of protagonist-in-context specifically recognizes at least one sense of this assertion of Marx's: "Men make their own history, but not as they please. They do not choose for themselves, but have to work upon circumstances as they find them, have to fashion the material handed down by the past" (cited by Ricoeur, 1988, p. 213).

Two other narrative concepts prove especially illuminating in this analysis: Linde's concept of *coherence system* (1993) and McAdams's concept of *ideological setting*. A *coherence system* is a "system of beliefs and relations between beliefs" (Linde, 1993, p. 163). An ideological setting is the "body of values and beliefs" (McAdams, 1997, p. 67) concerning "questions of goodness and truth" (McAdams, 1997, p. 81) that the individual encounters at a particular time and place. These narrative notions reveal specific aspects of context that proved especially influential in the etiology of the crimes these protagonists committed.

It matters that when they committed their crimes Raskolnikov was 23 and Power 20. One's personal ideology is generally formed during the adolescent and postadolescent years, and therefore is most influenced by the ideological setting in which one finds one's self at that period in life (Linde, 1993; McAdams, 1997). At that life stage, one's ideological setting "functions as a 'setting' for identity" (McAdams, 1997, p. 81), that sense of who one is and how one means to live one's life. Narrative analysis reveals then the significance of Raskolnikov's and Power's life stage as a time in life particularly ripe for drafting their own fledgling identities, their own life stories, in light of their ideological settings.

It matters that both Raskolnikov and Power conceived their crimes while students at universities, places where social critique typically flourishes. Dostoevsky takes pains to let his readers know that the idea for Raskolnikov's crime did not spring forth unparented from the admittedly twisted mind of Raskolnikov. The idea was in the very air of a time and place dominated by utilitarian and nihilist social theories. Similarly, Power committed her crime during a time that scholars of the Sixties describe as the peak of the militant phase of the antiwar movement (Gitlin, 1987), following immediately on the peak of the state's use of violence against dissenters. She committed her crime in 1970, the year the Black Panthers had declared "The Year of the Revolution" (Gitlin, 1987, p. 345), a time in which the phrase "make revolution" was being freely bandied about, especially at universities like Brandeis.

The Case of Raskolnikov

In *Crime and Punishment* Dostoevsky presents utilitarian theory as one of two ideas that directly influenced Raskolnikov's decision to commit his crime (J. Frank, 1995). Described in the novel as among "the latest ideas," utilitarian sentiments were said to have become so commonplace that Raskolnikov's friend, Razumikhin (one of the most praiseworthy characters in the novel), disgustedly refers to them as "these constant, incessant clichés, the same thing over and over again" (C&P, p. 194).

Dostoevsky has Luzhin, one of the two most odious characters in the novel, applaud the popular utilitarian case against helping those in need: "Science, however, tells us: 'Love yourself before all others, for everything in the world is founded upon self-interest.' " Dostoevsky is here portraying critically, in his own words, "the science of our day [that] has actually declared compassion a social evil" (C&P, p. 45).[1] Central to *Crime and Punishment* is a critique of the moral bankruptcy of this "scientifically" based, hyperindividualistic, egoistic utilitarian ideology (J. Frank, 1995; McDuff, 1991), an ideology that, when taken to its logical end, can justify eliminating individuals deemed "useless" or "parasitical."

The nihilist ideology that had emerged in Russia concurrent with Dostoevsky's youth was a second notion that much occupied Dostoevsky and that he also portrayed as directly contributing to Raskolnikov's crime (J. Frank, 1995; McDuff, 1991). As Raskolnikov construed the theory, a superior (that is, wholly "rational" and wholly self-sufficient) individual will "step across" (trans-gress) the "obstacle" of conventional moral "superstitions"—such as the belief that murder, except in self-defense, is always wrong. For

---

[1]These passages could have been written today, so well do they express an ideology that has bullied its way back into fashion in the America of the late twentieth and early twenty-first centuries.

Raskolnikov, Napoleon, who sacrificed countless lives in the execution of his egoistic goals, exactly personified this superior, extraordinary man.

According to Dostoevsky's biographer, Joseph Frank, nihilism often melded with utilitarianism to assert the "right of superior individuals to override the moral law at their own sweet will—in the interests of humanity as a whole, of course!" (1995, p. 76). Six months before his crime Raskolnikov had articulated certain ethical implications of this hybrid theory in an article he titled "On Crime." There he declared that "an 'extraordinary' person has a right . . . not an official right, of course, but a private one, to allow his conscience to step across certain obstacles, and then only if the execution of his idea (which may occasionally be the salvation of all mankind) requires it" (C&P, p. 312). In Bakhtin's (1994) view, all of Dostoevsky's major characters undertake to put themselves to the test. Certainly Raskolnikov supports Bahktin's interpretation, committing the murder primarily to test his own mettle, to discover whether he has what it takes, whether he is one of the extraordinary few or "a louse" like everyone else. This supremely complicated character is also motivated, however, by the utilitarian goal of achieving the greater good for the greater number by using the stolen money to save his sister from a despicable marriage and his mother and himself from abject poverty.

The Case of Katherine Ann Power

Power grew up the oldest daughter of seven children in a Catholic family, a straight-A student, and all-round "good girl." Like Raskolnikov, she happened to come of age in a time and place where social forces (religious, familial, educational, and geopolitical) facilitated her development as a political dissident.

As for the religious forces, Power's immersion in the coherence system of Roman Catholicism, including 12 years of parochial schooling, critically shaped her identity. Linde (1993), in fact, singles out Catholicism as the prototype of a coherence system likely to hold a vital place in the identity of someone exposed to it at a formative life period. As her therapist, Linda Carrol, later observed, "Katherine Power had been a young Catholic trained to seek a higher purpose" (Franks, 1994, p. 44).

Power specified to Lucinda Franks what she had believed this higher purpose might demand of her: "I grew up on stories of the saints—the ones who got their heads chopped off for the greater good. I always imagined how glorious that kind of sacrifice would be" (Franks, 1994, p. 48). As Linde pointed out, "an activity, an aptitude, or an ambition that goes back to early childhood must be seen as intrinsic to the self" (1993, p. 135) in that it manifests the temporal continuity typically expected of a well-formed life story. In Power we see ambitions of glorious self-sacrifice for the greater good rooted in her early childhood and continuing into her college years, when she saw herself as called on to put her life on the line to help end a war that she (and at least half the U.S. populace at the time; Gitlin, 1987) believed to be unjust.

In my conversations with Power, she has at times appeared to me to be embarrassed by or ashamed of these childhood and adolescent fantasies of heroic self-sacrifice, dismissing them as "grandiose." Elkind (1981, cited in McAdams, 1997, p. 80) and McAdams (1997) offer a more forgiving developmental understanding of such fantasies, or as Elkind (1981) called them, *personal fables*. McAdams wrote, "The personal fable may look like a delusion of grandeur, but in its proper developmental place it is normal and even healthy" (1997, p. 80). In fact, in its proper developmental place, adolescence, the personal fable, or "first draft" of a life story, *typically* incorporates grand ambitions that "celebrate the self's greatness, as when the young person spins fantasies about becoming the greatest scientist the world has ever known, writing the great American novel, or *changing the world in one glorious sweep*" (McAdams, 1997, p. 80, emphasis added). I would argue that the grand ambitions of Power's youth were not only developmentally normal but that she happened to be born into an entire cohort who, rightly or not, viewed itself as responsible for and capable of changing the world.

Power also happened to have been born to parents who modeled and directly taught principled nonconformity. First, as shown in this anecdote that Power (KP) related to me (JL) in our tape-recorded prison interview of August 1995, her parents had modeled activist nonconformity in their own behavior:

> **KP:** For the high school to be accredited, we had to have a guidance program. Sister Sheila, marvelous woman, hired this non-Catholic to set up our guidance program and to act as the guidance counselor for the first year. And there was some resistance to him because he was not Catholic, and I did not remember this, but he told me this story—of my parents being the activists in support of him. . . .

Power related to me in the same interview how her parents had explicitly instructed their children to resist mindless conformity:

> **KP:** . . . there's another piece of Catholic culture that is, was an explicit teaching in my life, in my home, and that is the culture of civil disobedience. The culture of nonconformity. My mother did deliberate . . . teaching of nonconformity to us. You know, the popsicle truck came down the street, we did not run out with all the other kids on the block to get popsicles.
> **JL:** Because?
> **KP:** Because . . . because that's part of thoughtless, reflexive, manipulated consumption. It's, it's, you know, it's wrong. She didn't object to us having popsicles. We went to the ice cream store and brought home

a package of popsicles which stayed in the freezer, and we could have a popsicle. But it was the mindless, mass activity of going out to the ice cream truck.

JL: That's incredible. That she would recognize that and instill that. . . .

KP: Yeah, explicitly. She codified it in words.

Besides the religious and familial influences, geopolitical forces were acting on Power as well. While she was in college, Presidents Johnson and then Nixon were waging a war that was killing hundreds of thousands of Vietnamese and Americans. In the spring of 1970, after having campaigned on a promise to end the war, President Nixon instead extended the war into Cambodia. Moreover, the government had begun to use mortal violence to suppress dissent: In the spring of 1970 four students at Kent State University were shot to death by Ohio National Guardsmen during a demonstration against the U.S. "incursion" into Cambodia, and two students were killed at a similar demonstration at Jackson State in Mississippi. The accumulation of these and other events radicalized a number of previously peaceable opponents of the war.

By mid-1970, during her senior year in college, Power had come to the conclusion, along with many others, that the avenues for resisting the evil of the Vietnam War peacefully and within the system had proved futile. She dropped out of classes and decided (in her words) "to go to war against the war" as a member of a group of five that included her roommate and friend, Susan Saxe, and three ex-convicts taking courses at Brandeis University in connection with a prison furlough program. This group spent the summer and early fall of 1970 carrying out "actions" designed to bring the war machine to a halt—for instance, firebombing and raiding an armory and robbing banks to fund the purchase of thermite to fuse military trains to their tracks (Franks, 1994).

How could such conduct jibe with Power's religious upbringing? According to Mario Savio (1995), another Catholic activist of the Sixties, Catholicism often socialized susceptible individuals of that generation to take on themselves a sense of personal responsibility to resist evil. As I (another susceptible Catholic of that generation) experienced it, two sets of events from our immediately preceding history contributed to this sense of responsibility: (a) the Holocaust, where for me the lesson was how far evil can go if no one resists it; and (b) the American civil rights movement, where the lesson was how evil can be stopped if individuals join together to resist it. For Power, the Vietnam War was the evil that she and her generation were called to resist.

No good narrative is without conflict (McAdams, 1997), and Power's includes her inner conflict between her identity as a "good girl" who did not break the rules and her sense that to continue to be a good person she would *have* to break the rules:

I've always been good, like the kind of good that's in quotes. I'm "nice." It's like, I'm a joke to the inmates here, because I don't break the rules. I don't do things that are going to make the grownups mad. And there I was feeling morally compelled to break the rules. There was this discomfort—it felt so disturbing, so not *me*. I was violating something but I was feeling that I had to do it, I had to do this to be an O.K. person. (Franks, 1994, p. 51)

Finally, it made a difference that Power was a student at a university that was a proverbial hotbed of unrest. Brandeis was the headquarters, for instance, of the National Student Strike Force, which organized antiwar protests around the country. Some of the professors were indeed urging their students to "make revolution." After Power's surrender, Allen Grossman, who had taught at Brandeis during those years, told Franks: "Impossible moral burdens were put on students. They were told that legitimate sources of money for the movement had dried up. Students like Kathy Power, in their enormous desire to be good, took it all as a personal mandate. . . . The liberal system and legitimate action within that system were denounced, with no thought about where this could lead" (Franks, 1994, p. 49). For Power, a sense of moral outrage against the evil of the Vietnam War remained the one stable feature of her life story during all those years as a fugitive, as Franks observed in her *New Yorker* article: "Running from one false persona to another, she clung to the only self that was constant—the warrior who represented the moral outrage of a generation" (1994, p. 43).

Clearly, both Raskolnikov and Power took the radical thought of their day and ran with it—with similar consequences. Their thinking and intentions were in crucial respects, however, diametrically opposed. Most important, for Raskolnikov killing was justified; for Power, killing was the great evil to be resisted. Deborah Cotton, a classmate of Power's at Brandeis, told Franks about Power: "I'll never forget a discussion several of us had about abortion. She [Power] was adamant that there was never a justification for taking a human life, no matter what the greater good was" (Franks, 1994, p. 48). Raskolnikov intended to commit murder. Power did not intend to commit murder, she herself did not directly kill, and she was and is actively opposed to murder.

Raskolnikov's goal in committing the murder was primarily egoistic—to test his own mettle, to prove to himself that he was an extraordinary person. In contrast, Power's primary "reason" for the bank robbery and her other crimes against property was moral opposition to the Vietnam War.

Still, there were other possible forms of action available to those who hoped to end the war. A group of prominent antiwar activists she then dismissed as "jet-set radicals" had sought out Power and her considerable gifts of mind and tongue, and attempted to enlist her as one of the "generals" (their word)—that is, a leader and spokesperson—in their "war against the war." They wanted her, among other things, to travel to Cuba, meet with the North Vietnamese, and return to the United States to speak out publicly against the war. The problem was that in Power's young Catholic mind that invitation constituted a great "temptation"—to the sin of grandiose egoism. When she renounced that "near occasion of sin," what was left to her (or so she thought) was the path of the "clandestine radical." She chose the way that seemed to her at the time both the most effective and the least grandstanding of the available options. Unlike Raskolnikov, Power's motivations were the opposite of self-aggrandizing.

THE PREDICAMENT: THE CRIME

Raskolnikov and Power did, however, share the crucial conviction that the greater good sometimes requires the independent thinker to engage in acts that lie outside of the law and conventional morality. Raskolnikov's reading of the social thought of his time led him to the belief that wrongdoing to the point of murder was permitted him. Hence he deliberately axed an elderly pawnbroker to death—and her sister as well, when she happened on the scene. Power's experience of her religious and familial upbringing, along with her reading of the social thought and public events of her time and place, led her to the belief that certain lesser wrongs—robbery and other crimes against property—were necessary to arrest a greater wrong— the wholesale murder that an unjust war is. The tragedy is that one of these crimes against property led to the unforeseen murder of a 42-year-old police officer, husband, and father of nine.

THE CONSEQUENCES/THE STRUGGLE
WITH THE PREDICAMENT

For both protagonists, their crimes resulted in an overwhelming sense of shame, which led them to attempt to hide. The shame-induced act of fleeing brought with it other enormously distressing psychological punishments, including a sense of profound alienation, regret, guilt, remorse, panic, apathy, and suicidal despair. In my view, the postcrime struggles of Raskolnikov and Power include these six aspects:

1. *Immediately following their crimes, both Raskolnikov and Power were flooded with* shame *so intense that it led them to attempt to hide themselves from the view of the world.* Mayman (1979) and Lewis (1971) identify a heightened sense of public exposure to an audience as a constitutive dimension of the experience of shame. Erikson defines shame as a "sense of having exposed

[one]self prematurely and foolishly," and as accompanied by wishes to become invisible, or to "destroy the eyes of the world" (Erikson, 1963, pp. 252–253).

In my 1995 taped interview with her, I asked Power a question that led to her reflecting on the shame she had experienced:

> JL: . . . . you said in your statement [upon surrender] that what you did was well-meaning and you thought it was right at the time, but it was naive and unthinking. I wondered whether you thought you were more naive than other people your age, more unthinking than other people your age?
>
> KP: No. I did at the time I wrote that statement. I have been helped to understand more of the dynamics of the situation since my return: ironically, what I needed to heal was only available if I picked up the thread of my story so people could tell me about the past. . . . that part of the shame that I carried for 23 years was: how could I think that up and go do it? What kind of horrible person am I that I could think that up and go do it? That's shameful!

In a televised interview in February 1994, soon after Power's imprisonment, Barbara Walters asked Power what her reaction had been on hearing on the radio about the shooting of Walter Schroeder. Power spoke of her profound shame and how it led to her fugitive status: "The depth of shame is unimaginable and my response was, of course, to flee."

Empirical research finds that shame is a far more painful emotion than guilt because guilt "merely" implicates one's behavior, whereas shame implicates one's very self (Tangney, 1990). So it was that for 23 years Power's shame overrode her sense of guilt, contributing to her remaining a fugitive.

2. Following the crime, both Raskolnikov and Power experienced an intense sense of alienation from family and community. The physical isolation required of a fugitive brought with it a concomitant emotional isolation. Immediately after the murders, Raskolnikov began to experience a state of terrible aloneness and alienation—as expressed by the narrator of the novel: "His soul had suddenly and consciously been affected by a gloomy sense of alienation, compounded with one of an agonizing, infinite solitariness" (C&P, p. 144). More vividly, he "felt as though, with a pair of scissors, he had cut himself off from everyone and everything" (C&P, p. 157). When Raskolnikov's beloved sister and mother visit him soon after the crime, it is clear that Raskolnikov's oppressive sense of alienation extends even to them: "It's as if I were looking at you from a thousand miles away. . . ." Raskolnikov says to his mother and sister (C&P, p. 281).

Like most people, Raskolnikov's reaction to this "intolerable" (C&P, p. 282) predicament is to withdraw further. But this "solution" leaves him tremendously conflicted and ambivalent. Raskolnikov responds to a later visit with his mother, for instance, by impulsively agreeing with her that, yes, they will very soon have a good long talk—only to regret it immediately:

> Having said this, he suddenly grew confused and turned pale: . . . it suddenly became quite clear and self-evident to him that he had just told a horrible lie, that not only now would there not be time for him to have a good talk—it was now out of the question for him to *speak* to anyone about anything ever again. The effect on him of this tormenting thought was so powerful that for a split second he almost lost consciousness altogether. (C&P, p. 279)

Midway through the story the narrator observes about Raskolnikov that "he was young, detached and, therefore, cruel" (C&P, p. 382). Raskolnikov's detachment grows so marked that his friend, Razumikhin, observes it and draws characterological conclusions about Raskolnikov, telling Raskolnikov's sister, "There's no one he loves; there probably never will be" (C&P, p. 266). Later in prison, Raskolnikov at first holds himself stonily detached from his fellow prisoners, who in turn heartily dislike him. The cold distance that Raskolnikov maintains extends even to Sonya, who loves him and has followed him to Siberia.

In her *New Yorker* article, Franks eloquently registers the physical and emotional alienation attending Power's flight: "When the war ended and her fellow-radicals dispersed and slipped back into the establishment, Power was left alone with the myth, a revolutionary without comrades or a revolution" (1994, p. 43). Or a family. To elude capture, Power refrained from all contact with her parents, siblings, and extended family for more than two decades. By 1974 when she separated from Susan Saxe, her friend, partner in crime, and fellow fugitive, Power's flight had cut her off from everyone she had known and loved before September 23, 1970.

3. *Both Raskolnikov and Power suffered intense emotional punishments of shame, alienation, apathy, panic, regret, and suicidal despair as a result of their crimes.* "Feelings play a prominent role in real predicaments," Robinson and Hawpe wrote (1986, p. 122). The narrator of *Crime and Punishment* describes Raskolnikov as tortured not only by the shame and alienation just discussed, but also by an increasingly volatile mix of terror, apathy, and a willfully blurred consciousness:

> When he remembered this time later on, long afterwards, he was able to perceive that his awareness must at times have been dimmed. . . . At times he was seized by a morbid and tormenting anxiety, which had even transformed itself into panic terror. But he also recalled that there had been minutes, hours and even possibly days full of an apathy that had taken hold of him as though in contrast to his earlier terror—an apathy similar to the morbidly indifferent condition of certain people

on their deathbeds. In general, during those final days he tried more or less to flee from any clear and complete understanding of his position. (C&P, p. 509)

There was depression as well: "My head's going round a bit, but that's not what it is. It's that I feel so sad, so sad! Like a woman, really" (C&P, p. 240). After a month of torment, Raskolnikov arrives at a psychological state of such profound despair that he believes he has only two choices: prison or "the river" (that is, suicide).

Dostoevsky's portrayal of Raskolnikov's depression as "womanish" links Raskolnikov with his female double in this analysis. Like Raskolnikov, apathy and depression plagued Power throughout her fugitive years: "The depression robbed me of so much energy and order," she told Franks (1994, p. 56). Her despair too reached suicidal levels, as Franks observed: "For years she has fought off depression—and the urge to do the job herself" (that is, kill herself. Here Franks is referring to death threats directed at Power upon her surrender; 1994, p. 42).

Like Raskolnikov, Power also engaged in psychological processes aimed at attempting to "flee from any clear and complete understanding of [her] position." As she told Franks, she had spent "years living only in the present and, quite literally, wiping out any memories of the past" (Franks, 1994, p. 42). This decision precluded the possibility during that time of her constructing a coherent and temporally continuous narrative—and therefore self.

When Franks asked Power about her reaction when she learned that Walter Schroeder had been killed in the robbery, Power described a state of horrified, traumatized shock:

> I couldn't believe it. . . . I was saying "What? What? How could this have happened?" It was a sharp, intense pain. . . . There was this overwhelming sense of wrongness. This wasn't supposed to be about taking lives—this was about stopping the taking of lives. [At this point in the interview with Franks, Power cried.] I have memorized that moment, replayed it again and again—so many times. I will never in my life ever forget it. (Franks, 1994, p. 51)

Even after all these years, Power weeps when she talks about the killing. She wept with Franks and more than once with me. She wept at her parole hearing on March 5, 1998. My observations concur with those of Franks that "every time Power tells her story, her guilt and remorse for Officer Schroeder's death are real" (1994, p. 58).

On this decisive dimension, Power departs from Raskolnikov, from whom we never hear a clear morally engaged admission of guilt or remorse for the murders. Instead, Raskolnikov shows amoral forms of regret—in his distress over having made a mistake, and amoral forms of shame—in his humiliation at having discovered himself not to be an extraordinary man after all.

4. *While evading capture, both Raskolnikov and Power threw themselves into frenetic activity to ward off despair and suicide.* "Living only in the present" and living only in action are, of course, time-honored modes of evading self-reflection and its associated painful thoughts and feelings. Even while Raskolnikov is working up his resolve to murder the pawnbroker, he simultaneously tries to conceal his intent from himself through self-distraction: "Almost unconsciously, prompted by a kind of inner necessity, he began with a kind of effort to scrutinize every object he encountered, as though in some desperate quest of some diversion" (C&P, p. 88).

The visit with his mother and sister fortuitously provides Raskolnikov with a goal absorbing enough to distract him from what is rightly obsessing him. Raskolnikov's need to take immediate action to dissuade his sister from marrying the despicable Luzhin temporarily succeeds in alleviating Raskolnikov's agony: "There was, however, one urgent practical matter that he must decide today, one way or the other—so he had determined earlier, on awakening. Now he felt relief in the *practical*, as a way out of the situation" (C&P, p. 282).

Like Raskolnikov, Power veered between periods of paralyzed depression and frenzied levels of activity during her fugitive years. She became a "workaholic," later describing herself with the song line, "I was in crazy motion" (Franks, 1994, p. 57). While a fugitive, she really believed that, for her, flight into activity was a matter of life and death, so much so that what she most feared about prison was its constraint on activity: "The central reason I didn't give myself up before is that I was so afraid that my frenetic activity was my only weapon against suicide" (1994, p. 42).

In choosing this particular way of managing their inner turmoil, both Power and Raskolnikov may indeed have succeeded in warding off suicide. At the same time they illustrate the truth of Proust's characterization of eternal busyness as a form of moral idleness. In fact, it is precisely their ultimate inability to distract themselves from their regret (and for Power, guilt and remorse) that proved crucial to the private aspects of their ethical transformation.

5. *Both sought to make atonement even while fleeing.* Raskolnikov's and Power's felt need for expiatory punishment during their postcrime, preprison period illustrates one of the four "ontologies of the self" first identified by Hungarian sociologist Agnes Hankiss and discussed by McAdams (1997)—namely, the tragic, *self-absolutory* ontology. In contrast with the other tragic lifestory identified by Hankiss (that is, the *compensatory* [in which "a good past gives birth to a bad present"]), the self-absolutory narrative portrays "a bad past giv[ing] birth to a bad present" (McAdams, 1997, p. 103). In these cases, the bad past of their crime gives birth to the bad present in which they are battered by psychological punishments, including the need to atone, or "pay the price" for their past transgressions (McAdams, 1997, p. 103).

It is notable that, although destitute, Raskolnikov spends not a kopeck of the money he stole from the pawnbroker during the murder. He hides the stolen money away, and en route to the police station to confess his crime he gives away all the rest of the money he has, money that his mother has just sent him at considerable personal cost. He insists on paying for the funeral of a brand-new acquaintance, Marmeladov, a good-hearted, hopelessly alcoholic husband and father of an impoverished family—which includes the saintly 18-year-old daughter, Sonya, who has been driven to prostitution as the sole source of income for the desperate family. Raskolnikov comforts Marmeladov's widow, and partly out of consideration for her dignity he fabricates a debt he supposedly owes Marmeladov: "Please permit me now . . . *to effect . . . the repayment of my debt to my deceased friend*. Look, here are . . . twenty rubles, I think—if they will be of any assistance to you. . . ." (C&P, p. 234, ellipses in original; emphases added). Overcome with gratitude, Marmeladov's 10-year-old daughter Polenka throws her arms around their savior, Raskolnikov, and kisses him. In affectionate response, Raskolnikov "told her his name, gave her his address and promised to come and see them again the next day without fail. The little girl went back upstairs completely enraptured by him" (C&P, p. 236). At this point, having reconnected himself with people and having made an act of atonement arguably double-layered in its personal meaning, Raskolnikov considers that perhaps life is worth living and decides against confessing.

Later, Raskolnikov carries on a lengthy discussion with Porfiry (the police official investigating the murders of the pawnbroker and her sister) about the criminal mind and about Raskolnikov's theory of what differentiates the extraordinary from the ordinary person. Raskolnikov explains to Porfiry that an ordinary person will sometimes make the mistake of conceiving of himself as belonging to the rare set of extraordinary individuals:

> But I do not believe that they represent any significant threat, and you really need not be anxious, as they never get very far. Of course, it would do them no harm to give them a thrashing now and then, to punish them for getting carried away and to remind them of their rightful place, but *they'll whip themselves*, because they're very well-behaved; . . . Moreover, *they impose various public acts of penitence on themselves*. (C&P, p. 315, ellipses and emphases added)

Here he is transparently referring to himself. He is pointing out the psychological truth that "ordinary" decent individuals who have transgressed the bounds of moral conduct will inevitably try to punish themselves and atone for their crimes. He is revealing his own desperate wishes for penitence and punishment.

While living as a fugitive, Power too made private efforts to atone for her crime, as she told Franks:

Power said that even as she was running from the law, she *tried to atone* for the damage she had done—for instance, by giving part of her income away. "In Catholicism, the catechism of forgiveness is that if you have done something very, very wrong, you can be forgiven by naming your act, knowing how it came to happen, and removing yourself from the environment that contributed to it. I did that and then *I vowed that I would make my life an act of contrition for my wrong to the Schroeder family.* (Franks, 1994, p. 54, emphases added)

What specifics went into living her life as an act of contrition? Among other things, Power lived a life of "voluntary poverty," the phrase Ron Duncan, her husband, used when speaking with Franks about his life with Power (1994, p. 44)—itself in part a program of self-imposed penitence. A former neighbor of hers describes instances of Power's kindness to her and her family: "Alice [Power's last alias] got me to walk for my health. She gave my daughter her car, and she wouldn't take a penny. Whatever Alice had, you were welcome to it" (Franks, 1994, p. 57). Then, while Power was negotiating her surrender, she sold her interest in the restaurant she co-owned and operated in Eugene, Oregon, and gave a quarter of the proceeds to the international hunger-relief agency, Oxfam (Franks, 1994).

Though there is good evidence that generosity was an integral facet of both Raskolnikov's and Power's (especially Power's) precrime character, these traits developed a postcrime life of their own in service of atonement.

6. *Related to their felt need to atone for their crimes, both Raskolnikov and Power manifested powerful urges to confess or be captured by the authorities. Crime and Punishment* famously abounds with instances in which Raskolnikov strenuously tries to give himself away. Quite conscious of this, Raskolnikov depicts the impulse with this metaphor: "The moth flies to the candle-flame of its own accord" (C&P, p. 298). The day after the murder, for instance, he is called into the police station. Panicked, at first he assumes that the police somehow know he's the murderer. On his way up the stairs into the police station, Raskolnikov thinks, "I shall go in, get down on my knees and tell them everything" (C&P, p. 135). Because he does not immediately go through with his confessional impulse, Raskolnikov finds out that the summons merely involves his landlady charging him with nonpayment of his rent. Even so, he has violent impulses to confess then and there:

A strange idea suddenly came to him: that of standing up right now, going over to Nikodim Fomich and telling him everything that had happened the day before. . . . The urge was so strong that he actually stood up in order to put it into action. "Shouldn't I think about it for a moment?" flashed through his head. "No, it's better to do it without thinking, and get it off my chest!" But suddenly he stood still like one thunderstruck. (C&P, p. 145)

What strikes Raskolnikov like thunder is overhearing two detectives discussing the very murder he had just committed; hearing this, he passes out on the spot, in the police station—something guaranteed to draw attention to himself.

On more than one occasion, Raskolnikov presents himself out of the blue to the investigators, Porfiry and Zamyotov. At one point he goes so far as to tauntingly "confess" to Zamyotov that he is the murderer—ending by laughing it all off as a joke, purposely leaving Zamyotov suspicious but bewildered.

Still later, Porfiry, who has by that time become all but certain of Raskolnikov's guilt, toys with Raskolnikov by letting Raskolnikov know that he knows the gory details of something else Raskolnikov has done to give himself away—that is, return to the scene of the crime. Porfiry taunts Raskolnikov: "If you go on like that you'll end up with brain-fever, and if you follow these impulses to overstimulate your own nerves, you'll be off ringing doorbells and asking questions about blood, sir!" (C&P, p. 406).

Like Raskolnikov, Power seems to have courted capture at times. She related, for instance, how seven years into her fugitive life, in 1977, she used to frequent a bar in Portland, Oregon, called, of all things, "The Slammer":

> Then, one night, I looked up from the long-neck Bud I was drinking to stare right into my own picture on a "Wanted" poster on the wall. The place was plastered with "Wanted" posters and jail bars. The customer next to me was a Portland police officer. I had let my hair grow long and it had gone back to its natural color, so I didn't even look that different from my poster. Now, did I stop going to the Slammer after that? No. Sometimes, in your despair, you invite change. (Franks, 1994, p. 54)

Or perhaps it was partly relief that she was inviting—the relief that seems so often to follow confession. Wilfred Sheed portrays this relief in his novel, *Transatlantic Blues*. Sheed has his British Catholic narrator regularly confessing his daily sins to his tape recorder, whom he calls Father Sony. The narrator muses about how the state of euphoric buoyancy he had always experienced as a child after going to Confession—"bouncing down the steps afterwards" (Sheed, 1978, p. 15)—seems to have created in him this confessional compulsion. Franks described Power after her confession in similar terms: "In fact, she had felt buoyantly light, disentangled at last from the heavy net of lies, aliases, and invented selves" (1994, p. 41).

OUTCOME/DENOUEMENT

Any good story makes us itch to find out how the predicament ends— that is, its *outcome* (Robinson & Hawpe, 1986), the *denouement*, or the "solution of the plot" (in McAdams, 1997, p. 26). *Both Raskolnikov and Power found that in the end prison offered the only way to resolve their intense shame, alienation, regret, despair, and other forms of emotional and ethical distress.*

At a crucial point in *Crime and Punishment* Raskolnikov is again discussing the murder with Porfiry, who asks Raskolnikov what his reaction will be when they catch the murderer. Instantly Raskolnikov answers: "He's got what he deserves!" Cunningly, Porfiry probes, "Well, sir, and what about his conscience?" To which Raskolnikov retorts, "If he has one, he'll suffer when he realizes the error of his ways. That's his punishment—that, *in addition to penal servitude*" (C&P, p. 315, emphasis added).

Later, after Raskolnikov confesses to Sonya, the same insight that before was merely intellectual and hypothetical suddenly hits home with Raskolnikov: "Life might really be better in penal servitude" (C&P, p. 494). These thoughts and feelings reflect Dostoevsky's view of suffering as redemptive (J. Frank, 1995)—a view that may come across as hopelessly quaint or even pathological in late-twentieth-century America, but a view nonetheless shared by Power.

Recall again Power's vow to make her entire life "an act of contrition" for her role in the killing of Officer Schroeder. Her use of Catholic terminology may have contributed to the pervasiveness of others' assumptions that she gave herself up and pleaded guilty out of "Catholic guilt," in the sense of being driven by some automatic, prereflective, masochistic, or otherwise pathological residue of childhood conditioning. Early on, I had assumed something like this, as well. My hypothesis was based on my insider's knowledge that her Catholic upbringing had included these potentially relevant beliefs: (a) that forgiveness is contingent on confessing and performing a tangible penance; and (b) that after death, most individuals will have to spend some time suffering the fires of purgatory to purify themselves before entering heaven. It seemed plausible to me that such powerful ideas might instill in someone raised a Catholic the need to suffer a tangible penance before that individual can feel forgiven. The Catholic-guilt interpretation has come to the fore at more than one point in Power's life story—with respect to her guilty plea, her acceptance of suffering in prison, and her parole hearing. For these reasons, I revisit it at each of these points.

I asked Power in our 1995 interview whether her *guilty plea* had something to do with her experience as a Catholic, specifically of the

> **JL:** . . . Sacrament of Penance in which you do a *tangible* sort of reparation, you know, like 5 Hail Marys and 10 Our Fathers. . . .
> **KP:** . . . you know, my friend Sandy from college. . . . She said look at . . . you know, you and your little Catholic conscience, you *wanted* to do this jail time. What I can tell you is this: I could have pleaded not guilty (ellipses added to indicate irrelevant material).

JL: Yes, you could have, and they might not have had a case.

KP: I know. In 1986, the *Boston Globe* . . .

JL: Why didn't you?

KP: carried an interview with the . . . with Ralph Martin's (Power's prosecutor's) predecessor in which he was quoted as saying he would not want to have to try this case.

JL: Yes, I've heard that a couple of times, that they said they knew he didn't have a case on you. So, . . . why *did* you plead guilty and choose to be put in prison?

KP: Because how could I . . . It was an act of redemption, not for the events of 23 years ago. God, I am just realizing at this moment as I answer this: it was an act of redemption for my dishonesty with the people I had to lie to in my fugitive life, the declaration in action that I understood the importance of authenticity, honesty, owning up, speaking, in order . . . in order to be, *in order to be somebody that anybody could trust ever.* I thought . . . that people would be very angry and very hurt that I was not what I seemed. What I didn't know is that they weren't confused, and I was exactly what I seemed, but I think part of that, part of why they know that is because I insisted on pleading guilty. How could they trust me? How could they not assume some sleazy level of inability to be honest and to act with integrity if I had said, "Oh, maybe I did it and maybe I didn't do it. What can you prove?" It would feel like disowning everything I had ever done. (Emphasis added; ellipses in original)

Despite my presuppositions, the sole whiff of "Catholic guilt" is Power's choice of words for her guilty plea as an "act of redemption." This is not a story about a mechanistic Catholic-guilt-induced wish to "buy forgiveness" with a concrete penance. Instead, the story Power tells is a thoroughly *relational* one. It is a story about the vital importance for her of ending the dishonesty about her identity. Because lying is a sin? No, because she sees that the lying had arrested her ability to construct a reasonably continuous and integrated self-narrative, and thus self—specifically a self worthy of others' trust. Ironically, her surrender, guilty plea, and imprisonment freed her to construct a better-formed self-narrative, one that shows "how the past reverberates in the present and how the present retrospectively illuminates the past's potential" (Rosenwald, 1992, p. 284).

The tragic self-absolutory narrative of atonement predominates in the middle chapters of Raskolnikov's and Power's stories. But it is not the whole story. As they pay the price exacted by society and by their own moral sensibilities, Raskolnikov and Power liberate themselves to reshape their life stories from a tragic to a romantic form, which ends with positive transformation (A. Frank, 1995).

EPILOGUE

A number of literary critics have assessed Dostoevsky's epilogue as a failure—a tacked-on, lame sketch of a magical, implausible religious conversion that fails to follow coherently from Raskolnikov's preprison character (J. Frank, 1995; Morson, 1994; Rahv, 1960). I agree. Furthermore, I argue that Power improves on Dostoevsky's version, writing a fuller, more coherent, more convincing, and more dramatic epilogue for her own life narrative. In prison she shows genuine change and development, change and development that, although anything but inevitable, does follow from her presurrender self.

Sketchy though it is, Dostoevsky's epilogue provides enough detail to support my argument that Raskolnikov and Power took both individual and relational paths to transformation. Their ethical transition was not complete until they moved outside of the secret grotto of their heads back into the world of other human beings.

At the *individual* level, the experiences of Raskolnikov and Power illustrate Spinoza's notion that the most effective way to overrule one emotion is by replacing it with another, stronger emotion—especially a self-transcending emotion such as wonder or love (Peters, 1970).

Raskolnikov never shows a direct, unequivocal acknowledgement of guilt or remorse over the murder of the pawnbroker. He does, however, as I have argued, suffer the emotions of regret, shame, despair, and alienation. Gradually, he supplants these painful emotions with another emotion, the preeminently *relational* emotion—*love*.

Just before Raskolnikov gives himself up, he visits his mother to reassure her, saying, "You must always remember that your son now loves you more than himself and that all the things you've thought about me, that I'm cruel and don't love you, all those things are false. I'll never ever stop loving you" (C&P, 591). The narrator comments, "It was as though after all this horrible time his heart had suddenly softened. He fell down before her, he kissed her feet, and both of them, clasping each other in their arms, wept" (C&P, p. 592).

While in prison he expands the range of his love and focuses it on a worthier object than himself, Sonya: "In these ill, pale faces [his and Sonya's] there now gleamed the dawn of a renewed future, a complete recovery to a new life. What had revived them was love" (C&P, p. 629).

On the second-to-last page of *Crime and Punishment*, the narrator describes Raskolnikov's blossoming connection with others as well:

> He had recovered, and he knew it, felt it completely with the whole of his renewed being. . . . That same evening, when the barracks had been locked for the night, Raskolnikov lay on the plank-bed, thinking

about her. Through that day he had even felt that all the convicts, his former enemies, now looked upon him differently. He had actually begun to talk to them, and they had replied to him in kindly tones. (C & P, p. 629)

Somehow, while in prison "he had recovered," we are told. But how? Dostoevsky tells us that it has a great deal to do with his love for Sonya, and he implies that it has something to do with his giving up his sense of superiority over the other prisoners and something to do with new-found Christian beliefs. Beyond that, we are not told or (better) shown precisely what went into his recovery. This is where Power improves on Raskolnikov's narrative. In Power's story we get to view the inside workings of the transition and its turning points as they are happening, as Power is living them— in prison.

Here is a second locus for revisiting the issue of the nature of Power's guilt, this time examining its specific role in her transition in prison from guilty criminal to priestly elder. At the time of her surrender, Power's attorney and friend, Steven Black, observed about Power that she was "obsessed with a desire to be punished, to seek expiation" for her acts (Franks, 1994, p. 45). In a similar vein, her husband, Ron Duncan, said then that Power had a need to experience suffering "in order to give her act of principle value" (Franks, 1994, p. 59).

I asked Power in our 1995 prison interview about these characterizations of her as someone who almost masochistically seeks out suffering. Again, my hypothesis, based on Black's and Duncan's characterizations of Power as well as my own Catholic background, was that a specifically "Catholic guilt" might have led her to seek out *extra* suffering as penance and purification. The interchange is illuminating enough to warrant extended quotes from the interview. My question was whether she had a particularly strong sense of deserving severe punishment, arising from her Catholic upbringing:

> **KP:** No, I'd hate to think of it that way . . . I don't feel like . . . no, I'll tell you something. . . . If I pursued this really uncomfortable course out of the sense that I deserved to be punished, I would say that that's a piece I've worked on in therapy since and have a healthier relationship with.
> **JL:** What about the concept . . . the concept of purgatory, the purification of guilt through suffering?
> **KP:** You know, the thing about suffering is . . . people who are addicted to suffering . . . no, to *comfort* . . . People who are addicted to comfort, and you must admit that's a theme of our culture . . . people who are addicted to comfort think that people who experience suffering have sought it out for a purpose. They don't understand that suffering just is. . . .

JL: Right.

KP: that suffering is something you put up with because it's the price of something that's important. Discomfort, I mean . . . cold is discomfort. Would I give up playing in the snow? . . . I have worked hard to recover that encounter with existence that people who are not afraid of discomfort have, and suffering is. I don't seek it, and I don't value it.

JL: Back to what we were just talking about. Something Ron was quoted as saying. . . . he was quoted as saying, I think by Lucinda Franks, that you seek out *extra* suffering. . . .

KP: It must seem that way. It must seem that way. The pain that I'm going to suffer, the awareness of suffering. . . . You know, something hurts somebody that you care about, you judge it and you want it to go away. It's hard to see why it could be valuable or important. You interpret it in a way that makes sense to you if you were doing it. I know that not everybody feels . . . at least seems to feel this open to awareness of suffering.

JL: Um hmm.

KP: I think that comes too, in the Catholic background. Yeah. . . .

KP: . . . and . . . you know what? And I still feel the pain, and I still say that it is a *priestly function to be willing to sit with the pain.* (First two emphases in original; last emphasis added)

In this interchange, we hear a story about a decision to surrender to imprisonment colored *in part* by the Catholic view of suffering as redemptive: "It is a priestly function to be willing to sit with the pain. . . ." The pain that Power has chosen to sit with, however, is the pain of her regret, shame, remorse, and guilt for causing pain to others—not gratuitous suffering and not suffering for its own sake. A "Catholic-guilt" explanation would trivialize and dismiss the very real change and development that she forged in the crucible of MCI Framingham prison during her years there.

What exactly went into this transformation? Like her fictional counterpart, while in prison Power supplanted certain lesser emotions with the self-transcending, *relational* emotion of love. Power has spoken of her son, Jaime, born in 1979, as "my first step in attachment to the world of humanity—a relationship that was permanent, that I couldn't walk away from" (Franks, 1994, p. 54)—much like Raskolnikov's renewed relationship with his mother. In fact, it was in part her son's objections to Power's urge to flee his home town that eventually led to her coming forth.

In 1984, Power and Ron Duncan had settled down to the extent of having bought a house in a small town in Oregon. But after living there several years, Power began again to be plagued with anxieties about being found. She therefore raised with the family the question of moving. As Franks told Power's story, that time Power's impulse to flee clashed directly with her love for her son: "It was Jaime's self-protective instincts that stopped her. 'He was just so deeply attached to his friends—fierce, really fierce,'

Power told me. 'He said, 'If you move away from here, you will have to leave me behind, because this is my home town and I'm going to stay here.' And, through some wonderful grace, we were able to hear him' " (1994, p. 56). The deep and reciprocal quality of the attachment with her son shines through in Jaime's response when Franks asked Jaime at age 15 how he felt about his mother's absence while she was in prison:

> "It's hard not having her here, but I'm just glad she did it now instead of five years from now, when I'll really need her," he says. He pushes away a newspaper article someone had sent him about Power. ". . . The way I like to remember her is when she took me and my friends swimming. She was great with my friends, and she would sit on the edge of the river in her little straw hat, smiling at us, smiling at all of us while we swam" (1994, p. 59).

Ron Duncan represented another step in Power's gradual reconnection to the world. When she met Duncan, Power trusted him enough to take the ultimate risk, to disclose who she really was: "He burned with this same vision that through his work he was taking care of people. I knew he would be a person that I could tell about myself" (Franks, 1994, p. 54)—much as Raskolnikov knew he could tell Sonya, the Marmeladov family caretaker, about his crime.

Power's presurrender reunion with her family of origin took her another step back to the human community. She received a letter from them in the spring of 1993 welcoming their prodigal daughter back home. Power later told Franks about the utter joy and release from shame that that welcome gave her: "In an instant, I was lifted of so much deep psychic shame. I thought they had written me off, condemned me. But even my uncle Ted, the priest, forgave me" (Franks, 1994, p. 58).

While in prison Power's love for her family also overcame her prior despair, as she told Franks: "My strongest weapon against suicide is my contract with God and my family. This time, I am going to come back—not like the other times, where I've walked away from my family and everyone that I knew in my life. Now I have said I will not leave anymore. I will not hurt anyone anymore" (1994, p. 42).

In the years I have known her, I observed another significant turning point in Power, as she replaced another negative emotion—in this case, anger—with love. When Franks spoke with Power just after her surrender, Power related how in her presurrender negotiations she had been assured that she could serve her prison term in Oregon (where her husband and son live and could afford to visit frequently) rather than in Massachusetts (where the crime was committed); but the Boston authorities had refused to honor that understanding. One result was that Power's suicidal despair was superseded not only by love for her family but also by anger on their behalf; in her own words: "Prison has taken the activity [her prior shield against suicide] away, but I have another weapon I never had before—anger" (Franks, 1994, p. 42). But in my visits with Power after Franks's published interview, it became clear that sometime during the early years of her imprisonment, Power's feelings on this matter had radically changed. The anger was gone, and in its place was a deep caring—for the Schroeder family.

This chapter of Power's life narrative now incorporates the conviction that it had turned out to be vitally important for her to have been incarcerated near Boston rather than in Oregon—for the sake of Walter Schroeder's family and her connection with them. Four years into her sentence, she told me how valuable it had been for her to be confronted with the depth and the severity of the damage she had done to the Schroeder family. As she explained it, had she been imprisoned in Oregon, her family and friends would have buffered her from the resentment and anger of the Schroeder family and many residents of Massachusetts. In prison in Massachusetts, however, she has had to feel that anger in full force, to the point of receiving death threats. Power's revised narrative includes the wish that her imprisonment in Massachusetts might palpably demonstrate to the Schroeder family that she has accepted the punishment demanded by society to redress the harm she did the family. Power's transition from anger to gratitude at the location of her incarceration represents a significant chapter in her epilogue. But there is more.

After having served 4½ years of her sentence, Power became eligible for parole. Her first parole hearing was scheduled for March 6, 1998. At this hearing she would stand alone, without an attorney, in the same room with the family she had so gravely damaged. Each side would present its case to the parole board.

Ever since her surrender, Power had sought some sort of reconciliation with the Schroeders, but they had always refused. As time went on and Power was faced with more of the specifics of the injuries suffered by this family because of the killing, her wishes for reconciliation grew. At the same time, Power has always believed that for her to *demand* reconciliation with or forgiveness from the Schroeder family would be to inflict another injury. Her clarity on this issue came through at my first interview with her in 1995, when she told me, "I felt obligated to offer restitution. I did, and I have their [the Schroeders'] answer, a refusal. I will always be open to any kind of reconciliation. But it would be out of line for me to say to them that *I need . . . anything*; it would be out of line for me to say that *they should . . . [do] anything*. I need to be respectful of them" (emphases and pauses in original interview).

By means of the March 1998 parole hearing, Power hoped to convey in person her profound remorse to the Schroeders. She hoped that her unequivocal statement of responsibility might help heal the wounds she had helped inflict on this family. Maybe she even hoped against hope for rapprochement with those she had become forever linked with through the harm she had done them.

She made her parole statement. There she spoke, among other things, of having used her time in prison to "sit unflinchingly in the presence of the reality that, because of my acts, another human being was dead" ("Legacies of Loss," 1998). She acknowledged having struggled those years in prison to (again, in the words of her written parole statement) "peel off the layers of . . . defensiveness, to get to the point where I could look squarely into the pained, accusing faces of the victims of my crime and say, 'I was wrong. I was wrong all along. Before God I am sorry. I will always be so sorry' " ("Legacies of Loss," 1998, p. D3).

Then she sat down and listened to the Schroeder family's response. She heard two messages. On the one hand, the Schroeders acknowledged that for the first time they could sense genuine remorse in and full acceptance of responsibility by Power. On the other hand, they felt that her statements could have been motivated by her desire for parole. At this point, Power tearfully withdrew her request for parole midproceedings. The *New York Times* wrote that Power's act had left those in the hearing room "stunned" (Goldberg, 1998, p. 6).

Power's withdrawal of her request for parole again evoked the dismissive interpretations of "penance" (by the *New York Times*; Goldberg, 1998, p. 6) and "Catholic guilt" (by an acquaintance of mine). Others, however, view Power's decision as a deeply ethical act. Attorney Rikki Klieman saw it that way, commenting after the parole hearing: "She [Power] is a woman of great moral fiber. . . . I don't know a person who is more moral than Katherine Ann Power" (Aucoin, 1998, p. F5). The narrative perspective on morality proves particularly revelatory here—specifically Morson's conception of morality as entailing "the ability to make oneself *the minor character in someone else's story*" (Morson, 1994, p. 74, emphasis in original). To me, this describes precisely what Power was doing in her withdrawal of her parole request— engaging in the profoundly moral act of making herself a minor character in the Schroeder family's story.

Ultimately, then, both Raskolnikov and Power find that authentic transformation is not only a private, individual matter, but also requires dauntingly strenuous repair work on the ruptures with family, victims (in Power's case), and the human community.

During their imprisonment, both Raskolnikov and Power succeed in transforming themselves for the better. That ethical transformation is reflected in the transmutation of both narratives from the tragic to the *romantic* form (Frye, 1957; Gergen & Gergen, 1986; Landman, 1993, 1995; McAdams, 1997). Both narratives take the realistically complex form of the romantic narrative in which the protagonist initiates a sudden decline, progresses upward from the depths, regresses downward more than once, and in the end embarks on what appears to be an ultimately upward movement (Gergen & Gergen, 1986).

Again, however, Raskolnikov's and Power's narratives not only converge but also diverge—and diverge in ways that are quite as revealing as the convergences. A. Frank's (1995) classification of narratives into restitution and quest (and chaos) stories reveals a final important distinction between these narratives.

Although restitution and quest stories both belong to the romantic or heroic genre, they otherwise differ. The restitution narrative presents a relatively personal and private tale: "Yesterday I was healthy, today I'm sick, but tomorrow I'll be healthy again" (A. Frank, 1995, p. 77). In contrast, the quest story presents a more communal and public tale, as demonstrated by the latter two of three features of the quest narrative: (a) it "recognizes that the old intactness must be stripped away to prepare for something new" (A. Frank, 1995, p. 171); (b) it is dyadic, not monadic; and (c) the storyteller stands as a "pivot point between microcosm and macrocosm" (A. Frank, 1995, p. 126).

Relative to Power's story, Raskolnikov's lacks these features. Instead, his story better fits the rubric of the restitution narrative—in particular the last two thirds of it in which the protagonist progresses from sickness to health.

In contrast, Power's story better exemplifies a quest narrative. Power graphically portrayed the first-noted feature of the quest narrative—the stripping away of the old intactness to prepare for something new—in her description at her 1998 parole hearing of how she had had to "peel off layers of defensiveness, to get to the point" where she could face the anger and pain of her victims and admit that she was "wrong all along" ("Legacies," 1998, p. D3).

Power's story manifests the second feature of a quest story in that it clearly conveys a sense of communion at least as strong as the sense of agency. As McAdams fleshes out Bakan's (1966) concepts of agency and communion, individuals motivated by agency most highly value power, action, individual rights, emotional detachment, and autonomy. Individuals motivated by communion most highly value social responsibility and interpersonal relationships (McAdams, 1997, p. 88). On the one hand, both Raskolnikov and Power manifest extremely agentic identities. Their self-conceptions as individuals willing to take action to the point of taking lethal power into their own hands in part moved them to commit their crimes: Raskolnikov as the Nietzschean superman (J. Frank, 1995) and Power as Pathfinder charting her own course (Josselson, 1996), or more agentically, Warrior [-Against-War] (McAdams, 1997).

On the other hand, there are important differences. First of all, Raskolnikov conceived and committed his crime alone. In fact, the agentic elements of individual power, autonomy, self-sufficiency, and emotional detachment represented *defining features* of Raskolnikov's would-be identity as an extraordinary man. Had he anticipated how excruciating the ensuing sense of alienation from other people would prove, Raskolnikov would have taken that as evidence that he was no extraordinary man but a "louse" like most everyone else.

In contrast, the communal elements of social responsibility and connection with others play a much stronger role in Power's identity than Raskolnikov's. Power conceived and committed the crime in cooperation with others. Despite the self-protective requirement to avoid deep and lasting attachments while a fugitive, she does not appear ever to have sanctified detachment. On the contrary, Power expressed to me in our 1995 interview her longstanding consciousness of the moral force of connection with others: "Only sociopaths are immune from fear of being cut off from connection. If there's something that's deeply wrong with our civilization, it's that we're so used to being disconnected that we think that this is the human existence."

As A. Frank pointed out, "People tell stories not just to work out their own changing identities, but also to guide others who will follow them" (1995, p. 17). The very act of Power's telling the story of her crime and punishment to me and others is a profoundly relational and generative act. In her first letter to me agreeing to tell me her story, Power clearly expressed the sense of "responsibility for testimony" (A. Frank, 1995, p. 166) characteristic of the protagonist of a quest story:

> I am willing to be open about these questions [regret, reparation, transformation]. I hope to be able to contribute something to thoughtful understanding of the ways people act, what constitutes responsibility, and what is owed to persons, the state, the universe as a result of acts that seriously damage. One of my hopes when I surrendered is that my willingness to "show up" and declare my responsibility could become a challenge to the nation . . . to do the same. We owe our children the story of the events of Viet Nam, but we haven't finished the process. We are collectively sort of in the same position as I was with my then-fourteen-year-old son [referring to the fact that son knew nothing about her former identity]. I had to bring out from hiding the shameful and terrifying "realities" of my life, digest and understand them, before I could pass on the wisdom-gained-from-experience which is the responsibility of the generation of elders. (Personal communication, July 22, 1995)

This letter also shows Power as a storyteller who stands as a "pivot point between microcosm and macrocosm," the final feature of a quest story specified by A. Frank (1995, p. 126). In this case, the microcosm is Power's set of personal regrets, and the macrocosm is her country's still unresolved regrets related to the Vietnam War. Buried in individualistic cultures like ours is the recognition that the ghosts of regret can haunt whole nations as well as individuals (Buruma, 1994). This insight permeates Power's deeply communal perspective.

One great good that seems to have accrued to Power out of the refiner's fire of all these years is a hard-won wisdom—the wisdom of a tribal elder. With her story, Power holds out to us the gift of this wisdom, a gift with the potential to help us as a populace lay to rest the uneasy ghosts of the Vietnam War.

CONCLUSION

How extraordinary that the old-fashioned morality tale "lived" by a male character in a mid-nineteenth-century Russian novel parallels in so many ways the morality tale of Katherine Ann (Alice) Power, a real-life twentieth-century American woman. Having two exemplars of this narrative of ethical transformation from two such different times, places, genders, and states of "factuality" has revealed a number of significant insights about the psychology of the crimes committed by the two and the process of their personal transitions and ethical transformation. If Raskolnikov's or Power's narrative had been read in isolation from the other, or in isolation from narrative concepts, these insights might have been missed.

First, juxtaposing these two narratives reveals what may be prevalent, if not universal, elements of ethical transformation. These stories show emotion, not reason, as the basis of morality. To their credit, Raskolnikov and Power "failed" the test that Rasknolnikov consciously undertook: Both ultimately lacked the stomach to suppress their moral emotions. In fact, it is their personal inability to circumvent so-called negative emotions such as regret, shame, and guilt that proved critical to their development as full human beings.

Whenever we ask "why" questions about people and their behavior, the answers tend to fall into two generic categories: internal (personal) or external (situational). However, in this highly individualistic culture, we tend to think first, last, and always of internal causes. The propensity is so strong and so pervasive that it has been called the "fundamental attribution bias"—the tendency to overestimate the internal or personal causes of behavior and underestimate the external or situational ones (Jones & Harris, 1967; Ross, 1977). Reading these narratives in the light of one another reminds us of a second important truth—the power of circumstances to shape a life, though not necessarily a life story that plays well in Peoria.

In a well-made life story, as in life, "history is seen as interactive—made as well as suffered" (Rosenwald, 1992, p. 284). Accordingly, to recognize that a crime is committed in a social and historical context is *not* to absolve the individual of responsibility. Dostoevsky leaves us with no doubt about this matter in his great novel. So does Power in her life story. Yes, Power did say in her first interview with me that she had not thought up what she did in isolation; in nearly the same breath, though, she acknowledged that "even if you didn't think it up, you learned it from your elders, *you* need to be responsible for your acts and resolve to change yourself." (See Landman, 1999, for elaboration of the intertwined roles of circumstance and personal agency in the regrets of the war resister, Katherine Power, and the war maker, Robert McNamara.)

Third, these fiction and nonfiction accounts both tell a story that challenges in another way the hyperindividualist sensibility—namely, a story of personal and ethical transformation that takes place in good part out of the confines of the head of the isolated individual. Raskolnikov proves unable to sustain living the heartless utilitarianism and hyperindividualistic nihilism demanded by his theory. Eventually he discovers what it appears Power always knew: It is not the self-sufficient, disconnected, hyper-"rational," hypoemotional, egoistic individualist but the person capable of self-reflection *and* feeling *and* attachment who is the extraordinary human being.

What happens inside the head—and heart—of these protagonists is a necessary part of the story. But it is not sufficient. What happens out in the human community—confession, atonement, expiation through acceptance of *society's* penance in a "penitentiary" and eventual reunion with humanity—proves at least as decisive in these narratives of transformation.

Despite the fervid assertions of radical individualism, no one is an island. We are storytellers. After their crimes Raskolnikov and Power could be described as "narrative wrecks" (Ronald Dworkin, cited by A. Frank, 1995, p. 54). Their respective life narratives function as "repair work on the wreck" (A. Frank, 1995, p. 54). Neither Raskolnikov nor Power could be whole again until they could bring themselves to tell a life story that was whole and coherent—a story that included their transgressions—and to tell this story out loud.

REFERENCES

Aucoin, D. (1998, May 3). The ascent of Rikki Klieman, legal-TV star. *The Boston Globe*, pp. F4–5.

Bakan, D. (1966). *The duality of human existence: Isolation and communion in Western man.* Boston: Beacon Press.

Bakhtin, M. M. (1994). *The dialogic imagination: Four essays.* M. Holquist (Ed.), C. Emerson (Ed.), & M. Holquist (Trans.). Austin: University of Texas Press. (Original work published 1975)

Bal, M. (1997). *Narratology: Introduction to the theory of narrative.* 2nd ed. Toronto: University of Toronto Press.

Buruma, I. (1994). *The wages of guilt: Memories of war in Germany and Japan.* New York: Farrar, Straus & Giroux.

Dostoevsky, F. (1991). *Crime and punishment.* (D. McDuff, Trans.). London: Penguin. (Original work published 1865–1866)

Erikson, E. (1963). *Childhood and society* (2nd ed.). New York: Norton.

Frank, A. W. (1995). *The wounded storyteller: Body, illness, and ethics.* Chicago: University of Chicago Press.

Frank, J. (1995). *Dostoevsky: The miraculous years, 1865–1871.* Princeton, NJ: Princeton University Press.

Franks, L. (1994, June 13). The return of the fugitive. *The New Yorker,* 40–59.

Frye, N. (1957). *Anatomy of criticism: Four essays.* Princeton, NJ: Princeton University Press.

Geertz, C. (1973). *The interpretation of cultures.* New York: Basic Books.

Gergen, K. J., & Gergen, M. M. (1986). Narrative form and the construction of psychological science. In T. R. Sarbin (Ed.), *Narrative psychology: The storied nature of human conduct* (pp. 22–44). New York: Praeger.

Gitlin, T. (1987). *The sixties: Years of hope, days of rage.* New York: Bantam Books.

Goldberg, C. (1998, March 7). Sorrowful radical abandons bid for parole at hearing, *New York Times,* p. 6.

Jones, E. E., & Harris, V. A. (1967). The attribution of attitudes. *Journal of Experimental Social Psychology, 3,* 2–24.

Josselson, R. (1996). *Revising herself: The story of women's identity from college to midlife.* New York: Oxford University Press.

Landman, J. (1993). *Regret: The persistence of the possible.* New York: Oxford University Press.

Landman, J. (1995). Through a glass darkly: Worldviews, counterfactual thought and emotion. In N. J. Roese & J. M. Olson (Eds.), *What might have been: The social psychology of counterfactual thinking* (pp. 233–258). Hillsdale, NJ: Erlbaum.

Landman, J. (1999, Summer). The confessions of the war maker [Robert McNamara] and the war resister [Katherine Power]. *Michigan Quarterly Review,* 393–423.

Legacies of loss, (1998, March 8). *Boston Globe,* p. D3.

Lewis, H. B. (1971). *Shame and guilt in neurosis.* New York: International Universities Press.

Linde, C. (1993). *Life stories: The creation of coherence.* New York: Oxford University Press.

Mayman, M. (1979). The shame experience, the shame dynamic, and shame personalities in psychotherapy. In J. Adelson (Ed.), *Cases* (pp. 57–71). Ann Arbor: University of Michigan, Psychological Clinic.

McAdams, D. P. (1997). *The stories we live by: Personal myths and the making of the self*. New York: Guilford Press.

McDuff, D. (1991). Introduction. *Crime and punishment*. (D. McDuff, Trans.). London: Penguin.

Morson, G. S. (1994). *Narrative and freedom: The shadows of time*. New Haven, CT: Yale University Press.

Peters, R. S. (1970). The education of the emotions. In M. B. Arnold (Ed.), *Feelings and emotion: The Loyola Symposium* (pp. 187–203). New York: Academic Press.

Pennebaker, J. W. (1993). Putting stress into words: Health, linguistic, and therapeutic implications. *Behavior Research and Theory, 31*, 538–548.

Pennebaker, J. W. (1997). *Opening up: The healing power of expressing emotions*. New York: Guilford Press.

Rahv, P. (1960). Dostoevsky in *Crime and Punishment*. *Partisan Review*, XXVII, 393–425.

Ricoeur, P. (1988). *Time and narrative*. Vol. 3. (Blamey, K., & Pellauer, D., Trans.). Chicago: University of Chicago Press.

Rieff, P. (1966). *The triumph of the therapeutic*. New York: Harper & Row.

Robinson, J. A., & Hawpe, L. (1986). Narrative thinking as a heuristic process. In T. R. Sarbin (Ed.), *Narrative psychology: The storied nature of human conduct* (pp. 111–125). New York: Praeger.

Roemer, L., & Borkovec, T. D. (1994). Effects of suppressing thoughts about emotional material. *Journal of Abnormal Psychology, 103*, 467–474.

Rosenwald, G. C. (1992). Conclusion: Reflections on narrative self-understanding. In G. C. Rosenwald & R. L. Ochberg (Eds.), *Storied lives: The cultural politics of self-understanding* (pp. 265–289). New Haven, CT: Yale University Press.

Ross, L. (1977). The intuitive psychologist and his shortcomings: Distortions in the attribution process. In L. Berkowitz (Ed.), *Advances in experimental social psychology* (Vol. 10, pp. 173–220). New York: Academic Press.

Savio, M. (1995, Summer). Two anniversary speeches. *Threepenny Review*, 33–35.

Sheed, W. (1978). *Transatlantic blues*. New York: E. P. Dutton.

Tangney, J. P. (1990). Assessing individual differences in proneness to shame and guilt: Development of the Self-Conscious Affect and Attribution Inventory. *Journal of Personality and Social Psychology, 59*, 102–111.

Wegner, D. M. (1994a). Ironic processes of mental control. *Psychological Review, 101*, 34–52.

Wegner, D. M. (1994b). *White bears and other unwanted thoughts: Suppression, obsession, and the psychology of mental control*. New York: Guilford Press.

Wegner, D. M., Schneider, D. J., Carter, S. III, & White, T. (1987). Paradoxical effects of thought suppression. *Journal of Personality and Social Psychology, 53*, 5–13.

3

DE PROFUNDIS: PRISON AS A TURNING POINT IN OSCAR WILDE'S LIFE STORY

WILLIAM TODD SCHULTZ

Some have divided playwright Oscar Wilde's life up into two discrete "acts." There is the ascent, marked by clear achievement, artistic success, and celebrity. Then there is the fall, beginning with a doomed relationship and ending in disgrace. Personologist Henry Murray (1981) once proposed the existence of an Icarus complex, a personality dynamic characterized by a rapid rise and an equally rapid descent. In broad outline, Wilde's story fits that theme. He flew too close to the sun, and he fell to earth.

Act One of the life augured nothing but unending triumph. Wilde attended Trinity and Oxford, winning several first prizes along the way, most notably the Newdigate Prize for his poem "Ravenna." He published a book of poetry and a scandalous work of fiction, *The Picture of Dorian Gray,* which gave voice to several of Wilde's subversive philosophies. His notoriety, already fairly well-established, grew into a kind of fame, and he embarked on a lecture tour in the United States, giving talks on home decoration, of all things, and the philosophy of aestheticism, which extolled beauty above all else. His plays, including his last, *The Importance of Being Earnest,* enjoyed success on the stage, and his essays, among them "The Critic as Artist" and "The Soul of Man Under Socialism," showed a daring and proliferating mind at work. Wilde was a shameless provocateur. His aphorisms—"Leading a double life is the only preparation for marriage" (Schmidgall, 1994)—tended to have a certain sting to them. If he sometimes found himself attacked in the press or made fun of, he still gave the appearance of feeling more or less bullet-proof. His sense of style and his intellect

*I am grateful to Dan McAdams for his generous attention to an earlier draft of this chapter and for his patience.

both were forces to be reckoned with, and for a time they sustained him. Even attacks on his assumed homosexuality met with resistance, because after all he was a married man and the father of two sons.

Act Two of the life is a story of the shift from fame to sudden infamy. Here Wilde's wit did not carry the day, and in fact may have hastened his fall. As the end result of a sequence of strangely fateful events described more fully later, Wilde found himself in prison, serving two years hard labor. He died broke, reviled, and largely alone. The shamelessness and daring on which he had staked his reputation finally fomented his ruin.

In this chapter I examine Wilde's "crash" narrative. Most straightforwardly, it represents an exemplary instance of a psychological turning point. He even described it as such. He speaks of an epiphany in prison, a self-realization in which he sees, for the first time, into his true nature. On the other hand, many have questioned Wilde's sincerity. Did prison really make Wilde into a different and better person, humbler and less attached to the charms of the shallow life, or was that simply a tale Wilde elected to tell about himself, a kind of "press-release" concealing connections between current behavior and personal history (Wiersma, 1988)?

I start the chapter by summarizing the features of the turning point episode Wilde constructed. After that, I compare Wilde's experience to what is known through research about turning points in general. I finish by highlighting the significant questions Wilde's case raises: To what extent is it representative, and to what extent distinctive? I begin with Wilde's self-analysis. By what combination of circumstances did he meet with his ruin, and how did he come to narrate it while in jail?

WILDE'S "CRASH" NARRATIVE

Wilde's fall resulted from what his principal biographer (Ellmann, 1968) called a "beserk passion," an affair with a volatile and by all accounts self-consumed young dilettante, Lord Alfred Douglas. This affair attracted more than the usual amount of interest, partly as a result of Wilde's celebrity and partly because of actions taken by Douglas's father, the Marquess of Queensberry. The story has received considerable attention in the past decade or so. A film, *Wilde*, was devoted to it, as were several plays, including *The Judas Kiss* and *Gross Indecency*. A number of biographies and scholarly monographs and papers also make it their focus (see, for instance, Buckler, 1989; Gopnik, 1998; Knox, 1996). All seem to portray Wilde either as a victim of repressive social forces or as the somewhat fatuous architect of his own ruin. Likewise, some regard Wilde's prison turning point as mostly genuine, and some see it as tendentious and artificial. I return to such questions later. For now, I simply want to set down the facts.

After urging his son to stay away from Wilde for fear of what the liaison might do to his family's reputation, the Marquess, meeting with no success, sent a card to Wilde's club accusing him of "posing" as a "somdomite" (sic). This Wilde apparently found both impudent and libelous. After much encouragement by Douglas, Wilde sued Queensberry, and lost—or to be more precise, Wilde dropped the charges after learning that the defense planned to produce witnesses (all younger men) who would testify to having sexual relations with Wilde. The press made much of this turn of events, the implications quickly became unignorable, and Wilde soon found himself charged with "gross indecency." The first trial resulted in a hung jury, and the second in Wilde's conviction to two years hard labor.

This outcome was disastrous for Wilde in several different ways. First of all, he lost everything one could lose. He never saw his sons again, his wife finally divorced him, he was bankrupted, and while he was imprisoned, his mother died. Second, the hard labor really *was* hard, a punishment Wilde must have been utterly ill-equipped to endure. He was made to exercise on a prison treadmill six hours daily. He slept on a plank bed. After one month, he began his work—either postbag-making, tailoring, or picking oakum. He could communicate with the outside world only after three months, and his visitations were few and far between. Following a transfer to Reading Prison, the source for a later poem titled, "The Ballad of Reading Gaol," Wilde was allowed to receive some books and to write one page of prose per day that, when finished, needed to be turned over to the warden each night. Capitalizing on this small privilege, Wilde initiated what was to become his sole personal statement about the causes for and meaning of his degradation. The statement assumed the form of a letter written to Lord Alfred Douglas, but was later published posthumously under the title *De Profundis*.

What follows is an examination of Wilde's effort to impose on his fall the organizing structure of a conversion narrative. But Wilde is up to more than just that. As a consequence, the text seems sometimes to be operating at cross purposes. On one hand, Wilde uses *De Profundis*, especially in its early sections, as a vehicle for attacking Douglas personally. He imagines Douglas will not have an easy time reading the letter, but urges him to go on, chiefly because he feels, or says he feels, Douglas needs to face certain unpleasant facts about himself. "If, as you read what is here written, [your pale face] from time to time becomes scorched as though by a furnace blast, with shame, it will be all the better for you. The supreme vice is shallowness. Whatever is realised is right" (Wilde, 1905/1996, p. 28). Wilde presumes to affect a therapeutic role. If he appears only to be indulging his rage at

Douglas's assorted weaknesses, then it is a rage with salutary potential—or so he says.

As Wilde goes on, however, Douglas drops out of the picture altogether, consigned to a mere off-stage presence. Soon the focus stays on Wilde himself, and the vitriol characterizing these initial segments of the work disappears. The impetus now seems to be of a different order. Wilde works to wring from his ruin a story not of disaster (though the disaster is never denied) but triumph—a triumph of the soul. That is, discarding the relatively simplistic trope of the Icarus tale, Wilde invents what for him may have been a necessary modification—he falls from a false grace to one that seems in hindsight much more true.

Central to all this is Wilde's use of the turning point metaphor. He invokes the term itself several times—as he must do, particularly if the tale's aim is salvation. Although he certainly dwells on "the tragically critical moment of all my life" (1905/1996, p. 7), "the crash of my life" (p. 21), "the ultimate and terrible moment" (p. 21), calling it a "gigantic psychological error [in which] my will power completely failed me" (p. 8), he does so only to set up a contrast between the tragic on one hand, and what he has made of it on the other. He is led to reflect on the "two great turning-points" in his life: when his father sent him to Oxford, an episode of great achievement, and when "Society" sent him to prison, an episode of great shame. But this shame gets immediately displaced by what Wilde calls his "ultimate discovery" (p. 45), the "starting point for a fresh development" (p. 45), a "new life" or "Vita Nuova" (p. 45), as Dante (whom Wilde was reading at the time) would have it. What precipitated such a momentous shift? Suffering, it seems. "Sorrow, then, and all it teaches one," Wilde writes, "is my new world" (p. 51).

Wilde speaks next of the characteristics of this world—its phenomenology—and of the psychological qualities of the turning point itself. First of all, it allows for a seeing into the essence of things. "It really is a revelation," he said. "One discerns things one has never discerned before. One approaches the whole of history from a different standpoint" (1905/1996, p. 52). It also defies intellectual determination, obeying an inscrutably internal logic. Wilde does not so much reach a conclusion but finds one ready-made, preformed. "It has come to me right out of myself," he wrote.

> So I know it has come at the proper time. It could not have come before, nor later. Had anyone told me of it, I would have rejected it. Had it been brought to me, I would have refused it. As I found it, I want to keep it. I must do so. It is the one thing that has in it the elements of life, of a new life, a Vita Nuova for me. Of all things it is the strangest. One cannot give it away and another may not give it to

one. One cannot acquire it except by surrendering everything that one has. (1905/1996, pp. 45–46)

In a sense, one waits for a dawning, because as Wilde also explains, "Everything must come to one out of one's own nature. There is no use telling a person a thing that he does not feel and can't understand" (1905/1996, p. 28).

Wilde also emphasizes the turning point's inevitability, invoking a clearly tragic-type narrative trope. He refers repeatedly to "my lot" and to the entire episode's "certain resolution." We all get meted out "different fates," Wilde says, and disaster seems to be his. This particular narrative choice deserves to be highlighted, because it determines the structure for Wilde's entire system of reference. Rather than adopting a psychological perspective, or one that might point up the essential randomness of life, Wilde asserts a more mystical framework. He imagines himself as a kind of puppet worked by "unseen hands." As he declares toward the end of the letter, "I am conscious now that behind all this beauty, satisfying though it may be, there is some spirit hidden of which the painted forms and shapes are but modes of manifestation, and it is with this spirit that I desire to become in harmony. . . . The Mystical in Art, the Mystical in Life, the Mystical in Nature—this is what I am looking for. It is absolutely necessary for me to find it somewhere" (1905/1996, p. 89).

The irrefutably interior quality of the experience guarantees its validity, according to Wilde. It cannot be embedded in or subjected to any kind of scientific or philosophical analysis. It is almost, for this reason, isolated from doubt. Morality, religion, and reason—Wilde explicitly rejects each. They cannot help him, he says. "I have to get it all out of myself. Nothing seems to me of the smallest value except what one gets out of oneself" (1905/1996, p. 46). He alludes to feeling an independence from "the external things of life" which have "no importance at all" (p. 46). The sense of the moment's individuality is enhanced, with Wilde portraying the experience as deeply personal, unique, and unrepeatable.

Finally there is the question of the turning point's momentariness. On this point Wilde seems to be of two different minds. If he chooses to play up the sudden explosiveness of his change of view, he still cannot quite resist a narrative based on gradualness. As he says at one point, "It is of course no new life at all, but simply the continuance, by means of development and evolution, of my former life" (1905/1996, p. 54). On the other hand, Wilde's manner of speech consistently implies an irreducible present. "*Now* I am approaching life from a completely new standpoint" (p. 50), and "*Now* for the first time since my imprisonment I have a real desire for life" (p. 51), or "I *now* see that sorrow . . . is at once the type and test of all great art"

(p. 52). He even, with all the benefit of hindsight, isolates (or invents) the decisive moment when the spirit opened up to him.

> I had absolutely nothing left in the world but one thing. I had lost my name, my position, my happiness, my freedom, my wealth. I was a prisoner and a pauper. But I still had my children left. Suddenly they were taken away from me by the law. It was a blow so appalling that I did not know what to do, so I flung myself on my knees, and bowed my head, and wept, and said, "The body of a child is as the body of the Lord—I am not worthy of either." That moment seemed to save me. I saw then that the only thing for me was to accept everything. Since then—curious as it will no doubt sound—I have been happier. It was of course my soul in its ultimate essence that I had reached." (1905/1996, pp. 58–59).

The mawkish drama of the scene, Job-like in its intensity, encourages more than a little doubt. Did it happen or did Wilde reconstruct it? He seems to anticipate the question, for he warns us of his story's curiousness. He doubts we will believe him. But by mixing his change metaphors, referring simultaneously to slow evolution and sudden *involution*, Wilde hedges his narrative bets. There is a stricken quality to his change, yet it results from the simple development of his former life. Looked at in this way, Wilde seems to be saying he is the same, only different. He discovered something— suffering—that he understood the meaning of, at least unconsciously, all along. He even speaks of how "all this is foreshadowed and prefigured in my books," through which a "note of doom" runs "like a purple thread" (1905/1996, p. 55).

We can now summarize the features of Wilde's individual turning point narrative with an eye toward comparing it to more nomothetic hypotheses. It is characterized by, as Wilde explains, an *irrefutably interior and inevitable seeing into the essence of things which defies all intellectual determination, and which gradually evolves into a moment of unmistakable discovery.* It leaves in its wake a new viewpoint, mirroring what philosophers of science refer to as a paradigm shift. But this comparison, too, has its qualifications, because Wilde wants to impress on us the emotional qualities of his shift, not its intellectual flavor. It is not something he thought himself into. It revealed itself to him only after everything else fell away.

I move next from Wilde to theory, partly to see whether or not Wilde's narrative can be assimilated into current research and partly to provoke that research, so to speak, into responding to the individual instance. This, after all, is one of the chief functions of psychobiography and what makes it, in my view, indispensable. By confronting theory in a way it alone can, the single case has the capacity to tell us what we know and what remains to be discovered. In fact, I would go so far as to say that genuine understanding of turning points can advance only if substantial use is made of actual lived lives in the process of eruption.

THE REPRESENTATIVENESS OF WILDE'S "TURN"

In outline, the facts of Wilde's case seem to square with much current thinking about the general structure of turning point experiences. Wheaton and Gotlib (1997), for instance, although admitting that turning points are difficult to define, are open to alternative formulations, and suffer from a definite lack of precision, do nonetheless describe assorted features of the concept that make for a good match with Wilde. According to these authors, a turning point is (a) a "disruption in a trajectory, a deflection in a path," (b) more than a temporary detour, and (c) knowable only after the fact, only postdictively (1997, p. 1). Turning points are narrated events with long-lasting consequences, in other words. Also, whatever change in the direction of the life course occurs, it must be nonnormative in the sense that we can define changes in direction only with respect to the individual's previous trajectory. The person is his or her own control group. His or her life is what preestablishes the baseline from which the departure occurs.

An idea of special relevance for Wilde's case concerns the role of psychosocial resources. Such supports in the face of trauma, something Wilde lacked entirely, having lost his family, his reputation, and his wealth, actually may mitigate potentially upsetting transitions, according to Wheaton and Gotlib. They "buffer," soften, or even prevent change (1997, p. 10). Having little or no psychosocial resources in place may have precipitated a more intense crisis for Wilde, it seems. Prison left no option but to change, or at least to imagine that possibility.

Wethington, Cooper, and Holmes see turning points as shifts in the meaning, purpose, or direction of a life and stress that they "must include a self-reflective awareness of, or insight into, the significance of the change" (1997, p. 217). Under this definition, "self-realizations or reinterpretations of past experiences may bring on a turning point" (1997, p. 217). What most frequently triggers such self-reinterpretations? Changes in important relationships, according to Wethington et al., including divorce or a serious breakdown in a close relationship, especially when reparation seems unlikely. In this scheme, turning points emerge out of a discovery of one's limitations. We learn how certain people are beyond our control, and we find we must "discover how to accept and adapt" (1997, p. 225). This describes Wilde's case nicely. He lost his lover, he lost his wife, and he lost his talent, at least for a time, and found in suffering a kind of peace, or a way of reenvisioning his life. The trigger is loss, and the turning point follows from figuring out how self needs to change to accommodate. Many of Wethington et al.'s respondents used the term "fresh start" to describe the kinds of identity shifts they made. So did Wilde, who spoke of his "ultimate discovery" being "the starting point for a fresh development" (1905/1996, p. 45).

Clausen (1993) regards turning points as perceptual reinterpretations or reorientations directed at the self and requiring changes in perceived identity. He listed four types—reformulations of life role, of life perspective, of life goals, or of self, the latter including profound realizations about one's strengths and weaknesses. Wilde's view of the world changed. He discerned things he had never discerned before, and he embraced a worldview revolving around the curative value of suffering. He also came to terms with the ways in which his preprison identity led him on a path toward ruin, and asserted in its place a postprison identity committed to forgiveness, love, sorrow, and humility.

So Wilde's case is not significantly anomalous, at least. In broad terms his epiphany jibes with current thinking. But what about in *specific* terms? Is Wilde's case as exemplary as it appears? Sometimes yes, sometimes no. In what follows I take up a number of subsidiary questions, beginning with the turning point's trigger.

The Narrative Spur

Loss of loved ones or of important relationships seems central to the narrative demand for a turning point. It forces a reevaluation of self and of life goals and values. It demands that we reassert who we are or make fresh commitments to what we believe in. It also can give rise to an explicit reconsideration of worldview in that we must somehow explain to ourselves and others why the loss occurred, why we or others have been singled out for suffering (for the effects of loss on personality and creativity, see Schultz, 1996, 1998, 1999). Of course, some people respond to loss not by redefining themselves in any way but by staying who they are, by becoming, one might say, even more the same. The story of Job comes to mind. In the face of unimaginable suffering of every possible sort, Job remains steadfast in his faith. He does not so much change as endure. So the obvious question is, "Why does loss lead to a turning point in some but not in others?"

Bruner (1999) sees, not loss exclusively, but "trouble" or jeopardy as the engine of narrative. Any kind of trouble will do, just so long as a "canonical state of the world" has been disrupted (1999, p. 324). If it is true that most mental acts, having grown automatic, go on without the benefit of consciousness, then jeopardy or error might force consciousness— the need for narrative—to spring into action. As long as the "same old story" succeeds, we feel no need to imagine a new one. But as Bruner writes, when faced with difficulties, "one may be forced to fashion an omnibus

Self [i.e., a completed, organizing, assimilating narrative] to cope with the jeopardy in which we have been put" (1999, p. 324). Moreover, trouble "may be not only the engine of narrative, but also the impetus for its elaboration" (p. 324).

This all seems persuasive, but the question remains (as Bruner himself acknowledges). Most people when in jeopardy tend either to justify the canon of the life or to make up excuses. Why do some reject these two options and author a new identity instead? Allowing that we know much too little about what predisposes us to such reflection, Bruner does offer a few hints. First of all, some have too little time for metacognitive activity of the sort required for significant alterations to identity. Second, some personalities apparently exhibit low needs for cognition; they are not motivated to exercise their mental faculties. Third, certain contexts may have the effect of heightening the agentive role, such that we experience a revival of self-agency not only in talk but also in behavior (Bruner, 1999, pp. 324–325).

The life of Wilde suggests additional possibilities. Another spur to identity reconsideration and the adoption of a turning point narrative might revolve around perceived guilt that, in the event, also would heighten the sense of self-agency, at least retrospectively. In *De Profundis* Wilde repeatedly asserts his culpability: "I will begin by telling you that I blame myself terribly. As I sit here in this dark cell in convict clothes, a disgraced and ruined man, I blame myself. In the perturbed and fitful nights of anguish, in the long monotonous days of pain, it is myself I blame. . . . " (Wilde, 1905/1996, pp. 2–3). If a subject implicates self in the very generation of jeopardy, that seems to call for "learning a lesson"; and in those who by dint of intelligence, temperament, imagination, or whatever, appear more driven to integrate selfhood, the end result of the "lesson" might assume the form of a turning point. Such seems to have been the case for Wilde, at least. His lack of will power sealed his doom—as he notes at different times during the letter—so he elevates this self-determined catastrophe into its own realization: He embraces the effect of his misguided and ill-considered agency. At the same time, it is as if Wilde seems to be saying, "I can't believe I could have been so stupid, so easily taken in, so heedless, so will-less, and it will never happen again because I *learned*." To not repeat the errors of the past virtually requires a new perspective.

As for Bruner's ideas, Wilde certainly had plenty of time for metacognitive reflection (prison has even produced a virtual genre of self-reflective writing), and his mind and context were such that there would have been a peculiarly high need for cognition. In fact, the tone of the letter conveys the impression of a strong desire to understand or explain something almost beyond understanding. In several different senses, then, Wilde's situation provided an optimal environment for self-realization. Its characteristics—

jeopardy, time for metacognitive reflection about self, desire and talent for such cognition, perceived blame and consequent need to learn from a mistake—might even make up a generalizable change "setting."

The Narrative Structure

Having been the kind of playwright who, according to one critic, "deliberately lets the machinery of his plots show until the plays become near-parodies," Wilde was certainly skilled at the manipulation of dramatic form (Brockett, 1977, p. 488). By imposing a structure on his experience, it comes as little surprise that Wilde seems to have scripted *De Profundis* and the events surrounding it very much like a play, right up to his enlightenment and catharsis.

Aristotle's *Poetics* includes a lengthy consideration of the characteristics of effective tragedy, among other things. In it he compares different types of action, and notes how "a complex action is one wherein the change of fortune is accompanied either by recognition (*anagnorisis*) or reversal (*peripeteia*), or by both," and how this recognition or reversal, when most successful, appears inevitable—it unfolds within the plot structure itself (1958, p. 21). Recognition is "a change from ignorance to knowledge of a bond of love or hate between persons who are destined for good fortune or the reverse" (pp. 21–22). Reversal "is a change of the situation into its opposite," which accords with the probable or unavoidable (p. 21). It means, even more specifically, that a situation that seems to or is intended to develop in one direction suddenly develops in the reverse direction. The third element mentioned by Aristotle is suffering or *pathos*. For Aristotle, the best kind of character is the truly tragic: "A man who is neither outstanding in virtue and righteousness nor [who through] wickedness and vice falls into some misfortune, but through some flaw. He should also be famous or prosperous . . ." (p. 24).

That Wilde's *De Profundis* makes use of these structural elements—consciously or not—seems almost impossible to deny. In prison Wilde comes to an *anagnorisis* about his love–hate relationship with Douglas, in the end affirming the power of love and forgiveness over the hate that can blind human beings. An initially promising situation—the affair itself—suddenly transforms into its opposite—ruin—and the outcome, as Wilde expresses it over and over again, has about it the aura of fatedness or inevitability. In other words, there is a clear *peripeteia*. Wilde also portrays himself as very much the tragic figure. He is neither virtuous nor wicked to begin with, and his suffering arrives by way of a flaw—in this case his utter lack of will power. In the event, Wilde even happens to be both famous and prosperous, so the resulting *pathos* becomes all the more gripping.

Even the basic categories of conflict typically met with in play structure seem evident. One person is at odds with another (Wilde versus Douglas/Marquess). One person—Wilde—also is pitted against a group, force, or idea; Wilde is the artist at war with a society bent on denying his individual expression. Finally, Wilde grapples with himself in the sense that, most fundamentally, he depicts a conflict between sensual and spiritual elements, between instinct and wisdom.

In a manual written for playwrights, Downs and Wright (1998) describe the "structure of formula." Most plays begin with an *event*, a moment of uniqueness or happening in the characters' lives—an unusual incident, special occasion, or crisis. There is a *basic situation* and a *disturbance* that causes an opening balance to come unglued. At some point the protagonist makes a *major decision* resulting in conflict. This comes to define what the play is about and forces the protagonist to move forward against great odds. Conflicts, crises, obstacles, and complications of different sorts intensify, action rises, and somewhere along the way a *dark moment* is visited on the protagonist—for a time his goal seems almost unattainable. The beginning of the end commences with an *enlightenment*, and according to Downs and Wright, this enlightenment (a) must not come out of the blue (no *deus ex machina*), (b) must not be immediately predictable, and (c) must emerge naturally out of a developing plot line. The play then concludes with a *catharsis*.

Wilde plots *De Profundis* in a similar fashion. There may be various ways to fit Downs and Wright's template over Wilde's narrative, but one such possibility might go something like this: The event or happening is Douglas's word to Wilde that his father, the Marquess, is taking every opportunity to trash their coupling and wants them to desist. Already a crisis of sorts, the basic situation gets even further "unglued" when the Marquess accuses Wilde of being a sodomite. The leaving of the calling card, then, functions as the "disturbance." Now comes a major decision leading to overt conflict, this being Wilde's suit against the Marquess for libel. The protagonist—Wilde—presses forward against great odds. He stands up for his right to be an individual. Action rises as Wilde drops the charges, then gets tried himself. The guilty verdict seems like the best candidate for the dark moment. Here Wilde begins to wonder whether his goal—self-understanding—may elude him. Prison looms, and Wilde, though many encouraged or even expected him to do so, chooses, like Socrates, not to escape via exile. Then comes enlightenment, the recognition of the value of sorrow and suffering; a naturally emerging revelation given the basic plot line, yet not immediately predictable. For Wilde, this realization does come more or less out of the blue, except for the fact that he tells us he intuited it all along. It was, as he himself declares, "foreshadowed" in his early life.

As for the turning point or enlightenment specifically, locking one's self into generic plot structure almost requires it. Wilde, of course, naturally thought like a playwright. But in doing so, there is a sense in which he predetermined the outcome of his narrative. There would be no curtain call until he found some way of imagining the protagonist's triumph. It is as if his life demanded a play. And who better to script it?

The Epiphany

This question has most to do with how to *analogize* turning points and with which analogy best captures Wilde's case. As Wheaton and Gotlib note, the turning point concept seems "essential" yet "problematic" (1997, p. 3). Comparing it via Wilde to other clearly established tropes of change— some applied to personality, some not—may suggest potential refinements.

Kuhn's (1970) notion of a paradigm shift comes immediately to mind. Paradigms are conceptual frameworks or models that, much like perceptual sets or gestalts, create a tendency to "see" some data and not others. More than that, the paradigm actually preselects certain facts as meaningful, because "in the absence of a paradigm or candidate for paradigm, all of the facts that could possibly pertain . . . are likely to seem equally relevant" (Kuhn, 1970, p. 15)—an untenable state of affairs. Under conditions of what Kuhn called normal science, paradigms tend to be relatively binding, appropriately open-ended, and oriented toward the solution of minor puzzles or problems within a given field, scientific progress amounting to a tinkering with the mostly "known."

Why do paradigms shift? When "existing rules" persistently fail to make the puzzles "come out as they should" (Kuhn, 1970, p. 68). As this failure continues, a search for new rules begins, and the new rules eventually get assembled into a new paradigm. Change is a function of unsuccessful efforts to make meaning—in other words, because existing in a state of thwarted meaning-making constitutes a paradigmatic crisis. This sounds very much like Bruner's notion of canonical disruption. In both instances an accepted story has broken down and a need for story-making has been mobilized.

This analogy seems partly to capture Wilde's predicament in *De Profundis*. The old story, the old personal myth, no longer meets Wilde's needs. Though he had once espoused the "trivial in thought and action," the "froth and folly of life," and "lived entirely for pleasure," in prison he feels a need to shape new views and ideas: "I see fresh developments in art and life, each one of which is a fresh mode of perfection. I long to live so that I can explore what is no less than a new world to me. . . . [Before prison] I shunned suffering and sorrow . . . I resolved to ignore them, to treat them, that is to say, as modes of imperfection. They were not part of my scheme of life.

They had no place in my philosophy" (1905/1996, p. 51). But now Wilde comprehends the lessons "hidden in the heart of pain" (p. 52).

Under the old paradigm, suffering was ignored. Wilde's scheme of life demanded that it be treated like an inconsequential datum. It was not relevant for understanding. In the wake of his ruin, however, it became anomalous, and a new scheme of life was created to accommodate it. This new scheme, once established, allowed Wilde to discern things he had never discerned before. It opened up a new world, just like a new paradigm brings with it "new" perceptions.

On the other hand, Wilde did not think himself into his new view. It descended on him. He speaks as if he found it, not as if he assembled it to deal with puzzles that were not working out as they should. Wilde places himself squarely in the realm of revelation, of religious awakening, not in the realm of science. This fact recommends two different modes of understanding, Christian conversion and Zen satori.

William James takes up conversion in a pair of chapters from *Varieties of Religious Experience*. He identifies what he feels to be two forms, the volitional type and the type by self-surrender, but then essentially discards the former because even when conversion seems willed and deliberately sought after, "The very last step must be left to other forces and performed without the help of [the will's] activity" (1997, p. 230). James considers self-surrender the vital turning-point of the religious life. To relinquish control is to throw our conscious selves on the mercy of powers, such that "when the new centre of personal energy has been subconsciously incubated so long as to be just ready to open into flower, 'hands off' is the only word for us, it must burst forth unaided!" (James, 1961, p. 175). Revelation "sweeps in like a sudden flood" (p. 179).

In James's scheme the feelings that "fill the hour" of the conversion experience include (a) a sense of higher control (in illustrating this he describes a case strikingly similar to Wilde's, in which a man throws himself on his knees and prays as he had never prayed before); (b) a state of assurance, trust, and confidence; (c) a perception of truth not known before whereby "the mysteries of life become lucid" (p. 200); (d) an intuition of "clean and beautiful newness within and without" (p. 203); and, most characteristically, (e) an ecstasy of happiness (James, 1961).

It is hard not to be struck by how very closely James's account resembles Wilde's reconstruction. Religious conversion, it seems, may represent a primary narrative form with which to construct sudden identity change. Wilde certainly speaks of having surrendered to an incubated truth that burst forth: "Whatever beauty of life still remains to me is contained in some moment of surrender" (1905/1996, p. 71). He recounts a sense of higher control in the form not of God but of destiny or Fate. He tells Andre Gide, "I knew there would be a catastrophe . . . I was expecting it . . . Prison has completely changed me. I counted on it for that" (1949, pp. 20–21). He calls his insight irrefutable, he talks of perceiving reality for the first time, and he realizes that now, by virtue of his epiphany, he can at last be truly happy.

Like conversion, the Zen notion of satori—a seeing into the true essence of things—also requires self-surrender. One achieves the state not by thinking or relying on logic or reason but by cultivating a frame of mind consisting of openness and a readiness to receive truth. Satori is intuitive in nature. It is a realization rather than a solution. It is interior and personal and cannot be imposed from without. Because it seems to those who receive it like a mental upheaval or catastrophe, its effects on one's moral and spiritual life are nothing short of revolutionary—it gives rise to a lasting change of character. The world no longer looks the same (Suzuki, 1956, p. 84). In Zen, koans (deliberately provocative and paradoxical riddles) are sometimes used to precipitate the satori—they uproot thought and by virtue of their apparent insolubility encourage shifts of understanding—but as a stimulant, really anything will do. In fact, satori generally comes totally unexpectedly. It "strikes at the primary fact of existence, and its attainment marks a turning point in one's life" (Suzuki, 1956, p. 97). Suzuki summarizes satori's qualities in terms resembling those James proposed for conversion. It is (a) nonintellectual, unwilled, and conative; (b) irrefutably authoritative or doubtless; (c) impersonal in nature; (d) a feeling of exaltation; and (e) sudden or abrupt.

That such qualities can be observed in Wilde's account of his epiphany seems self-evident. As summarized already, Wilde's turning point assumes the form of an *irrefutably interior and inevitable seeing into the essence of things that defies all intellectual determination and that gradually evolves into a moment of unmistakable discovery*. Wilde notably was not unfamiliar with Eastern ideas. Early in his career he reviewed a work by the Chinese sage Chuang-tzu, so he may have made use of such knowledge when it came time to construct his transformation. Whatever the case, one thing seems clear—Wilde's favored analogy for change is religious in nature. His turning point is best understood as a conversion or satori, a profound self-discovery precipitating a brand new way of looking at the world. There is no process of induction, no effort to piece together an alternative model for reality such that the data of life assume a different shape or form. In other words, in this instance the paradigm shift template does not seem apt. More so, a new view incubated and burst forth, just as James described. Or did it? James and Suzuki both highlight the abruptness of conversion/satori. In fact, Suzuki goes so far as to declare, "If it is not abrupt and momentary, it is not satori" (1956, p. 108). This returns us to a question posed earlier. Was Wilde's turning point a gradual unfolding, or was it a "mental catastrophe," striking suddenly at the very heart of existence?

The Suddenness of the Turning Point

If turning point experiences can be said to vary phenomenologically—and it seems like they must, because they emerge from an ongoing life-story—then one form they might assume, maybe even a preeminent form, is conversion or satori. In some ways these structures seem like turning points *par excellence*. As such, they might come quickly to mind whenever subjects cast about in pursuit of narrative strategies with which to construct tumultuous change. They simply fit the bill like nothing else does. But they do impose on the change narrative one particular demand: It must be imagined as a sudden explosion of identity. This gives rise to a certain ontological–epistemological quandary. Is the turning point *really* sudden, or is it just convenient to depict it that way? Or to put the question a little differently: Does abruptness make for a more effective change narrative?

Wilde seems to have struggled with this very question, because as we have seen he alludes to both possibilities—gradualness and abruptness. The same struggle can be found in James and Zen. Conversion's volitional type, which James has a hard time taking too seriously, suggests an effortful, willed process, an evolution toward awakening. Some Zen thinkers, unpersuaded by Suzuki's insistence on the momentary nature of satori, speak of a gradual unfolding of consciousness. It would appear, then, that this kind of question recurrently arises whenever attempts are made to conceptualize personality upheaval. On one hand, the difficulty has a lot to do with what Bruner (1999) calls the "qualia" of selfhood, and with how those qualia reflectively cohere. Qualia indicators signal the feel of a life, its mood, pace, zest, weariness, and so forth. They express subjectivity—what we experience inside—and because they tend to be unsituated with respect to external events, "they are notoriously subject to contextual interpretation" (Bruner, 1999, p. 311). We look "outside" as a way of explaining what we feel to ourselves and to others. Coherence indicators "reveal the internal structure of a larger self-concept and are presumed to indicate how the particulars of various endeavors cohere into life as a whole" (p. 311). So there is the subjective feel of a turning point, on one hand, and there is, on the other, the attempt to narrate it, to construct coherence through reflective activity.

This would suggest a number of possibilities. The qualia of a turning point might include a feeling of abruptness, but on reflection, one might construct a continuity rather than a discontinuity. Of course, the opposite might be true too, and in fact seems more likely, especially if sudden upheaval in the form of conversion–satori makes for a more compelling narrative structure, a better turning point tale. Or the qualia may match the narrative: The feel of abruptness gets told as abruptness, for instance. In addition, to complicate things still more, it seems possible to reflect ourselves into the memory of a subjective feel that never existed to begin with. After all, turning points are always retrospectively adduced, "the embodiment of wisdom in hindsight," as Wheaton and Gotlib pointed out (1997, p. 3). If we do not necessarily recall the feeling of epiphany, we might simply talk ourselves into it, convince ourselves that it must have been there whether we recall it or not. Some events almost require at least hypothetical personality change—trauma, divorce, death, crisis, loss. When external circumstances call for it, we may feel obliged to imagine that we profited from them in some way by becoming different and, more important, better people—or that we learned something useful, at least, or acquired a slightly changed perspective. It is not hard to imagine the inclination to invent a turning point, in other words, even when the requisite experience seems to be missing.

In trying to assess Wilde's epiphany, one inescapable fact presents immediate complications: The subjective feel is embedded within the narrative construction of the event. What we know about the qualia indicator is what Wilde tells us about it. As a consequence, any effort to pass judgment on its "reality" seems problematic from the start. Was it really abrupt or was it really gradual? Wilde tells both types of stories, although he favors the former. But does he favor it because the change truly was abrupt, or does he favor it because suddenness makes for a better story? There would appear to be two answers to such a question. First, if who we are is what we say we are, then the question assumes a false division—self *is* story (McAdams, 1993). Second, if who we are differs from what we say we are, then the question is probably unanswerable because its solution can only be sought in the narrative Wilde himself proposes.

Bruner covered the same ground, wondering about his research participants: "Did the people involved actually *experience* their lives in this way, or is this just in the telling?" (1993, p. 47). Clearly the story form affects the organization of experience just as surely as it affects memory recall. We impose meaning postdictively. We hone and mitigate as required. "Adventures happen to people who know how to tell it that way," as Henry James once put it (quoted in Bruner, 1993, p. 48). Bruner offered a sensible conclusion. "Rather than regarding [turning points] simply as 'true reports' about 'what happened,' we [would] do better to consider them as preternaturally clear instances of narrative construction that have the function of helping the teller clarify his or her Self-concept. They are prototype narrative episodes whose construction results in increasing the realism and drama of the Self" (1993, p. 50). They are real because they have real effects on self-understanding, which often translate into real effects on behavior. Indeed, all analyses of turning point experiences, including those of James and Suzuki, stress the turning point's durability. Durability may even represent the one true hallmark of a legitimate turning point event, because if the turning point produces no lasting behavioral outcome, then it probably did not happen. Something has to "turn." We need to ask of Wilde, then, whether or not he "turned." Did the epiphany really lead to a *vita nuova*, like Wilde says it did? Answering this question requires looking into Wilde's life after his release.

The Durability of the Turning Point

It is not at all uncommon to wonder about those who proclaim sincere change. It is one thing to *say* it, yet another to *show* it. We tend, I think, to be on the lookout for signs of hypocrisy. Having been a dramatist and having celebrated the artistry of the well-fashioned "pose," Wilde certainly leaves himself open to just such charges. How to know when the faker is not faking? Is the liar telling the truth when he declaims his lies?

No one doubts that Wilde emerged from prison a broken man. He had a great deal of trouble writing. He worried about money, and he relied on friends for loans. "His hat was no longer so glossy. His collar had the same shape, but it was no longer so clean. The sleeves of his frock coat were slightly frayed," Gide related (1949, p. 31). Wilde perceives a clean break. "My life before prison was as successful as possible. Now it's something that's over" (quoted in Gide, 1949, p. 21). Moreover, "One should never go back to the same existence. My life is a work of art. An artist never starts the same thing twice" (pp. 20–21).

Gide, for his part, remains brutally unconvinced. He observed not a "spiritualisation of the soul," but delusion and decay. "His will had been broken. The first months [out of prison], he could still delude himself, but he very soon gave way. It was like an abdication. Nothing remained in his shattered life but the mournful musty odor of what he had once been, a need every now and then to prove that he was still thinking—wit, but artificial, forced, crumpled" (1949, p. 30). To Gide, Wilde's artistic silence was not the pious silence of a Racine, just as his humility was "only a pompous name that he gave to his impotence" (p. 38). In his very depths the "bursts of his former pride" (p. 38) remain.

Richard Ellmann (1988), too, though he considered the writing of *De Profundis* to have been "regenerative," nonetheless questioned Wilde's sincerity. "Humility is a slippery term in the letter" (1988, p. 514), implying that Wilde's insights were more rhetorical than real.

A close look at Wilde's postprison letters suggests a different conclusion. Although he is reeling from the experience—he complains of terrible loneliness, and because of his infamy must use a pseudonym when checking into hotels or receiving mail—still much of what he says and does seems like a clear departure. After prison Wilde published just three pieces of work. All three express deep feelings about the horror of imprisonment, and all three are filled with sympathy for the downtrodden, a sentiment not at all met with in preprison Wilde. The poem, "The Ballad of Reading Gaol," recounts a prisoner's execution for the murder of his wife. As he awaits his sentence he maintains a Christ-like equanimity and fearlessness. Apart from this, Wilde managed just two published letters—on the subject of children, the insane, and prison reform. Such concern, sincerely expressed, would have seemed uncharacteristic of Wilde before the turning point. The letters therefore mark what I consider an obvious change of priority.

Along similar lines, though Wilde was often virtually penniless, he committed himself to sharing the small loans he received with a number of men from his prison gallery. One note reads in part, "My dear Friend, I send you a line to show you that I haven't forgotten you. . . . Don't, like a good little chap, get into trouble again. You would get a terrible sentence. I send you 2 pounds just for luck. I am quite poor myself now, but I know you will accept it just as a remembrance" (1962a, p. 580). Another fellow prisoner he devotes time to helping reenter business. These actions also speak to Wilde's heightened sense of humanity. They seem in keeping with the insights contained in De Profundis.

In self-reflective letters to friends, too, Wilde takes pains to assess his change and to clarify its precise nature. "Perhaps I will be a better fellow after it all," he says (1962a, p. 567). He insists he is not at all embittered; he alludes to having learned the importance of gratitude, humility, and friendship, which he sees "with changed eyes" (p. 596). He says he does not require riches or wild profligacy anymore. "I want peace, and have found it" (p. 595). Again he rejects his previous life. "My reckless pursuit of mundane pleasure, my extravagence, my senseless ease, my love of fashion, my whole attitude towards life, all these were wrong. . . ." (p. 595). To Will Rothenstein he wrote, "I was all wrong, my dear boy, in my life . . . [But] in many ways I have gained much. I am not really ashamed of having been in prison. I often was in more shameful places. But I am really ashamed of having led a life unworthy of an artist" (p. 604).

Wilde especially emphasizes gratitude, saying "I learned in prison to be grateful. . . . For *me* to use such a word shows an enormous development in my nature. Two years ago I did not know the feeling the word denotes. Now I know it, and I am thankful that I have learnt that much, at any rate, by having been in prison. But I must say again that I no longer make *roulades* of phrases about the things I feel. . . . Violin variations don't interest me" (1962a, p. 607). Moreover, "To think of the feelings and happiness of others is not an entirely new emotion in my nature. . . . But I think of those things far more than I used to do" (p. 607). Now Wilde determines he needs rest, quiet, and solitude. He looks "to a simple mode of existence" (p. 607). He even grows bored with himself, and notes how "it is pleasanter to me, now, to write about others" (p. 609). All things considered, Wilde says, "I am in many respects a much better fellow than I was, and I now make no more exorbitant claims on life. I accept everything. I am sure it is all right" (p. 621).

Some friends detect subtle differences, too. Robbie Ross's comments are representative. They speak to something of a new viewpoint. "He enjoyed the trees and the grass and the country scents and sounds in a way I had never known him to do before. . . . It was natural to Wilde to be artificial as I have often said and that is why he was suspected of insincerity. I mean when he wrote of serious things, of art, ethics, or religion, of pain or of pleasure. [But] Wilde in love of the beautiful was perfectly, perhaps too, sincere. . . ." (Wilde, 1962a, p. 565). This can be read as a comment on Gide. While raising doubts about Wilde's change may be understandable, it still seems unkind and unfair to rule out the possibility altogether. Even the habitually insincere must be granted the opportunity to express sincere thoughts and feelings.

Before concluding, one last fact needs addressing. A year or so after his release Wilde did reunite with Douglas, much to the consternation of friends and of his ex-wife, Constance, who responded with a threatening letter promising always to keep him from his sons and to withhold money. Wilde refused to budge. He needs companionship, he says, and he says he truly loves Douglas. Some felt that this revealed an absence of true insight, for why else would Wilde reconcile with the object of his ruin? The trouble is, in the final pages of *De Profundis*, Wilde alludes to just such a possibility. He preaches forgiveness and love as opposed to retaliation and hate. "To humility," he writes, "There is nothing that is impossible. . . . No one can possibly shut the doors against love forever" (1905/1996, p. 91). Bearing these kinds of remarks in mind, Wilde's willingness to stand by Douglas, despite all the obstacles, suggests that he *did* live his new truth, not that he exposed its falsity.

On balance, then, it appears Wilde's epiphany endured. The narrative translated into real effects on behavior. There may have been occasional backslidings and relapses, but to focus on those alone "misses the point of serious interest," as James explained. What is truly important in conversion, according to James, "is not so much the duration as the nature of these shiftings of character to higher levels. Men lapse from every level—we need no statistics to tell us that. . . . So with the conversion experience—that it should for even a short time show a human being what the high-water mark of his spiritual capacity is, this is what constitutes its importance— an importance which backsliding cannot diminish" (1961, p. 209).

CONCLUSION

We are now in a position to gather what we have learned from Wilde's case. It has its distinctive qualities yet at the same time seems representative—it may typify a generalization. In response to catastrophic loss, Wilde made use of traditional dramatic formula to script a new identity. Casting himself in a tragic role, as one neither irredeemably wicked nor thoroughly good, he virtually ensured himself the required epiphany. In Wilde's instance, as in many others apparently, the spur was jeopardy and—something possibly unique—perceived blame and the consequent need to profit from self-engineered disaster. Bruner noted how some turning points function as second chances. This holds true for Wilde. Trouble, loss, and culpability in combination can be mobilizing. They call for metacognitive self-awareness and narrative. Why? Because we need to interpret them. We need either to assimilate them into preexisting models of self or to reimagine them reflectively and creatively as a means of fashioning a new self-story, as did Wilde. It seems Wilde really had two choices. He could either deny blame by blaming others and in so doing remain the same as he always was, or he could accept blame and profit from ruin by becoming a different person. Clearly he chose the latter option. In some ways it was the more creative and the more courageous. It required that he jettison his former views and leave himself open to charges of hypocrisy or insincerity.

To the extent that Wilde's case is prototypical, then, he (a) engaged in a clear act of self reorientation and metacognitive self-reflection which was (b) spurred by a sense of jeopardy, loss, self-blame, and an absence of "softening" psychosocial resources and (c) fashioned through the use of conventional dramatic formulas. He also (d) achieved his insights via self-surrender, and (e) recounted his experience in terms closely resembling conversion–satori. This set of features, not strikingly unusual in any way, may surface in other turning point narratives. That is, lessons learned from examining Wilde's realization might prove useful when there comes a time to inspect similarly epiphanous experiences.

What may make Wilde unique is his tendency to stress the interior, impersonal, and nonintellectual nature of his realization. As he said, it simply unfolded itself. It followed its own timetable. It was, so to speak, fated. This fact seems significant. In choosing a change narrative, appeals to destiny may be somewhat expectable. Trauma lends itself to the identification of omens, signs of some force at work in the universe. Wilde posits what might be called a natural law of self-correction. His wasteful, heedless life predetermined a reckoning. It came, as he said he knew it would. He had counted on it. There is the sense that things could not have been otherwise. In more general terms, those who experience turning points may emphasize the struggle, the difficult effort of coming-to-terms, of reviewing the life and reaching hard-fought conclusions. One thinks, for instance, of the psychotherapeutic process and the battle against resistance and self-deception. Wilde paints a different picture. His was a visitation, a flash, a sudden knowing. It was, as might be expected, far more dramatic.

With respect to qualities of suddenness and durability in the turning point narrative, Wilde's case raises various immensely important questions. The forms a turning point may assume must be multitudinous. At the same time, not everything counts as a legitimate turning point event. In my view, Wilde represents one particularly recognizable type, a type marked by sudden explosion and catastrophic change. One might even call this the "dramatic" type, to distinguish it from types marked by a slow unfolding. Why do some prefer dramatic narratives? In Wilde's case the answer is clear. He was a dramatist. He was peculiarly aware of story form. He knew how to tell his tale this way, and he possessed the requisite gifts. In addition Wilde may have had more of an impetus for change—and not just any change but one that would leave him an entirely different person. One way to rectify our mistakes is to metamorphize into a person utterly unlike the one who made those mistakes in the first place. Wilde's turning point tale may have functioned as something of a confession. He revealed his sins, and in so doing folded them into a new vision. His was a guilty *mea culpa*. His ruin required that he profit from it, and spectacularly.

As for durability, it does seem like a necessary accompaniment. But at the same time, James is right in recognizing the possibility of occasional relapse. Insisting too strictly on colossal and consistent alterations of self risks the commission of a "Type II" error—some true turning points might be written off as insufficiently lasting. Life is complex. There will be slippage. Even when change is relatively modest or fitful, the turning point concept may apply. It seems important to acknowledge that some turns might be more momentous than others, more sustaining.

In jeopardy, suffering from loss, guilty of weakness and temptation, virtually friendless, Wilde marshaled all his skills in an act of supreme artistry—he remade a self in both prototypical and somewhat atypical fashion. Apart from all his other accomplishments, Wilde still is best known as a playwright. But his most compelling script may have been his last. In the end, his life was his play.

REFERENCES

Aristotle. (1958). *On poetry and style*. Indianapolis: Bobbs-Merrill.

Brockett, O. (1977). *History of the theatre*. Boston: Allyn & Bacon.

Bruner, J. (1993). The "remembered" self. In J. Singer & P. Salovey (Eds.), *The remembered self*. New York: Free Press.

Bruner, J. (1999). Narrative and metanarrative in the construction of self. In M. Ferrari & R. Sternberg (Eds.), *Self awareness: Its nature and development* (pp. 308–331). New York: Guilford Press.

Buckler, W. (1989). Oscar Wilde's aesthetic of the self: Art as imaginative self-realization in *De Profundis. Biography: An Interdisciplinary Quarterly, 12*(2), 95–115.

Clausen, J. (1993). *Gender, contexts, and turning-points in adults' lives.* Washington, DC: American Psychological Association.

Downs, W., & Wright, L. A. (1998). *Playwriting from formula to form.* San Diego, CA: Harcourt Brace.

Ellmann, R. (1968). *The artist as critic: Critical writings of Oscar Wilde.* New York: Random House.

Ellmann, R. (1988). *Oscar Wilde.* New York: Knopf.

Gide, A. (1949). *Oscar Wilde: In memoriam.* New York: Philosophical Library, May 18.

Gopnik, A. (1998). The invention of Oscar Wilde. *New Yorker,* 78.

James, W. (1961). *The varieties of religious experience.* New York: Collier Books.

James, W. (1997). *William James: Selected writings.* New York: Book of the Month Club.

Knox, M. (1996). *Oscar Wilde: A long and lovely suicide.* New Haven: Yale University Press.

Kuhn, T. (1970). *The structure of scientific revolutions.* Chicago: University of Chicago Press.

McAdams, D. P. (1993). *The stories we live by: Personal myths and the making of the self.* New York: Guilford Press.

Murray, H. (1981). American Icarus. In E. Shneidman (Ed.), *Endeavors in Psychology: Selections from the Personology of Henry A. Murray* (pp. 535–556). New York: Harper and Row.

Schmidgall, G. (1994). *The stranger Wilde.* New York: Dutton.

Schultz, W. T. (1996). An 'Orpheus Complex' in two writers-of-loss. *Biography: An Interdisciplinary Quarterly, 19*(4), 371–393.

Schultz, W. T. (1998). Finding fate's father: Some life-history influences on Roald Dahl's *Charlie & the Chocolate Factory. Biography: An Interdisciplinary Quarterly, 21*(4), 467–485.

Schultz, W. T. (1999). The riddle that doesn't exist: Ludwig Wittgenstein's transmogrification of death. *Psychoanalytic Review, 86*(2), 1–23.

Suzuki, D. T. (1956). *Zen Buddhism: Selected writings of D.T. Suzuki.* New York: Anchor Books.

Wethington, E., Cooper, H., & Holmes, C. (1997). Turning points in midlife. In I. Gotlib & B. Wheaton (Eds.), *Stress and adversity over the life course: Trajectories and turning points* (pp. 215–231). Cambridge: Cambridge University Press.

Wheaton, B. & Gotlib, I. (1997). Trajectories and turning points over the life course: Concepts and themes. In I. Gotlib & B. Wheaton (Eds.), *Stress and adversity over the life course: Trajectories and turning points*. Cambridge: Cambridge University Press.

Wiersma, J. (1988). The press release: Symbolic communication in life history interviewing. *Journal of Personality, 56*(1), 205–238.

Wilde, O. (1962a). *The letters of Oscar Wilde*. New York: Harcourt, Brace & World.

Wilde, O. (1962b). *The picture of Dorian Gray*. New York: Signet. (Original work published 1891)

Wilde, O. (1996). *De Profundis*. New York: Dover. (Original work published 1905)

4

EVER UPWARD AND NO TURNING BACK: SOCIAL MOBILITY AND IDENTITY FORMATION AMONG FIRST-GENERATION COLLEGE STUDENTS

J. SCOTT ROBERTS AND GEORGE C. ROSENWALD

What will happen to Cinderella after she marries the prince? Will she slide into her regal role as smoothly as he, who has been groomed for it all his life? Following her rise in social status, will she retain a saintly generosity toward her family? And when an occasional courtier snickers about the parvenue princess, as once her stepsisters snickered about her wish to attend the ball, how will she react? Can we really be so sure she will live happily ever after?

Of course, Cinderella's is an unusual case of social mobility; others cannot rely on supernatural assistance in "turning upward." Yet we may also wonder about the ultimate well-being of those upwardly mobile individuals coming of age in contemporary America: How will their tales of social advancement turn out? The question is certainly not a novel one. Upward mobility has long played a prominent role in both our social science and cultural mythology, often celebrated in the latter as a point of national pride. Horatio Alger's "rags to respectability" stories and present-day politicians'

This study was supported in part by grants from the Department of Psychology at the University of Michigan, Ann Arbor. Several study participants were recruited through the Michigan Study of Adolescent Life Transitions (MSALT; Dr. Jacquelynne Eccles, principal investigator). Discussions with Deborah Carr, John Lynch, Sherrill Sellers, and Jennifer Stevens helped us greatly in clarifying the conceptual, methodological, and historical aspects of this project. We would also like to thank the following people for their practical assistance: Debra Josefowicz, for helping coordinate recruitment of MSALT participants; and Meredith Englander and Meredith Lee, for transcribing interviews.

references to the "American Dream" are just a few of the ways in which social mobility has been romanticized in our culture.

Proponents of a marginality thesis, by contrast, have pointed out that such upward mobility is apt to be accompanied by multiple strains (e.g., Durkheim, 1951; Sorokin, 1927). Outdoing the previous generation both financially and educationally can bring about disruption in relations with family and friends, as well as the discomfort and uncertainty of moving into an alien world. More simply put, one does not escape society after leaving the social class of one's origins. All along the upward journey, the mobile person experiences changes in class-specific norms and the subjective effects of dislocation. Such processes—that is, those engendering the psychological costs of upward social mobility—were what we wished to learn more about in this study. We did so primarily through life-historical interviews of upwardly mobile individuals. Yet before we could adequately conceptualize these processes, some background was in order.

THE PSYCHOLOGY OF UPWARD SOCIAL MOBILITY: A BRIEF RETROSPECTIVE

The personal consequences of social mobility attracted considerable interest among social scientists in the 1950s and 1960s. Domains of interest at that time included racial prejudice (Bettelheim & Janowitz, 1950), political orientation (Barber, 1970), mental disorder–neuroticism (Hollingshead, Ellis, & Kirby, 1954), and psychological adjustment (Ellis & Lane, 1967). The standard method in these studies involved the quantitative comparison of upwardly mobile with socially stationary individuals to determine if and how the two groups differed. In the 1970s this stream of investigation dried up rather suddenly. Critics pointed out that differences obtained in various dimensions, although often attributed to the stresses of upward mobility, could also be accounted for by the groups' differing conditions of origin. To this day, it is not clear whether mobility's psychological effects occur in forms eluding the demanding statistical tests of contemporary social science (Jackson & Curtis, 1972). Partly as a consequence of this method-ological impasse, partly because of an interest in social structure rather than social psychology, researchers shifted their focus from the consequences to the predictors of intergenerational mobility. Innovative multivariate statisti-cal analyses prompted an explosion of studies on "status attainment," an area that remains a mainstay of sociological research (Savage, 1997). The puzzle of mobility's psychological effects remains, however, and is one stimu-lus for this study.

Although psychological studies of upward mobility have been rare in recent decades, we are beginning to see a revival of interest in the topic, manifest in qualitative research and retrospective autobiographical accounts of working-class academics (e.g., Dews & Law, 1995; Grimes & Morris, 1997; Tokarczyk & Fay, 1993). Such work has shown us the power of narrative approaches in illuminating the psychological complexities of upward mobility. This work also suggests a wave of mobility different in important respects from earlier decades, as women and racial and ethnic minorities have moved into social positions largely inaccessible to them previously. An important psychological implication of this cohort difference may concern the public visibility of mobility. Women and minorities who move up within society today are visible to each other for mutual support and can draw on special resources offered them in many institutions. Within universities, for example, they may find student organizations and academic disciplines related to their gender, racial, and ethnic identities. As a result, upward mobility, although still a great challenge for many (and compounded by the pernicious effects of sexism and racism), may be a less isolated and isolating process than it once was (Higginbotham & Weber, 1992). This cohort difference, with its attention to social factors other than class, may mask some of the effects of mobility per se. The theme of invisibility with regard to upward mobility's psychological costs has long been noted in qualitative research (Newman, 1988; Sennett & Cobb, 1972). Our belief that these costs remain underappreciated was another impetus for this study.

SOCIAL MOBILITY AND THE OCCUPATIONAL DOMAIN: LESSONS FROM A SCARCITY OF RESEARCH

It seems curious that even before the aforementioned shift to status attainment research, psychological investigations of social mobility rarely focused on well-being within the occupational domain. This, after all, is a central issue for those who leave their working-class backgrounds behind; they want a different, "better" kind of work. Yet studies in this area generally have not been reported. We can make out several reasons for this seeming oversight. First, the overcoming of educational and occupational barriers is, by definition, the forte of the upwardly mobile. The sheer resolve to succeed may discount the frustrations and privations along the way (and those who do not complete the ascension because of its stresses would not even be represented in mobility studies). Second, an individual who pursues "membership" in a higher social class does so in pursuit of certain powerful incentives. Once these are realized, well-being may be determined by strains and satisfactions having little to do with mobility per se. Indeed, its psychological effects may not operate in a sufficiently uniform fashion to be detected in aggregate data (Marshall & Firth, 1999).

Given the difficulties of researching the occupational domain, it seemed wise to explore instead the beginning phases of upward mobility—that is, the experience of the higher educational domain, a transition point where mobile individuals separate themselves from working-class families and peers. This domain may allow a clearer view of the social–psychological aspects of upward mobility. There is another important reason for this focus. In discussions of mobility, sociologists since Sorokin have attended mainly to the disruption of existing relations and the difficulty of achieving a new social integration. To this, we believe, must be added the implications of mobility for the individual's sense of ego identity.

SOCIAL MOBILITY, HIGHER EDUCATION, AND EGO IDENTITY

As famously elaborated by Erikson (1968), ego identity is a developmental challenge whose outcome is largely realized (at least in Western society) by the end of the years in which young people attend college or prepare themselves in other ways for a productive adulthood. It is a challenge in that it requires the integration of many components: "an evolving configuration [of] constitutional givens, idiosyncratic libidinal needs, favored capacities, significant identifications, effective defenses, successful sublimations, and consistent roles" (Erikson, 1968, p. 163). Two aspects of ego identity are especially relevant to the study we report. First, the components temporarily synthesized at each point in ego-identity development are *psychosocial*. That is, each component is socially relevant and socially shaped. This is obviously true of sublimations, identifications, and roles. But it applies no less to defense-effectiveness and to the seemingly elementary constitutional and libidinal ingredients of identity; these, too, are under the intense and pervading influence of socialization. Second, the synthesis of these components is an *evolving* one, always subject to revision but never so urgently topical as in adolescence and young adulthood. This period witnesses identity struggles in part because this is the time during which young people define the occupational role they may take on for the rest of their lives. The centrality of occupation in ego identity is a main reason why the study of identity formation is especially interesting in the case of upwardly mobile individuals.

Taken together, the psychosocial and evolving aspects of identity imply that its formation involves a tension between (a) the adaptive demands of new external tasks that the individual encounters and (b) the restraints imposed by earlier workings of identity components and syntheses. When this tension between these innovative and conservative forces is optimal, producing neither paralyzing immaturity nor a headlong rush into incoherent impersonations, the individual enjoys "a sense of psychosocial well-being:

a sense of knowing where one is going, and an inner assuredness of anticipated recognition from those who count" (Erikson, 1968, p. 164). As Erikson implies, identity is contingent not only on achievement in the occupational domain but also in that of social and family relations.

It is not hard to imagine how upward mobility via higher education might influence identity formation. A young working-class person's commitment to higher education signals to herself as well as to "those who count" that she is seeking a life different from theirs in important respects. As we know from research on first-generation college students[1] (Billson & Terry, 1982; London, 1989; Piorkowski, 1983), significant others may greet this departure from the historical family norm with a range and intensity of reactions: pride and joy, to be sure, but also sadness, bewilderment, and envy. Emerging tensions in these crucial relations may then bring about in the young person feelings of guilt, confusion, bitterness, and loss. Especially important during identity formation are relations with parents, and previous research has found that working-class parents tend not to be as supportive of formal education as their professional-class counterparts (see chapter 5, this volume, for a review). Given this potential tension between the pull of significant others and the demands of a consciously chosen discontinuous future, it is perhaps not surprising that working-class students may experience more intensely than others the challenges of social integration and acculturation in higher education (Granfield, 1991; Stewart & Ostrove, 1993).

Strains in family and peer relations are not the only possible sources of difficulty during identity formation for the upwardly mobile in higher education. Others may stem from the aforementioned dispositions referenced by Erikson. While studying reasons for attrition in higher education, Trent and Medsker (1968) found that college "persisters were more selective in choosing their colleges and saw more reasons for attending. . . . They tended to be more intellectual . . . and open-minded before entering college" (p. 126). These traits are manifest signs of a certain kind of ego identity. They represent a set of cultivated capacities, values, styles, and outlooks, or what Bourdieu[2] (1977) might call a "habitus": that is, a class-influenced personal code of taste, knowledge, and behavior, as mediated by childhood experience. Actual or perceived deficits in one's habitus—which may become more apparent for the upwardly mobile in the life transition of higher education—

---

[1] Exact statistics are not available on this group's enrollment in higher education, but a survey of incoming U.S. freshmen (Dey, Astin, & Korn, 1993) indicated that at the university level 22.5% of students' fathers and 27.7% of their mothers were not educated past high school.
[2] In Bourdieu's argument, not only do working-class individuals have less economic resources than professional-class counterparts, but they are also hampered by deficits of "social and cultural capital." Examples include in-group membership conferring the advantages of social networking and "connections" (social capital), language skills and information about manners, fashion, and style (embodied cultural capital), cultural items such as books and paintings (objectified cultural capital), and academic credentials (institutionalized cultural capital).

can have manifest implications for social relations, career development, and, therefore, the formation of ego identity. The importance of attending to processes of identity formation among the upwardly mobile seems further underscored by research suggesting that identity resolution influences overall adult well-being (Vandewater, Ostrove, & Stewart, 1997) and, with perhaps even more enduring consequence, intimacy and generativity (Stein & Newcomb, 1999).

IMPLICATIONS OF THE LITERATURE REVIEW

Given the relative inattention to the subjective costs of social mobility—both in the research literature and society at large—we wished to provide a detailed and inclusive portrait of its psychological challenges. We decided to explore the experience of upward mobility in individuals whose lives were subject to the cultural and social dislocations of mobility, who had not yet settled into careers whose specific characteristics might obscure the experience of mobility as such. Our focus was on the experience of higher education, often a "turning point" in the lives of the upwardly mobile. Given the complex interaction of social and personal factors in determining the experience of upward mobility, we did not expect uniform aggregate effects and offered no predictions concerning these. We especially wished to understand upward mobility in regard to ego identity formation; this meant evaluating mobility as a process rather than as an outcome.

METHODS

Logic

Studying ego identity formation as a process, rather than as a product, calls for a suitable method. Outcomes can be framed as "ego identity status" and represented quantitatively (Marcia, 1980). But the *development* of identity involves a continual balancing of multiple components, negotiating of tensions, and resolving of contradictions. We have stressed thus far the psychosocial aspect of identity formation, referring to the values and attitudes of significant others that the young person internalizes. Narrative methods are ideally suited to represent internalization. It is their essence to bring the context into the main action, the past and future into the present. Central events are, as it were, irradiated by the ambient situation; "before" and "after" give meaning to, and gain meaning from, the here and now. It seemed to us, therefore, that a *contemporaneous* narrative account of the young person's experience was the most advantageous medium for exploring the identity development of upwardly mobile youth.

In making this choice, we have the support of Savage (1997), who, in a methodological review of the upward mobility literature, concluded that life historians can best "tease out the complex interplay between people's strategies, values, and their mobility, a set of connections which has been rather elusive within virtually all survey-based approaches to the subject" (p. 321). In his even-handed review, Savage mentioned possible drawbacks of biographical methods as well. But given our special focus on the interaction among identity's ingredients, on the internalization of values and attitudes, and on the tracing of sameness-within-change, these drawbacks mattered less than the evident strengths. Our methodological decision was further eased in that we had neither hypotheses to test nor empirical generalizations to establish—tasks that would have required sampling and inferential statistics. Rather, the scholarly literature on upward mobility and identity formation sensitized us to certain focal topics, which we explored in our interviews.

Participants

Participants were four-year college students and graduates whose parents' highest level of education was high school or less ($N = 15$; 8 women, 7 men; age range: 19–27 years; 12 European Americans, 2 African Americans, 1 Asian American). Six participants from southeastern Michigan, all of them known to be first-generation students, were recruited from the subject pool of the Michigan Study of Adolescent Life Transitions (Eccles et al., 1993). The remaining nine participants were recruited in the Durham, North Carolina, area through newspaper advertisements specifying the first-generation criterion. At the time of the interviews (1994–1995), five participants were enrolled in college, six had graduated college in the past year, and four were enrolled in a graduate or professional school program. Eleven different state and private colleges and universities were represented in the participants' schooling.[3]

Procedure

After informed consent was obtained, participants were interviewed on three occasions and financially compensated for their efforts. Interviews covered a wide range of topics, in keeping with our earlier discussed interests. Topics included (a) how the pursuit of higher education had shaped, and

---

[3] Although our theoretical introduction refers to upwardly mobile students' working-class backgrounds, this constellation was not found in every case. For example, two respondents' fathers were wealthy businesspeople with a high school education.

been shaped by, the participants' longstanding relationships, especially those with parents, siblings, and hometown peers; (b) how respondents experienced the transition to higher education, including the challenges of moving into an environment new to them, their families, and peers of different class background; and (c) how participants negotiated occupational choice. Although we made sure these topics were taken up in each set of interviews, we followed no fixed interview schedule. Rather, we began interviews with open-ended questions and allowed participants substantial freedom to proceed in their own ways.

Interview Analysis

Interviewing an individual to collect a clarifying narrative is itself an act of interpretation preceding the more notorious one of culling from what is gathered the excerpts to be reported (Runyan, 1982). Interpretive choices multiply as we survey a collection of narratives. The interpretive challenge of a multiple-case study is always to synthesize an abstract social object—in this case, "upward social mobility"—out of the respondents' perspectival accounts. But this challenge is somewhat lightened as we focus our interest on certain favored rubrics. Because we concentrated on identity formation, we could select the portions of each set of interviews relevant to this developmental task and bring them into conversation with one another. The resulting syntheses are not offered as hypotheses to be tested on other upwardly mobile individuals—though there is no reason *not* to do so—but as tentative interpretations of the seemingly disparate accounts offered by the given group of respondents (Rosenwald, 1988).

A common hazard in dealing with life-historical narratives is to take them at face value. Yet if one keeps in mind that adolescents and young adults are noted for their volatile characterizations of others, especially parents (Marcia, 1980), then one can allow for the possibility that these significant others might have described the narrative's events, interactions, and relationships quite differently from the participants themselves. Whether a narrative study can ever shed sufficient light on the objective conditions of subjectivity is a complex question in any case. But our interest was in the students' own experiences and interpretations.

The interview sets were taperecorded and transcribed for analysis. After several readings of transcripts, the first author wrote case synopses for each participant, with relevant themes and illustrative quotations identified. These case synopses were then synthesized into the summary we shall present. We organized the interview syntheses under two main headings of identity theory: relatedness and career development (another major component of identity, ideology, was not considered separately). It will become clear that the narratives were analyzed primarily through the sociological lens of class.

This does not imply that race, gender, ethnicity, and region are not powerful influences in this group's identity formation.[4] Yet their extensive treatment was beyond the scope of this chapter.

THEMES OF IDENTITY

Relatedness

Parental Relations

All students are apt to experience significant changes in family relations on entering higher education; the physical and emotional separation that this move usually entails alters relationships between the two groups regardless of class background. For first-generation students, however, pursuing higher education means entering a formative world that their parents have never inhabited. This move had important consequences for participants' parental relations, especially for those respondents whose pursuit of higher education represented dramatic upward mobility. Value clashes and communication difficulties marked these relations in ways that seem directly related to their movement in class. For example, many noted that their parents had "no clue" about how college worked or what they did there, that "they don't ask a lot about it . . . [and] don't even know what to ask about it." Discussing an experience so foreign to one's parents can prove frustrating, as in the case of Lisa.[5] A recent graduate of a selective state university, Lisa said that her parents were very supportive of the idea of higher education and at her graduation ceremony told her "thousands of times" how proud they were of her. Indeed, like many other respondents, she felt that her parents enjoyed a vicarious sense of achievement through her higher education. Yet despite their praise, Lisa found it hard to relate the specifics of her college experience with them.

> My mom is very supportive. But I don't know if she is necessarily interested. I was doing an oral history project, and I was so into it that whole semester; it was a graduate class. That was just my life, and I think she thought it was cool that I was in a graduate class [and] that I loved it, but when I would try to tell her what I was doing, she would start talking about something else, or she would get this kind of glazed look in her eyes.

---

[4] Higginbotham and Weber (1992), for example, found that African Americans may be more likely than Whites to view upward mobility as a *family* rather than an individual goal. This group may experience greater family support and less isolation from kin during upward mobility.

[5] Names of all participants have been changed for the sake of confidentiality; other identifying characteristics have also been altered or otherwise obscured.

Lisa worried that her father was even more thoroughly dismissive of her "impractical" studies. He has often forgotten Lisa's major and has reportedly questioned the wisdom of her course selection, with his "big question" being, "Are you learning anything that's going to help you in the real world?" Lisa has not felt comfortable sharing her classroom experiences with him.

> It's just so hard to explain to them what you're doing. . . . Here's my dad who's just gotten off working ten-hour days, six days straight. To tell him that in Medieval History I'm learning about the Goths and the architecture—even though he didn't try to make me feel guilty, or make me feel that things were irrelevant—just looking at him, I'm like, it's interesting to me, but it won't be interesting to him.

Other participants reacted with anger to this perceived lack of interest in and understanding of their college experiences. For example, Kevin, a recent graduate of a prestigious state university, expressed his frustration at his parents' alleged lack of support:

> I looked at it as I'm the first person in this entire—not this immediate family, this entire—family to ever go to school, and they don't seem to be really supporting me as much as they can. . . . I would ask for things and my dad would be like, "You're on your own right now" . . . My dad, every single time that I talk to him, he asks me about a job. He didn't seem to care how I was doing in school; it was just like, "Are you working?" . . . I'm like, "Dad, I got straight A's." [He'd reply,] "You need a job" . . . That made me want to talk to them less about college. I was like, they don't care how I'm doing. All I ever hear is "Money that, money this." I'm just like, fuck it, I just won't talk to them.

Despite his bitterness, Kevin followed his father's advice and for most of college worked at least 40 hours a week while maintaining a full courseload. Yet he rarely called or made the short trip home during his undergraduate years. Another participant, Frank, spoke of similar dissatisfaction, which has grown through encounters with friends' college-educated parents.

> [They] know what going through college is all about and what it's like to be in my shoes. . . . Some of my friends' parents. . . . I love them to death, and I'm like, "God, if my parents were just as supportive as they were." It's not just financial support either, but it's, "Yeah, I can see you doing this. I can see you doing that" . . . To this day I wonder if, [my parents] think, "Wow, you did a good job. You know, we're really proud of you for putting up with a lot" . . . I just wish that people could look at my achievements as commendable as opposed to, you know, "You could be doing a little bit better."

Frank's hunger for approval was striking; he spoke proudly about earning a recommendation letter from a reputable corporation and gaining acceptance into a college fraternity. His need for validation may be related to the perceived lack of parental recognition that has accompanied his pursuit of higher education.

Also complicating participants' parental relations at times during higher education was a shared sense of shame regarding family class background, one that seemingly became more pronounced as the students interacted with peers and professors from more moneyed and formally educated families. For example, some participants noted that their parents were reluctant to have their occupations revealed or homes shown to their children's college friends. Meanwhile, a few respondents expressed great embarrassment regarding their parents' alleged sexism and homophobia, intolerance that was attributed in part to class background. Returning to Lisa's case, we learn how perceptions of family prejudice prevented her from sharing an important piece of her education with her parents.

> My parents, especially my dad, [given] the generation they are in, being from the South, there is like definite racism. I can kind of console myself by saying, "Well, I have this education and he doesn't, he just hasn't been in any environment where he can see another side." [But] it is kind of awkward sometimes. I took a History class and I wrote this paper about Black laborers and my teacher was like, "A plus." I felt so good about that. He had written a really great comment about it like, "You should consider doing graduate work in history and I don't know if I could have written this paper." I was just like, oh my gosh, I hadn't had that kind of feedback. Anyway, the first thing I want to do is tell my parents about it . . . but then I didn't want them to read it because it's all about the injustices that these men felt as African-Americans. My dad would take one look at it and say, well, what about this and what about this. So I never let them read it.

Such an incident might not have been as disturbing if Lisa did not greatly respect her father, a hard-working mechanic who helped finance her education. Managing conflicting emotions about loved ones is a universal task but one distinctively shaped by upward mobility.

Several respondents felt that their pursuit of higher education prompted defensiveness in their parents. Many parents were described as self-deprecating about their own educational achievement or belittling of their children's coursework (e.g., emphasizing how "book smarts" are overrated and intellectuals are "out of touch" with the "real world"). Often the growing educational disparity between parents and students was reflected through vocabulary differences. Mary, a graduate student whose mother has an eighth-grade education, elaborated, "We just don't talk the same language. I make a conscious effort to bring the vocabulary down to a certain point. . . . In the past we've had fights because she thinks I'm being condescending to her, treating her like a child." Respondents suggested that their parents sometimes addressed such differences by making them feel that in asserting their new-found knowledge they were "putting on airs." Henry recalled "getting picked on for using certain words. Like the summer I worked for my dad, one time I used the word 'eschew,' and they called me 'eschew' all day, the workers and my dad." The students reported tailoring their vocabulary to avoid such scenes and hiding knowledge gained in college for fear of appearing arrogant or overshadowing relatives.

Of course, disruption in these crucial relationships adds to the developmental burdens already present for students in college, those involving formation of career and relational identities. Some respondents and their parents may become closer after they have gained more perspective on this tumultuous period in their relations. Yet Mary's case suggests that, for other students and their parents, the distance will remain.

> I go home, we talk about the weather, talk about people in the family, people in the neighborhood. . . . The stuff I would like to talk about, [my mother] can't. She doesn't understand it. Stuff she'd like to talk about I think would be incredibly boring. . . . I learned very early on that they couldn't discuss [school]. To try to discuss it with them would be very frustrating to me, and embarrassing for them. . . . I realized I had far educated myself past my parents. There's like this vast gulf between us. It's never been able to be crossed.

These stories illustrate a range of discomfitingly perceived parental reactions—from approval without substantive comprehension to outright, sometimes cruel disparagement. From the standpoint of identity formation, one must consider the consequences of these students' vividly experienced outsidership with respect to their families. For example, Lisa may feel that, no matter what studies she undertakes, she will remain well-loved by her parents. But will she feel loved as Lisa the historian? How will she cultivate this affection if she must withhold cherished intellectual and moral preoccupations from the family conversation? How wide must she cut the swath of silence in their relationship? We do not know enough about the effects of such secrecy to make forecasts about the maintenance of "psychosocial well-being." Kevin, at least, is evidently unhappy about the silence he has imposed on himself. As we saw, such silence separates students not only from their parents but also from their peers, when they protect their parents from shame. The long-term consequences of such students' attenuated moral support and of their intellectual self-fragmentation deserve further attention.

Sibling Relations

Higher education significantly alters students' relations with siblings as well. For first-generation students with younger siblings, their college experiences can enable them to counsel those brothers and sisters who might also pursue an advanced degree. In this way, they might lend the kind of guidance they wish others had provided them. Yet many participants did not feel their siblings saw them as dependable guides through higher education. Instead, some worried about how their academic success might alienate them from brothers and sisters. Henry described relations with his younger siblings:

> They knew that regardless of how they performed, they could only do as well as me, they could never do better than me, and in all likelihood they wouldn't do as well as me. . . . My brother excelled at sports, partly in reaction to my academic achievements. He wanted to make his own path, a name for himself. My sister, she tells my mom, "Any club I join, Henry was the president" . . . she feels like everything has been taken away from her. She talks very openly about not wanting to finish high school and not wanting to go to college. It's a really awkward situation right now. Part of me feels guilty, like if I hadn't done so well she would at least go to a college and make a name for herself and get out of the trap that my mother's in of working at a dead-end job.

One might point out how Henry's guilt over his hard-won achievements is irrational, as is his sister's belief that all has been "taken away" from her. Yet guilt over having outdone the family by too much seems a real risk of upward mobility. Henry, attuned to potential family tensions, said that he does not share his summa cum laude success with his siblings for fear they might become discouraged in their own academic pursuits.

Of course, siblings are not always threatened by mobile students' rise. Many participants reported that siblings encouraged their academic exploits, feeling that the "good of one [family member] was for the good of all." Furthermore, some siblings are upwardly mobile themselves. Still, those who are not may have negative reactions to being "left behind," heightening students' sense of isolation from family and decreasing motivation to proceed further upward. Kevin's case illustrates this point. Though an A student at a prestigious university, he described himself as the "black sheep of the family in that I've gone on and pursued higher education."

Understanding this peculiarly negative spin becomes easier when one considers his relationship with his younger brother, who did not go to college but remained with the extended family and took over its landscaping business. His family's first college graduate, Kevin now finds himself out of touch with the gang back home—and scoffed at by his brother.

> Everyone's always told me, you know, "You gotta go to college to succeed, to make money. You'll be a success, go to college, you're smart." Now I've gone to college and I have nothing but debts. . . . On the other hand, here's my brother who just sort of coasted through high school, didn't even care . . . got the business right after he graduated basically and he's making three, four thousand dollars a month. . . . He tells me, "You never had a TV that big. You're not making anything

and you graduated from college." Now that he's got money, he takes me out to dinner once in a while and he shoves it all in my face.

This contentiousness might be chalked up to sibling rivalry, but it seems a rivalry made all the more intense by Kevin's educational rise.

As we know, parents play a unique role in identity formation as caretakers, authorities, and purveyors of value. Siblings, meanwhile, at least for those who separate themselves from the family via higher education, can represent the traditionalist alternative. Socially stationary brothers and sisters embody what the upwardly mobile might have, could have, or should have become (or remained). Not only for Kevin but for other first-generation students siblings can serve as the enduring reminder of the road not taken. Identity formation always involves choices effected through identification processes. But for the upwardly mobile student, the sibling who pursues what he abandoned and spurns what he idealizes may remain like a *doppelganger*, painfully recalling to consciousness alternate choices and possibilities that would otherwise be consigned to the margins of awareness.

Relations With Hometown Friends and Peers

Also often "left behind" during upward mobility are close friends from the precollege years. Although many participants drew their friends in high school from a college-bound crowd, several bonded with those who did not pursue higher education. For those whose close childhood friends were primarily of working-class origin, there seemed more a danger of, to quote one respondent, "losing that connection between an original set of friends because you chose such different paths in life." For example, upward mobility shaped the decline of Sam's old friendships during higher education. Sam dropped out of high school but later enrolled in a community college where he flourished academically. Now a student at a prestigious law school, he has kept in touch with high school friends, some of whom went to college but few of whom stayed there. Sam has the sense that his success makes his friends feel answerable to him for lagging behind educationally, deference that, though flattering, makes him uneasy.

> There is definitely something different within me. Law school does change you [and] the way other people look at me, or at least the way I feel I'm being looked at. When I see people now, even though I don't want any justification from them as to what they are doing now, they feel the need to give it to me: "I'm going back to school to do this, I'm going to do that" . . . That's just how our society is, and I try not to buy into it, that somehow doctors and lawyers and Ph.D.'s are better than friends of mine who are landscapers and construction workers. But some of them do want to make those kinds of comparisons. It makes me feel good when they ask for advice, like "where is a good place to

go to school?" or "how can I get started again?" But I don't feel comfortable being asked to judge what they are doing just by virtue of me being in law school.

Sam questions the moral valuation of success in Western society. He understandably feels that his education does not warrant the distinctions others make between him and his friends. Nevertheless, the higher his educational rise, the more pronounced these judgments become. Success is thus not only a source of pride but also of inner conflict. Despite their apparent admiration, Sam worries about his friends' suspicions that he is no longer "one of them."

> I don't know if they think I'm looking down on them, but sometimes that's the feeling I get. . . . If I'm around and it's a big party or something, and people are getting drunk and smoking pot or whatever, and I'm not doing those things, you add that to it as well and they start wondering, "Who is this guy any more?" Why you're not doing some things that you used to do. . . . People just wonder why you care about this type of thing so much. Higher education in my case, law in particular. "Why do you care about that?"

Sam's friends seem to interpret his ambition as a judgment of their own important life decisions. The result, predictably, is strain in key social relationships.

After higher education, upwardly mobile individuals often leave their hometown without turning back. Practical career concerns can motivate such a departure, but so, too, can unfavorable attitudes toward the people within it. Frank spoke of his disdain for the hometown in which he was reluctantly spending his summer.

> There's a lot of lower-class people. I didn't want to start ragging on the town with my parents here [but] I just don't like all the trash. There are a few college kids, but there's no one I can really hang out with. . . . I don't want to say I feel superior. That sounds terrible, but I don't know, it kind of limits me socially. . . . There's nothing for me here, everyone knows your business. . . . It's just kind of a dead town, a bunch of drunken idiots, you see them waxing their cars and gearing up to cruise down Main Street.

We see again how thickly moralism can pervade discussion of class and educational differences.

Harriet is another student for whom financial constraints have precipitated a move back home after college. Though a tough, independent, self-described "beer and pretzel" person, she recalled beginning to cry after spotting the city limits sign on her return drive to her hometown. "I really just want to get out of here. I just hate it, I absolutely hate it here. I don't fit in [Hometown], and I've been wanting to get out forever . . . [but] I got trapped here again. It's so depressing." Revulsion for one's hometown is not necessarily tantamount to rejection of one's family and old friends, but some respondents admitted that motivation for leaving was a desire to escape the lifestyle and influence of these important others. This departure may ultimately prove pivotal in the estrangement of the upwardly mobile from their families and hometown friends.

It appears from these excerpts that upwardly mobile students may unexpectedly be cast into the limelight by old friends and peers. Ironically, these students—who may feel at sea in their new surroundings—find themselves approached for direction by those still with the firm ground of familial continuity and class tradition under their feet. These supposed pacesetters must cope with loneliness—and may do so, as we have seen, by disdaining old companions still enjoying one another's affirmation or cutting themselves off altogether from this group. To put it tritely, the grass on the other side of the class boundary seems greener; Sam's old friends' admiration of his new position is evident, and Harriet, on the other side of the fence she erected, finds her success a source of alienation.

Relations With Professional-Class Peers

Higher education brought most participants into more extensive contact with peers from more moneyed backgrounds. Living among them in college often made class differences readily apparent. Several respondents commented on this financial disparity with bitterness. Harriet, a recent graduate of a state university, elaborated.

> There were some hard times. I only slept like four hours a night in college 'cause I had to work and go to school and study 'cause I was gonna try to get into law school. . . . Most of the people that I became friends with, their family paid for everything. . . . I never had that luxury. I always paid for everything, even in high school I paid for everything. I was bitter about that for a long time. I'd be like, "You had things handed to you on a silver platter and I worked my ass off for it!"

Class tensions were especially pronounced for participants at private or "elite" institutions. These respondents expressed outrage at their wealthier peers' alleged reckless spending and sense of entitlement. These peers were also criticized for a lack of appreciation for working-class employees on campus and ignorance of student differences in class background. Henry, a senior at a highly selective private university, detailed the personal effects of the latter.

> People complain that I'm cheap . . . that when we can't go to a nice restaurant for steaks [if I come along]. They complain and they probably don't even think about it. It's really irritating. It seems like they've

been given things their whole lives, everything they've needed. I find it disgusting that people drive $30,000 cars around campus, probably never having worked a day in their life. Their parents gave them their car [and] they complain that their parents yelled at them because they had a $200 credit card bill [that the parents also paid for]. . . . I have so much more of my time every week taken up by things like work. It's frustrating, it's aggravating.

Such a dynamic can take its toll on working-class students as they try to finance their education, compete academically, and achieve pleasurable social relations. These demands are considerable enough without having to be endured in silence, and yet participants did not seem willing to articulate their financial concerns to peers. Their embarrassment about not having money (or their pride in not wanting to complain about it) meant they were often reluctant to explain in detail why they could not in good conscience be a part of the costly fun. So when college friends and acquaintances joined Greek organizations, went to concerts or fine restaurants, or traveled to the beach or ski slopes on spring and winter breaks, many of the students interviewed could not come along, increasing the isolation and jealousy some of them felt at school.

Some participants discussed how relations with professional-class peers made them more self-conscious about perceived deficiencies in cultural capital and what Bourdieu calls the "habitus." Mary, who attended social functions in the professional world as a graduate student, office worker, and spouse of an engineer, elaborated.

> I'm very conscious that I don't spend a lot of money on clothing. . . . [I'll think] I look like White trash, I can't wear that. . . . At the office Christmas party, everyone else shows up in drop dead dresses. . . . I show up in something I happen to find at Goodwill. . . . You put me in front of a classroom, no problem. You put me in a room full of people all dressed better than I am, all sipping champagne, all talking about a favorite kind of wine and why it tastes the way it does, and I'll feel about that big. I'll just want to go shrink in a corner. . . . When people start talking about their vacations in Europe, I just look at them and go find someone else to talk to. . . . When the party's over with, I'm so tired. What have I got in common with these people?

For Mary, concerns about sharing values and background with peers— not salient issue for her as an undergraduate—have emerged as she has moved into the professional world. She, like other respondents, seems at an impasse, one with distinct class cultures on either side. In the thick of such adaptational struggles, the upwardly mobile person's sense of rightness about her accustomed style and values is apt to be severely tested.

Career Development

Class Disadvantage and Its Psychological Effects

Conservative views of upward mobility suggest that increased access to higher education in the postwar era has "leveled the playing field" for working-class individuals with high occupational ambitions. Yet participants detailed how class-related disadvantages often shaped their college experiences. For example, because of financial constraints, most participants' higher education options were much more limited than their professional-class counterparts'. Furthermore, their parents' insistence on self-reliance meant they were often "on their own" when applying for and financing their higher education.

Family limitations in social capital were also demoralizing for students. Some participants, because of a lack of guidance or other resources, found their college experiences disrupted. Henry, for example, reported that his parents advised him to set his sights on community colleges near home. Neither they nor he realized he was capable of attending more competitive schools. Henry dropped out of college once he decided he did not want to pursue engineering. During a year away, he worked 80 hours a week to pay off college loans and support himself. He seriously considered not returning to college, but eventually matriculated at a private university with a financial-aid package. Although he developed into an accomplished premed student, the earlier events still frustrated him.

> Neither of [my parents] really knew about college. They didn't really know about how to apply, about how to get money, even that you should visit and find out what's there. I think if my parents were more supportive, if we had gotten our act together, all three of us, I think I wouldn't have wasted my time at [Engineering University]. I didn't really blame them or feel that it was their responsibility. I guess part of that comes from having it drilled into me all my life that it was going to be up to me, whatever was to happen. . . . Five of my friends from high school just graduated. It was hard on graduation day when all their family was here and they were all wearing their caps and gowns. I was thinking, of all my friends, there's no one who has worked harder to get to college and to get where I am and they are. I felt like I deserved, I should be graduating now.

Henry realizes the unfairness of his class-based disadvantages but seems unsure about whom or what to fault for this injustice. An obvious target of blame is not available, but bitterness remains; this dynamic was common among respondents.

Their families' lack of acquaintance with college culture often made participants' transition to higher education particularly difficult. To quote

Ray, a rising college senior, "[I didn't know] what to expect socially. I didn't know what to bring, I didn't know anything about a dorm experience, I didn't know anything about setting up presentations for seminar classes. I was just completely unfamiliar with what I had to learn." Of course, not only working-class students feel trepidation about their initially unfamiliar school surroundings. Yet the potential for a crisis of confidence would seem greater among those whose loved ones had never before made the trek into higher education. Doubts about ability can combine with pressure to succeed in creating significant anxiety. "The first to go to college" may represent the mobility aspirations of the entire family and thus greatly fear "letting down" those back home. Jill, a case in point, reported that she "panics" during big exams and "feels terrible" about having a low class rank after her first year of school: "It's always been, 'Get out of this, have a better life than I do' . . . I guess that's why I started freaking out because I'm right in the important stages, and I mess up." Several students evidenced such a self-critical style. A lack of professional role models in the family may further shake confidence. As Tanya noted, "My parents don't have connections. You become aware of that when you are at someplace like [Private U]. Everybody's parents seem to be able to get everybody else jobs."

Occupational Choice

One of the major developmental tasks for any student in higher education is refinement of career goals and skills. Psychologists in the Eriksonian tradition have long suggested the suitability of the college years for allowing young adults a "psychosocial moratorium" to experiment with various career identities at a relatively leisurely pace. However, for many participants, their financial responsibilities and internal and family pressures to seek out practical vocational preparation made engagement in such moratoria quite difficult. Participants who were able to integrate preprofessional training into their education managed to quell concerns about its practical pay-offs. Others, whose career interests changed in college, found that the occupations to which they had tentatively given allegiance (and that their parents advocated) no longer seemed so apt. The process of occupational choice seemed especially difficult for those respondents who chose not to pursue family-approved job options.

A case in point is Kevin. Like many other respondents, he reported that his family viewed college as a means to an occupational end rather than as learning for learning's sake. As he became less enchanted with his law school plans and found validation from professors and peers for his creative talents, Kevin strayed from the occupational path his family endorsed.

[My parents] were always telling everybody, "You know, he wants to be a lawyer." So everyone was always asking me, "Oh, you're the future lawyer; how's it going up there at [State U]?" And I couldn't bring myself to say, "Well, uh, that's actually not it anymore. I have no interest in law whatsoever." Because all of my uncles were like, "So man, are you going to represent me later on?" And it was like, "Uh . . ." So I started lying to them, saying I was going into environmental law for a little while just because they didn't know what the hell it was. So they stopped asking me questions anyway, they're not the inquisitive type. . . . But [my parents'] view of college was just a period of time that it took to get a really stable job. They didn't think of it as a time where I need to find myself. . . . When I started figuring out more about what I wanted to do and realizing that it was farther away from what I had originally said I was going to do when I got in, it just became harder to communicate with them. . . . They're pushing me in all these [other] directions . . . [and] that hurts in that I feel if I go to try to pursue [acting and writing] that I won't have any help. . . . They didn't seem to want to listen to that part of it.

Respondents with interests in areas such as fine arts and philosophy seemed to have difficulty committing to these fields, partly because of perceptions that such a decision would elicit derision from relatives. Indeed, several noted family concerns about "impractical" careers with intangible fruits of labor. Ed, who was working on a PhD in the social sciences, elaborated.

It might be hard for them to understand just the concept of being in school as long as I've been. . . . At 21 my dad had his business . . . [at 25] I'm still at school making next to no money. So they are all waiting for me to finish my education. . . . They don't really understand it. They are just waiting for me to be a doctor or something.

Many respondents seemed to have internalized suspicions of unconventional careers. Emily's science prowess prompted her to consider briefly advanced studies in biology, but she came to feel that she would "rather die the death of a thousand screams" than follow this course (she now avoids such a scenario in medical school). Sam, meanwhile, became more politically aware in college and contemplated a doctorate in political science. He chose law school instead because "it's just less time and the sooner I can get to doing something: less money and also less questioning by other people of 'why are you doing that?' " What Sam wanted to hurry up and "get doing" was public service law that could benefit those like his father, whose own attempt at an American Dream—running his own car dealership—ended in near bankruptcy.

A big part of my personality and motivation has been for years thinking about how difficult it has been for my parents. . . . I couldn't see myself writing a bunch of academic crap to go in some law review somewhere that's going to sit on the shelves of the law library and maybe one person in every ten years is going to read that article. That's going to be a great thing for that one person to find, but to me that is not very much action.

What was striking in such interviews was not the common concern about whether or not one's work would "make a difference." Rather, the interviews impressed us with how little moral freedom these respondents felt in arguing inner conflicts out with themselves. The pressures toward what Erikson calls "identity foreclosure" seem powerful, leaving little room for deliberate exploration of one's work possibilities.

THEORETICAL IMPLICATIONS

Upward Mobility and Relational Identity

Our findings demonstrate upward mobility's multiple influences on family and social interactions. An "internalization of class conflict" (Sennett & Cobb, 1972) seemed to mark many participants' relations. As Ochberg and Comeau (chapter 5, this volume) found, academic ambition tends to strain family bonds more for working-class college students than their professional-class counterparts. Indeed, many respondents perceived that their educational advancement had disrupted family communication and heightened a sense of estrangement from important others.

The interviews begin to fill in the details of related research, including that which shows that strains in family attachment may lead to a variety of negative educational outcomes, including lower academic achievement and poorer college adjustment (Cutrona, Cole, Colangelo, Assouline, & Russell, 1994; Rice, Cole, & Lapsley, 1990). Results also specify the manner in which problems in family relations can affect identity formation. In terms of Josselson's (1994) model of relational identity, upward mobility seems to present special challenges in achieving successful *eye to eye validation*, *idealization and identification*, and *embeddedness*. As seen earlier, those students perceiving family indifference (and at times, hostility) toward their aspirations found this lack of validation profoundly disquieting. Similarly, many students noted problems in the dimension of idealization and identification, as higher education brought into focus their families' difficulties in providing models for achievement in the professional world. Working-class students can compensate by finding supportive peers and professors in college (that a few described instructors as second mothers or fathers perhaps bespeaks their considerable desire for mentorship), but many respondents often felt alone or confused as they navigated the transition to the professional class.

Another important dimension of relational identity is embeddedness, which, according to Josselson (1994, p. 98), "involves finding and taking a place with others; it encompasses belonging. . . . Where might there be a place for me?" Erikson placed embeddedness at the heart of identity by noting that during this developmental task the young person must grapple with the challenging question, "How do I fit into the adult world?" Distanced from families and hometown friends, yet feeling like intruders in the professional-class world, many participants felt betwixt and between two subcultures, with their deracination overshadowing often dramatic achievements. For instance, Sam, once a high school dropout, had gained entrance to one of the nation's most prestigious law schools. But rather than celebrating his story as one of personal triumph, he described his first year in professional school as follows.

> I'm not part of the community. I don't feel very accepted by it and I'm not sure that I want to. I don't have many friends there in the sense of other people I know as friends. . . . I was definitely utterly alone this past year. There really was no one that I could talk to about what I was doing and why it was so frustrating to me. Part of that is law school. More so was just my view of things and my not being accepting of how things are as most people there are. There really wasn't anyone, no one in my group of family or friends who could relate to that. I just didn't feel real connected.

Upward Mobility and Occupational Identity

As implied earlier, difficulties in relational identity can complicate efforts to achieve occupational identity. Ideally, young people pursue careers with the guidance and recognition of important others. Failures in the relational dimensions of validation and identification, however, can burden their pursuit of rewarding work. Marcia (1980) has conceptualized identity formation according to the quality and extent of occupational exploration and commitment. Respondents' accounts suggested that it may be difficult for upwardly mobile individuals to sustain an extended period of exploration (e.g., via graduate school); in doing so they would risk not only financial stress but also family scorn. As Ochberg and Comeau (chapter 5, this volume) summarized,

> Fathers who have less education and less prestigious careers often feel that graduate school encourages frivolous occupational fantasies: careers with poor pay and security or no specific career goal at all. Further, many less-educated parents feel that graduate school encourages young people to put off adult responsibility: starting a family of one's own and paying one's own way. In contrast, parents with more education and

more prestigious careers may take for granted a longer period of exploration and preparation.

Not only their parents express such concerns; the respondents themselves desired more immediate pay-offs from their educational endeavors. Settling quickly on a prescribed career would therefore be tempting, yet such identity foreclosure may ultimately represent an unsatisfying solution to this developmental dilemma.

It should be clear by now that the struggle of occupational choice for upwardly mobile individuals often represents a clash of values: the hard-headed practicality of their working-class background versus the intellectual idealism fostered by higher education. Conflict may arise as the upwardly mobile student adopts "professional-class" work values that are at odds with family notions of what constitutes a worthwhile occupation. Where values clash, moral judgments are soon to follow. Participants' disparagement of hometown peers who "go to beauty school and marry the guy at the gas station" was reportedly countered by family ridicule of "nerd schools" and exhortations to "get a real job." As the interviews suggested, an inflexible and threatening moralism often marks discussion of class and educational differences. What concerns us most is that by internalizing these rigid judgments, upwardly mobile students may miss an opportunity to integrate their talents and motives during a suitable period of career exploration.

Continuation of Conflict Into Adulthood

What will happen as these students move more fully into adulthood? The study design does not allow us to know whether these themes of conflict would remain prominent beyond higher education. One might expect that certain tensions reported would die down over time. For example, some difficulties in parental relations may be explained by the general adolescent tendency in moratorium to use parents as negative models (Erikson, 1980). That is, to facilitate differentiation, parents may be temporarily cast in an unflattering role as the antithesis of what the young person wants to become. Parental relations may become less stormy once the young person's individuation is more complete.

Still, many of the psychological costs of mobility mentioned may encumber identity development well beyond the college and graduate school years. We were struck by how themes of adult conflict in the autobiographical reflections of working-class intellectuals (e.g., Dews & Law, 1995; Grimes & Morris, 1997; Ryan & Sackrey, 1984; Tokarczyk & Fay, 1993) paralleled those in our interviews. For example, Rodriguez (1982), a Mexican American writer with a PhD in Renaissance literature, discussed how education "shattered the intimate bond that once held my family close" (p. 30). And Podhoretz (1967), in his discussion of the "prices to be paid for the rewards of making it in America" (p. ix), recounted his own journey from working-class Brooklyn to the professional-class publishing world of Manhattan (pp. 3–4):

> It appalls me to think what an immense transformation I had to work on myself in order to become what I have become: if I had known what I was doing I would surely not have been able to do it, I would surely not have wanted to. No wonder the choice had to be blind; there was a kind of treason in it: treason toward my family, treason toward my friends. In choosing the road I chose, I was pronouncing a judgment on them, and the fact that they concurred in the judgment makes the whole thing sadder but no less cruel.

We found again in such accounts the difficulty of explaining work to family, the sense of social dislocation (feeling "caught in the middle," "nowhere at home"), anxiety about professional competence and social grace, resentment of professional-class peers' privileges and assumptions of class homogeneity, and guilt about having advanced well beyond family and friends. For these authors, the costs of upward mobility in adulthood seemed largely the same as those encountered in our interviews; the difficulties of identity development—of integrating disparate class personas—remained.

Qualifications

It is clear that our presentation focused on the psychological "dark side" of upward mobility. Yet mobility per se is not always necessary or sufficient to bring about many of the conflicts discussed. Furthermore, within these difficulties lie possibilities for creative and productive resolution. Indeed, respondents made the point that their relative lack of financial and emotional support in college has bred independence and responsibility that they are thankful to possess. They noted that straddling the professional and working classes has allowed them to find common ground with an impressive diversity of people. They said that they have developed uncommon work ethics, and that they have an appreciation of achievements and possessions for which they have worked harder than most peers. We should not lose sight of the fact that many upwardly mobile students achieve unusually mature relational and occupational identities.

Our focus on conflict may also have created the impression that participants generally viewed their parents and families with scorn or pity. This was not the case. Most students expressed at least some admiration and affection for their families. In fact, it was their closeness before college that made negative developments in family relations especially unnerving for some; these changes were not experienced as trivial, predictable annoyances but as deeper and alarming losses. Perceptions that their families no longer appreciated their achievements or approved of their plans were particularly stinging—in part because these judgments were from respected loved ones and also because respondents' academic success had previously been a less ambiguous source of personal and parental pride. Such conflicts did not mean, however, that respondents necessarily perceived their family relations as abnormal.

A final qualification: Although our discussion at times implied otherwise, we realize that first-generation students are hardly a homogeneous group. As was only briefly acknowledged in this chapter, differences with regard to race, gender, ethnicity, region, and college institution can shape identity development in powerful ways. Especially interesting to us was the intersection of issues of race and class. For example, a few White respondents mentioned masking aspects of their class background in efforts that might be described as "passing" for someone from a wealthier and more educated background—much as racial minorities may feel pressure to mute their backgrounds in "White" America. It may not be far-fetched to apply DuBois's classic concept of "double consciousness" to the upwardly mobile (DuBois, 1903).

We noted other parallels between the accounts of White and Black participants. In characterizing the experience of Black students at her university, one participant, Tanya, described stresses similar in nature to those White respondents reported.

> We didn't get here very easily. People say that to get here we are meeting quotas, that we got an easier ride and we are all here on scholarships just so we can add color to the campus. . . . [But] we aren't here to chill and then go work for Dad's oil company. It just doesn't work like that. If we fail here, we don't have things to fall back on. We don't have a back-up plan. It's either we make it or we don't and we go home and be poor.

Tanya implied the primacy of race in her identity, discussing her involvement in Black student groups and describing "the posse," her close-knit group of five Black women college friends. All of these women were reportedly first-generation students, but according to Tanya, "it never really occurred to us that none of our parents went to college." Still, when asked to describe what bonded this group together, Tanya mostly referenced issues of class.

> What united us? A lot of times we would talk about the fact that we had no money, and how if we had money we would get straight A's. We were like, I don't understand how people can have money and not

do well because you don't have to go to work and you'll have all your time to study. . . . We would vent our bitterness . . . talk about how everybody around us had [money] and had no appreciation for it.

We expect that the increasing attention on social mobility within research on African Americans (e.g., Fordham, 1995; Higginbotham & Weber, 1992) will yield fruitful insights.

The Still Hidden Injuries of Class

As mentioned earlier, a lack of financial, social, and cultural resources often left participants with a sense of injustice; in jockeying for position within the social structure, they knew that the race was, in a sense, rigged. Although they could recognize how their backgrounds had shaped their experiences, participants seemed not to have conceptualized the frustrations of upward mobility in terms of social class. Who was to blame for the unfairness of it all? Respondents sometimes accepted their disadvantages as the "way of the world." At times they expressed anger at their families or complained about being unable to take advantage of institutional minority preferences. Most often, they blamed themselves for an inability to make the most of their educational experiences. Rarely did they link their difficulties to class structure. That they may have lacked class consciousness is not surprising given that admitting social stratification contradicts the American national faith in equal opportunity.

Yet viewing the obstacles to upward mobility as systematic, rather than idiosyncratic, barriers could be liberating for these students. Other campus groups have benefited from such collective sociological imagination. For example, student organizations for women, racial and ethnic minorities, and gay and lesbian students speak out against social injustices and provide supportive communities for their members. Perhaps most important, such organizations support the development of ego identity, offering peer validation and identification along with a sense of belonging. Still, the notion of a "First-Generation Students' Association" or an "Upward Mobility Club" seems peculiar, perhaps because the view of a rise in class as potentially alienating hardly commands the attention of the American public. Class background did seem to bond several first-generation students interviewed, but its potential for drawing peers together is often overlooked. As Lisa commented about her best friends at a selective university, "It was just kind of ironic that a lot of us are from working-class backgrounds. We didn't even talk about it until we were pretty close, which I think is pretty interesting. . . . It's not like you introduce yourself, 'Hi, my name is Lisa and my parents didn't go to college, but I'm at [State U] anyway.'" Such material reinforced Fussell's (1983) view of class as "America's dirty little secret."

CONCLUSION

It was also Fussell who claimed that "the number of hopes blasted and hearts broken for class reasons is probably greater in the world of colleges and universities than anywhere else" (1983, p. 141). Indeed, the potential psychological costs of upward mobility via higher education seem considerable, with implications for the crucial task of identity formation. Respondents found their personal and academic progress undermined in various ways: through the pains involved in leaving family and friends behind, the uncertainty of entering a foreign educational world, and the confusion of pursuing a career without obvious role models or a wealth of financial and cultural capital. One worries about the challenges these costs pose to the further development of relational and occupational identities.

It is worth noting that higher education can provide serious challenges for all students, regardless of class background. We do not claim that the difficulties presented in this study are unique to first-generation students, that their higher education is only a time of inner struggle, or that its intellectual and social rewards remain unavailable to them. What we do assert is that this group's path to success is psychologically more complex and demanding than is generally imagined. Fuller consideration of the emotional costs of upward mobility seems imperative in a society that champions this process while often denying the antagonisms within its class structure.

We offer this discussion with the hope of prompting a larger public conversation on the psychology of upward mobility. Multiple-case studies are not designed to provide the "last word" on the phenomenon of interest. Ideally, they involve the "quest for good examples . . . displaying the generality and comparability of seemingly private experience, articulating the social sources of fate and the systematicity of what seemed random and inexplicable, [and] enriching public discourse about previously occluded issues" (Rosenwald, 1988, pp. 263–264). These are lofty goals, to be sure, but we hope that this chapter helps spark dialogue among educators, counselors, policymakers, and, perhaps most important, upwardly mobile individuals themselves. Such discourse only seems appropriate in a nation that claims the permeability of class boundaries as proof of greatness.

REFERENCES

Barber, J. A. (1970). *Social mobility and voting behavior*. Chicago: Rand McNally.

Bettelheim, B., & Janowitz, M. (1950). *Dynamics of prejudice*. New York: Harper.

Billson, J. M., & Terry, M. B. (1982). In search of the silken purse: Factors in attrition among first-generation students. *College and University, 58*, 57–75.

Bourdieu, P. (1977). *Outline of a theory of practice*. Cambridge: Cambridge University Press.

Cutrona, C. E., Cole, V., Colangelo, N., Assouline, S. G., & Russell, D. (1994). Perceived parental social support and academic achievement: An attachment theory perspective. *Journal of Personality and Social Psychology, 66*, 369–378.

Dews, C. L. B., & Law, C. L. (Eds.). (1995). *This fine place so far from home: Voices of academics from the working class*. Philadelphia: Temple University Press.

Dey, E., Astin, A., & Korn, W. (1993). *The American freshman*. Los Angeles: Higher Education Research Institute.

DuBois, W. E. B. (1903). *The souls of black folk*. Chicago: A. C. McClung.

Durkheim, E. (1951). *Suicide*. Glencoe, IL: Simpson.

Eccles, J. S., Midgley, C., Wigfield, A., Buchanan, C. M., Reuman, D., Flanagan, C., & Mac Iver, D. (1993). Development during adolescence: The impact of stage–environment fit on young adolescents' experiences in schools and in families. *American Psychologist, 48*, 90–101.

Ellis, R. A., & Lane, W. C. (1967) Social mobility and social isolation: A test of Sorokin's dissociative hypothesis. *American Sociological Review, 32*, 237–256.

Erikson, E. (1968). *Identity: Youth and crisis*. New York: W. W. Norton.

Erikson, E. (1980). *Identity and the life cycle*. New York: W. W. Norton.

Fordham, S. (1995). *Blacked out*. Chicago: University of Chicago Press.

Fussell, P. (1983). *Class*. New York: Summit Books.

Granfield, R. (1991). Making it by faking it: Working-class students in an elite academic environment. *Journal of Contemporary Ethnography, 20*, 331–351.

Grimes, M. D., & Morris, J. M. (1997). *Caught in the middle: Contradictions in the lives of sociologists from working-class backgrounds*. Westport, CT: Praeger.

Higginbotham, E., & Weber, L. (1992). Moving up with kin and community. *Gender & Society, 6*, 416–440.

Hollingshead, A. B., Ellis, R. A., & Kirby, E. C. (1954). Social mobility and mental illness. *American Sociological Review, 19*, 577–584.

Jackson, E. F., & Curtis, R. F. (1972). Effects of vertical mobility and status inconsistency: A body of negative evidence. *American Sociological Review, 37*, 701–713.

Josselson, R. (1994). Identity and relatedness in the life cycle. In H. A. Bosma, T. L. G. Graafsma, H. D. Grotevant, & D. J. de Levita (Eds.), *Identity and development: An interdisciplinary approach* (pp. 81–102). Thousand Oaks, CA: Sage.

London, H. B. (1989). Breaking away: A study of first-generation students and their families. *American Journal of Education, 97*, 144–170.

Marcia, J. (1980). Identity in adolescence. In J. Adelson (Ed.), *Handbook of adolescent psychology* (pp. 159–187). New York: John Wiley and Sons.

Marshall, G., & Firth, D. (1999). Social mobility and personal satisfaction: Evidence from ten countries. *British Journal of Sociology, 50*, 28–48.

Newman, K. (1988). *Falling from grace*. New York: Free Press.

Piorkowski, G. K. (1983). Survivor guilt in the university setting. *Personnel and Guidance Journal, 62*, 620–622.

Podhoretz, N. (1967). *Making it*. New York: Random House.

Rice, K. G., Cole, D. A., & Lapsley, D. K. (1990). Separation/dividuation, family cohesion, and adjustment to college: Measurement validation and test of a theoretical model. *Journal of Counseling Psychology, 37*, 195–202.

Rodriguez, R. (1982). *Hunger of memory*. New York: Bantam Books.

Rosenwald, G. C. (1988). A theory of multiple-case research. *Journal of Personality, 56*, 239–264.

Runyan, W. (1982). *Life histories and psychobiography*. New York: Oxford University Press.

Ryan, J., & Sackrey, C. (1984). *Strangers in paradise*. Boston: South End Press.

Savage, M. (1997). Social mobility and the survey method: A critical analysis. In D. Bertaux & P. Thompson (Eds.), *Pathways to social class: A qualitative approach to social mobility* (pp. 299–325). New York: Oxford University Press.

Sennett, R., & Cobb, J. (1972). *The hidden injuries of class*. New York: Vintage Books.

Sorokin, P. A. (1927). *Social mobility*. New York: Harper and Brothers.

Stein, J. A., & Newcomb, M. D. (1999). Adult outcomes of adolescent conventional and agentic orientations. *Journal of Early Adolescence, 19*, 39–65.

Stewart, A., & Ostrove, J. (1993). Social class, social change, and gender. *Psychology of Women Quarterly, 17*, 475–497.

Tokarczyk, M. M., & Fay, E. L. (Eds.). (1993). *Working-class women in the academy: Laborers in the knowledge factory*. Amherst: University of Massachusetts Press.

Trent, J. W., & Medsker, L. (1968). *Beyond high school*. San Francisco: Jossey-Bass.

Vandewater, E. A., Ostrove, J. M., & Stewart, A. J. (1997). Predicting women's well-being in midlife. *Journal of Personality and Social Psychology, 72*, 1147–1160.

5

MOVING UP AND THE PROBLEM OF EXPLAINING AN "UNREASONABLE" AMBITION

RICHARD L. OCHBERG AND WILLIAM COMEAU

"Let me tell you about the very rich. They are different from you and me . . . soft where we are hard, and cynical where we are trustful."
—F. Scott Fitzgerald ("The Rich Boy," 1926).

"He remembered poor Julian . . . and how he had started a story that began, 'The very rich are different from you and me.' And how someone had said to Julian, Yes, they have more money."
—Ernest Hemingway ("The Snows of Kilimanjaro," 1938).

This chapter describes a study of college seniors who are looking forward to graduate school. Some of them have become much more educated than their parents; they say that they have entered "a different world." By this, they mean several things. Their classmates and instructors assume that higher education will pave the way to better careers—careers that will not simply pay more but that will offer more scope for creativity or service. (Their parents—so these students say—are skeptical about both these careers and whether more school will lead to them.) Even when their parents value advanced education, they often do not know enough about it to offer meaningful advice or reassurance. This is part of what upwardly mobile students mean by a different world—but there is something more.

At times, they suggest that they are engaged with their parents in a fierce debate about character. Given that the world is a certain sort of place—and they disagree about what sort of place that is—what sort of person should one be to make one's way in it? In particular, working-class parents sound troubled by their children's sense of entitlement: This seems to them irresponsible and self-indulgent. Upwardly mobile students agree that they feel entitled, but they put a wholly different construction on this. Their parents, so these students say, do not feel entitled to anything—they pride themselves on their responsibility and stoicism, but these seem to our informants too close to servility.

Of course, arguments about character are much less obvious than those about, say, the cost of tuition. In fact, students and their parents rarely spell out this argument in so many words—this sometimes makes them appear to be talking past each other. Yet it seems to us that this moral issue may be the bitterest point of contention—and the ways in which it goes unacknowledged may be the most interesting sense in which upwardly mobile students and their parents really do live in different worlds. The privileged, it appears, are different—not just because they have more money but because they take for granted a way of being that offends those less privileged. The aim of this chapter is to bring out what this entails.

When we began this study we were not sure what we would hear. One possibility was that upwardly mobile students would feel strongly supported by their parents: Their academic careers might have become a family project. We imagined their parents saying, "We never had the chance to go to college, but by God you will." Higginbotham & Webber (1992) suggested that this is especially true of women and African Americans. However, we also imagined an opposite scenario. Upwardly mobile students might tell us that they developed their ambitions without their parents' support, that in fact their ambition has driven a wedge between them and their families. In this vein we imagined their parents saying, "We never went to college— who do you think you are?" Either story would have been interesting—and no doubt both exist (London, 1989). The optimistic "family alliance" version might suggest how some working-class students escape the narrow horizons of their milieu; the pessimistic, "family estrangement" story might add to our understanding of cultural constraints.

Why did we imagine that working-class parents might be disturbed by their children's academic ambitions? Consider these issues: College and graduate school are very expensive, not just in tuition but also in time. The years spent earning a degree might otherwise go to building a career; working-class parents may doubt whether this investment will be recouped. However, this pragmatic calculation is only the beginning.

Most working-class families regard college as a means to a better job (Clark, Heist, McConnell, Trow, & Yonge 1972); many college instructors and advisors, on the other hand, disparage this vocational focus as plebeian. Winston Churchill, for example, remarked, "The first duty of a university is to teach wisdom, not a trade." A working-class student who brought this attitude home might well seem supercilious.

Working-class families may wonder what sort of nonremunerative "wisdom" college confers. One common idea is that it teaches students to appreciate great books, fine art, classical music, and so on. This sort of cultivated taste is important in some circles. Coleman and Rainwater (1978, p. 86) reported, "Men and women of Upper-American standing gave most attention [to] breadth of interest and information, familiarity with the arts ...and comfort in interaction with people like themselves" (see also Lamont, 1992). Other sociologists suggest that "cultural capital"—that is, familiarity with highbrow music, art, literature—defines membership in an elevated class and fosters social mobility (Bourdieu & Passeron, 1977; DiMaggio, 1982; DiMaggio & Mohr, 1985; McClelland, 1990). However, not everyone holds cultural sophistication in such esteem. Coleman and Rainwater continued, "[Working-class] Americans emphasized character more than culture when judging themselves socially above others. Having 'good morals' and 'initiative' were the prime virtues they credited themselves with in contrast to those of lower standing" (see also Kahl, 1953, pp. 189–205).

We might take this a step further. Intellectual sophistication is not just a matter of what one knows but of one's attitude toward knowing. Perry (1968) suggested that liberal education teaches students to question ideas. Students who attain a relativistic view of knowledge assume that any set of facts are only what one can observe from a particular perspective—and that perspectives should be debated. This entails not just an approach toward abstract knowledge but also toward its purveyors. However, this attitude toward knowing and learning may be linked to social class. The upper middle-class style—which encourages students to debate ideas with their instructors—may run counter to the working-class emphasis on respect for authority (Kohn, 1977). Anyon (1987) suggested that sharply different styles of teaching can already be distinguished in working-class and upper middle-class grade schools.

In short, college and graduate school are not just stepping-stones to better paid jobs, they belong to an upper middle-class culture. (No doubt this is more true of some schools than others.) A number of studies have documented how alien this culture may feel to working-class students— and professors (Ellis & Lane, 1967; Granfield, 1991; Ryan & Sackrey, 1984; Wegner, 1973). In turn, upwardly mobile students who adopt the values of this new milieu may seem to their parents irresponsible and patronizing. College may seem to these parents not only a bad investment but a corrupting influence, one that teaches students to disdain their parents' concerns and values.

Of course, these are only possibilities; with these ideas in mind we turn to our study. This chapter is divided into two sections: The first part draws on a traditional questionnaire; the second, on some less structured interviews. Let us be clear about how we regard each of these.

We are chiefly interested in using upwardly mobile students to clarify the moral contours of their world. Our approach is a variation on an old device: One can often bring to light the tacit rules that govern a system by examining the charges laid against those deemed deviant. Upward mobility is a kind of deviance; the family arguments it provokes may reveal what normally goes without saying in working-class families.

From this perspective, the estrangement of upwardly mobile students from their families would be important even if it were comparatively rare. Would we really lose interest if only a substantial minority—rather than a majority—felt so estranged? At the same time, it would strengthen our case if we could show, statistically, that the experience of upwardly mobile students differs from that of their privileged classmates. To set the stage for the argument we will eventually make, consider the possibilities that follow.

Upwardly mobile students may report much less encouragement from their families than do their more privileged peers. Scores of previous studies have found this to be the case; many of them go on to show that young people who are encouraged by their parents are more likely to become academically ambitious. This helps to explain the well-known fact that among students with approximately equal high school grades, those from more privileged families are far more likely to attend college (Alexander, Eckland, & Griffin, 1975; Conklin & Dailey, 1981; Sewell & Shah, 1968).

Notice that this finding would tell us only that privileged students receive more encouragement. It would not, however, indicate any difference in how family encouragement and academic ambition affect each other in different kinds of families. Suppose, however, that we found a substantially lower correlation between family encouragement and academic ambition among less privileged students. This might lend credence to two ideas.

Students from less privileged backgrounds may feel that their parents do not really understand the whole system of higher education; if so, they may discount their parents' advice. Some may regard their parents as overly optimistic: They may be restrained in their ambitions despite the fact that their families encourage them. Others may feel that their parents are excessively skeptical: They may insist on their ambitions despite their parents' discouragement. If this is the case, then the correlation between family encouragement and academic ambition should be lower among less privileged students than among more privileged ones.

Finally, students whose academic ambitions far exceed their parents' expectations may provoke their skepticism and resentment. If so, we may actually find a *negative* correlation between family encouragement and academic ambition. Presumably, this is most likely among highly ambitious students from less privileged families. In contrast, we might expect privileged parents to be enthusiastic about their children's academic ambition—those privileged students who are most ambitious should report the most family encouragement. (Notice that we are suggesting that family encouragement and academic ambition may influence each other, much the way confidence and success are often said to do.)

When we began this study we expected that more privileged students would report more family encouragement; this, after all, has been shown repeatedly by others. In addition, we hoped to find a different correlation between academic ambition and family encouragement among students from different backgrounds. This would lend credence to the idea that family encouragement means something different to upwardly mobile students than it does to their privileged classmates—and academic ambition means something different to less privileged parents than it does to their more privileged neighbors.

This much said, it seems to us that statistical comparisons can take us only so far. What we really want to know is how upwardly mobile students understand their disagreement with their parents. The best way to get at this, we believe, is by examining in close detail the conversations that our informants report.

THE SURVEY

The aim of this section is to test whether the experience of upwardly mobile students differs from that of equally ambitious students who start from more privileged backgrounds.

1. Do more privileged students experience more family encouragement?
2. Is there a different relationship between family encouragement and academic ambition among students from different backgrounds?

Sample

We conducted this study at an urban, nonresidential state university that draws students from a wide range of socioeconomic backgrounds. No doubt we would have found a different population of students (and parents) at an Ivy League university, a Jesuit college, or a community college—and of course, students at any of these schools would have encountered a different campus culture. This should be borne in mind in extrapolating from our results.

We surveyed 160 college seniors (74 men, 86 women), age 30 or less (mean age = 24). About 80% were White; approximately equal numbers of African Americans, Latinos, and Asians made up the balance. We recruited informants at various locations in the university to ensure a range of majors, and paid them $5 to participate.

We focused on the plans that college seniors have for graduate school. This is unusual; most investigators have studied undergraduate education. However, we wanted to hear from students whose parents are skeptical of higher education; we thought that graduate school would be more likely than college to provoke this reaction. (We also thought that graduate education may be replacing college as the boundary between upper middle-class and less prestigious careers. Today, many careers that were once attainable with a college degree require more advanced certification: teaching, nursing, many human service occupations, even many business careers.)

Measures

Before designing a questionnaire we interviewed six students. We also drew ideas from research on family attachment (Armsden & Greenberg, 1987; Grotevant & Cooper, 1985; Josselson, 1980; Lapsley, Rice, & Fitzgerald, 1990), and on class differences in family support for education.

Family Background: Parents' Education and Occupation

Our informants scored each parent's education on a six-level measure, from "Did not finish high school," to "Doctoral study." They also described each parent's occupation, which we scored using the latest revision of the Socioeconomic Index (SEI; Stevens & Cho, 1985). Because many students did not list any occupation for their mothers we eventually dropped this variable from our analyses. To present some of our findings visually (and to facilitate some statistical analyses), we will divide the sample using fathers' education. Fathers who had no more than a high school education ($N = 71$) had an average SEI score of 34.7; typical occupations at this level include police and skilled trades supervisors. Among fathers who had at least started college ($N = 89$) the average SEI was 58.2; typical occupations include business managers and technical writers. We will refer to students with high school-educated fathers as "less privileged," "working class," or as "upwardly mobile" and to the rest as "privileged." (Many students describe their parents as working-class—by which they seem to mean a mixture of occupation, education, values, and *savoir faire*. At the risk of oversimplifying things, we will follow their lead.)

Family Support for Education. Lareau (1987) suggested that working-class parents value education but do not become actively engaged in supporting it. (Doubting their own ability to offer good advice, these parents leave the job to their children's teachers and school counselors.) Therefore, we assessed two aspects of family support.

1. *Family engagement* (mean = 3.49; SD = .78; Cronbach's alpha = .88) measures whether students feel that their parents are engaged with them in their academic ambitions (see appendix).
2. *Valuing education* (mean = 3.37; SD = .54; Cronbach's alpha = .72) measures students' perception of the value that their parents place on higher education (see appendix). We asked students rather than the parents themselves because we are interested in how students make sense of their family experience.

Graduate Plans. We also assessed two aspects of students' plans for graduate school.

1. *Academic ambition*: Students scored their graduate plans on a five-level measure, from "No current plans for graduate school," to the PhD or an advanced professional specialization. To discourage unrealistic estimates we described how long each degree usually takes. Nevertheless, 88 students (54%) hoped to earn a master's degree, and another 50 (31%) hoped to receive a terminal degree (4 to 8 years of graduate study). Because it seems unlikely that this many students will actually apply to graduate school, we use the scale to compare ambitiousness rather than as a literal prediction.
2. *Commitment* (mean = 3.73; SD = .77, Cronbach's alpha = .70): This scale asks students how prepared they are to make substantial sacrifices to further their education or career (see appendix). For example, are they prepared to postpone getting married or having children, move to new cities or invest several years in poorly paid apprenticeships to gain experience? Certainly not all graduate plans require such sacrifices, but many do. Students who are prepared to make such sacrifices may be more committed to their graduate plans.

We also asked students to report their gender, age, ethnicity, grade point average, academic major, marital status, and whether or not they were living with their parents.

Results

Privileged Students Report More Family Support

Students who come from more privileged backgrounds say that their parents place greater value on education. (Remember that this is the students' view of their parents; we do not know what the parents themselves would say.) More specifically, students say that their parents value education more if they have better educated fathers ($r = .30$, $p < .01$), better educated mothers ($r = .20$, $p < .05$), and fathers who are employed at more prestigious occupations ($r = .28$, $p < .01$). (Our three measures of family background correlate highly with each other; combining them does not significantly improve the variance predicted by fathers' education alone.)

Family engagement presents a more complicated picture (see Figure 5-1). Students with better educated fathers report more family engagement; however, most of the difference is concentrated among those who are most ambitious. Fathers' education makes no significant difference in engagement among students who aspire to master's degrees. However, the disparity among students from different backgrounds grows steadily as they become more ambitious. Among those who aspire to terminal degrees, those with college-educated fathers report significantly more family engagement than do those with high school-educated fathers ($R^2 = .19$, $F = 11.5$, $p = .001$).

Family Engagement Influences the Graduate Plans of Privileged Students but Not Those of Upwardly Mobile Individuals

Figure 5-1 indicates that among students with college-educated fathers, those who are more ambitious feel more engaged with their parents ($r = .38$, $p < .01$). In marked contrast, there is no linear relationship between ambition and family engagement among students with high school-educated fathers ($r = .02$). However, this may not be putting the matter strongly enough. Figure 5-1 suggests a curvilinear relationship between family engagement and academic ambition among students with high school-educated fathers. If true, this would be quite interesting: It would suggest that beyond a certain point academic ambition actually leads to a reduction in family engagement. Unfortunately, our sample is too small to demonstrate this statistically.

We found a similar pattern when we examined the interaction among family background, family engagement, and commitment. Among students with college-educated fathers, those who are most committed report the most engagement ($r = .43$, $p < .01$). There is no relationship between family engagement and commitment among students with high school-educated fathers.

Of course, it may be that the pattern we have described so far is influenced by other variables that are regularly associated with students' backgrounds or aspirations. We tried to tease apart the most likely of these.

Gender. We expected that family engagement would be more important to women than to men, but we found no evidence for this. Women reported slightly more engagement than did men. However, family engagement did not influence women's ambition or commitment any more than it did men's.

Family Engagement

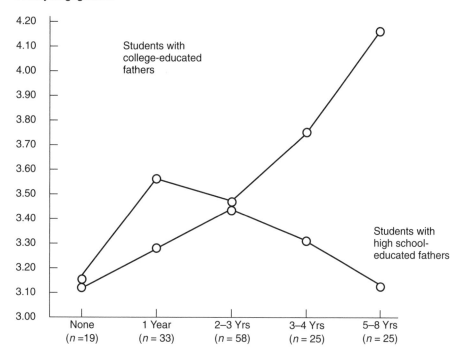

Academic Ambition
(Length of Anticipated Graduate Study)

Variance in family engagement explained by academic ambition and fathers' education

All informants ($N = 160$)				
Source	Sum of Squares	df	F	Significance of F
Within and residual	83.86	156		
Fathers' education	1.28	1	2.40	.124
Academic ambition	3.20	1	5.99	.015
Fathers' education times ambition	2.83	1	5.29	.023

Students Who Hope to Receive at Least a Three-Year Master's Degree ($N = 108$)				
Source	Sum of Squares	df	F	Significance of F
Within and residual	53.90	105		
Fathers' education	4.63	1	9.10	.003
Fathers' education times ambition	6.14	1	12.07	.001

Figure 5-1. Academic Ambition and Family Engagement Among Students With High School- and College-Educated Fathers

Previous Academic Success. Not surprisingly, students who had done well in college had more ambitious plans for graduate school. We wondered whether students from less privileged families had done less well as undergraduates. If so, their graduate ambitions might be less realistic—this in turn might explain why their parents are less enthusiastic about those plans than are more privileged parents. This was not the case. At every level of graduate ambition, students from less privileged families reported grade point averages that were as high (or slightly higher) than those of more privileged students. Controlling GPA did not alter the essential finding: Academic ambition receives much more support in privileged families.

Ethnicity. Unfortunately, we did not have enough African American, Latino, or Asian students to test whether academic ambition is more (or less) encouraged in ethnic families. Controlling for ethnicity did not alter our results. (This seems a promising direction for future research. It might be especially interesting to explore the experience of recent immigrants. Popular belief holds that this is the population in which children receive the most encouragement to exceed their parents' education. It would be interesting to see whether—and why—this is true.)

Other Potential Confounding Variables. Finally, we examined students' age, marital status, and whether or not they were living at home. None of these affected our central findings.

Summary of the Survey

We find that the experience of upwardly mobile students differs from that of their more privileged classmates. First, privileged students say that their parents value education more. Second, it seems that these students become ambitious and committed partly because they have their parents' encouragement. Nothing of the sort is true of upwardly mobile students. In fact, those who are most ambitious and committed are unusually likely to feel disengaged from their parents.

These results present us with a puzzle. We find no evidence that upwardly mobile students pay any price for their lack of family support. If family engagement leads privileged students to be more ambitious and committed, why does not family disengagement injure the ambitions and commitment of the upwardly mobile? (As a matter of fact, we struggled with these numbers for many months before deciding that we were trying to go in the wrong direction. We planned to show how family disengagement puts upwardly mobile students at risk; at this point, the interesting question seems to be, why are they so implausibly resilient?) Various possibilities come to mind.

It is possible that family engagement does affect less privileged students, but at an earlier point than we were able to observe. At our school only

38% of all entering freshmen graduate within six years (this is not an unusual rate of attrition). Students would seem more likely to remain in school if they feel encouraged by their parents. It may be that many less privileged students, and especially those who felt disengaged from their families, dropped out before they became eligible for our study. Of course, even if this is true we might still wonder how our informants survived this winnowing. How have they managed to remain unaffected by their disengagement from their families?

Perhaps they have found other mentors or circles of like-minded peers. It would be interesting to know more about this. But whatever encouragement these students draw from others, they must ultimately convince themselves. Somehow, they must tell themselves a story, one that justifies the choices they have made—and avows their intention to persevere—despite the fact that their parents are not engaged with them in their ambitions. With this idea, we turn to the interviews.

THE INTERVIEWS

So far we have seen that upwardly mobile students feel less supported by their parents than do their more privileged peers. However, these scores do not convey the subjective experience. For example, we do not yet know much about the tone of family discussions. Upwardly mobile students may feel that their parents are interested in their plans, eager to help as best they can, but simply lack the experience to do so. This would be a rather different portrait than that of parents who are disinterested, derisive, or jealous.

Then, too, we do not yet see how students understand their parents or themselves. Upwardly mobile students may simply disagree with their parents about whether higher education is a good investment. Of course, such arguments may be important in themselves—they certainly may be vehement. However, these students and their parents may disagree about more than monetary costs and benefits; they may disagree about what one can legitimately expect: in an education, a career, a life. If so, family arguments about education might suggest that upwardly mobile students have crossed a cultural boundary.

Therefore, we interviewed 56 of these students for about one hour each. We focused chiefly on those with high school-educated fathers who planned to pursue at least a three-year master's degree ($n = 34$). For comparison, we also interviewed a similarly ambitious group with college-educated fathers ($n = 22$).

We first asked our informants about their experience with jobs or further education since leaving college and about their plans for the near future. We then asked how well their parents understood the details of their plans for graduate school: how various programs differed, how long each might take, what the chances were of being accepted, what graduate school might cost, and what possibilities existed for financial aid. Finally, we asked about the more personal side of discussing their plans with their parents. Did they talk to their parents about their own doubts and anxieties? Did their parents seem to have faith in them? After talking to their parents, did they feel a sense of shared enthusiasm, or did they feel angry and misunderstood? We also asked what issues they did not discuss and why: This proved especially interesting. Throughout the interviews we encouraged our informants to give detailed examples of these conversations.

Shared Enthusiasm

Although we are chiefly interested in upwardly mobile students, their experience is more striking if we compare it to that of their middle-class peers. We therefore begin with a group of informants whose college-educated parents provide vigorous encouragement and practical assistance. Listening to them, we get the impression that higher education has become a family project.

> **Mike:** My father would say, "Have you heard anything from the schools yet? Well, maybe you should call them. Isn't it getting late? We have to figure out a financial plan for the year. How much is it going to cost?" All that kind of, you know, dealing with logistical stuff.
> **Sarah:** There were times when I needed emotional support or I didn't have time to do my laundry or run to the library or the post office. They are supportive in that aspect, and of course it makes it very easy. My mother says, "What is the worst case scenario? What if you don't get in, how can we get you in?"

These informants describe the practical help that their parents offer: running to the library, figuring out a financial plan. At the same time, they point to something more: a sense that their parents are engaged with them in their ambitions.

> **Interviewer:** What happens when you and your family talk about graduate school?
> **Robert:** I go from the sublime to the very bleak. I say, "If this happens it could be very good. But it could also be bad, like this. . . ." And they offer their input, and it ends up being a conversation that is somewhat emotionally charged with hope and expectation, you know? They're very happy to see that I know what I think I want to do with the rest of my life.

Several students mentioned that their parents' reassurance seemed grounded in experience. If these parents sound, at times, hardheaded, they also make the steps toward a viable profession seem less mysterious. This, as we will show in a moment, differs sharply from the experience of upwardly mobile students.

> **Elizabeth:** It is not so much like they are giving me a big hug and telling me everything is going to be okay. My father, he's a surgeon, and he makes good money. I was raised to buy things when I wanted and not worry about whether I could afford them. That is my biggest doubt, will I be able to afford what I want? And my father will point out that he makes a lot of money, but he has to work on Saturday and Sunday, and that you have to work extra hours, if that is what it takes. My father is very level-headed, so I have a more realistic outlook after talking to him.

Of course, parents who turn graduate school into a family project may seem intrusive. Some of these students needed to make clear to their parents, and maybe to themselves, that their ambitions are their own. Mike, with whom we began, described his parents "pushing, poking and prodding, sometimes basically pushing me out the door and saying, 'Go to the mailbox.' I knew their intentions were to be helpful, but it was not. So I was like, 'Get out of my life.'"

> **Sean:** I didn't tell them I was going to law school; it wasn't open for discussion at all. I didn't want them to expect that I was going to get in to a good law school or something, and I wanted to make sure that they knew it was my choice, and if I wanted to, like, bag it in the middle, I could just do that. So I made sure that they knew I was just doing it for me.

Despite their parents' occasional intrusiveness, most middle-class students were grateful for their support. Having a strong sense of connection to their parents helped these students feel that their plans are worthwhile and likely to succeed. This contrasts markedly with the experience of the upwardly mobile.

Benevolent Misunderstanding

The second group consists of upwardly mobile students who feel that their parents value higher education and try to support their ambitions. However, these parents do not understand the details of graduate school or the careers to which it leads. These students feel that their parents lack the experience to offer meaningful advice or reassurance. Although students in this group do not disagree with their parents about fundamental values, many of them end up feeling isolated in their families.

> **Interviewer:** Is there anything that your parents don't understand about your plans or about graduate school?

Ann: You know, I don't think they understood a whole lot about college. When I was in high school I would hear other students talk about their parents contacting schools, doing this and doing that, making the kids sit down and write out their application. As important as it was to my Dad for me to go to college, he took absolutely no part in the process, and I think it was just that they had no concept of what it involved.

Not only were these parents unable to advise their children, they could not provide meaningful reassurance. Several students were frustrated by their parents' unwarranted optimism.

Interviewer: Is there anything your parents don't understand about graduate school?
Pat: The whole damn thing. My parents have no concept of what undergrad is, what nursing school applications are. They don't know that kind of stuff. My Dad is just a Dad, and his little girl can just about do anything, you know, walk on water, the whole bit.
Beverly: I think they're under the impression that if you're bright and you apply yourself you'll just be accepted. They don't realize that for every 100 slots, 7,000 people apply.

In a poignant reversal of roles, many of these students, recognizing that their parents cannot offer meaningful reassurance, refrain from talking about their own worries.

Interviewer: Is there anything in particular that you find yourself keeping to yourself?
Barbara: I think the struggle of it; the financial strain. They see my life as being easy and carefree, they don't see the strain.
Interviewer: Why don't you tell them about the struggle?
Barbara: There is nothing they can do about it. They would just worry and be concerned and I don't want them to do that. They struggle with so much on their own, and I think we all just really take care of ourselves, out of mutual consideration and concern, because we don't want to burden one another. The funny thing is that we end up withdrawing from each other so as not to overburden the other.

Once again, we hear a connection between the practical side of family support and the more personal sense of a family bond. Students whose parents could not help them with applications or with realistic encouragement often ended up feeling isolated within their families.

Interviewer: How do you end up feeling after you talk to them?
Joanne: Probably more distant. They think if you have a degree as a nurse, there will always be a job. And that is no longer true; hospitals are laying people off; it is so hard to find jobs. So a lot of times I'll walk away from a conversation and I'll be like, "These people, you just don't understand what's going on out there."

Interviewer: How do you end up feeling after having a conversation with your family?

Frank: I guess a little distant. Like if I bring up a thought about the type of school I am interested in, they won't go into it much, or talk much about it. And so I'll just sort of back off, and realize that it is up to me. I might be looking for an answer from them that they don't really have.

Jeff: I got a paper accepted at a conference and they were happy for me but they didn't really understand the magnitude of that achievement, that it was my first paper accepted at a conference, being a very special thing and a big deal. I am starting to keep things to myself because I have come to expect my parents' support and understanding through high school and undergraduate but now with the PhD I find that when I discuss things with them it's like flat soda. I am expecting a fizzy soda and I'm getting a flat soda.

Estrangement

Our final group is composed of students who seem more profoundly estranged from their families. If the dominant mood among benevolently misunderstood students is sadness, the characteristic mood in our last group is anger. Misunderstood students feel that their parents value higher education and want to help but do not know how. Estranged students say that their parents deride graduate school (and often college, too); they refuse to help even when they can.

Many of the arguments in these families center on whether higher education is a good investment—or at least, this is where they begin. Of course, some academic subjects seem more likely to pay off than others; working-class parents are particularly irritated when—as they see it—their children waste time and money studying subjects that have little connection to any job.

Interviewer: Say you sit down with him and say, "I want to go into Art History." How would the conversation go?

Todd: He'd say, "What the fuck do you want to do that for? What kind of a job is that going to give you?"

Karen: If I said, "Dad, I want to get a master's in philosophy," he'd be like, "Why, that's silly. Why are you going to waste your money doing that; you're not going to be able to find a job; didn't you learn anything from getting a BA in English, and not having a minor in business or marketing? When I couldn't find a job he used to throw it up in my face. "Well, what did you expect, what were you doing being an English major anyway? I told you so."

Jim: My Dad thinks I am a complete idiot.

Interviewer: Why is that?

Jim: Oh, just because I am very idealistic, and I am not practical, and I tend to get started on things that, that are stupid. Like going to school and.... You know, I have been involved in activism too, like going to Greenpeace, an organization that "really doesn't do any work," just things like that.

Not surprisingly, parents who consider their children's graduate plans irresponsible are reluctant to pay for them. Of course, finances are tight in many of these families. However, our informants insist that the amounts in question were easily within their parents' reach—and obviously justified.

Kim: My car broke down my last semester of school and I couldn't get to work, I couldn't get to finals and I needed my father to wire me some money to get this car out of the shop. And I begged my father and he said, "If you had a job you wouldn't be where you are right now." So, that was the only time I broke to ask. I just never asked, and the one time I did he said, "No." So, I just haven't. I won't let them say, "No" again.
Interviewer: How would they feel about your wanting to become a teacher or a high school guidance counselor?
Chris: My father has no understanding of that. He thinks it is some pointy-headed liberal sort of bullshit. I would have needed $800 a semester to go to Columbia, because everything else would have been paid for through grants and loans. So I would have needed some help on the rent, but he just thought it was way too much money. I never asked him for money to get through college until then. He said, "You're not a bum."

These vignettes sound angrier than anything we have heard so far— this suggests to us that arguments over money may have triggered some deeper dispute. These parents sound outraged by what they regard as their children's presumption of entitlement. In contrast, the parents advocate the virtue of hard work and self-reliance.

Bill: The decision in my family was that they weren't going to help to pay for college. You were on your own once you graduated from high school; that was just the way. My old man was one that, he came up from the ranks and struggled, and you were going to do the same. That was his idea, you had to struggle to know what life was all about.

Naturally, upwardly mobile students respect hard work and self-reliance—don't we all? At the same time, they point out how tough their parents' lives have been, and suggest that they want something very different for themselves.

Sam: My father is one of those "pulled myself up by the bootstraps and so everyone else should" type of people. "When I was your age I was working in a donut shop at four in the morning," and this, that, and the other.

Interviewer: Why do you think he tells you this story?

Sam: To show me how hard work like that will make me successful like him. But I don't really want to be like him. I respect and thank him, but his idea of succeeding in life is going out, working hard, and not being happy.

One way to read these passages is that upwardly mobile students regard their fathers as rigidly moralistic. They are obsessed with character—especially the virtue of making one's own way—to the expense of everything else. Chris's father, refusing to help with tuition, tells him, "You're not a bum," Chris himself emphasizes the wasted opportunity. Kim's father punishes her for what he sees as her improvidence; Kim herself focuses on his intransigence in an emergency. Sam acknowledges his father's stoicism but underscores his unhappiness, and Bill doubts whether there is any larger lesson to be learned from struggling.

However, it would be inexact to say that upwardly mobile students regard their parents as preoccupied with character and they themselves are simply pragmatic. Upwardly mobile students make their own judgments about character; however, their judgments seem to be organized differently. For working-class parents, the crucial distinction may be between responsibility and indulgence; for upwardly mobile students, however, the salient distinction may be between self-assertion and humility. In the following passage Kim draws a vivid picture of the gulf between herself and her family, both in terms of how they live and how they think.

Kim: Neither of my parents thought I should go to college. I am the only one in my family to go to college. My mother's ideal child would've got married and had children like the rest of the girls did. I wasn't interested in that and so therefore it's "What are you doing? You are wasting your time. You are never going to get in; you are not smart enough, you are not this enough, you're going to be an old maid." If I am not standing up to what she thinks is par then I have disgraced her.

Interviewer: How does that make you feel? The disgraced part?

Kim: I just feel, you know my sisters got married and had children at 18, 19 years old, and that is crazy. I mean, my sisters are living in trailers, working in grocery marts, you know, like for $5 an hour. I would take my life before I would take that kind of life and yet my mother looks at them as if "they are married, they have children, they're. . . ."

Interviewer: Successful?

Kim: Exactly. That's success, and what I'm doing is not successful, and I'm just like, "What are you guys, crazy?" Sometimes I feel like the whole world is crazy, my family, and I'm just like, "that's so abnormal." So I think I'm the only sane one, sometimes.

When Kim says that she would sooner die than live like her sisters she is, in part, talking about material well-being. Yet it seems to us that what Kim finds horrifying is not only her sisters' dead-end lives but their passive acquiescence. This sort of life seems normal to them—desirable, even—this is what makes her family seem, to Kim, "crazy," and she seems to them "disgraceful." We might say much the same about Sam. The problem is not merely that his father got up each morning at four to make the donuts but that, (according to Sam) "his idea of . . . life is . . . working hard, and not being happy." Two further quotes make much the same point.

> **Annette:** I am just in a different world from what they are in. In the working-class world, you know, you are to be humble and thankful for what you have, and by criticizing what you have you are basically criticizing everyone around you. By saying, "I don't want this life" you are telling them, "What you have is not good enough for me." I wish we agreed more. They don't mean to be mean or hurtful but there is an unspoken accusation that I think I am better than they are. I can't even state my opinion without being accused. I am like, "Give me a break, all I said was. . . ." So I watch what I say. I can't go home for long stretches of time, just for the sheer intellectual isolation of it, I suppose.

Another young woman, who dropped out of a master's program in education when it seemed intellectually superficial, said that she would never try to explain her reasons to her family.

> **Barbara:** There is that sense of, "What do you want; who do you think you are?" They see it as kind of an arrogance: "You think you are better." So I try to avoid anything that can be misconstrued as that. There have been so many hurtful, name-calling sorts of things. I'll comment on buying into some kind of media gimmick, and ridicule it, innocently, in the way I would just with friends, "how can people be so stupid?" And I am sitting with a table of people who have totally bought whatever line it was. And they are really resentful. My sister has had real problems, getting angry with me, telling me I am demeaning. Like coming out of a movie and deconstructing things, people get really irritated back home, because you don't go to a movie to think. A week ago my younger sister started talking about a critic that she just happened to catch on the radio, a feminist, criticizing a film. She told me the plot, and I said something sarcastic, and she said, "That's what the critic said, and I kind of got it." I was ready to say, "Yeah!" And she looked at me and said, "You think that way all the time," and I said, "Kind of. . . ." And she said, "It can get kind of annoying when you do it all the time." And I said, "How do you think it feels for me that around here, no one ever does it?"

These passages raise a mixture of issues. All of these informants tell us that they want a better life than that of their parents and siblings. Part of what they have in mind is material well-being: Kim does not want to end up working in a grocery mart and living in a trailer. In addition, many of them want lives in which there is a larger place for ideas: Barbara wants an education, not just a credential; she notes that "back home . . . you don't go to a movie to think." As we heard earlier, some hope to pursue careers that offer scope for creativity and public service. All of them tell us that these aspirations seem impractical to their families.

But to say only this is not enough. These students feel that their parents regard them as not only impractical but irresponsible and self-indulgent. From this perspective, there is something wrong not just with their view of the world but with their character. If our informants are right, we understand more of their parents' anger. How dare Barbara drop out of a master's program that will supply her with perfectly good teaching credentials just because she finds it intellectually lightweight? Who does she think she is? In the same vein, how can any responsible person waste time on art history, or philosophy, or Greenpeace—and expect someone else to pick up the tab?

In turn, these upwardly mobile students render a corresponding judgment against their parents: not merely that they have lived tough lives (for this in itself might be honorable) but that they have made a virtue of being satisfied with their meager portion. Our informants are appalled by the sort of personality that could find such dreary lives acceptable. This is a moral failing of a different sort: a failure of nerve, or imagination, or perhaps simply of desire. Annette says, "In the working-class world you are to be humble and thankful." Barbara describes inadvertently ridiculing "people who have totally bought whatever line it was." Kim concludes, "That's success . . . and that is crazy."

We are finally ready to see how upwardly mobile students and their parents speak past each other. The issue—both sides might agree—is entitlement. Further, they agree, one's sense of entitlement reflects not only one's judgment of opportunity but one's character. However, entitlement carries opposite valences for the students and their parents. If one regards the world as a difficult place, and if, in consequence, one regards character in terms of responsibility versus self-indulgence, then to feel entitled is a moral failure.

However, the picture changes if one sees a wider range of opportunity, and if one thinks that some people make the most of their chances whereas others settle—humbly and gullibly—for less. From this perspective entitlement is not just an accurate assessment of one's chances, it is an index of character. The alternative is to acquiesce, passively and humbly, in one's own disenfranchisement—it is to be servile not just in one's material condition but in one's soul.

This, we think, is the charge that upwardly mobile students level against their parents—never, perhaps, in so many words, but in their actions.

We suspect that parents recognize this (though again, perhaps without ever putting the matter so explicitly), and this may explain the anger behind their incredulity. "Who do you think you are?"—and who do you think I am, if I have chosen differently?

CONCLUSION

In these last pages we want to underline some ideas and also suggest how this discussion might be extended. Upwardly mobile students face a problem. Somehow they must explain, if only to their own satisfaction, why the world into which they were born—and that seems world enough to their parents and siblings—seems to them inadequate. This is a variation on a standard problem—one that personal narratives are supposed to help us solve: How do we justify the choices we have made, and intend to keep on making, when those choices seem unreasonable to those who matter to us? We may start by considering two very different answers. Years ago, C. Wright Mills (1959) outlined one kind of understanding that he thought might help people see their way forward:

> Nowadays men often feel that their private lives are a series of traps. They sense that within their everyday worlds, they cannot overcome their troubles. . . . They are bounded by the private orbits in which they live; their vision and their powers are limited to the close-up scenes of job, family, neighborhood; in other milieux they move vicariously and remain spectators. And the more they become aware, however vaguely, of ambitions and of threats which transcend their immediate locales, the more trapped they seem to feel. . . . What they need . . . is a quality of mind that will help them . . . to achieve lucid summations of what is going on in the world and of what may be happening within themselves. It is this quality . . . that may be called the sociological imagination. (p. 3)

To be accurate, Mills was concerned with a different problem than are our informants. He was interested in the kind of insight that helps people improve the social system in which they live—upward mobility improves only the life of each individual. Nevertheless, Mills's observation may be pertinent. Even if one is changing only one's own station in life, one needs to justify this change. Mills suggests one way to do this: by framing one's disenchantment with "close-up scenes of job, family, neighborhood" (p. 3) in the context of a larger social vision.

Sociological insight may strike many of us as an ideal—nowhere more so than when we are trying to explain why some people end up with more of the pie than others. The alternative—explanations framed in terms of individual character—is likely to disguise the source of our trouble and immunize us against social change. (Plato suggested that the lower orders may be reconciled to their station if it is explained to them that at birth their souls were mixed with lead instead of gold or silver. In our day, theorists more concerned with mobilizing the disenfranchised than pacifying them make the converse recommendation. Garfinkel (1981), for example, notes that in trying to explain why some individuals do better than others, we divert attention from the more important question: Why do we have so skewed a distribution of winners and losers?)

Yet if sociological explanations seem more liberative (at least to theorists) they may also seem abstract, bloodless, and therefore less urgent than explanations framed in terms of character. Linde (1993) found that ordinary people justify their careers by pointing to longstanding personal interests. In contrast, explanations couched in terms of life circumstances seem, to speakers and audiences, insufficient. "An explanation rooted within the self . . . is preferable to one rooted outside . . . [which] invites attribution to either accident or determinism" (p. 131).

Ideally, our informants might find a way of combining perspectives. Like Mills's puzzled subjects, they are trying to see beyond their immediate situation—and therefore, perhaps, need to understand themselves sociologically. At the same time their explanations must carry the kind of conviction that counts in our culture. However, this combination does not come easily; usually, we describe our choices as reflecting either our personality or our circumstances. (Linde found that we attribute our successful choices to our personality and our failures to circumstance.) We prefer monochromatic explanations because each offers a distinct justification. By explaining at least our happy choices in terms of "selfhood" we claim that we were bound to act as we did to be true to ourselves. Our "selves" seem irrevocable—therefore, choices made in their name cannot be impeached. The force of this argument would be lost (or so it often seems) if, instead, our choices seemed dictated by our situation—because of course our situation might have been different.

Yet even if we appreciate the rationale behind the rhetoric of selfhood, we can imagine alternatives. Psychosocial theorists routinely point out that the "self" that each of us has come to be was shaped by our milieu—and might conceivably seem no less precious to us for this influence. What makes our upwardly mobile students interesting is that they illustrate—if only in a tentative, preliminary way—how psychosocial understanding might help in ordinary life. Our informants have developed hybrid accounts in which sociology and personality are woven together. Both of these threads seem essential to their motivation.

Upwardly mobile students see a connection between a social milieu (the working-class world) and a certain kind of personality—more exactly, some assumptions about what sort of person one *should* be. That is, they suggest not only that their parents have ill-paid and uninspiring jobs, that they have little appreciation of certain kinds of ideas, that they do not know how to pull the levers that get one into a better school or job. Certainly, all this is important, but there is something more. In addition, our informants say their parents are constrained by their attitude. The problem is not just that they do not know how to seize the world and shake it but that they regard as indecent the presumption that one should. In short, upwardly mobile students feel that they have entered a world where people not only have more and know more but one that takes for granted a different notion of character.

At the same time, these stories mobilize change because they are not only about character but about the relation between character and social class. One is "humble and grateful" not only as a matter of individual temperament but because this is what one's culture expects. Because one is humble, or grateful, or stoic—instead of appropriately demanding—one is likely to remain in that demeaning position. Telling the story this way, to us and to themselves, our informants not only explain how they differ from their parents, they commit themselves to a different trajectory. They will continue their education, get different jobs, live in different neighbor-hoods—not just because these will pay better or be more prestigious—but because in this way they hope to realize a different way of being.

We want to emphasize how important this connection—between character and culture—is to our informants. By focusing on character they invest their choices with an urgency and a legitimacy that they might otherwise lack. Kim's rejection of her sisters' lives might seem narrowly materialistic if she pointed only to their dead-end jobs. By underscoring their complacency, she makes her rejection of their world morally unassailable. Of course, we do not mean that character is more important to our informants than anything else; the point, rather, is that a certain way of thinking seems to them an inseparable part of the working-class world and a significant reason why it is intolerable to them.

In underscoring the connection between psychological and sociological self-awareness we are repeating a point made years ago by Erikson. Identity denotes "the whole interplay between the psychological and the social," and therefore "it would be obviously wrong to let some terms of personology . . . on the one hand . . . and [purely sociological theories], on the other, take over the area to be studied. . . ." (1968, p. 23). Like Erikson, our informants explain how class and character are twin faces of one coin.

Erikson, however, was chiefly interested in how people feel when they have found their niche in life. Therefore, he regarded the goal of identity development (if not its intermediate steps) as the conviction that one's personality and one's cultural membership are "identical" (1968, p. 22). Or, as he said elsewhere, it is the half-surprised recognition that one's community is prepared to embrace the person one has become.

Upwardly mobile students face a different problem—they have to explain why the niche that threatens to absorb them is the wrong sort. If they allowed themselves to be embraced by their parents' community, this would come at the expense of their character. (Of course, upwardly mobile students hope to be embraced by a new community—in this sense they are moving toward a new identity. Yet to say only this would not be strong enough. These students seem urgently motivated by what they are leaving behind. To see this, we need ideas that capture the power of recognizing—intensely—the disparity between one's character and the milieu that one is trying to escape.)

Part of what makes Erikson's theory interesting is that it traces the convoluted turns by which young people resolve an identity and the risks of doing so without testing one's limits and the limits of one's milieu. In the same spirit we might wonder what sort of developmental history has led our upwardly mobile informants to their present self-understanding. In asking this question we are going beyond anything that we heard. Whatever we say on this point, then, should be regarded as speculative—more a description of what we would like to hear than a prediction.

We assume that people develop a psychosocial perspective gradually. It seems likely that when our informants were younger they understood themselves and their parents in more purely psychological terms. Perhaps they were seen by their families, and saw themselves, as dreamy or bookish, lacking talent or interest in the things their families valued, perhaps as loners, malcontents, snobs. No doubt (especially as they grew older) these students regarded their parents in reciprocally unflattering ways: as having little imagination or drive, or as superficial and prejudiced, sad, bitter—or unreasonably complacent. (In short, much the way Kim describes her family.)

Gradually some of them came to regard things more sociologically. They saw that the choices their parents made and the judgments that they render (on their own lives and their children's) are not simply a matter of individual personality but of their culture. (Like Annette, they started to say, "In the working-class world you are supposed to be. . . .") Seeing their family disputes in more cultural terms may have allowed our informants to be more tolerant of both their parents and themselves. Yet this would by no means have made them any more willing to accept such lives for themselves. Instead, they may have reached the conclusion that to be working-class is not just a matter of one's job but a way of being—one that seemed intolerable—and that they needed to escape.

To repeat: These are only speculations (but see Ochberg, 1992; Wiersma, 1992, for examples). We cannot say how many students would tell us anything like this history. We can, however, say why such a story would be important: It would illustrate how a certain kind of development matters. At one time (we imagine) the way forward would seem blocked—not just because it seemed difficult but because it seemed illegitimate. Then at another time the way forward would seem more open—not just because one has found a pragmatic solution (say, going to graduate school), but because one has come to understand differently the relationship between one's character and one's milieu—and this makes a new trajectory seem both reasonable and urgent. Were students able to tell us such a story it would illustrate how a certain kind of insight comes about and how it may transform one's life.

APPENDIX: MEASURES USED[1]

FAMILY ENGAGEMENT

College students sometimes feel that their experiences at school have changed their relationship with their families—sometimes for the better, sometimes for the worse. Here we would like to know how you feel that you and your family are getting along these days.

1. My family often doesn't understand the ups and downs of my life.
2. I wish my family could offer me more helpful advice.
3. Even when we disagree my family takes my point of view seriously.
4. Sometimes my family seems disappointed in the choices I'm making.
5. My family seems pleased that I am finding my own way.
6. My family doesn't really expect me to accomplish the things I want.
7. My family doesn't even know what kind of courses I am taking.
8. The differences between me and my family could never change how close we are.
9. Sometimes I feel I am turning my back on everything I was taught.
10. I hardly ever talk about school or my plans for the future with my family.
11. My family would be more likely to tell me the problems with something I want to do than encourage me to do it.
12. Often, my family and I just don't know what to say to each other.
13. Too often my family doesn't seem interested in what I am doing.
14. Sometimes I feel confused about whether I still believe the things my family taught me.
15. Sometimes I feel a little embarrassed by things people in my family think or say.
16. My family supports who I am and how I am different from them.

THE VALUE OF EDUCATION

Some people see higher education as a way to guarantee a good life; others are much more skeptical about whether college or graduate school are really worthwhile. Here we want to find out how your family feels about the value of higher education. Score each item as you think your parents

---

[1] All items were scored on five point Likert scales.

would answer it. If you think your parents would disagree, choose the one whose opinion matters most to you.

1. College teaches you to appreciate the finer things in life.
2. The chances of a good life are slim without a college degree.
3. Well-educated people seem to lead more fulfilled lives.
4. The people who get the best grades are not necessarily those who do best in the real world.
5. People today need more education to get good careers.
6. A lot of well-educated people are really snobs.
7. Education doesn't seem to help people tell right from wrong.
8. Most employers are more impressed by hard work and intelligence than academic credentials.
9. The more educated you are, the more tolerant you are of other points of view.
10. Well-educated people not only know more, they somehow seem more cultured.
11. There is some truth to the stereotype that the best students are often unattractive in other ways.
12. A college education changes the way you work out your problems.
13. A lot of what you learn in college has little practical application.
14. People with more education treat each other with more respect.
15. What you need to know to do a job well you never learn in school.
16. When you consider how much time and money you sacrifice, college or graduate school are not such great investments.
17. College is a way to gain prestige and independence.

COMMITMENT

Often students feel that although they have some ideas about the sort of work they enjoy, they are not sure about the practical details of getting started on a career once they leave college—or about the sacrifices they may have to make before their long-term plans work out. In this section we would like to find out how far you have gone in working out the details of your future plans.

1. I would be willing to borrow a substantial amount of money to pay for the additional education I may need for my career.
2. I am willing to move to another state in order to pursue the career I want.
3. I am prepared to postpone getting married in order to get started on my career.

4. I am prepared to go to graduate school for several years in order to prepare for the career I want.
5. I would work for a year or two at a low-paying job just to get the experience I need for my career or graduate plans.
6. I am prepared to put off buying my own home for 5–10 years in order to get my career established.
7. I won't sacrifice many more years just to prepare for a somewhat better career; I want to start living an adult life soon.
8. I am not willing to move away from the people I love just to pursue a better job or more education.

REFERENCES

Alexander, K., Eckland, B., & Griffin, L. (1975). The Wisconsin model of socioeconomic achievement: A replication. *American Journal of Sociology, 81*, 324–342.

Anyon, J. (1987). Social class and the hidden curriculum of work. In E. Stevens & G. Wood (Eds.), *Justice, ideology, and education.* (pp. 210–225). New York: Random House.

Armsden, G., & Greenberg, M. (1987). The inventory of parent and peer attachment: Individual differences and their relationship to psychological well-being in adolescence. *Journal of Youth & Adolescence, 16*, 427–454.

Blustein, D., Walbridge, M., Friedlander, M., & Palladino, D. (1991). Contributions of psychological separation and parental attachment to the career development process. *Journal of Counseling Psychology, 38(1)*, 39–50.

Bourdieu, P., & Passeron, J. (1977). *Reproduction in education, society, and culture.* Beverly Hills, CA: Sage.

Clark, B., Heist, P., McConnell, M., Trow, M., & Yonge, G. (1972). *Students and colleges: Interaction and change.* Berkeley: University of California, Center for Research and Development in Higher Education.

Coleman R., & Rainwater, L. (1978). *Social standing in America.* New York: Basic Books.

Conklin, M., & Dailey, A. (1981). Does consistency of parental educational encouragement matter for secondary school students? *Sociology of Education, 54*, 254–262.

DiMaggio, P. (1982). Cultural capital and school success. *American Sociological Review, 47*, 189–201.

DiMaggio, P., & Mohr, J. (1985). Cultural capital, educational attainment and marital selection. *American Journal of Sociology, 90(6)*, 123–161.

Ellis, R., & Lane, C. (1967). Social mobility and social isolation: A test of Sorokin's dissociative hypothesis. *American Sociological Review, 32*, 237–253.

Erikson, E. (1968). *Identity: Youth and crisis.* New York: Norton.

Fitzgerald, F. (1926). The rich boy. In *All the sad young men*. New York: Scribner.

Garfinkel, A. (1981). *Forms of explanation: Rethinking the questions in social theory*. New Haven, CT: Yale University Press.

Granfield, R. (1991). Making it by faking it: Working class students in an elite academic environment. *Journal of Contemporary Ethnography, 20*, 331–351.

Grotevant, H., & Cooper, C. (1985). Patterns of interaction in family relationships and the development of identity exploration in adolescence. *Child Development, 56*, 425–428.

Hemingway, E. (1938). The snows of Kilimanjaro. In *The fifth column and the first forty-nine stories*. New York: Collier.

Higginbotham, E., & Webber, L. (1992). Moving up with kin and community. *Gender & Society, 6(3)*, 416–440.

Josselson, R. (1980). Ego development in adolescence. In J. Adelson (Ed.), *Handbook of adolescent psychology* (pp. 188–210). New York: Wiley.

Kahl, J. (1953). *The American class structure*. New York: Rinehart & Company.

Kohn, M. (1977). *Class and conformity*. Chicago: University of Chicago Press.

Lamont, M. (1992). *Money, morals, and manners: The culture of the French and American upper-middle class*. Chicago: The University of Chicago Press.

Lareau, A. (1987). Social class differences in family-school relationships: The importance of cultural capital. *Sociology of Education, 60*, 73–85.

Lapsley, D., Rice, K., & Fitzgerald, D. (1990). Adolescent attachment, identity, and adjustment to college: Implications for the continuity of adaptation hypothesis. *Journal of Counseling and Development, 68*, 561–565.

Linde, C. (1993). *Life stories: The creation of coherence*. New York: Oxford University Press.

London, H. (1989). Breaking away: A study of first generation college students and their families. *American Journal of Education*, 144–170.

McClelland, K. (1990). Cumulative disadvantage among the highly ambitious. *Sociology of Education, 63*, 102–121.

Mills, C. W. (1959). *The sociological imagination*. New York: Oxford University Press.

Ochberg, R. (1992). Social insight and psychological liberation. In G. Rosenwald & R. Ochberg (Eds.), *Storied lives*. New Haven, CT: Yale University Press.

Perry, W. (1968). *Forms of intellectual and ethical development in the college years*. Cambridge: Harvard University Press.

Ryan, J., & Sackrey, C. (1984). *Strangers in paradise: Academics from the working class*. Boston: South End Press.

Sewell, W., & Shah, V. (1968). Social class, parental encouragement, and educational aspirations. *American Journal of Sociology, 73*, 559–572.

Stevens, G., & Cho, J. (1985). Socioeconomic indexes and the 1980 census occupational classification scheme. *Social Science Research, 14,* 142–168.

Wegner, E. (1973). The effects of upward social mobility: A study of working status college students. *Sociology of Education, 46,* 263–279.

Wiersma, J. (1992). Karen: The transforming story. In G. Rosenwald & R. Ochberg (Eds.), *Storied lives* (pp. 195–213). New Haven, CT: Yale University Press.

6

SERENDIPITY AND AGENCY IN NARRATIVES OF TRANSITION: YOUNG ADULT WOMEN AND THEIR CAREERS

MARCY PLUNKETT

The choice of career and process of entry into the adult world of work is complicated for women, and the subjective experience of that process is little understood (Phillips & Imhoff, 1997). A significant body of research exists on topics of external as well as internalized factors of career development in women. Yet more is needed to understand the internal experience of career entry for women—that is, how young women themselves make meaning of their choices and actions. To date, much of the research on career development has been psychometric and trait-oriented, rather than focused on the meaning created by the individual as she or he constructs it in a social context (Young & Collin, 1992). This study focuses on the construction of meaning concerning career identity development in the narratives of college-educated women seeking professional careers.

The challenges young women now face in choosing and entering adult career paths are different from those of earlier cohorts of women who had more restricted choices available to them, but they remain considerable nonetheless. The process of arriving at a commitment to a career and the strategy for pursuing it can be painful, gradual, and uncertain in our time of rapid changes in work–family roles, where multiple options are possible but role models and mentors are limited, and there is intense competition for graduate school and careers (see Erikson, 1968; Josselson, 1987; Larson, Butler, Wilson, Medora, & Allgood, 1994; Levinson, 1996; Stickel & Bonett, 1991; White, 1966). Erikson has characterized this process as particularly problematic: "In general it is the inability to settle on an occupational identity which most disturbs young people" (Erikson, 1968, p. 132). Although he was referring primarily to men, the observation now fits young women as well. For both men and women, the process is complicated by the coexisting process of seeking and achieving intimacy in stable adult relationships. With most educated young women expecting to combine career and marriage, this process in early adulthood may well be more complex than ever (Goldin, 1997; Plunkett, Hassinger, & Hollenshead, 1995). A considerable body of work beginning in the 1920s concerning educated women's adult development points to the internal value placed on relational ties and sees it as a major factor in women's complicated career pathways, contributing to the subordination of individualistic career goals (Angrist & Almquist, 1975; Arnold, 1993; Douvan & Adelson, 1966; Gilbert, 1993; Gilligan, 1982; Helson, Pals, & Solomon, 1997; Hulbert & Schuster, 1993; Jordan, Kaplan, Miller, Stiver, & Surrey, 1991; Josselson, 1987, 1990, 1996; Larson et al., 1994; Lieblich, 1987; Luzzo & Hutcheson, 1996; McClelland, 1975; Miller, 1976; Plunkett et al., 1995; Roberts & Newton, 1987; Stickel & Bonett, 1991; Veroff, 1983).

This study proposes to illuminate the career identity process by following the lives of a small number of young women from college graduation into their mid-20s via a combination of quantitative and qualitative methods: intensive, open-ended interviews and questionnaires. Their material reveals the narratives or "inner scripts" (Conway, 1998) constructed by these young women to describe and guide their lives in the crucial transition from late adolescence to adult identity development that takes place in the early 20s. This developmental period, aptly titled the "novice phase" (Levinson, 1996), is one in which the main parameters of the adult identity are laid down, often through a process of experiential trial and error. In this study the narratives are conceived of as the subjective accounts rendered by the women to describe their passages from adolescent to committed, adult career identities. These narratives are compared, in turn, with some objective, behavioral data of actual career choices made in this period.

People often hold personal accounts of their lives that are in some ways dissonant with observers' accounts to meet the multiple demands of contemporaneous cultural conventions as well as personal defense mechanisms. For women in particular, it has frequently been noted that personal ambition and agency may be perceived by the outside observer but minimized or overlooked in the subjective experience of the individual to conform to gendered expectations of women. For example, Heilbrun (1988) and Conway (1998) have pointed to the absence of personal ambition and the dominance of uncertainty in the autobiographical narratives of some outstanding women such as Golda Meir and Eleanor Roosevelt. In addition to the complexity inherent in synthesizing gendered, historical, and individual personality aspects into the formation of a subjective narrative of career identity, we would expect that each developmental period of life would influence the content of the preferred personal narrative.

SERENDIPITY AND AGENCY

In reviewing the contemporary scholarship on career development for women we find an ongoing discussion of two important contrasting concepts, agency and serendipity. Agency is the easier concept to describe. Introduced into the psychological literature by Bakan (1966), it is used synonymously with intentionality and instrumentality and is thus embedded in a "quest" narrative, implying the existence of a clear goal, strategy, and unflagging ambition, impervious to temporary setbacks and distractions. It includes a determination to create educational and career opportunities, not only a willingness to respond to such opportunities (Betz & Hackett, 1987). It is a highly individualistic notion in which relational considerations are clearly secondary in priority, regarded as interferences that must be resisted, or at best, delayed. Not surprisingly, this is widely regarded as a model based on men's development and not characteristic of most women's lives (Bateson, 1990; Heilbrun, 1988; Josselson, 1990).

The presence and nature of agency in women's career development has been a major focus of psychological research. It is defined in the research literature as the existence of internalized behaviors and competencies that further one's career. This includes taking initiative in creating and respond-ing to opportunities, risk-taking, persistence, and ability to assess and modify plans to achieve a better fit between goals and choices (Ancis & Phillips, 1996; Betz & Fitzgerald, 1987; Betz & Hackett, 1987; Clausen, 1991). Nu-merous studies have linked career agency to self-efficacy expectations, or inter-nal self-confidence that one will actually undertake or use career-agentic be-haviors (Ancis & Phillips, 1996; Betz & Hackett, 1981, 1987; Phillips & Imhoff, 1997). Accumulated research as well as clinical experience suggest that young women are hampered in their career agency—in other words, the focused pursuit of educational and career goals. External constraints and sex-role stereotypes, manifested within academic environments, family of origin, and the culture as a whole, presumably play a role in women's behavior. Lack of appropriate mentoring and inadequate training of career agency skills for women in college have also been suggested (Helson et al., 1997; Phillips & Imhoff, 1997). As described previously, the importance women place on de-veloping close relational ties, existing and expected in their futures, also act to impede or complicate young women's career agency (Larson et al., 1994).

Serendipity is less elaborated and researched in the field of psychology than is agency. I would propose that it offers multiple insights into the career identity experience of contemporary young women and is particularly relevant to the process of identity formation in times of developmental transition. With its emphasis on the unplanned aspects of experience, it can serve to illuminate the creative process that is inherent in developing a personal identity.

A major problem in describing the role of serendipity in women's careers is the lack of consistency and clarity in the use of the term by researchers, which tends to confuse the issues. *Webster's Unabridged Dictionary* defines it as "an assumed gift for finding valuable or agreeable things *not sought for*" (italics added; p. 2072). Allegedly Horace Walpole coined the word in a letter in 1754, referring to the ancient Persian fairy tale of the fifth century, "The Three Princes of Serendip," in which three young men on the brink of adult life are sent on a quest by their father to save the kingdom as well as to prepare them for the adult responsibilities they would soon shoulder. Walpole was referring to accidental scientific discoveries, and in fact the term serendipity is used in the history of science to describe unexpected scientific discoveries or inventions, such as Fleming's famous discovery of penicillin from mold in an improperly closed Petri dish (Austin, 1978; Kantorovich, 1993; Roberts, 1989).

Within the career development literature, serendipity has found its most explicit expression in feminist, narrative scholarship on women (Bateson, 1990; Tomlinson-Keasey, 1990, 1994). Its use implies an internal stance that is in many ways the obverse of agency: the absence of a preconceived intent, goal, or strategy to achieve a predetermined result. Self-awareness of power and motivation as emanating from within is muted, and external factors such as chance, accident, or circumstances are stressed. Relationship demands are among the external factors thought to contribute, and in some cases, underpin a serendipity orientation. In general, serendipity is used to connote fortunate or positive occurrences. The Oxford English Dictionary defines it as "the faculty of making happy and unexpected discoveries by accident" (cited in Kantorovich, 1993, p. 154).

In understanding serendipity, there is a subtle but important distinction to be kept in mind between those discoveries or creations that are unexpected means to achieve a desired end, which are more precisely labeled "pseudoserendipity" (Roberts, 1989, p. 3), and those findings that are truly "accidental discoveries of things not sought for" (p. x). Seeking an answer to one question, the scientist finds the answer to another he or she was not pursuing. For the unintended discovery to have an impact, however, the scientist or scientific community must be able to recognize its significance. According to Kantorovich (1993) on the history and philosophy of science, the development of science rests on serendipitous discoveries in much the same way that evolution rests on natural selection. His theory of evolutionary epistemology elaborates the necessarily unintentional quality inherent in major breakthroughs in scientific, indeed all, knowledge:

> At times, an activity intended to solve a given problem leads to unintended results. This pattern of discovery might still keep us within normal science. However, it might initiate a process of scientific revolu-

tion. In fact, blind discovery is a necessary condition for scientific revolution; since the scientist is in general 'imprisoned' within the prevailing paradigm or world picture, he would not intentionally try to go beyond the boundaries of what is considered true or plausible. . . . he is blind to any territory which lies outside the one governed by his world picture. . . . Thus, one of the major ways of transcending an established state of knowledge is to do it unintentionally while trying to solve some problem within the confines of the prevailing paradigm. (1993, pp. 153–154)

Characterizing one's own experience as serendipitous in the precise sense would imply an absence or minimizing of conscious, articulated goals, not simply an unexpected or improvisational means toward an end, which is more properly understood as ingenuity or resourcefulness. Serendipity and pseudoserendipity are frequently used interchangeably in everyday speech as well as in the psychological literature. By extension, one cannot be sure that the women in this study consistently used the term in the most precise sense. However, when participants used serendipity or related terms, the researchers observed them to mean that ultimate career goals or destinations were subjectively perceived in only the most general terms at best, conveying the impression that a particular outcome was still to be discovered. The affective tone connected to the serendipitous process, although often positive, could also be ambivalent or indeed negative. In much the same way that Kantorovich explains scientific process, the young women were conscious of seeking career definition in a general way but experienced a particular outcome as accidental and unintentional. However, for a potential choice to be meaningful it must be recognized and used by the individual.

Furthermore, a subjective narrative describing one's process as serendipitous, unintended, or "blind luck" might well run counter to an observer's viewpoint of that same process, but still be a meaningful indication of the internal reality of the individual at that time. This relates to the fact that whereas the inner narrative is a conscious phenomenon, the individual very often holds an unconscious or preconscious sense of her goals and process, hidden from her own awareness for complex reasons, but nonetheless evident to the astute observer. Similarly in science there may be a readiness for novel discovery that exists "below the threshold of awareness" (Kantorovich, 1993, p. 173). This is what is meant by Pasteur's well-known observation that "chance favors the prepared mind."

A review of the use of serendipity in describing women's career development suggests that often it has been used in the imprecise manner described or without a clear reference as to viewpoint, leading to oversimplifications and generalizations that do not properly account for the subtle ways that in fact serendipity and agency are both aspects of the multilayered process of career development, particularly in the transitional or novice phase of life. In this analysis, serendipity is used to describe a subjective, conscious, and affectively varied characterization of one's experience as being driven by chance or accident, with goal and means not fully, consciously articulated or owned by the individual. It does not exclude the possibility of the coexistence of other inner narratives stressing agency.

There is conceptual overlap between serendipity and other concepts in psychology. It is related to passivity, in the sense of reactivity to external forces, but without the largely pejorative connotations of that term, particularly for women. One could also compare it to a defense mechanism that operates against an awareness of conflicts concerning individual will, ambition, or ideals. These defensive configurations are not uncommon in late adolescent development. However, serendipity is understood in this instance as a particular theme in an "inner script" or narrative, and as such is operating at the level of conscious awareness, unlike a defense mechanism, which is by definition an unconscious phenomenon. Serendipity is a conscious ego construction that serves certain purposes for the individual at a particular point in development, and although those purposes may include tolerating and containing unconscious conflict they are not limited to them.

There is also overlap between serendipity as a narrative construction and the concept of locus of control. Locus of control describes the attribution of events to external (e.g., luck, chance, fate) versus internal factors (e.g., ability, skill, effort). In relation to career decision making, "internally locused individuals may take both an active role in the direction of their educational/ vocational futures and personal responsibility for decision making and for gathering the kinds of information necessary to such decisions. Externals, on the other hand, may believe that vocational plans are largely influenced by chance factors and thus fail to invest time and energy in information-gathering and vocational decision-making activities" (Taylor, 1982, p. 319). Using well-established psychometric measures, a large body of research reveals this relationship between locus of control and career decision making (Fuqua, Blum, & Hartman, 1988; Larson et al., 1994; Taylor, 1982) and women's external locus of control (Lopez & Staszkiewicz, 1985). Recent research, however, has failed to document the presence of consistent overall gender differences on locus of control and career decision making in young adults (Larson et al., 1994; Luzzo, 1995). These findings suggest the need to examine how career-related external locus of control may appear in different guises and in different arenas for men and women. For example, compared to men, women appear to focus on expected conflicts between career and family and thus frame their whole career vision in a "dichotomous" framework (Larson et al., 1994).

Explicit references to serendipity in career development appear primarily in some feminist and narrative scholarship on women lives. Heilbrun

(1988) and Conway (1983, 1998) have noted the absence of personal ambition and the dominance of uncertainty in women's autobiographical narratives. More recently, Bateson (1990) and Tomlinson-Keasey (1990, 1994) have explored this phenomenon in their research on women. Bateson's focus on the narrative construction of meaning in women's lives is of particular relevance to our concerns: "Composing a life involves a continual reimagining of the future and reinterpretation of the past to give meaning to the present, remembering best those events that prefigured what followed, forgetting those that proved to have no meaning within the narrative" (1990, pp. 29–30).

In their writings, Bateson and Tomlinson-Keasey have described women's career processes as typically interrupted, discontinuous, and responsive to external circumstances or the needs of others rather than individualistically driven. The terminology used to describe these processes are "serendipitous," "improvisational," and "contingent." Bateson's highly popular book (1990) describes five prominent women whose careers are marked by discontinuity and reactivity, yet in spite of that succeed brilliantly in their careers.

Although Bateson's writing convincingly captures the experiences of many women of her generation and clearly resonates with readers, there are some problems in her inconsistent use of the term *serendipity*. On the one hand, she has emphasized serendipity in its precise meaning when she suggests that a personal sense of intentionality or agency is reconstructed only in retrospect: "We tend to reshape our pasts to give them an illusory sense of purpose" (1990, p. 17). On the other hand, Bateson has defined the central task of her study to be the identification of "more abstract underlying convictions that have held steady" in women's lives (1990, p. 15). There is a contradiction that goes unacknowledged. How can there be lifelong, guiding convictions as well as serendipity, "an illusory sense of purpose"? The answer, it would seem, is that there exists a more complex subjective narrative that includes elements of agency and serendipity, an intricate and evolving interdependence and oppositional dialogue of the two approaches. In fact at one point Bateson herself implies this process in referring to men's narratives becoming more like women's: "Men no longer organize two fully separate narratives, one domestic and one professional; women's narratives are half autonomous and half contingent" (1990, p. 88).

Tomlinson-Keasey's use of serendipity is quite close to my own. Based on an analysis of 40 women from the Terman Genetic Studies begun in the 1920s, Tomlinson-Keasey (1990, 1994) identified several major themes in women's career development. Pertinent among them is the lack of self-confidence in their own abilities, the embeddedness in relationships, the importance of social context and roles, and serendipity, or the lack of individualistic career planning. Serendipity is defined in her writing mostly by example or by metaphor, as in "a player being pulled helplessly along"

(1994, p. 236), and is not portrayed as a positive or happy subjective experience. Improvisers appear to be quite similar: "persons [who] do not set individual goals, but who assess their life situation and improvise to establish a life path that meets their needs" (1994, p. 236). As the following passage makes clear, Tomlinson-Keasey means to contrast these approaches with intentionality and to minimize the latter's importance in women's lives:

> A description of the life paths of adult women must confront the complexity of lives in which relationships, intimacy, and commitment are a primary responsibility. It must allow for discontinuity in the flow of women's lives and recognize that serendipity and improvisation are substitutes for goal setting when the woman's life path is not clear. (1994, p. 239)

Although Bateson and Tomlinson-Keasey offer valuable insights about women's careers based on close narrative studies that fit with other scholarship and undoubtedly resonate with many women's experiences, I would argue that the emphasis on serendipity and related ideas of uncertainty and reactivity as the *overarching* narrative for women's career development is too sweeping. For one thing, although they suggest it, they do not go far enough in exploring the possibility of more nuanced and multilayered career strategies that include elements of planfulness and intent as well as flexibility and reactivity. Another shortcoming is insufficient emphasis on cohort effect. Bateson's sample drew on her own and earlier historical cohorts, and Tomlinson-Keasey's was based on the Terman sample from the 1920s, several decades before the women's movement. Perhaps their analyses no longer fit so well for current college graduates, whom we would expect to be less restricted by traditional gender roles that privilege marriage and family and more capable of acknowledging professional ambition and pursuing it than were women who came of age in previous decades. Stewart and Ostrove (1998) suggested the special role played by historical context in the late adolescent period in shaping women's conscious identity and later midlife functioning. They argue that earlier cohorts of women had fewer rewards for consolidating a strong sense of individual agency in their identity in early adulthood than women in more contemporary cohorts, who by and large expect careers as well as families.

DEVELOPMENTAL CONTEXT

Another shortcoming in previous work describing serendipity in women's career approaches is the failure to emphasize and differentiate developmental context. The particular challenges and imperatives of each developmental phase give shape and meaning to the narrative one is likely to use at that time. Although the plot line of each individual's narrative will differ by necessity, there will be some consistency to the essential struggle requiring resolution, within a given historical period. The women in our study were in various stages of transition from late adolescence to early adulthood. Levinson has a more inclusive term for this period, the "novice phase" (Levinson, 1996). A review of the literature concerning this period of life suggests why it lends itself to a personal narrative emphasizing serendipity, even in the midst of agency in thought and deed.

The novice phase requires the college graduate to consolidate a sense of identity through interactions with real-world activities, with work or career choice being a central area of identity. Initially, choices in work and relationships need to be provisional as young adults test out their suitability and satisfaction. For men as well as women, many young people in the novice phase do not complete college with a well-developed sense of their career identity. Our sample can be seen as representative in this respect. Josselson (1987) has commented on the "built-in flexibility" of college seniors' identities in her similar study of women's identity development in young adulthood (p. 39). At the university where the current study took place, the office for career planning that serves the large undergraduate student body reported that only 30% of graduating seniors who seek their services go on directly to graduate or professional school (Simone Taylor, personal communication, January 23, 1998). In this context, the benefits of a period of personal exploration beyond the academic walls can be considerable. The women in our study referred to this as "time-out." Erikson (1959, 1968) has written about the value of a "psychosocial moratorium" that allows for the suspension in late adolescence of permanent career choices to integrate aspects of personal identity and explore options before making adult commitments in work and relational choices. He wrote that "strong individuals create their own 'psychosocial moratorium'" (1959, p. 638). Time-out allows young people to experiment and practice in the real, occupational world outside the classroom, with relative freedom from evaluation and responsibilities.

Yet even within the relative freedom created by a time-out phase, there are internally derived conflicts and pressures as well as external circumstances that heighten the young person's sense of uncertainty and lack of control over outcomes, making serendipity a particularly meaningful and relevant personal narrative.

Externally, the structure of college life with its explicit guidelines for personal progress (courses, grades, etc.) no longer operates, and a young person has to construct her own from a much wider array of conceivable options. The absence of uniform rites of passage to adulthood in contemporary culture adds to the burden on the individual to forge her own way (Hatcher, 1994). She may or may not know, or choose to seek out, knowledgeable adults to help her, and even if she does, no one has a crystal ball to foresee the future. Barriers to entry in many careers for women have eroded, providing more choice but also what Erikson has called the "dilemma of choice" (Erikson, 1959). Outcomes that involve other people, as in intimate relationships, necessarily limit one's subjective sense of power.

Internally, this period of identity formation involves several complex and emotionally charged processes: the formation of personal goals or ideals that feel personally derived rather than inherited from parental or other external sources; assessment of one's real achievements in relation to these goals and ideals; and increasing independence from family.

Even for those young people who achieve a satisfactory outcome of commitment to a career path that feels reasonably consistent with personal goals and history, this is a developmental period in which awareness of the limits of one's power to achieve goals is salient even when one must be active in formulating and pursuing them. Psychological strategies are needed to deal with this state of tension. Josselson (1990) has commented on "toleration of uncertainty" as a critical and understudied aspect of identity formation (p. 182). In a related way, young adults may choose and construct serendipity as an inner narrative because it helps to explain as well as to tolerate and contain the doubt, uncertainty, and disappointment inherent in the flux of the novice phase at the same time as it opens up the possibility of flexibility and experimentation.

There is an interesting connection to consider between identity formation in the novice phase and the creative process. Following Kantorovich's compelling theory of the evolutionary nature of knowledge development, it is possible to note a number of parallels with individual growth: Change is most likely to occur in periods of flux or crisis that demand answers to new problems, leading in turn to a new stable configuration. Although development builds on preexisting knowledge–structure and the activity of the seeker, there is no specified endpoint. And just as breakthroughs in science require that the community of scientists respond and validate the novel finding, so the young adult needs the validation of meaningful others for career identity to be established. Identity cannot be achieved in a vacuum any more than can creative breakthroughs in knowledge.

PLAN OF THE STUDY

This study is an extension of an earlier in-depth action–research project of 40 college women on the brink of graduation from a large, midwestern public university (Plunkett et al., 1995). The participants were interviewed and completed questionnaires concerning their goals, ideals, and strategies for future career and relationship plans, both before and after participating in a five-week small group experience designed to encourage a reflective, proactive approach to career planning. The women were self-selected, mostly White, from middle-class to upper-class economic backgrounds, but represented a range of academic majors and career choices. By self-report and grade point average, they were all in good standing at the university. All were in their junior or senior years. The original research revealed that although most were planning to go on to graduate study and pursue serious careers, nearly three quarters were planning to first take a time-out. With varying degrees of purposiveness and clarity, they foresaw the purpose of time-out as helping them to sort out professional and relationship issues. Some were clear and directed about how their choices could lead to specific outcomes such as graduate school entry in a particular field, but most were not, although they had broad outcomes in mind. This situation provided the opportunity to closely follow how elements of agency and serendipity are used and conceptualized by young women in the period of early career development.

For this current study, the original cohort of women were recontacted in the summer of 1995, five to six years after graduation, depending on the individual's time of participation in the original study. Out of the cohort of 40, 24 completed the follow-up questionnaire.

Measures

Questionnaire

The follow-up questionnaire instructed women to write extensively about their activities and subjective experiences in the years since graduation. The questionnaire was divided into four major domains of experience:

1. Education and career choices;
2. Presence and purposes of a time-out phase;
3. Relationship considerations; and
4. Perceived continuity of career interests since college.

In each domain, questions were designed to elicit both objective information, such as activities and timing of certain choices, as well as women's subjective process of the reasons for making certain choices and how they contributed to the development of career identity. Most of the questions were posed in an open-ended manner, inviting personal reflection. These were assessed for the frequency of certain responses amenable to coding and for recurrent themes in the narrative data. Two coders, including the author and an undergraduate woman student in psychology at the university, independently reviewed the data after establishing a reliability of 93% on 56 variables.

The following are the key dimensions of the questionnaire material selected for the subject of this chapter, the interplay between agentic goal-directed behavior and thinking and nonagentic self-presentations:

1. Success or failure to establish an initial career commitment;
2. Continuity, change, and discontinuity of career fields since graduation;
3. Presence or absence of goal-directed narratives related to this period;
4. Predominance of relationship considerations over individual agency, defined as a pattern of decision making in which priority is given to the desire to be with or accommodate to a partner's needs that sets a limit on career, educational, or geographic options.

The Interviews

Out of the group of 24 who returned completed questionnaires, eight women were chosen to be interviewed in depth about their lives and thinking during this period. All of those chosen had taken a time-out and returned to graduate school, and hence could be seen as having successfully achieved an initial career commitment after a phase of exploration. Beyond this commonality, they were chosen to reflect a range of career choices, activities, and expectations at the time of graduation. At graduation, four had planned to take time-out and were relatively certain of career goals; they indicated at that time a commitment to a particular field or career, a plan for the type of graduate program to enter within five years, and an explicit timetable for meeting their goals. Another two also had planned a time-out but were quite uncertain of their career goals and timetable. The final two were chosen because they had not planned to take a time-out, yet took one in the intervening years, and both were relatively certain of career goals, plans, and timetables. Given the geographical mobility typical of this age group, and the subsequent difficulty in locating individuals, the final sample is limited but reflective of the larger group of 40 in most respects.

The interviews lasted between two to four hours over several sessions, and were conducted by the researcher, either in person or over the telephone when necessary. They were audiotaped for purposes of thematic content review. The interviews were flexibly constructed to elicit narratives concerning choices, planning, and uncertainties for the period since graduation. It is important to note that the term "serendipity" was *not* introduced by the interviewer. The flexibility of this approach, coupled with prior knowledge of each individual and her history, allowed the interviewer to pursue promising lines of inquiry in the spirit of ongoing conversations. The fact that the women had earlier participated in a program with the researcher likely deepened their sense of trust and a shared history.

The final step was an integration of the various sources and forms of data to compose the life story themes of the eight participants who were interviewed. The researcher and an experienced, female psychologist reviewed all the interviews, the written questionnaires, and some interview material from the original study at graduation with instructions to track themes related to agency, power, relationships, serendipity, continuity and discontinuity of career development, and dominant conflict and feeling tones. The coders met to discuss each woman's protocol and to develop ideas about the life story themes that emerged across the data sources. Themes were agreed on by consensus between the coders.

RESULTS

Questionnaire Results

We found that most women in the overall pool of 24 achieved an initial commitment to a career field during this period of early to mid-20s and that there was evidence of exploration and initiative leading up to it. Commitment was indicated by entrance to graduate or professional school. Within 5 or 6 years postgraduation, 92% had entered graduate training, which was a marked increase from the number declaring this intention at the point of graduation (67%). Of those entering graduate training, 68% chose the same field cited at graduation or a field within the same general domain. Clearly the intervening period must have contained experiences that fostered the achievement of this landmark in career development. Our data gives us indications of what this included.

Women used the period between graduation and graduate school, the time-out period, to pursue activities that helped them to establish or confirm a career direction. Seventy-nine percent assented to the broad statement that it was a period that helped them to sort out their goals. The same number reported that they spent time preparing to apply for graduate school. The major activity of the women in this group was paid employment (92%), and they judged their experiences to be beneficial in making a career choice. They wrote about choosing jobs or volunteer activities that were in the same or related field to what they ultimately chose (67%). A few others believed their activities were helpful in eliminating career areas (8%). It is noteworthy that only a few indicated no relation at all between their time-out activities and their career choice (17%).

Our overall ratings of whether each woman's entire questionnaire indicated a sense of deliberateness in making choices since graduation bear out the impression of considerable goal-directed or agentic behavior. We found that most women (83%) were judged to include narratives and behaviors indicative of deliberate approaches (i.e., containing articulated goals, evidence of seeking out counsel or advice, choosing experiences deemed relevant to goals, or self-reflection concerning one's reactions and feelings to an experience).

In addition to career development, this period also revealed an emphasis on fostering or pursuing intimate relationships. Close to half of the women chose to live in locations to be with or near a significant other during their first year out of college (38%). In addition, 46% were judged to have included relationship considerations in making decisions regarding academic or time-off activities in the entire period after college. Although this was substantial, the rating of a predominance of relationship considerations over career was lower (29%).

The general continuity and evident pursuit of career interests between college graduation and graduate choice that we found in the questionnaires runs counter to any objective characterization of serendipity dominating the lives of these young women in this developmental period. On the other hand, our findings do suggest that many women did experience within themselves a sense of serendipity in the midst of apparent agency. That they did so was much more apparent in the interviews than in the questionnaires, indicating the value of combining qualitative and quantitative methods in approaching a complex topic such as this.

Interview Results

We found that the interviews provided a deeper, more nuanced appreciation of the subjective experience of early career identity than did the questionnaires alone. It is likely that the personal relationship developed in an extended dialogue fostered the awareness and sharing of conflicts and uncertainties.

Although most of the women had a general sense of their career interests that held steady throughout this period, and in objective terms made or used choices that aided their commitment, the outcome was by no means preordained in the minds of the women themselves. The specific map for each woman's quest had to be developed as she went along, much like the princes in the old Persian fairy tale. Unforeseen events, specific opportunities, disappointments and restrictions, juggling relationship needs, and finding that a conceptual interest did not translate into satisfaction with the reality of a particular job or program were all part of the journey referred to as accidental, undirected, or serendipitous, even when there was evidence of considerable planning and goal-setting activities. Furthermore, unresolved internal, often unconscious or preconscious, conflicts concerning choices lent themselves to a narrative script highlighting luck or accident in some instances. For some women, serendipity language seemed to convey a lack of "goodness of fit"—in other words, those choices did not feel authentic or ideal to them. Still others seemed pleased with the outcome and used serendipity to imply good fortune.

Thus a paradox of the coexistence of agency and serendipity in early career development repeated itself in many forms, with differing personal connotations. The term *serendipity* arose spontaneously at many points; it was not present in the interview protocol. What follows are some samples of how themes of serendipity appeared in women's narratives. In some cases, it is the final outcome that is perceived as accidental. In others, it is the means toward that end, and in many a combination of the two. What is common in these subjective narratives, however, is the person's own inner experience of lacking or minimizing clear, personally derived objectives or strategies during this period of transition and experimentation and experiencing the process and outcome as based largely on chance rather than self-directed agency.

One woman who finished college unsure of her career direction, wanting "a break from full-time work or school," first did some waitressing at a western ranch and then decided to volunteer at a Native American reservation. She spoke of this move as something that "fell into my lap," which minimized the overall agency implicit in her long-term interest in "finding something to help people, perhaps in social work." Her experience there helped her to settle on nursing as a helping field that was "a more tangible way to help, also more marketable." In the middle of her nursing program, she met and fell in love with a man in another state and decided to move there. She said it was doubtful she would have made such a move if there had not been a comparable nursing program available. Once again, she used vocabulary of chance to describe that process: "I fell in love with someone and serendipitously there was a program there." She has graduated and is working at a job about which she feels ambivalent. The romantic relationship did not last. All in all, she reflected that "a lot in my life has been serendipitous. It's possible to be a little more conscious of goals and write them down. I tend to take a job because it's there and stay with it if things are going along okay." For her, language of serendipity seemed to imply a sense of lack of control over events as well as a questioning or dissatisfaction with outcomes.

Another woman in the study described her journey from graduation to social work school several years later as a "process of discovery . . . of chance what I fall into." On graduation, "I didn't know what I was looking for . . . I needed to have experience and see where it led me." She had "a vague idea of social services" and began to look for all sorts of jobs through family contacts. At the time of graduation, she told us that "it's okay to let it be by chance—we don't have as much control as we think." She moved home to be near her family, including a young relative who was struggling with a life-threatening illness. Later she moved to another city to be with a boyfriend she ultimately married. There "by chance," as she put it, she found a job that clinched her decision to go to social work school. The fact that her own mother was a social worker and her close relative was gravely ill were not emphasized in the account of her particular process of pursuing her career but seemed highly relevant to us. In her rendition, she seemed to "happen on" her career rather than to actively choose it. This is an example of how unacknowledged personal conflicts may be translated into a conscious script of serendipity.

A third woman who went on to enter a doctoral program in English spent some years in a large city after college. On graduating with a degree in English, "I didn't know what I wanted to do." In what she described as "a conflicted moment," she moved to be near a boyfriend. "I wanted to be where he was. I had no sense of a job. I pounded the pavement looking for work at women's magazines." With the aid of her connections in the office where she had volunteered as a research assistant as an undergraduate, she found a position at an institute for women's issues. This clear continuity in experience and intentional use of connections in a strategic fashion was portrayed paradoxically as a serendipitous event: "Oddly enough, my position at the women's center led to my job in a serendipitous way."

Her experience at the job, with the aid of some influential women mentors, "consolidated [my] desire to go to graduate school." Although she remains uncertain about a career in academics versus publishing, she feels she has "charted her own course" professionally, deviating from her family's "program" for her career. What remains most uncertain and troubling for her is the absence of a committed relationship. She says that her future plans remain open "because I don't know whom I will be attached to." For this young woman, serendipity was applied to the uncertainty inherent in finding a job and, perhaps even more important, the lack of control involved in establishing a romantic, long-term relationship.

A fourth woman illustrates a career narrative that is more clearly agentic. Her approach to her career after college was deliberate and analytic. She articulated a long-range vision of her ultimate career and location, and at each step of the way considered opportunities in light of her final goal. She considered new opportunities in school or work using a process of articulating her needs, gauging her feelings, weighing alternatives, and seeking out trusted advisors. She also permitted herself ample time to explore new territories and took time off in the midst of her graduate training. Her process in choosing an internship illustrates the strong presence of agency in her approach:

Working for the judges this past summer was a very deliberate political and career move. I'm considering moving back to my home town and if I do this, I want to be very precise in how I choose the first place I work after I graduate from law school. . . . In choosing this, I wanted to sort of buy time, in a professional way, to see for myself whether I thought I was better suited to do public defense or prosecution. The summer enabled me to meet nearly all of these goals.

This young woman did encounter professional disappointments and modified her original goals. Yet she always conveyed a sense of self-authorship and direction in her planning. When she did refer to "luck" in her life, she also reflected that her own activity was pivotal: "Yes, I'm sort of lucky with that. . . . It happened to work out that way . . . that when I go looking for something else there was something else there. Partly it's a factor that I go looking and partly that it existed too."

It is interesting that although she had romantic relationships after college, she seemed to expect that they would ultimately fit into her own long-range vision. Romantic involvements rather than career goals were thus placed in the contingent position.

ANNE'S NARRATIVE

I have chosen to present one young woman's career narrative in greater detail. Anne[1] was chosen from among other possible narratives for a number of reasons. She is someone I know particularly well, having spoken with her at least eight hours over the years beginning at graduation about her decisions and emotions. The narrative is full, detailed, complex, and articulate. Her story illustrates the rich interplay so apparent in the interviews—using a language of serendipity or chance side by side with language and behavior implying the opposite: goals, strategy, and planfulness. Although she recognized both agency and serendipity in her choices, when asked to consider how much of her career development had been planned versus unplanned, she summed up the total experience as follows: *"I jumped off the dock without a plan."* (Italics added) Anne's narrative reveals how serendipity as a conscious narrative serves to explain to the self those issues in the process of identity consolidation that remain uncertain or conflicted and to provide the possibility for further change.

Six years after graduation and well into a demanding doctoral program in psychology, Anne described a great deal of self-questioning about her choice of graduate school and career. It is important to note that not only

---

[1]Not her real name.

does she have regrets and conflicts about how some aspects have turned out, but that she feels she made these decisions "blindly" and "without a plan." In her retrospective analysis, the process was "made by default and not consciously thought through." This overall characterization of serendipity is striking because most observers would think that she accomplished what she had deliberately set out to do.

At the point of graduation she articulated a desire to move back to her hometown, be with her boyfriend of many years, and be accepted to a nearby graduate school in psychology or a related field working with children. She married soon after graduation and a baby was planned and arrived two and a half years later. At the time of this study, she was working on her dissertation and seeking a required internship. She perceived her marriage as strong albeit strained by the demands of parenthood. In the midst of apparent success in both career and relationships, she describes herself as "frazzled" and "desperate for closure," questioning many of her career choices.

Always a motivated and hardworking student, after high school Anne left her home and originally went to a prestigious private college, thinking she would follow in her father's footsteps and become a physician. Her mother also worked in the health field. Her parents encouraged her to do well and pursue a career, and the choice of pediatrics combined her love of children and her desire to serve and be overtly successful. She went off to college with this as her career goal. Like many students, she changed her mind about her major. After two years, she also decided to transfer to another university, in order to be closer to family and her high school boyfriend. This is where I first met her, during her junior year.

Anne considered a number of different majors before settling on psychology. She says she was attracted to it so that she could work with children in a "helping field" and because it was intellectually stimulating. She had always intended to get a PhD or MD degree, "something that would be a real accomplishment." Furthermore she felt the need to be "self sufficient and career minded" from a young age based on her mother's experience of getting divorced and raising two young children on her own. Anne was the oldest child. She remembers being very proud of her mother, who went back to school and landed a responsible position in her field, but also somewhat resentful of the extra household and child care responsibilities she shouldered as a result of the situation. She felt that the divorce experience left her with a dread of uncertainty about the future and a conviction that doing well in school was "the prescription for success." She did extremely well in her classes in psychology, both in the academics and the practica. Interpersonally, she was skilled in connecting with people; seen as open, caring, and responsible in her interactions. Doing childcare as a part-time job during college, she became close to the family where she worked. The mother was a clinical psychologist working part-time in a private practice and juggling the demands of career and children. Anne says that she felt drawn to this way of life.

At the point of graduation Anne was in the process of formulating her career and relationship goals. Compared to other participants in the original study, she was relatively if not absolutely certain of her career goals and articulated a timetable and reasonable plan for achieving them. To all observers she appeared self-motivated, agentic, and directed. She did not seem like someone "jumping off the dock without a plan," as she retrospectively described herself. She saw her time-off year as an opportunity to work in her general field of interest, make contacts with faculty in specific graduate programs, and live near her family and boyfriend. He was already launched professionally and was not flexible about relocating, although it was not clear she herself wanted to relocate at the time.

All in all Anne enjoyed her year off. To earn money but mostly to bolster her intended application to graduate school, she worked as a preschool teaching assistant and made contact with a professor in a desirable graduate program, volunteering to be his research assistant. He was impressed with her work, and this undoubtedly helped her application.

She was excited when she was admitted to her top choice school. "I figured when I got in that I was meant to be a psychologist." Yet she found it to be more research-oriented and less clinical than she had hoped. It has been "grueling and demanding," taking energy away from her personal life. There are few colleagues or faculty who strive for the balance between professional and family life that Anne seeks. Few of her peers are married or have children. Indeed she says she feels "almost embarrassed to acknowledge that this is the life I want."

It is easy to understand why Anne would feel stressed and "frazzled" at this point in her life. She is in a period of exceptional demands in graduate school and family life, and feeling insufficient support in either realm. She is also evolving in a more clinical direction within the field than her faculty and wishes she had taken more time before graduate school to explore more options.

In retrospect Anne feels that she did not plan her course well but went forward "blindly." If she had not "felt that graduate school was her only option," she would have tried other things, possibly move to a different city for awhile, apply to more graduate schools, and investigate more fully the nature of graduate school life. Because she was admitted "so easily" she felt that her commitment to this career choice "wasn't really tested."

From the observer's viewpoint, Anne's retrospective characterization of her career process as "accidental and unplanned" is puzzling, because it minimizes the clear intentionality in her behavior and her success in achieving a desired outcome, albeit one that she later came to question. Yet there are a number of reasons that may help to explain why this narrative feels subjectively compelling to her, at this time of transition in her life, as it does for many others in this stage of development.

Above all is Anne's implicit expectation that she must plan her life to avoid insecurity, and she followed one major, family-derived script in her prompt pursuit of a career and stable family situation after graduation. She was not, however, in touch with another set of needs that became apparent to her as time went on that were at variance with the dominant narrative that she had constructed from her childhood. These needs involved allowing herself more uncertainty and exploration to develop her own personal, unique identity. Her narrative of serendipity thus reveals the subjective sense that what she is doing is not sufficiently self-derived and authentic, and thus to her feels "blind" and "unexpected."

At the same time as serving to explain and tolerate disappointment and confusion, Anne's choice of a serendipity narrative serves to open up the possibility of growth in the future. By acknowledging the mismatch between her emerging self and her choices to date, she opens up the space to evolve in a direction that feels more self-directed and genuine.

Anne's experience underscores the point that for identity formation to be successful, the set of goals and commitments emerging from the novice phase of exploration need to feel essentially self-derived and authentic, as well as be attainable and realistic. This process is never fully conscious and is often conflictual. Levy-Warren (1996) has reminded us that identity commitment includes loss and struggle as it implies limits, a letting-go of "the possibilities represented by old fantasies" (p. 28). Idealized views of parents and internalized parental expectations need to be modified or rejected and replaced by self-images grounded in self-knowledge.

Anne's narrative illustrates the interplay of agency and serendipity narratives in a very successful, directed person in the novice phase of development, and thus how a subjective narrative that uses serendipity captures an essential aspect of contemporary women's career identity development in this phase of life, with its mixed elements of risk-taking, uncertainty, relational expectations, and self-exploration. Each woman will of necessity bring her own individual stamp to the experience and will need to address those issues that matter most to her personally. As observers, we have to expect that words used in common, serendipity in this case, will include nuances and shades of meaning for each individual.

DISCUSSION

Our study demonstrates the existence of a rich tapestry of the distinct, opposing themes of agency and serendipity in women's experience of early career development. In this sample of educated young women, intent on combining future careers and families, we found that agency was apparent in the general continuity of career goals and purposeful use of life experiences in the period after college for career exploration and experimentation. Indeed most women concluded this phase by entering graduate school in a field related to their interests in college and spent considerable thought and energy getting there. This group is small and not representative of the general population of college women, but in many respects representative of the privileged, ambitious, career-focused women who will be the leaders of the next generation of women striving to combine career and personal goals.

In this context of expectation and opportunity, we were intrigued by the frequent appearance of an inner script or narrative emphasizing serendipity, essentially the opposite of intentionality and planfulness, existing side by side with agency in many cases. Anne was a good example of someone who articulated a narrative including elements of both agency and serendipity and made a number of agentic choices, yet felt serendipity to be the truest to her in a deep emotional sense. In some ways, the persistence of serendipity as an inner reality is consistent with earlier research on serendipity (Bateson, 1990; Tomlinson-Keasey, 1990, 1994) and external locus of control in career development. Yet there are at least three critical distinctions to be kept in mind in interpreting the meaning of serendipity for this particular group in this generational cohort. It is only one strand of the tapestry, which also includes agency and self-determination; indeed from an observer's viewpoint it is debatable that serendipity in the precise sense dominated the lives of earlier cohorts either. Relationship considerations still matter but do not necessarily predominate as they once did for women; and above all, serendipity should be understood as a subjective aspect of experience embedded in a particular developmental stage. There are a number of factors that help explain why young women use this narrative of serendipity at this time and why it can be psychologically adaptive.

The transition from late adolescence to early adulthood is a phase full of opportunity and it is fraught with uncertainty. One is asked to be decisive and bold and make choices for a lifetime, yet tolerate ambiguity and disappointment. To take charge but to live with limits. To realize one's ideal self but also to question and reframe that ideal closer in line with one's own desires. This is essentially a creative process, with one's identity as the work-in-progress. The creative process requires one to combine elements of planfulness and exploration and to tolerate the state of suspense of not knowing the final outcome, all the while moving toward it. Creativity is enhanced when one can be open to surprises and make good use of them.

These tensions are perhaps more true than ever for young people in today's rapidly changing, postmodern culture. Career-oriented young women are encouraged to explore alternatives and be successful professionally. Most also desire to forge long-term relationships and include those considerations in their visions of the future. These high expectations, coupled with pro-longed adolescent exploration, provide rich opportunities, but also present psychological risks, such as confusion, shame, and loss if goals are delayed or not realized. Serendipity is a creative way to express and tolerate this complexity and to keep psychological risks and tensions contained. Positive or useful serendipity permits a suspension of commitment in the service of ultimately attaining a satisfying personal fit between self and opportunity. Negative serendipity would involve a sweeping denial of agency and ambi-tion in the pursuit of goals with the possible failure to ever achieve one's goals.

It would be interesting to explore differences between women in the nature and persistence of serendipity in their personal narratives, in light of identity formation. Josselson's work (1990, 1996) suggests that tolerance of change and uncertainty is related to "identity status" formulated along lines suggested by Erikson (1968), Marcia (1980), and others. Optimally, in the case of healthy identity achievement, one would expect serendipity to be balanced by an attitude of agency and emotional resiliency and a conscious acknowledgment of and attachment to goals, and to diminish with the achievement of a more adult identity. One would not expect it to characterize the whole of women's lives but to resurface in periods of life stress and transition. In our own material, those young women with the best sense of subjective career fulfillment did show this mix of qualities, and those with more exclusive emphasis on serendipity showed less. Further, larger and longitudinal studies of women would help address these hypotheses.

In addition, the importance of relationships was clearly demonstrated in these women's interviews and questionnaires. Many decisions following graduation were made with the intent of furthering important relationships. Although we did not find relationship considerations to supersede or deter-mine career considerations, as earlier research has suggested (Bateson, 1990; Tomlinson-Keasey, 1990, 1994), they were clearly an important part of the equation. A narrative of serendipity can be understood as one way to explain, and enable accommodation to, the needs of an evolving important relation-ship. The interplay between serendipity and agency that we found has multiple meanings and implications, however, and should be understood as a creative approach that fits the developmental requirements of many young women, with differing nuances and emphases for each person.

REFERENCES

Ancis, J., & Phillips, S. (1996). Academic gender bias and women's behavioral agency. *Journal of Counseling & Development, 75,* 131–137.

Angrist, S., & Almquist, E. (1975). *Careers and contingencies.* New York: Dunellen.

Arnold, K. (1993). Academically talented women in the 1980s: The Illinois valedictorian project. In K. Hulbert & D. Schuster (Eds.), *Women's lives through time: Educated American women of the 20th century* (pp. 393–414). San Francisco: Jossey-Bass.

Austin, J. (1978). *Chase, chance and creativity: the lucky art of novelty.* New York: Columbia University Press.

Bakan, D. (1966). *The duality of human existence.* Boston: Beacon Press.

Bateson, M. (1990). *Composing a life.* New York: Penguin Books.

Betz, N., & Fitzgerald, L. (1987). *The career psychology of women.* Orlando, FL: Academic Press.

Betz, N., & Hackett, G. (1981). A self-efficacy approach to the career development of women. *Journal of Vocational Behavior, 18,* 326–329.

Betz, N., & Hackett, G. (1987). Concept of agency in education and career development. *Journal of Counseling Psychology, 34,* 299–308.

Clausen, J. (1991). Adolescent competence and the shaping of the life course. *American Journal of Sociology, 96*(4), 805–842.

Conway, J. (1983). *Convention versus self-revelation: Five types of autobiography by women of the progressive era.* Northampton, MA: Project on Women and Social Change, Smith College.

Conway, J. (1998). *When memory speaks: Exploring the art of autobiography.* New York: Vintage Books.

Douvan, E., & Adelson, J. (1966). *The adolescent experience.* New York: Wiley.

Erikson, E. (1959). Late adolescence. In S. Schlein (Ed.), *A way of looking at things: Selected papers from 1930 to 1980* (pp. 631–643). New York: Norton.

Erikson, E. (1968). *Identity: Youth and crisis.* New York: Norton.

Fuqua, D., Blum, C., & Hartman, B. (1988). Empirical support for the differential diagnosis of career indecision. *The Career Development Quarterly, 36,* 27–29.

Gilbert, L. (1993). *Two careers/one family: The promise of gender equality.* New York: Sage.

Gilligan, C. (1982). *In a different voice: Psychological theory and women's development.* Cambridge, MA: Harvard University Press.

Goldin, C. (1997). Career and family: College women look to the past. In F. D. Blau & R. G. Ehrenberg (Eds.), *Gender and family issues in the workplace* (pp. 20–58). New York: Russell Sage.

Hatcher, S. (1994). Personal rites of passage: Stories of college youth. In A. Lieblich & R. Josselson (Eds.), *The narrative study of lives: Exploring identity and gender* (vol. 2, pp. 164–194). Thousand Oaks, CA: Sage.

Heilbrun, C. G. (1988). *Writing a woman's life.* New York: W.W. Norton.

Helson, R., Pals, J., & Solomon, M. (1997). In R. Hogan, J. Johnson, & S. Briggs (Eds.), *Is there adult development distinction to women? Handbook of personality psychology* (pp. 291–314). San Diego, CA: Academic Press.

Hulbert, K., & Schuster, D. (Eds.). (1993). *Women's lives through time: Educated American women the 20th century.* San Francisco: Jossey-Bass.

Jordan, J. V., Kaplan, A. G., Miller, J. B., Stiver, I. P., & Surrey, J. L. (1991). *Women's growth in connection: Writings from the Stone Center.* New York: Guilford Press.

Josselson, R. (1990). *Finding herself: Pathways to identity development in women.* San Francisco: Jossey-Bass.

Josselson, R. (1996). *Revising herself: The story of women's identity from college to midlife.* New York: Oxford University Press.

Kantorovich, A. (1993). *Scientific discovery: logic and tinkering.* Albany: State University of New York Press.

Larson, J., Butler, M., Wilson, S., Medora, N., & Allgood, S. (1994). The effects of gender on career decision problems in young adults. *Journal of Counseling and Development, 73,* 79–84.

Levinson, D. (1996). *The seasons of a woman's life.* New York: Alfred A. Knopf.

Levy-Warren, M. (1996). *The adolescent journey: Development, identity formation, and psychotherapy.* Garden City, NJ: Jason Aronson.

Lieblich, A. (1987). Preliminary comparison of Israeli and American successful career women at mid-life. *Israel Social Science Research: Special Issue, 5*(1–2), 164–177.

Lopez, L., & Staszkiewicz, M. (1985). Sex differences in internality-externality. *Psychological Reports, 57,* 1159–1164.

Luzzo, D. (1995). The relative contributions of self-efficacy and locus of control to the prediction of career maturity. *Journal of College Student Development, 36*(1), 61–66.

Luzzo, D., & Hutcheson, K. (1996). Causal attributions and sex differences associated with perceptions of occupational barriers. *Journal of Counseling & Development, 75,* 124–130.

Marcia, J. (1980). Identity in adolescence. In J. Adelson (Ed.), *Handbook of adolescent psychology* (pp. 159–187). New York: Wiley.

McClelland, D. (1975). *Power: The inner experience.* New York: Irvington.

Miller, J. (1976). *Toward a new psychology of women.* Boston: Beacon Press.

Phillips, S., & Imhoff, A., (1997). Women and career development: A decade of research. *Annual Review of Psychology, 48,* 31–59.

Plunkett, M., Hassinger, J., & Hollenshead, C. (1995). *Women looking ahead: Life and career planning for college women.* Ann Arbor: University of Michigan, Center for the Education of Women Research Reports.

Roberts, R. (1989). *Serendipity: Accidental discoveries in science.* New York: John Wiley.

Roberts, P., & Newton, P. (1987). Levinsonian studies of women's adult development. *Psychology and Aging, 2,* 154–163.

Stewart, A., & Ostrove, J. (1998). Women's personality in middle age: Gender, history, and midcourse corrections. *American Psychologist, 53*(11), 1185–1194.

Stickel, S., & Bonett, R. (1991). Gender differences in career self-efficacy: Combining a career with home and family. *Journal of College Student Development, 32*, 297–301.

Taylor, K. (1982). An investigation of vocational indecision in college students: Correlates and moderators. *Journal of Vocational Development 21*, 318–329.

Tomlinson-Keasey, C. (1990). The working lives of Terman's gifted women. In H. Grossman & N. Chester (Eds.), *The experience and meaning of work in women's lives* (pp. 213–240). Mahwah, NJ: Erlbaum.

Tomlinson-Keasey, C. (1994). My dirty little secret: Women as clandestine intellectuals. In C. Franz & A. Stewart (Eds.), *Women creating lives: Identities, resilience, and resistance* (pp. 227–245). Boulder, CO: Westview Press.

Veroff, J. (1983). Contextual determinants of personality. *Personality and Social Psychology Bulletin, 9*, 331–343.

White, R. (1966). *Lives in progress.* New York: Holt, Rinehart & Winston.

Young, R., & Collin, A. (1992). *Interpreting career: Hermeneutical studies of lives in context.* Westport, CT; Praeger.

7

THE SETBACK OF
A DOCTOR'S CAREER

VARPU LÖYTTYNIEMI

> There are unquestionably times—particularly when we interpret our-
> selves—when a vision of the whole, of a center, is appropriate and
> necessary. (..) But the quest for the whole (..) must not be undertaken
> at the expense of difference and multiplicity. (Freeman, 1993, p. 144)

Lassi (as I call him) is a young Finnish physician, one of the 30 who
shared with me their life stories in the context of a research interview. I
interviewed Lassi in late 1996, almost one year after he had completed his
training and graduated. At the time of the interview, Lassi was at a crossroads:
There was no obvious trajectory to the future, his previous career expectations and the foundations on which these expectations were laid had more
or less given way to ambivalence. Lassi needed to ask once more, "Where
am I heading?" My request for an interview, therefore, was fortunately timed.[1]

A change in his personal self and professional motives seeks an articulation in Lassi's story—this is the plot of the story in my reading it. The
change is not located in the story where his life course takes turns that are
most easily recognized as turning points in Western culture; Lassi chooses
his profession, graduates, and starts a family without verbally challenging

I wish to thank Matti Hyvärinen, Vilma Hänninen, Liisa Rantalaiho, and the postgraduate seminar
at the Department of Women's Studies, University of Tampere, for wise words that can be heard
throughout my chapter, even though I have merged them with my own voice. David Kivinen has
given it all, including the English language, the finishing touches; without him Lassi's narration
would have lost too much of its vitality when deprived of its original language.
[1]Originally the reason why I set out to collect stories by 1995 graduates was that they (as I myself)
belong to a generation of doctors who were confronted with unemployment and consequential
uncertainty while they were still medical students during the recession in Finland in the early 1990s.
They (we) had to orientate themselves to an insecurity of life and career that was previously
unknown for Finnish physicians. At the time of the interview, Lassi was still not sure whether he
would be able to find his next job in his hometown; however, unemployment rates among doctors
were steadily decreasing, and Lassi could count on finding some work, sooner or later.

the continuity of his self. In Lassi's story, transition takes place where he narrates his way through his advanced studies research project, a part of his medical education that he once expected to become a first step in a scientific career. The arguments of the past hero are now dialogized by a critical voice and vocabulary assigned to his present self, and transition takes place in and through this dialogue.

EPIPHANIES AND KEY EPISODES

Epiphanies of life, Norman Denzin wrote, are transformational experiences for the one experiencing them; after these often problematic interactional situations or turning points, a person will never be quite the same again. Because of their profound meaning, these episodes of life are remembered and told time and time again, and once they are given a thick description as parts of personal stories, they are brought alive with all the density of emotion and interaction (Denzin, 1989a).

Yet one life bears potential for untold stories and for continuous retellings. Turning points are not necessarily moments in personal lives as the lives are lived. Instead, turning points are moments in personal stories about those lives, stories that are told to give meaning to experiences. Life transitions become life transitions that are meaningful and constitutive of selves only when they are articulated and given meaning—that is, in retrospect (Denzin, 1989b, p. 71).

Discussing Denzin's concept of epiphany, Matti Hyvärinen points out that not all personal transformation is clothed in the style of thick description; stories and narrators are not all alike (Hyvärinen, 1998, p. 162). Instead of pure description, a story constructing an ethical self must evaluate what has happened, and do so against what the teller expected to take place. Knowing our expectations about the world and our living in it are an essential part of knowing, or constructing, our selves, and this is why the key episodes of our stories—that is, episodes where the construction of self or identity is at its most intense—are often episodes that are thick in expectation (Hyvärinen, 1994, 1998). Furthermore, expectations are not only textual or narrative guidelines, they have a political dimension as well and therefore serve as a link between agency that takes place in the material world and aims at reaching its goals and the narratives that are told about that agency (Hyvärinen, 1994, p. 63; 1997, p. 36).

A key episode often produces transformation, but instead of thick description, transition may only be found in the vagueness of linguistic hedges and false starts that both hint at an expectation guiding the telling. Hyvärinen redefined *epiphany* or *key episode* as an episode of a life story that usually manifests both thickness of expectation and a breaking-down of the expectation structure. In the tumult of a key episode, previous expectations give way to and are replaced by new ones (Hyvärinen 1998, p. 162).

Besides expectations, key episodes often reveal the key rhetoric with which the teller constructs the self and builds a relationship to this self, to life, the world, and the other–listener (Hyvärinen, 1994, pp. 55, 63). Katri Komulainen further highlighted the importance of the key rhetoric in constructing selves. The "plot" of the story, she wrote, is not so much about external turning points in the *life lived* but about changes in the vocabulary and metaphors in the *life told*, because these changes embody changes in the self and the world as it appears to this self (Hyvärinen, 1994, p. 121; Komulainen, 1998a, p. 156; 1998b, p. 302). She gives an example of a story that can be read as a transformation narrative: The narrator, a Finnish woman in her 40s, tells her story using a key rhetoric that is characterized by a contrast between her past and present selves; the present self is constructed as advancing and autonomous, the past dependent self as being its opposite. This transition in rhetorics and the self told with it is the plot of the story.

Besides expectations about themselves and the world where they have experienced what their stories will be about, tellers have expectations about social situations. The structures of expectation help us figure out what all the different situations in which we get involved are about and how we should act in them and how we should relate to other people (Tannen, 1979/1993).[2] Usually it is not one structure but many, sometimes contradictory, that meet in the same situation; for the young doctors in my study the situation was at once a research interview, a discussion between two colleagues, and an occasion for telling a life story. Lassi attempted to resolve his dilemma by concentrating on the telling: He did not spend too much time wondering what he was supposed to tell or what I, the researcher, wanted to know.

By telling about his expectations, Lassi is narrating an ethical self. At the same time, expectations draw from the mutual understanding and social knowledge that make his telling and my understanding possible. Expectations represent the cultural other, the listener who is present in the story. Expectations, even when I take them to be mine, originate from the shared (discursive) reality; they are both my expectations and others' imagined words. Sometimes others' words make speech double-voiced in a hidden polemic way (Bakhtin, 1984, pp. 195–199); the other's word does not have an immediate presence in the speaker's discourse, but it is possible to hear traces of it, the speech is directed toward it, and the speaker is in dialogue with the expected response.

---

[2]Tannen (1979/1993, p. 19) referred to F. C. Bartlett when discussing the concept of structure: From the sociological point of view, structures of expectation are not static, cognitive structures that are

In key episodes of personal stories the tellers are most passionate in their aspiration to present one self, to construct sufficient unity out of multiplicity (Hyvärinen, 1994, p. 121). In dialogues of key episodes, it is possible to trace both multiple voices and the quest for a unified identity. As Ruthellen Josselson (1995) noted, to allow the narrator personal change or unfinalizedness of the self, we need to hear the dialogic parts of the story. We will regard the dialogues as processes in which the narrators are asking themselves who they are, could be, and could become. Josselson argued that as researchers we should be sensitive to *whole* people, including their dialogic moments. The concept of whole becomes problematic, though, if we accept that these dialogues take place "in the boundaries of self and other" (de Peuter, 1998, p. 39). Our stories and selves are not as coherent and unified as the Western, masculine ideal suggests. The many voices given to them are not our own but others' (Bakhtin, 1981, 1984; Sampson, 1993). Whenever new voices, other points of view, are allowed to enter the dialogue, they will change us and make possible something that was not a choice before. If we question the myth of the unified self we will see fragmentation as a viable standpoint for another kind of authenticity: situational authenticity that allows the multiple voices to be heard (de Peuter, 1998). Our glimpses of the whole, fleeting experiences of continuity and coherence are nevertheless real and true.

EVIDENCE OF EXPECTATION

Narrating is never pure description, but it is colored with evaluation that may be direct or included in linguistic choices—for example the choice of wording. By means of evaluation the teller attempts to answer the listener's "so what?" before the question is even put, determined to make distinct the point of the story, explain why this particular story was worth telling (Labov, 1972, pp. 366–371). Evaluation is hence inseparably linked to what is unexpected and what is everyday experience in the narrator's culture. *Evidence of expectation* is indeed Tannen's (1979/1993) concept for many of those linguistic devices that Labov calls *evaluative elements*. After finding these evaluations or evidence of expectation on the surface of language, it is possible to dig further and (re)construct the background expectations, ideas about the world and its relations (Hyvärinen, 1998, p. 161).

The evidence of expectation alerts the analytical reader to ask what the background expectations are, but the (re)construction of these expectations still remains the reader's interpretative task. Where evidences are dense, the

---

built once and for all. *Structure of expectation* refers to the dynamics of relations in which the structures are continuously realized and reconstructed.

reader is invited to "turn over this stone, deliberate upon the underlying expectations" (Hyvärinen, 1994, p. 60). Hyvärinen has combined Tannen's and Labov's evaluative elements into the following list of evidence of expectations (Hyvärinen, 1994, p. 59). In my analysis, I use the same list myself:

1. Repetition, especially repetition of whole utterances;
2. False starts;
3. Backtracks, breaking-down of the temporal order of telling;
4. Hedges that flavor the relation between what was expected and what finally happened: *indeed, just, anyway, however*;
5. Negatives. As a rule, *negative* is only used when its affirmative is expected (Labov, 1972, pp. 380–381);
6. Contrastives;
7. Modals;
8. Evaluative language;
9. Evaluative verbs; and
10. Intensifiers, including laughter.

THE KEY EPISODE: THE FIRST SETBACK OF LASSI'S CAREER

The key episode in Lassi's story is about his advanced studies, a 10- to 14-credit unit that is included in the doctor's examination and often means an excursion into the world of science and personally conducted research. The project is carried out under the supervision of a tutor (a senior physician), and it is not unusual for the advanced studies project to lead to scientific publications and later to a doctoral thesis (Halila, 1998). Lassi, too, had had the idea of writing a thesis somewhere in the back of his mind when he chose his field of study. However, as it turns out, his "scientific career didn't really get off to any start."

In the interview I partly missed Lassi's experience of disappointment, even though he says straightaway that his advanced studies were the "first setback" in his career. Although I did not say so, I thought during the interview that Lassi was mostly just gaining time when he protracted his narrative about his advanced studies; many interviewees only mention them in passing, if at all. In other words, I noticed that in my cultural understanding a doctor's story should not (not even on this time scale, within just one year of graduation) include a highly detailed account of one's advanced studies. This is actually quite strange inasmuch as advanced studies are the foundation for one's relationship to scientific work during pregraduation education and often for one's doctoral thesis later on. Scientific work is a merit even for postgraduate medical training, and in some specialties it is quite difficult to obtain a university hospital training post without a published thesis and a doctoral degree. That I missed Lassi's point is stranger still if I think about my own doctor's story (such as I tell it today), whose trajectory was set by what I did for my advanced studies.

I think at least part of the reason for my deafness in this matter was the lightness in Lassi's tone of voice. Even now as I listen to the original tape instead of reading my transcription, I hear him telling a pure comedy. It was only when I transcribed Lassi's interview that I found other interpretations and the tragic fibers in the story (Murray, 1989, pp. 182, 198–199). I even noticed that listening to the way he makes the transition from the Lassi he was before to his present understanding, between his two voices in the story, opened up the whole of his life story in a new way—that is, I picked this single episode as a *key episode* even before I could name it as one.

Applying Labov's (1972) narrative structure, the episode is actually a collection of several short narratives. The narrative structure is not really very well-suited to analyzing this kind of longer story. Nonetheless I will keep the structure in mind, to remind me of narratives having structural elements with different functions. I will find abstracts, orientations, complicating actions, evaluations, results, and codas (Labov, 1972) in the subnarratives of the episode, even if I am not systematically looking for them. Lassi's words are translated as close to verbatim as possible, with much of the haziness that is so characteristic of oral speech when the speech is forced to take the form of written text. It is problematic to give only a translation of the text analyzed (Fairclough, 1992). However, I have chosen to do so because the interview extract presented is long and it is unlikely that there are very many readers who would benefit from the Finnish text anyway. Furthermore, I am not doing a very detailed textual analysis; what I have attempted to preserve in the translation is what I concentrate on in my analysis: evidence of expectation and the (ironic) style. Many details in the contents have been changed for reasons of anonymity. (See Exhibit 7-1 for transcription conventions.)

Orientation

At the outset Lassi orientates his listener to the characters and their activity in the story (Labov, 1972). Lassi's research project would be tutored by his uncle's former colleague.

1. But the first the first setback like a bit more *clearly*—
2. or I don't know whether it was in any way like in my career but—well in my personal career perhaps it was
3. that I had started my advanced studies with pretty high exp-expectations .. tutored by my uncle's old colleague, so uhm,

EXHIBIT 7-1
Transcription Conventions

- Short overlapping utterances are marked in slashes //I: Mm// within the embedding utterance. I = I, the interviewer
- Longer simultaneous utterances are marked with a bracket in the ongoing utterance at the point [where the overlap begins. The second utterance starts on the line below.
- —Marks a false start.
- Two dots indicate a short pause.
- Three dots—...—indicate a clear pause, from about two seconds.
- Unclear or inaudible words(?) are indicated by a question mark.
- Where another voice (including the past Lassi's voice) enters the narrator's discourse without merging with his own, it is inserted in quotation marks (").
- Stress is <u>underlined</u>.

> I was working with this stomach cancer stuff in the surgery
> department then and .. hh ...
> 4. the research plan it was prepared and written up and
> 5. it seemed perfectly okay,

On lines 1–3, in the abstract of the whole advanced studies episode, the narrator explicates what the following story is going to be about: the first real setback in his career. But Lassi has to dialogize his words. First, the hedge *a bit* says that despite the violence of the setback, he does not want to make too big a deal of it. The background expectation may be guiding him not to tell a doctor's career out of past difficulties or setbacks, or he may want to keep a backdoor open in case I, the listener, do not get the point of his story and think it is not really worth the trouble of telling. For me Lassi's major hardship may be nothing more than appropriate professional growth and coming to know the rules of science. The false starts on line 2 can support either explanation. By defining his advanced studies as a setback in his "personal career," Lassi retains the right to evaluate their meaning and, on the other hand, makes known his being aware of telling a story that may be banal and not worth telling (Linde, 1993; Tannen, 1979/1993) when valued against what a doctor's career is expected to include.

The language is double-voiced in a way that Bakhtin called hidden polemic (Bakhtin, 1984, pp. 195–199). In hidden polemic, the other's word is not present in the speaker's discourse as such, but the whole discourse is directed to taking the (perhaps hostile) word into account, to discussing with it. Hidden polemic speech takes a sideward glance at the other speaker it has included, and the shadow or trace of this other word can be heard even if the word cannot (Bakhtin, 1984, p. 208). The speech is full of interruptions, reservations, repetitions, diminutives (Bakhtin, 1984,

p. 211)—that is, evidence of expectation. The linguistic phenomena that Tannen (1979/1993) and Hyvärinen (1994, 1998) called evidence of expectation are not only our own but *others'* expectations as we assume they are, evidence of others' voices and dialogue within the discourse. When I choose to analyze key episodes that are expectationally dense parts of a story, I hence choose to analyze the hidden polemic parts.

The hedge *a bit* and the false start on line 1 are a reply to the medical audience whose assumed reaction is something like, "Aren't you exaggerating this a bit, saying that advanced studies were a setback in your career, or do you really let such minor hardships upset you?" According to the medical "superaddressee" (Bakhtin, 1986, p. 126), there is a strict order of events that can or cannot be defined as setbacks. No wonder I was surprised during the interview about Lassi protracting his narrative about advanced studies.

COMPLICATING ACTION

The story would probably not be elicited in its full length and fascination if Lassi did not tell of conflict. The original setting is now thrown into a different light, and Lassi's evaluation of "perfectly okay" (line 5) is challenged.

6. I did have one idea myself on what I could have done my advanced studies

7. but it was like rejected out of hand so I thought—at that time my reaction was like, (")yeah, yeah,

8. okay, fair enough, he probably knows wh- what it should

9. I: Mm [what was this subject you had in mind?

10. be on(")

11. I was thinking of doing like pretty much what my uncle my uncle had advised ...

12. so that I would have done it on this .. ulcer or gastric ulcer perforation, a comparative study between laparoscopic versus .. open surgery,

13. and then like discussed it from .. many different angles, financially and so on, and so many complications etc., you know,

With the listener oriented by Lassi's "pretty high expectations" about pursuing research (line 3), the first complicating action (Labov, 1972) in the story follows from line 6. Lassi had had his own idea for a research subject, but that had been "rejected out of hand" (line 7; the Finnish metaphor is *tyrmätä*, that is, knock out). The phrasing implies a strong evaluation about what happened as well as an expectation of the opposite. According to my interpretation, what Lassi had expected was respect for his idea, but he was turned down instead. He says that at the time he accepted that his tutor must know better, but now in his telling he ironizes this past self: "Yeah, yeah, okay fair enough." The false start on line 7, too, ("I thought—at that time my reaction was") highlights the difference between his past thoughts and the present. Today Lassi would no longer have such blind faith in a senior colleague's better understanding.

It is interesting to note that Lassi's own idea turns out to be his uncle's (line 11). There are two different rhetorics of the self, two different language games in play. "I did have one idea myself" is needed to make a central point in the story: Lassi's ideas were rejected, whereas the uncle's advice was given to the past Lassi who still depended on authorities. His uncle's voice can be heard on lines 12–13, where Lassi lets it merge with his own as he describes what the original idea was about: Lassi's words are double-voiced (Bakhtin, 1984). Like words, ideas become our own after first being someone else's. We let others' ideas enter our own inner dialogues, we give them new meanings and interpretations so that they can be reinvented as innovations. Likewise, when we reject ideas we once recognized as our own, we may bestow them on others.

Lassi had been "quite enthusiastic" about his own idea for his advanced studies, an idea that had crystallized during his practical period in surgery. Lassi used to consider surgery as a possible future career, it had a special place among all specialties because his uncle was a surgeon. Where Lassi says this in the interview, he is ironic about his past self, who wanted to follow in his uncle's footsteps into the world of surgery and take his advanced studies in surgery as well, "of course." Now, in the narration of the episode of advanced studies, surgery is being carefully reevaluated.

Lassi tells about his growing interest in surgery during a practical period of his education. It was, he says, "pretty good fun," "quite easy" for a trainee who was not responsible. He could enjoy what was "nice" about the surgeon's work and watch all the "super tricks" being done. His expressions play down the importance of surgery, even allowing for the influence of spoken language and Lassi's style. At the time of the interview surgery was still one alternative direction for Lassi's career, so this can hardly be taken as a sign of his devaluing the specialty or surgical work in general. Rather, it is a narrative device that tells about the breaking-down between the past Lassi and the present conscious thinker, the former of which showed uncritical admiration of surgery and surgeons. The reasons why the past self wanted to be a surgeon were different from those of the present Lassi, and these former grounds are here subject to reevaluation by Lassi-the-narrator in the present. (Lines 14–20 omitted.)

21. but it still didn't—Pekka (Pekka) who was my tutor he had something completely different in mind
22. and he had everything set up
23. and he had like—he just picked this book from the bookshelf like (")take this, start working on that, you get to know something about it first but do it anyway("),
24. and I didn-—yeah of course I started working on it,

On line 21 Lassi returns to the story that my question interrupted on line 9. *But* says that his own idea did not get the reception he had expected, but his tutor had "something completely different in mind," had "everything set up" (lines 21–22). On the following line (23) Lassi again reveals his sense of style. Skilfully, without any direct evaluation, he makes it clear that his present self does not accept the way he was once treated by the tutor; his language is highly evaluative instead. If Lassi and his scientific work had been taken seriously, his tutor would not have "just" picked some book and said "take this, start working on that," and he would not have been told to "get to know something about it first," just for the sake of it. "Do it anyway" captures all the disparagement Lassi experienced in his relation to a (former) authority (line 23). The expectation was still to do as he was told to do, "of course," and so Lassi, as he puts it, "yeah of course started working on it."

TAKING ACTION

Lassi started working on the project his tutor suggested to him, and he still means that it was the right thing to do.

25. there was this old dissertation from 1970 or something, Heikki Virtanen had written his thesis on gastric carcinoma and Pekka said that (")no one has done any work on this subject in Finland for twenty-five years so someone should take a look at what's been happening there.(")
26. I thought (")well why not,
27. this is perfectly okay,(")
28. and I mean it was okay and no doubt still is,
29. you could probably I'm sure you probably could have got almost anything out of it but .. I mean
30. I was really excited when I started working on it,
31. in the first phase like in the very first phase Pekka said something like (")we'll go through all the patients in this region(") //I: Mm//

32. I was like (")yes(") I said (")yeah yeah yeah we'll go through them //I: (laughter)// that's okay by me,
33. I'll work alright("), and uhm that (")yeah we do what you say(")
34. and so we started from the university hospital surgical patients and (laughter), I still—it was all new to me
35. and I didn't really understand much about anything
36. and I just asked Pekka what do I do and he just said that (")yeah you begin with the—outline your research plan a bit(")
37. and I outlined it a bit,
38. I didn't know really what it was all about and he practically wrote it for me, this research plan
39. so in that sense he was a good tutor (laughter), //I: Mm mm// helped me a great deal in the beginning
40. and then he just said that (")you go over to the operating ward and start leafing(?) through the operation diary and pick out all the patients who have been operated for CA ventriculi.(")

Lassi was supposed to review the data of all patients who had been diagnosed with advanced cancer of the stomach during the past 20 years and see what had happened to them. He first gives (lines 26–27) the evaluation of his past self of this new subject assigned by his tutor, and then agrees in his present voice, with his present judiciousness (lines 28–29). He thus constructs a narrating "I" who is capable of evaluating, capable of deciding whether the subject was good, and in this way he presents to me a socially acceptable and valuable young physician. If I were not aware of the professional competence of the Lassi of today, I might think I was sitting face to face with a colleague who still does not "really understand much about anything" (line 35).

After his initial disappointment, Lassi regains his enthusiasm on line 30, where the seriousness of Lassi's experience is given a voice in the story, and the tragic potential of the story is revealed. Further on, a comical setting (Burke, 1984, p. 41) is created, the past Lassi as the foolish hero; he was a beginner in the world of science, he did not understand much, and was not responsible for much either (lines 32–38). The hero is benevolently ironized. Whatever the tutor suggested, the past Lassi could only uncritically comply: "yeah yeah yeah we'll go through them that's okay by me" (line 32). Once again I accept the irony and give Lassi a laugh, and by laughing Lassi intensifies his past indiscretion as well (line 34). Even if the expectation may have been otherwise, Lassi "didn't understand much about anything" as he was supposed to write his research plan and get his project off the ground. In general, a negative statement is made only if its affirmative was expected to take place (Labov, 1972; Tannen, 1979/1993, p. 44). The important thing is that the one who does not meet the expectations, the one who does not understand, is the past Lassi; the present Lassi understands more comprehensively.

That the tutor "just" told Lassi what to do (lines 36 and 40) is a very effective means of evaluating his action. Lassi *"outlined* a bit" his research plan as instructed by his tutor (line 37), but he did not really know what it was about: Eventually his tutor *wrote* the plan. Is this not a good tutor? In a way yes, says Lassi at the beginning of line 39, he "helped me a great deal in the beginning." Tutors are supposed to help their students in the beginning, but is that enough? Lassi answers this question by laughing on line 39, suggesting that a question remains to be answered: The tutor was good in one way, what about others? "In that sense" (line 39) invites the listener to narrate on for other interpretations, different stories.

41. and so (laughter) I was really excited when I went there // I: Mm// the first evening to sit there
42. I noticed that there was like //I: (laughter)// a whole wall covered by these diaries
43. and then I started leafing through the pages like (")no bloody hell,(")
44. I started counting how much time I'll be spending on this // I: Mm mm mm//
45. I mean it was an absolutely terrible job to look them all up,
46. there was this old handwriting that was really difficult to read at first,
47. I mean it did get easier but //I: Mm mm// it took an awfully long time,
48. well then I like put my nose down to the grindstone,
49. at first there was this excitement and then it went a bit faster
50. but then it slowed down and slowed down,
51. I thought I'm never going to get to the end,
52. well I did get them done from 1970 to 1990, the operation diaries, so I had the diagnoses and the or the patients' names,
53. then you had to go to the hospital archives and bla bla bla and then you browsed through and tried to find these patients,

Things get complicated again from line 41: Lassi had been "really excited" when he went to spend his first evening on the operating ward. He did this on his tutor's instructions, which left little room for questioning: "And then he just said that you go over to the operating ward and start leafing through the operation diary" (line 40). Besides being thick with expectation, from line 41 on the telling is also rich in details and thick of description (Denzin, 1989a). One can almost see the wall covered by operation diaries and feel the despair of Lassi sitting there, surrounded by dust-covered books, with night falling, trying to decipher the next to illegible handwriting (lines 41–46). Lassi, now the fighting hero, takes on his next to hopeless task, "puts his nose down to the grindstone" (line 48), and it "takes an awfully long time" (line 47). Initially he is driven by a sense of enthusiasm, but a turning point is waiting just around the corner. The enthusiasm is replaced by despair: "But then it slowed down and slowed down, I thought I'm never going to get to the end" (lines 50–51). Yet the Lassi who "started counting" how much time it would all take (line 44) and who "put his nose into the grindstone" (line 48) shows more activity and commitment than the one who was not responsible or really involved in the early stages of the project (lines 31–40).

Now that Lassi is telling the story, he can evaluate his past activity and its rationale. Again, evaluation is found in his choice of words. Once he had found the patients' names in the diaries, Lassi had to dig out their case records from the hospital archives, and "bla bla bla and then you browsed through" the records (which is not a serious scientific activity compared with reading them; line 53). "Bla bla bla" can be used to cut the story short when the listener is supposed to know what a researcher does in the archives, yet as far as I can tell it is not really included in the terminology with which doctors describe scientific work. Lassi's past self thought he was conducting scientific research, but Lassi the narrator has serious doubts.

In the archives Lassi ran into difficulties again. It was "an awful lot of work" to find all the records he needed, some of them were on microfilm and others were never found. At this stage of the story the past Lassi also begins to realize that even in university hospitals, not all records are "really accurate."

58. and I always asked for Pekka every now and then and he didn't have time
59. and then I was supposed to—and then I really started to get bogged down,
60. well I got it all done [at] the hospital and then he said, (")well the thing is this, you're going to go to Herttala hospital,(")
61. I thought (")wellwell("), so it's off to Herttala then, the same thing, plowing through all them twenty years in the books, // I: (laughter) oh no//
62. well I did them and then looked up the patients,
63. well that I did like in one big crunch, I actually did it, at that stage it looked pretty good and

64. I got them it went pretty quickly and painlessly and then I
   was like really pushing ahead,

Lassi did not know how to interpret all of his data and he tried to ask his tutor for help. The tutor was not available, however (line 58), and Lassi "really started to get bogged down" (line 59). When he was finished with one hospital Lassi went on to another and yet another.

TURNING POINT

In the fourth hospital, the turning point of the story and the breaking down of Lassi's expectations will finally take place.

68. and uhm . and then the last one was the Old Hospital
69. and so I went over to the Old Hospital,

In the fourth and last hospital, after countless hours in the archives, Lassi met for the first time "a real scientist," a chief physician who had the time to sit down and go through Lassi's research plan. Lassi defines *scientist* through a definition of its antithesis: The other chief physicians, not real scientists, were busy and did not have the time for detail. They gave the support they absolutely had to but were not really interested in Lassi's project.

75. but this Simo Luukko over at (laughter) the Old Hospital
   he was like that, when I went over there I noticed straightaway that (")okay, right this is something completely different here,(")
76. it was really like—first we sat down and had a look at the
   research plans,
77. he was a bit surprised that it wasn't really like polished and
   carefully prepared
78. it was kind of a bit like an advanced (advanced) study sort
   of thing, the research plan, and it hadn't really been—
79. he straightaway asked an awful lot of questions for which I
   had no answers and
80. then I started to realize that (")yeah perhaps it hadn't been
   very well planned this thing of mine after all,(")
81. and then he like said (")okay like what shall we(")
82. and I said (")yes, I'd need to have these—uhm where do
   you keep—I'd probably should have to get your operation diaries(")

83. so he looked at me for a while and said (")no-o, we have these discharge (discharge) registers, just give the diagnosis number and he'll get them all for you,(") //I: Mm//

84. then I realized—it was then that I started to realize that (")no-o bloody hell all that work I've done looking them up over there,(") they have these same registers everywhere at least at the university hospital, you could have got them directly for example there

85. but you just like can't—and you don't—and like a-—

86. I had spent no end of time on what like on what could have been got just by asking

The turning point of the episode is getting closer as the "real scientist" finally takes his time and gets acquainted with Lassi's research plan. The plan turns out to be an "advanced study sort of thing," "not really polished and carefully prepared" (lines 77–78), whereas Lassi had had a scientific career and doctoral thesis in mind. Lassi makes a false start on line 78 and does not complete his direct evaluation of the plan; the evaluation would be problematic. If the listener still remembers that it was Lassi's tutor who actually wrote the plan, she will catch Lassi's disappointment with the tutor's scientific orientation and, first of all, with the tutor in which Lassi had put all his faith. The assistance Lassi received at the beginning of his research project turns out to be illusion now that he is faced by a "real scientist," and Lassi is unable to answer his many questions (line 79). On line 80 the present Lassi steps forth: "Then I started to realize." The eyes of the foolish hero are finally opened; Lassi started to realize he had wasted countless hours, instead of plowing through operation diaries he could have found everything with one register search. On line 85, Lassi (as I hear his words) comes close to naming the guilty party, but again it remains a false start. "Could have been got just by asking" on line 86 does not explicate who should have asked.

The "real scientist's" voice enters Lassi's story and provides his present self the courage to emerge. What this figuration of true science lacks, though, is a supportive word and emotional warmth. The scientist's task, besides informing about the discharge registers, is to point to the mistakes made, and he leaves Lassi with a final sense of failure, now knowing what went wrong. The voice of true science knows no mercy.

90. and then in the end they were about one-hundred-and-eighty patients whose case records I had read more or less from cover to cover and done awful a lot of different and so on,

91. and it took an awful lot of time and I'd gathered quite an extensive data set,

92. but ... it was kind of like...—
93. I got this feeling somehow that since it hadn't been planned
   so very carefully and
94. and I mean even if I thought I'd done a pretty careful job
   I—it still turned out that I hadn't done it nearly as carefully
   as it should have been done and,
95. I don't know if it was just like my own self-criticism that ...
   all these interpretations when you read the records of one-
   hundred-and-ninety patients and you've got certain things
   you're collecting on them,
96. they're not all //I: Mm mm// that unambiguous, you've got
   to put it somewhere and on the other hand you don't always
   have the time to ask ...
97. and you can't always be bothered to go and ask your tutor
   how is this
98. and then it may change a bit over time, that they should all
   be done in one go and preferably gone through one more
   time //I: Mm mm mm// to make sure they're correct and all

The next subnarrative begins on line 90 where Lassi starts to review
the case records of 180 patients with carcinoma of the stomach. It took "an
awful lot of time" to find and take the notes he needed, but in the end he
had assembled "an extensive data set" (line 91). The story gets complicated
on line 92, which is marked with *but*: Lassi is again faced by the inadequate
planning of his research. He evaluates the planning, but with false starts
(line 92) and hedges (*kind of* on line 92 and *somehow* on line 93). I take
his hesitation to mean that he still cannot concede explicitly that the
planning had really been inadequate. He speaks about his own feeling
instead. He is not expected to give a direct negative evaluation of a research
plan written by his tutor—that is, by someone who is supposed to know
better. He continues to use the passive voice, which also hints at a problematic explanation. In his own opinion, Lassi had taken his notes carefully,
but as it turns out not "nearly as carefully as it should have been done"
(line 94). Yes, he had been careful, which he soon asserts again on line
102, but how could he have been careful enough when he "didn't really
understand much about anything" (line 35) in the beginning. He had trusted
his tutor and followed his advice.

When he was reading the case records and taking notes, Lassi did not
always have time (line 96) or could not always be bothered (line 97) to
find his tutor and ask him for advice even if he needed it. He repeats that
it was not possible in practice to ask whenever in doubt. Now it is Lassi
who does not have the time or who cannot be bothered—that is, he cannot
and does not want to run to his tutor with questions. On line 58 he still

asked the tutor who "didn't have time." Has the tutor's lack of time been transmitted to Lassi, too? Maybe so, but I would still suggest another interpretation: The turning point of the story is situated between the two explanations, and Lassi has now adopted a new rhetoric of the self and new expectations about this acting self, instead of the past self, line 58, who could not get the support he asked for. That is why Lassi no longer has the time.

RESULT

After things start getting complicated, the result of the narrative terminates the series of events and reveals what finally happened (Labov, 1972).

   99. and then I realized that (")no-o that .. no this thing is not as valid as I(")—

100. but on the other hand it was still reasonably—

101. I still think it is quite—

102. I did do a careful enough job

103. and it didn't—

104. it did sort of get bogged down in the summary bit, as the result was that like in twenty years there had been no development, //I: (laughter)// that they all die (laughter) of it anyway, so //I: Mm//

105. so there wasn't really any sensible nothing sensible was like [found]

106. I: Mm well that's a result I suppose [as well

107. Yeah it was quite a good result

108. but I wasn't—I was expecting something a bit different // I: (laughter)//, that it would have produced some kind of—

109. I don't even know what I expected but

110. well it was a result anyway and then I .. scribbled something up in a couple of evenings, out of these results

111. and so that was my advanced studies then

112. but somehow there did remain something of an aftertaste of doing science,

113. mainly I mean I had put in an awful lot of work,

114. and then what did I get out of it, advanced studies,

The key episode proceeds from line 99: Lassi, the protagonist, has learned that what he had taken to be scientific research was not as valid as he had first expected. The explanation is highly problematic, though. On line 95 he suggests that it was all down to his own self-criticism. However, he wants to reestablish his honor and value (from line 100). His research was not valid, yet he knew he "did do a careful enough job" (line 102).

From line 99, he makes four false starts, he is really struggling to find the right words for what he has to say. There is a conflict between Lassi both having (line 102) and not having (line 94) worked thoroughly enough. Yet Lassi-the-narrator will stand up for his past self.

On line 104 he reattunes his ironic voice when he tells about his final report being delayed. I quickly intervene to try and heal the lesion in his doctor's honor (line 106) and say that his result was good enough. But Lassi had expected something more, even though he makes a false start out of it on line 108. He had expected a lot, but it is problematic to admit; the past Lassi must not be told to have been all too unwise or his expectations excessive. There was no reason for a real commitment any more, and Lassi "scribbled something up in a couple of evenings" (line 110). Indeed, the excitement of the past hero pushing ahead to reach what for him was an aspiration would, if assigned to the Lassi now finishing the project, make him seem more or less foolish. The final fullfilment was never allowed to the poor hero, but the whole effort had suddenly atrophied instead. All that remained was "something of an aftertaste of doing science" (line 112).

Lassi's expectation structure has broken down, but what had he expected? On line 99 he points to his expectation of doing scientifically valid research, which did not materialize, at least in his own opinion. His project was good enough to give him the credits he needed for the completion of his advanced studies, but it was not much of a base for a future scientific career (lines 114, 130). Further, he is disappointed with the result he finally got (line 104); he had, I think, expected a result that would have clarified the preferential treatment for the disease instead of finding that "there had been no development"—which, as I point out, is as good a result as any. The broken expectation that lies behind the others and that is most carefully hidden in evaluative language—hedges and false starts—is the one about getting the amount and kind of support Lassi needed from his tutor.

Lassi hints at an ironic reading throughout the story; his style (like the "bla bla bla" on line 53) is not one a doctor is supposed to use in a serious account of scientific work. Yet it is only now that the listener knows enough to see clearly the incongruity between Lassi's original ambitions and the outcome of the project. The intended irony in his story is revealed as it becomes obvious that Lassi's words about his endless nights on the operating ward cannot be taken as a straightforward description of a brave hero that finally overcomes all the hardship and triumphs.

Lassi is a skillful narrator with a sense of irony, but what the ironic tone in his telling implies is more than just narrative competence. Irony will not be used unless the speaker feels confident that the listener knows when his words are not to be taken literally. The listener–reader must share some beliefs, and this shared understanding of what is not explicated connects the narrator and his listener with the ties of a relationship. Irony has a social character (Booth, 1974; Perelman & Olbrechts-Tyteca, 1971, p. 208). While Lassi was telling his life story, I was under the impression he was talking more to himself than to me. During the first of the two hours that the interview lasted, he paid hardly any attention to me at all. But Lassi's turning inward and speaking, as it seemed, pretty much to himself, were ironic actions: They were to be taken the roundabout way. Lassi spoke to me, too, or rather to the implied listener in me as he could not know my beliefs particularly. Lassi's audience was, besides himself, any (young) colleague that, with her presumed understanding, now became palpable in me (Hyvärinen, 1994, p. 125).

Lassi's story is a good example of how form and style are not just decorative elements pasted on to the story, but an integral part of message and meaning of the story. The point of irony is to expose how reality often fails to meet the expectations about it, and how individuals and social orders are not as noble as they may first seem—it is sometimes a fine line between irony and cynicism (Murray, 1989). Unlike hidden polemic speech, in parodistic discourse and ironic style the other's voice and viewpoint is heard, but is then made into an opponent whose otherness is emphasized and who is finally turned against itself, to give support to the speaker's original voice (Bakhtin, 1984, pp. 193–194). Parody accepts multiplicity of voices but not their parallelism; it creates hierarchic relations between voices and makes one a servant of the other.

Lassi parodies both his tutor (for example line 23: "He just picked this book from the bookshelf like take this, start working on that, you get to know something about it first but do it anyway") and his own past self (line 32: "yeah yeah yeah we'll go through them that's okay by me"). He lets both of these voices be heard in his story, but by ironizing them, his tutor's lack of attention to detail and his past self's lack of will, he turns them against themselves: The present Lassi's own voice, the true scientist's in origin, resounds loudest, and that is how he manages to question the tutor's authority.

OUTCOME

By the end of the story, the point of narrating shifts from explicating what happened to evaluating the significance of it all to the narrator's present and future.

116. and then .. Pekka would have wanted me to go on doing research there, //I: Mm//
117. he kept calling me here for a long long time and all, you know like (")come on over here and see us and work there's all sorts here(") (unclear)

118. and I just tried you know somehow politely //I: (laughter)//
     like no thank you like no, yes no,
119. now he's given this up, I haven't heard from him for a long
     time that //I: Mm mm mm//
120. so that that job that's all over with
121. that I'm not going to I won't d- I'm not going to start doing
     anything there .. and I won't—
122. it just was that I have certainly not ruled out the possibility
     of doing science
123. but it still it wasn't my thing, //I: Mm mm mm//
124. it started out perhaps a bit on the wrong foot from the
     beginning so that I didn't
125. even though I was in a sense excited about it but
126. I wasn't excited about it in that way because I mean on
     the one hand I didn't really understand these things at
     the time,
127. I think that Pekka should have—
128. although he was an okay tutor and really—he always had
     the time when you wanted to but
129. I didn't know what to ask and he somehow didn't know
     what to tell me, //I: Mm mm mm//
130. so I mean I think the whole thing got off a bit on the wrong
     foot so that a scientific career didn't really get off to any
     start here.

Lassi tells about his own competence as a potential researcher with
his tutor's voice. The tutor kept calling him and wanted him on his research
team even after Lassi had completed his advanced studies project (from line
116). However, Lassi had now become an actor himself and could turn
down the offer. He has not given up his anticipation of research in the
future (line 122), where the negative statement refers to the background
expectation that doctors should do research. For the moment, though, Lassi
is aware that this is not his thing anyway (line 123). He has to give accounts
for this statement, not least because he is sitting face to face with a colleague
who is conducting an interview for her doctoral thesis. Once again he finds
himself at a loss trying to explain why he, for the moment, has chosen not
to meet the expectation. Lassi did not develop a strong enough interest
because at the beginning of his scientific career he did not really gain an
insight into what he was doing. "I think that Pekka should have" remains
a false start on line 127, and Lassi goes on to confirm that Pekka was a
good tutor who always had time to spare. The problem was that Lassi did
not know the right questions and the tutor did not give him the answers,

but this evaluation of what went wrong can only be given by the present Lassi in the context of the interview.

131. so I decided at that stage that no that I'm not going to—
     that now,
133. that from now on I want to take a closer look at the job first
134. now I have like a couple of times before, I went to medical school and got my advanced studies started pretty much in a rush
135. so it's been pretty close a few times that I've regret—regretted this decision (decision) that it's come a bit too quickly a major decision
136. so that I'd really like to if I may w- may express my wish
137. and if there's any chance then,
138. in the future I'd gather (gather) experience in as many fields and specialties as possible and if it only—
139. it is (it's) hard to know what—
140. you change your mind quickly if you find something you like.

The story and the present time meet and project to the future from line 131 in the coda of the episode (Labov, 1972, p. 365). By going through the setback of his advanced studies in his early career, Lassi the hero has grown to presence of mind. He does not want to rush into major decisions any more, but he wants to look around first and gain experience working in different places. According to my interpretation, the episode of Lassi's advanced studies is a key episode in his story, an episode in which Lassi's aspiration to construct a consistent self out of discordance of life and life story is intensified (Hyvärinen, 1994). He uses his past experience to articulate a self, and he does this with a key rhetoric of present and past selves (Komulainen, 1998a, 1998b), the latter of which lived his life following others' advice and example, without giving too much attention to motives or consequences.

The present self, by contrast, is left with a new kind of ambivalence and no self-evident trajectory to follow to the future. In the turmoil of the episode, Lassi's future plans for career and specialty change or give way to suspense, not so much because he was disappointed by surgery or science as such but because his past grounds are no longer valid. At the same time, his present self is capable of reflection and of evaluating and being critical of former choices and authorities. I would argue that one of the firmest expectation structures that is broken down in the episode is the expectation about absolute collegiality, which includes respect for anyone higher up in the hierarchy and, equally important, responsibility for a colleague who is lower down and in need of support. Nevertheless, it is extremely problematic for Lassi to show his own social value by maintaining that his failure in the advanced studies project was partly the fault of his tutor, who did not assume responsibility. Lassi comes close to slipping into uncollegiality himself. He makes one false start after another and hides his evaluation in evaluative language and ironic style. It is only at the end of this long episode that he finally shares the responsibility between his past, uncritical self and the tutor who "didn't know what to tell" him.

LASSI'S QUEST FOR COHERENCE

Having started out from parallelism of the whole and multiplicity, it seems that I am ending up celebrating the former: Lassi's search for one self. I read for others' multiple words and expectations in Lassi's story, but only to see the final coherence dawn. Before we departed after the interview, Lassi said it had been necessary for him to work through his past. In this I hear him expressing his own quest for a narrative identity or a vision of the whole. With his actual questions in mind, Lassi turned to his personal past, choosing to tell what seemed important from the viewpoint of today (Freeman, 1993). It was these experiences that elicited the story and that were articulated by the story he told (Widdershoven, 1993).

When the interview was conducted in late 1996, Lassi had in his life and career come to a crossroads: He liked working in the collegial atmosphere of a health center, but as to the work itself he sometimes longed for something else. The unemployment situation that had been a real threat for (young) doctors in the early 1990s had already taken a turn for the better, yet Lassi could not take it for granted that he would find another job in the city where he lived. From this present Lassi looks back. However, despite the sudden turns of the surrounding world, my cultural understanding tells me that neither discontinuity nor ambivalence are expected in too great a measure in a doctor's self, life, and career. By telling, as he could do, simply about a doctor who has given up his previous ambitions to become a surgeon and a scientist and who is just waiting and seeing and, in his own words, "does not even get round to" looking for his next job, Lassi would risk appearing improper in his own eyes and mine.

I do not think that Lassi's own personal identity is based on a rhetorical transition between his past and present selves, though. Another reading of his story is possible with Lassi as other than a product, but rather the subject of his personal dialogue. Listening to Lassi interpreting his own life, I hear in his story an expression of personal change and professional growth. He works through his past, plots his way from his advanced studies to his present doubt, to see how his experience of frustration finally provides him with an explanation, a justification, for his "waiting and seeing" and a vision of a future that is not fixed. From line 131 onward in his key episode, he joins his memories, his acting (and narrating) self in the present, and his anticipation of the future in a coherent whole that bridges the fractures in the continuity of his life, experience, and identity (Crites, 1997).

READING FOR THE TRUTH

"Concordant discordance" (Ricoeur, 1984, pp. 65–66) between the story as a whole and all the sudden reversals is, according to Hyvärinen (1998, pp. 165–170), needed in the story to construct the character and the depth of the story. The story needs a sufficient amount of coherence to be understandable and a sufficient amount of diversity to be interesting; I guess so does a self. In the analysis I may "analytically bracket" (Gubrium & Holstein, 1998, p. 165) one and read for the other. However, while privileging the diversity and multivoicedness of narrative identity, it is hard to deny we experience ourselves as more or less authentic, coherent, and continuous (de Peuter, 1998, p. 43). The further I move from reaching for Lassi's experience toward reading textually for expectations that guide Lassi's telling or the diversity of voices in his quest for the self, the more I feel I have a dialogue with the story text; Lassi who once sat with me in his own livingroom and shared with me his life experiences draws further away.

Our life stories are the fiber with which we are connected to others. We share with others our stories, often just pieces and fragments of them, to tell others something about ourselves and to construct ourselves as moral actors in others' eyes. Coherence is not an absolute property of the person narrating or an absolute property of the story text. Instead, coherence is achieved situationally where the story succeeds in convincing the addressee about the narrator's moral and social value. The listener's task is to approve and understand, or sometimes negotiate, the moral point made and the ethical self represented in the story (Linde, 1993).

As a researcher I am supposed to take seriously the dialogics and multivoicedness of the self, but as a partner in concrete dialogue, I should be sensitive to the point of the story, to the narrator's truth. This point may vary in the intensity with which it strives for unity and in its openness to diversity; the interviewees who see life as a great dialogue probably *want* to be made contradictory; only then do they experience that I have heard their multiple meanings. The process and dialogue of searching itself is important for Lassi, too. Still he is narrating for a solution, albeit not a final one. He is also narrating for my understanding what it meant to him to fall from the height of expectations and how his present consciousness about himself grew out of this disaster.

In a dialogic relationship, I am supposed to respect the other's own consciousness about him or herself. I can only listen to the other and extend that other's points of view "to the outside limits of plausibility" (Bakhtin, 1984, p. 69). The other's consciousness cannot, Bakhtin argued, be reached and analyzed as an object; it can only be related to in a dialogue. To think about the other's inner world of meanings is to talk *with* it (Bakhtin, 1984, p. 68). Denzin (1989b, p. 81) wrote that "there is no truth in the painting of a life," saying that personal stories are always fictions, constructions whose meaning is not to be found in their correspondence with factual truth. Life stories are true in another sense: They are told to image the real, "the truth such as it appears to me" (Lejeune, 1989, p. 22). When working with life stories, it is next to impossible to push into the fading background the human beings, the concrete others who once told me their stories and shared with me something of their privacy. It has an impact on my relationship to my interviewees, and perhaps to the other in general, if I see the personal truth in a life story or if I do not. It is only when I do that I become a conarrator of the teller's story and self in the dynamic relationship between synthesis and dispersion, identity and difference.

To relate to the other dialogically does not mean an illusion of complete understanding, or knowing the whole person. Bakhtin wrote that every word we utter is directed toward an answer and understanding. The word only has a meaning when it is given one by the listener—that is, when it is heard and assimilated into the listener's inner dialogue where it meets with other words and gets a reading (Bakhtin, 1981, pp. 280–283); this is what Bakhtin called active understanding (1981, p. 282; 1986, pp. 68–70), living conversation in which meanings and identities are never fixed but always open to change. For example, in my inner dialogue, I listen to the dialects of my own past, my generation, and my profession, because these dialects construct *me* (Booth, 1986, p. 153). Understanding does not mean, therefore, that there *is* one single truth in the other's words; rather it means relating to the other's words as a personal truth I can never completely reach. We can never know the other, we can only listen to the words of the other, imagine what the other might be like (Josselson, 1995), and be surprised by the other (Morson, 1986). Josselson calls this the research paradigm of discovery.

Life transitions become life transitions only when they are given that meaning. If Bakhtin is right, the one who gives the meaning is in the end not the narrator him or herself but anyone who listens to the words and takes them seriously. It is the listener who either allows or denies the narrator coherence and personal change. What a responsibility.

REFERENCES

Bakhtin, M. M. (1981). *The dialogic imagination. Four essays by M. M. Bakhtin.* (Eds. & Trans. M. Holquist, C. Emerson, & M. Holquist). Austin: University of Texas Press.

Bakhtin, M. (1984). *Problems of Dostoevsky's poetics. Theory and history of literature,* Vol 8 (Ed. & Trans. C. Emerson). Minneapolis: University of Minnesota Press.

Bakhtin, M. M. (1986). *Speech genres and other late essays* (Eds. C. Emerson & M. Holquist; Trans. V. W. McGee). Austin: University of Texas Press.

Booth, W. C. (1974). *A rhetoric of irony.* Chicago: University of Chicago Press.

Booth, W. (1986). Freedom of interpretation: Bakhtin and the challenge of feminist criticism. In G. S. Morson (Ed.), *Bakhtin. Essays and dialogues on his work.* Chicago: The University of Chicago Press.

Burke, K. (1984). *Attitudes toward History* (3rd ed.). Berkeley: University of California Press.

Crites, S. (1997). The narrative quality of experience. In L. P. Hinchman & S. K. Hinchman (Eds.), *Memory, identity, community: The idea of narrative in the human sciences* (pp. 26–50). Albany: State University of New York Press.

Denzin, N. K. (1989a). *Interpretive interactionism. Applied social research method series* Vol. 16. Newbury Park, CA: Sage.

Denzin, N. K. (1989b). *Interpretive biography. Qualitative research methods Vol. 17.* Newbury Park, CA: Sage.

Fairclough, N. (1992). Discourse and text: Linguistic and intertextual analysis within discourse analysis. *Discourse and Society, 3*(2), 193–217.

Freeman, M. (1993). *Rewriting the self. History, memory, narrative.* New York: Routledge.

Gubrium, J. F., & Holstein, J. A. (1998). Narrative practice and the coherence of personal stories. *The Sociological Quarterly, 39,* 163–187.

Halila, H. (1998). Finland. In G. Eysenbach (Ed.), *Medicine and medical education in Europe* (pp. 148–169). Stuttgart: Georg Thieme Verlag.

Hyvärinen, M. (1994). *Viimeiset taistot* (The Last Fights). Tampere, Finland: Vastapaino.

Hyvärinen, M. (1997). Rhetoric and conversion in student politics: Looking backward. In T. Carver & M. Hyvärinen (Eds.), *Interpreting the political. New methodologies* (pp. 18–38). New York: Routledge.

Hyvärinen, M. (1998). Thick and thin narratives: Thickness of description, expectation, and causality. In N. Denzin (Ed.), *Cultural studies: A research volume* (Vol. 3, pp. 149–174). Stamford, CT: JAI Press.

Josselson, R. (1995). Imagining the real. Empathy, narrative, and the dialogic self. In R. Josselson & A. Lieblich (Eds.), *The narrative study of lives, vol 3: Interpreting experience* (pp. 27–44). Thousand Oaks, CA: Sage.

Komulainen, K. (1998a). Naisten naissuhteet. Kerrottu ja puhuteltu sukupuoli itsenäistymiskertomuksissa (Relations of women to women: Told and addressed gender in independence narratives). In M. Hyvärinen, E. Peltonen, & A. Vilkko (Eds.), *Liikkuvat erot: sukupuoli elämäkertatutkimuksessa* (pp. 153–185). Tampere, Finland: Vastapaino.

Komulainen, K. (1998b). A course of one's own: The rhetorical self in educational life stories by women. English summary in Katri Komulainen, *Kotihiiriä ja ihmisiä: Retorinen minä naisten koulutusta koskevissa elämänkertomuksissa* (pp. 299–312). Publications in Social Sciences n:o 35. Joensuun yliopistopaino, Finland: University of Joensuu.

Labov, W. (1972). The transformation of experience in narrative syntax. In W. Labov, *Language in the inner city* (pp. 354–396). Philadelphia: University of Pennsylvania Press.

Lejeune, P. (1989). *On autobiography. Theory and history of literature, Vol. 52* (Ed. J. P. Eakin; Trans. K. Leary) Minneapolis: University of Minnesota Press.

Linde, C. (1993). *Life stories and the creation of coherence.* New York: Oxford University Press.

Morson, G. S. (1986). Preface: Perhaps Bakhtin. In G. S. Morson (Ed.), *Bakhtin. Essays and dialogues on his work.* Chicago: The University of Chicago Press.

Murray, K. (1989). The construction of identity in the narratives of romance and comedy. In J. Shotter & K. Gergen (Eds.), *Texts of identity* (pp. 176–205). London: Sage.

Perelman, C., & L. Olbrechts-Tyteca (1971). *The new rhetoric. A treatise of argumentation.* Notre Dame, IN: University of Notre Dame Press.

de Peuter, J. (1998). The dialogics of narrative identity. In M. M. Bell & M. Gardiner (Eds.), *Bakhtin and the human sciences.* London: Sage.

Ricoeur, P. (1984). *Time and narrative, Vol. I.* Chicago: University of Chicago Press.

Sampson, E. E. (1993). *Celebrating the other: A dialogic account of human nature.* New York: Harvester Wheatsheaf.

Tannen, D. (1993). What's in a frame? Surface evidence for underlying expectations. In D. Tannen (Ed.), *Framing in discourse* (pp. 14–56). New York: Oxford University Press. (Original work published 1979)

Widdershoven, G. A. M. (1993). The story of life. Hermeneutic perspectives on the relationship between narrative and life history. In R. Josselson & A. Lieblich (Eds.), *The narrative study of lives* (Vol. 1; pp. 1–20). New York: Sage.

8

WOMEN'S UNDERSTANDINGS OF THEIR OWN DIVORCES: A DEVELOPMENTAL PERSPECTIVE

AMY M. YOUNG, ABIGAIL J. STEWART, AND KATHI MINER-RUBINO

Marital dissolution has been the focus of considerable social science research, and much of that research has conceived of the ending of a marriage as a life transition or a turning point (see, e.g., Ahrons, 1980, 1995; Ebaugh, 1988; Hetherington, 1979, 1989; Weiss, 1975). For example, Stewart, Copeland, Chester, Malley, and Barenbaum (1997) reviewed seven psychological constructs often used in studying divorce, five of which suggest that divorces are often transitions and turning points: trauma, loss, life stress, opportunity for growth, family transformation. Research has recognized that divorces often involve enormous pain for some or all of those involved, and at the same time they sometimes permit considerable release from strain or personal growth for some or all of those involved. A large proportion of research on divorce has focused on the impact of parental divorce on children (see, e.g., Amato & Keith, 1991; Emery, 1988; Kurdek, 1987; Wallerstein & Kelly, 1980; Wallerstein & Blakeslee, 1989) or on the transformation of the family as a system as a result of parental divorce (Ahrons, 1980; Stewart et al., 1997). Some research does focus on the perspective of individual adults who divorce, and some of that research explores adults' constructions of their experiences in the context of marital dissolution (see especially Riessman, 1990). However, even those studies rarely take a developmental or lifespan perspective on the adults' experience.

In this chapter we will consider the value of a developmental or lifespan perspective for examining adults' experience with divorce. A significant

We would like to thank the members of our research group (Alison Climo, Pamela Hartman, and Isis Settles), as well as David G. Winter, for ongoing feedback about this project and an early version of the manuscript. We are also grateful to the women in the Radcliffe Longitudinal Study who have shared their perspectives on their lives so generously.

body of theory and research suggests that adulthood is not a monolithic period; instead it is marked by periods in which particular preoccupations or life tasks dominate as others recede in importance (see, e.g., Erikson, 1980; Gould, 1980; Levinson, 1978, 1996; Wrightsman, 1988). Although there are no rigid age boundaries to adult "stages" and even no rigid sequence to them, there is reason to believe that the early adult years are dominated by concerns about finding one's place in the adult social world. For middle- and upper-class adults this may involve finding a "vocation" or "calling"— a professional identity; for poor and working-class adults it may involve finding secure employment that fits one's skills and knowledge and is reasonably satisfying (Erikson, 1968; Josselson, 1987, 1996; Marcia, 1980).

Most adults also seek to establish a satisfying personal life (perhaps at the same time, perhaps a little earlier or later). This may include an intimate partner, children, a friendship network, and/or an extended family. But most people spend some part of early adulthood developing relationships to which they become committed—relationships that they hope will persist through much of the rest of life (Erikson, 1980; Josselson, 1992; McAdams, 1985).

Finally, many adults seek to make a contribution beyond their work and family. They may be involved with neighborhood or community events, take part in political processes, engage in cultural activities; or pursue this goal in other ways. Sometimes the wish to make a contribution is expressed partly or wholly through family or work activities, but often it is expressed in participation in activities that have a wider or broader frame of reference (Erikson, 1980; McAdams & de St. Aubin, 1998; Peterson & Stewart, 1990, 1993, 1996; Stewart, Franz, & Layton, 1988).

It seemed to us that adults who were primarily focused on one or another of these major developmental tasks would approach their primary relationships, as well as endings of them, from different perspectives. Although these different perspectives might not influence their relationships per se, we did expect that they would affect the meaning of those relationships to them. Thus a lifespan developmental perspective could be useful in understanding how people make sense of their own divorces, at the time and retrospectively. Because there is so little research articulating different meanings or implications of divorces at different ages or life stages, we did not articulate detailed hypotheses and set out to test them. Instead, using our general understanding of important themes in adult development, we conducted an exploratory qualitative analysis of women's accounts of their divorces. These accounts were gathered in the course of collecting data for an ongoing longitudinal study beginning in 1974 when the women were 31, through 1996, when they averaged 53. These data permitted us to compare the accounts of women who divorced in their 20s, 30s, and 40s using data collected over most of their adulthood. We approached the data with an awareness of the adult developmental theories that cover these years, particularly the themes that Erikson (1950, 1968, 1980) identified with this period—identity, intimacy, and generativity.

AVAILABLE DATA ABOUT WOMEN'S VIEWS OF THEIR OWN DIVORCES

The participants were a subsample of a larger study of women who graduated from college in 1964 and have been part of a longitudinal sample studied extensively by Stewart and her colleagues (see Stewart & Vandewater, 1993, for an overview). In 1964, 244 women were part of an initial research project concerning liberal arts education for males and females (see Winter, McClelland, & Stewart, 1981). Follow-up questionnaires were mailed to the women of this initial sample in 1974, 1979, 1986, 1991, and 1996, when the women were ages 31, 37, 43, 48, and 53, respectively. More than 100 women completed each follow-up wave, with data collected in at least one of these waves by 170 women, or 70% of the original sample. In each wave of the study, the participants were asked basic demographic questions; a number of open- and closed-ended questions about their well-being, personality, work, and family lives, and previous life experiences. In responding to broad questions (e.g., about the high and low points in their lives and about their activities and hopes for the future), as well as in more direct questions (e.g., about their marriages and divorces), women often gave us a good picture of their marriages and their divorces. Because the data were open-ended, some women were more detailed and forthcoming than others, so naturally the data vary in richness across different women. Because we are depending on data not designed to gain a detailed picture of women's ideas about their divorces, our findings must be viewed as exploratory and preliminary in nature.

It is also worth noting that these women are part of a particular cohort of women (and men). Stewart and her colleagues (Stewart & Healy, 1989; Stewart & Ostrove, 1998; Stewart & Vandewater, 1993) have outlined the ways in which this sample was part of a "transitional" cohort—raised with "traditional" White middle-class values about gender roles but influenced by the women's movement and other social changes they encountered in their young adulthood. That encounter sometimes confirmed personal dispositions to resist conventional gender socialization, sometimes catalyzed personal transformation, and sometimes produced resistance (see, e.g., Stewart, 1994).

The fact that this cohort slightly predates the "baby boom" generation means that it has generally experienced disjunction between the world of its rearing and the world of its young adulthood. In the area of marriage and family, the world of its rearing was certainly conservative and traditional, stressing the importance of avoiding divorce and of performing the conventional roles of providers (for men) and of wives and mothers (for women; see Coontz, 1992; Skolnick, 1991). However, legal restrictions and constraints on divorce were loosened in the period of this cohort's young adulthood, coinciding with continually rising divorce rates until about 1988, when they plateaued (Rice, 1994; Thornton, 1989). As a result, we may expect that the women in this sample were raised to view divorce as rare and catastrophic, but experienced both knowledge of the rising probability of divorce and its increased acceptability in their young adulthoods (Amato & Keith, 1991). The women in this cohort who divorced in their 20s divorced at the beginning of this period of liberalization, and those who divorced in their 40s may have felt some of the backlash that emerged in the 1990s against divorce (see Stacey, 1991). In any case all of them were part of the broad national trend for divorce rates to increase and then plateau in the period from the mid-1960s to the early 1990s.

Women were selected for inclusion in our analyses for this chapter if they had been legally married and subsequently divorced ($N = 78$ by age 53). Of these 78 women, 27 were excluded because they provided little or no information on their first divorce (i.e., they left questions about marriage and divorce blank or did not participate in a wave near the time of the divorce), leaving a total sample of 51 women for analysis. These 51 women were divided into three groups by age; women who divorced in their 20s ($n = 18$), women who divorced in their 30s ($n = 22$), and women who divorced in their 40s ($n = 11$). Even though some of the women were married and divorced more than once (14% of entire sample), the analyses were based on accounts of the first divorce for all of the women.

Files containing all of the open- and close-ended questions from all available waves of data for 30 women (10 from each group) were separately reviewed by each of the three authors to identify themes that seemed to distinguish the three groups from each other. This process yielded a total of 25 consensual themes, with examples; this coding scheme was then used by the first author to systematically content-code whatever data were available from all waves, from all 51 women, with women from the three groups mixed together. Fifteen percent of the files were also coded by the second author (interrater percent agreement = .95). Of the 25 themes, 18 differentiated the three groups, 4 were infrequently coded in all three groups, and 3 were frequently coded but did not differentiate the groups (see Table 8-1 for a list of all of the themes).[1] When we illustrate themes by quoting

---

[1] It is important to note that percentages of women showing evidence for each theme is presented in Table 8-1 as well as throughout the chapter to provide the reader with a sense of the extent to which each theme was expressed by women in each group. This information should not be used to draw inferences about the larger population.

TABLE 8-1

Themes and Percentage of Endorsement for Women Who Divorced in
Their 20s, 30s, and 40s

Theme		Women who divorced in their		
		20s	30s	40s
Frequently reported and differentiated groups				
Self	Period of self-questioning and depression	50%	14%	18%
	Adaptable/flexible personality	0	23%	27%
	Strong self-definition	67%	18%	9%
	Ongoing depression	6%	32%	18%
Marriage	High conflict divorce	6%	18%	0
	Difficulties with spouse's behavior or personality	6%	41%	18%
	Marriage served earlier purpose	0	0	36%
	Marriage hampered individual pursuits	11%	5%	45%
	Incentive to marry early	17%	0	9%
	Unfair/unequal labor distribution within marriage	0	18%	0
Other Relations	Issues with intimacy	0	18%	18%
	Children experience emotional difficulties	6%	21%	9%
Education/Work	Uncertainty about vocation	33%	9%	36%
	Volunteer activities	0	0	36%
	Analytic occupation	47%	24%	0
	Helping profession	5	33%	0
Views	Mentions of 1950s norms	0	0	18%
	Negative view of role combination for women	0	5%	27%
Infrequently reported				
	Marriage focuses on parenting	0	0	0
	Husband has midlife crisis	0	0	9%
	Companionnate marriage	0	0	9%
	Feels need to try to be more independent	0	9%	0
Evenly distributed among groups				
	Husband leaves marriage	17%	18%	27%
	Lack of closeness, availability of husband	11%	9%	9%
	Relationships in general are important	11%	22%	18%

from women's files in this chapter, we have edited identifying information to conceal individual identities; alterations are indicated by brackets for additions ([ ]) or ellipses for deletions (. . .) in the text.

CONTEXTUAL DIFFERENCES AMONG THE GROUPS

Although the focus of this chapter is on the correspondence between adult development and constructions of marital dissolution, it is important to recognize that the contexts of the women's lives varied at different stages of their development. Table 8-2 provides a general picture of the contextual differences between these women at the time of their divorces. Most of the women who divorced in their 20s had married very young, were married for a short time, had already accumulated postcollege degrees, and were working full-time at the time of the divorce. They usually did not have children; the few who did had preschool-age children. In contrast, women who divorced in their 30s had married only a little later but were married nearly twice as long on average. Though they were equally well-educated

TABLE 8-2
Demographic Characteristics of Women Who Divorce
in Their 20s, 30s, and 40s

	20s Divorces (*n* = 18)	30s Divorces (*n* = 22)	40s Divorces (*n* = 11)
Average age at marriage (range)	21 18–26	22 18–27	25 20–35
Average age at divorce (range)	27 23–29	35 31–40	46 42–49
Average years married (range)	6 3–9	14 8–20	21 15–28
Education level at time of divorce	37.5% BA; 35.7% MA; 28.6% doctoral	50% BA; 37.3% MA; 12.5% doctoral	62.5% BA; 25% MA; 12.5% doctoral
Work status at time of divorce	66.6% employed full-time; 25% student	58.3% employed full-time; 41.6% employed part-time	75% employed part-time
Percentage with children at divorce	25%	89%	89%
Average age of children at time of divorce (range)	5 3–6	9 3–19	17 12–22

and likely to be working full-time at the time of their divorces, they were much more likely to have children, and those children were typically elementary school-age or adolescents. Women who divorced in their 40s had married quite a bit later, had even longer marriages, but were less well-educated and most likely to be employed only part-time. Though these women were equally as likely to have children as the women who divorced in their 30s, their children were typically adolescents or older at the time of the divorce. These differences underscore the fact that these three groups of women differ not only in terms of their age or developmental life stage at the time of the divorce but also inevitably in life circumstances. As will be discussed later, these contextual factors surely worked in conjunction with personality development to shape women's thinking about their divorces.

One other contextual factor deserves discussion: women's own preferences about the ending of their marriages. It is interesting to note that all three groups included both women who initiated the divorce and women who were unwilling partners in the divorce: Despite this fact, all women appeared to be able to connect their divorce experiences to their individual development, whether this development occurred in the domain of identity, intimacy, or generativity. We believe this speaks to the fact that it was not the features of the divorce per se—at least not those surrounding initiation— that were associated with the women's development; instead, it was the meaning the women made of the experience that reflected their developmental preoccupations.

THEMES IN WOMEN'S ACCOUNTS OF THEIR DIVORCES

Before discussing themes that differentiated the three groups, it is important to recognize the commonalities among the groups. First, the three groups did not differ in terms of their account of which spouse initiated the divorce or who was the first to leave the relationship. In all three groups, there were both husbands and wives who initiated or were the first to actually leave the relationship. Second, there were no differences among the groups in the extent to which they reported emotional distance in their marriages. On the basis of our initial review of files, we had expected that the women who divorced in their 30s would be more likely than women in the other two groups to report feeling a lack of closeness to their partner. It seemed to us at that point that women who divorced in their 30s emphasized interpersonal relationships, including the marital relationship, more than their counterparts. However, systematic coding indicated that many women from all three of the groups reported feeling emotionally distant from their partners. It may be that the groups actually do differ in how they defined closeness (e.g., shared goals, shared interests, shared intimate conversations), and that women who divorced in their 30s differed from the other groups on a particular definition of closeness. However, our coding approach was not subtle enough to capture any such difference, if it exists.

Women Who Divorced in Their 20s

Women who divorced in their 20s emphasized a period of self-questioning, uncertainty, and depression surrounding the time of their divorce, which eventually led to a dramatic restructuring of their plans for the future. Fifty percent of the women who divorced in their 20s reported such a period of self-reflection and personal change, whereas only 14% of the women who divorced in their 30s and 18% of the women who divorced in their 40s reported such a period. Some of the women who divorced in their 20s emphasized the positive aspects of the upheaval and change: "[It was a] period of intense personal and social experimentation. [I] would probably consider it a turning point in terms of personal growth." However, most of the women who divorced in their 20s focused on how the period of self-questioning felt distressing and overwhelming. For example, the following woman who divorced at age 27 noted four years later that the low points over the past 10 years of her life had involved a sense of "aimless, undirected floating—in my marriage and career and (husband's) career—our lifestyle—there was no direction. I seemed unable to break through my husband's and my refusal to face the future." Similarly, another woman who divorced at age 28 recalled at age 53 that during her 20s, "I had no very clear expectations, leaving college. I was ultimately very happy in my choice of a husband (her second husband) and my daughter; that was not even faintly visible in 1964, I wasted the entire decade of my twenties trying to find a direction. . . ."

A central component of the self-questioning had to do with choosing a career and settling into an occupation. Women who divorced in their 20s more often reported being uncertain about their vocational choices than women who divorced in their 30s (33% versus 9%). Often uncertainty about career choices was demonstrated by voicing the feeling that their occupational choice poorly suited who they were as individuals, yet they did not know what would be a more appropriate choice for them. In other cases, the uncertainty was voiced in terms of confusion or regret over college majors and planning for future employment while in college. For example, one woman, when asked about how her college experiences affected her career choices, stated,

> Negatively. In high school, I had done well in foreign languages and wanted a career in the foreign service or UN—found that these were not the best at [her school]—switched to English major—and have not found that to be very enjoyable. Also was interested in music, but was too timid to try a music class, so put that off for years.

Regardless of whether the questioning focused on their college major choice or their poor job choice following college, women who divorced in their 20s expressed a sense of urgency about their need to figure out what they were going to do with their lives. Often psychotherapy played an important role in helping them sort out who they were and how they wanted to structure their lives in terms of occupational and relational roles. For example, one woman wrote at age 31 about the previous decade in her life: "Most of [these years were] a blur. Along the way I managed to continue with graduate school and keep going, but the general memory is pretty much a painful one. I finally got myself into analysis and began to work things out."

Finding the uncertainty in their lives intolerable, women who divorced in their 20s had often gained a sense of certainty by getting married, a decision that they soon regretted. For example, one woman who divorced at age 28 noted, "Marriage was mostly an escape from being alone, useless, unwanted, general anomie, after college. Somehow getting off the east coast revealed a completely different world and I raised my expectations dramatically within a few months."

In fact, the women who divorced in their 20s were more likely than the women who divorced in their 30s and 40s to report that they believed there were special incentives to getting married early (17% versus 0 and 9%, respectively). For example, one woman who divorced at age 27 talked about how the role of "wife" gave her a sense of purpose or meaning. When asked what was the most enjoyable event at college, she replied,

> I have to say getting married [while in school]. Friends came to our apartment; I had a special position as a married woman . . . girls signed out overnight to our apartment; I was free of parental regulations; I had a role as a wife, unlike most people I knew; . . . I had acquired a sense of identity (later revealed as false). . . . At the time I thought getting married was great, but I now regret profoundly not having stayed single through the 4 years.

Like this woman, generally women who divorced in their 20s realized that the decision to get married was a mistake soon after doing so and wanted to "correct" their mistake before they wasted too many years of their lives. They seemed to have felt that it was possible to do an "about face" with their lives, with relatively fewer complications than if they stayed married longer.

Not only did the women who divorced in their 20s describe different life experiences than the women who divorced in their 30s and 40s, they also appeared to have different personality characteristics. Most noteworthy is the strong sense of self that was articulated by the women who divorced in their 20s. Fully 67% of the women who divorced in their 20s described themselves later in terms reflecting a strong, clear, or agentic self-definition, whereas only 18% and 9%, respectively, of the women who divorced in their 30s and 40s did. Evidence of a strong sense of self emerged in a variety of ways, such as stressing the importance of "knowing oneself," or "following one's own instincts," or thinking of oneself as being "independent," "set in one's ways," or "strong-willed." For example, one woman who divorced at age 28 described herself as "independent, knowing what I like and don't like and having that clear between me and others." Another woman, who divorced at age 28, when asked about how her divorce affected her work and family activities, stated that, "[I have] much more freedom to make my own decisions. I wouldn't like to be married again because I like a close relationship but enjoy being relatively free from complications of someone else's life."

These expressions of a strong sense of self may appear contradictory to the self-questioning and uncertainty women who divorced in their 20s emphasized when describing themselves and their divorces. How is it that these women appeared confused about what they wanted for their lives during that period, yet still came across as having a strong sense of self? One possible explanation is that women who divorced in their 20s had a strong need to feel certain about who they were and what they wanted for their lives. It may be that women who divorced in their 30s and 40s were just as uncertain about their identities as women who divorced earlier; however, they may have felt less distress than women who divorced in their 20s over their identity uncertainty, and therefore less likely than the women who divorced in their 20s to voice concern over these issues. It may be precisely because women who divorced in their 20s focused so intensely on identity concerns that they were able to develop and therefore articulate a clearer sense of who they were and what they wanted for their lives than the women who divorced later.

Content coding also revealed that women who divorced in their 20s were less likely to describe themselves, or be seen as, adaptable or flexible than women who divorced in their 30s or 40s (none versus 23% and 27%, respectively). For example, one woman who divorced at age 27 gave the following advice to recent graduates of her college: "Know who you are and what you want before you start. Don't follow him, put him through school, type his dissertation—see if you can find someone who will type yours."

These differences in personal characteristics among the groups were also evident in the types of careers the women pursued. Women who divorced in their 20s were more likely to have jobs that involved analytic skills— such as researchers, statisticians, or technical writers—than the women who divorced in their 30s and 40s (47% versus 24% and none, respectively). It may be that women who divorced in their 20s were drawn to these professions because these occupations were less likely than others to require them to adapt to the needs, demands, or tempos of other people. The fact that women who divorced in their 20s differed from the other groups in the types of careers they pursued suggests that the personality distinctions we found through the content coding may have affected the way they interacted with others in general, rather than that differences in the marital relationship led them to be more independent or less adaptable.

Women Who Divorced in Their 30s

Whereas women who divorced in their 20s tended to conceptualize their divorces in terms of their own development as individuals (e.g., self-questioning, reorganization of personal goals), women who divorced in their 30s tended to focus on issues within the marital relationship. For example, women who divorced in their 30s often emphasized difficulties they were having with their spouses' behavior, whether it was because of his personality traits, mental health issues, or unwillingness to assume responsibilities or participate in family activities. Content coding of the data revealed that 41% of the women who divorced in their 30s described such difficulties, whereas 6% of the women who divorced in their 20s and 18% of the women who divorced in their 40s did. For some of the women who divorced in their 30s, a problematic spouse meant that he was uncooperative or dishonest. For example, one woman who divorced at age 39 described her husband as "not responsible, aggressive, sometimes truly crazy, often unreasonable, not dependable, a spend thrift. . . ." Another woman who divorced at age 36 stated that the contributing factors of her divorce were "husband's deteriorating mental health—characterized by pathological lying and sexual promiscuity, long absences, abandonment of responsibilities. . . ." As in this case, mental illness on the part of the husband was prominent among the women who had conflictual divorces. For example, one woman who divorced at age 37 mentioned the following when asked about noteworthy events that had occurred over the past decade:

> Husband had a manic phase in spring (what I later realized it was—at time had no idea what was going on: aggressive, spending wildly, probably hallucinating, probably an affair, not sleeping, etc.). . . . I did not understand pattern of what was happening so was subject to reacting to individual actions and trying to make sense of them in a rational/logical way, which of course was impossible. Husband reacted by protecting, blaming and anger to what was going on inside of him. . . .

For other women, having a difficult husband took the form of a partner who was unwilling to share responsibilities. For example, one woman who divorced at age 34 performed all of the household labor and child-raising responsibilities while her husband read and wrote. They were able to survive financially because of her inheritance. However, after a decade of doing so she began to feel resentful about this arrangement. When asked at age 31 what had been the low points over the past 10 years, she wrote, "Feeling resentment sometimes that my work is so constant and [husband] is freer. He reads and reads while I do laundry." Another woman who divorced at age 36 listed the major factors contributing to her divorce: "My husband did little besides watching TV and reading. Poor sex life. I did ALL the work in the house and yard." Other women who divorced in their 30s emphasized how their husbands degraded them. In response to a question about the least satisfying things about her marriage, one woman, who divorced at age 34, wrote, "He stuttered and suffered from some insecurity—always needed to drown me out (People thought me shy.)." Another woman, who divorced at age 36, said, "My husband was emotionally difficult/controlling. My life is happier without him."

In addition to focusing on difficulties they were having with their spouses, women who divorced in their 30s spoke about conflict, strife, and hostility between them and their spouses during the divorce. Instead, women who divorced in their 20s or 40s were able to find amicable resolutions to their marital problems, despite the fact that these resolutions entailed the dissolution of their marriages. Whereas 18% of the women who divorced in their 30s showed evidence of conflictual divorces, very few of the women who divorced in their 20s and 40s did (6% and none, respectively). At times, a conflictual divorce simply meant that the woman had difficulty getting her husband to cooperate with the divorce proceedings. For example, one woman who divorced at age 39 stated in her record of annual events: "Filed for divorce, husband failed to appear for divorce hearing and I received divorce by default. Spent much of the fall trying to get him to sign a settlement." For other women, a conflictual divorce meant that their husbands fought ruthlessly during the divorce proceedings for monetary possessions or custody of the children. For example, one woman, who divorced at age 39, recalled years later:

> Looking back I realize that husband really did want what he said he wanted (He had been hospitalized for mental illness at an earlier point in which he said he wanted a divorce). [When he returned home] his heart was not into picking up old life and doing something with it. [He was] also probably moving toward divorce. [He] did not want to improve his financial situation. Money he saved by working went to private things of his that he could move with him. I found out later that he did not pay federal tax for 3 years. From divorce point of view more debts and fewer traceable assets the better. As a [professional involved with divorce] he knew this.

For other women who divorced in their 30s, conflictual divorces meant that they had difficulties convincing their husbands that the relationship was over, despite the fact that their husbands might have initiated the breakup. For example, one woman described the low points of her late 30s this way: "Trying to keep my ex-husband from hanging on my heels. . . . trying to work out comfortable ways for (my children) to see their father without bringing him back in my life. He is still around too much." The higher rate of conflictual divorces among the women who divorced in their 30s in contrast to the women who divorced in their 20s and 40s suggests that there may have been greater interpersonal strife during these marriages than during the others. It is not clear why women who divorced in their 30s were more likely to experience interpersonal conflicts with their spouses than the two other groups. Other differences among the groups that emerged from the content coding of their files provide suggestions, though.

We found that women who divorced in their 30s were more likely than women who divorced in their 20s or women who divorced in their 40s to show evidence of having struggled with intimacy issues with others in general (i.e., both within and beyond the marriage), particularly with establishing interdependence with others. That is, these women were more likely than the women of the other groups to report having difficulty establishing a balance between recognizing and fulfilling their needs and the needs of others. Often women who divorced in their 30s found it difficult to find a balance because the needs of others consumed their lives to such a great extent that they were unable to identify exactly what their own needs were. For example, one woman discussed a realization about herself and relationships that occurred following her divorce:

> I am in the middle of [realizing how women] avoid autonomous decisions about one's own life and self. I have a notion that women—[women who graduated from our college] are no exception—are very prone to doing what others want them to and then calling it their own decision— or rather, to successfully avoid becoming conscious of what they themselves want (to take innocent revenge if doing what others want does not satisfy own needs). I would like to stop pretending to do what I think others want me to.

Even if they did recognize their needs, perceptions, or reactions, they did not validate them and did not expect others to do so. For example, one woman who divorced at age 37 described how disappointed she was with herself for feeling jealous that her husband spent large amounts of time with another woman while she was alone at home with her children. After years of trying to learn how to be more tolerant of the situation, she discovered that her husband and the woman actually had been having an affair. The "uncomfortable feeling" she had about the amount of time spent between her husband and the other woman was actually well-founded and was not simply a reflection of her inability to be tolerant of her husband having friendships outside of the marriage. In a sense, the feeling represented her need to have her husband remain faithful to her and their marriage—a need that she did not feel she could insist on within the relationship.

It is important to recognize that the intimacy concerns expressed by women who divorced in their 30s may not have caused these women's marital conflicts. It is more likely that the combination of these women's difficulties with balancing their own and others' needs and their husbands' problematic behavior was particularly challenging to work out. Thus women who divorced in their 30s may have tolerated more difficult behavior on the part of their husbands longer because of their reluctance to recognize and validate their own needs. Women who divorced in their 20s or 40s, or for that matter women in the sample who remained married, might not have been as tolerant of the same behaviors as the women who divorced in their 30s were.

An alternative explanation, however, is that women who divorced in their 30s may have recognized and validated their own needs but were more willing than women who divorced at other ages to work on a troubled marital relationship. Supporting this explanation is the fact that the women who divorced in their 30s were more likely than the women who divorced in their 20s and 40s to be in "helping professions," such as nursing, social work, or teaching (32% versus 5% and none, respectively). It may be that women who are in helping professions are particularly attuned to the needs of others and are willing to be responsive to others' needs. Or it may be that women who divorced in their 30s felt that they were particularly skilled at dealing with interpersonal problems and therefore tried to work on marital problems longer before finally divorcing. However, the fact that women who divorced in their 30s both held jobs in helping professions and expressed intimacy concerns suggests that although they may have been especially attuned to interpersonal issues, they were not able adequately to address the issues in the marriage.

Although women who divorced in their 30s stayed in their marriages a long time, their remaining in the marriage appears to have exacted a considerable toll on their well-being and the well-being of their children. One third of the women who divorced in their 30s suffered from persistent depression, whereas none of women who divorced in their 20s did. One woman who divorced at age 38 recalled the high points over the past decade of her life as:

> (solving) my mental problems by divorce and remarriage. I finally ended a 16 year marriage when my ex-spouse decided for a brief time that we (i.e., he) were better off apart. Prior to that I had been needing but afraid of the split, and worked very hard (and successfully to a certain extent) to maximize the good in the marriage. However, actually experiencing a sense of escape, guilt-free . . . made me realize how the relation-

ship had been continually depressing and devaluing me, so when he changed his mind again I did not.

Not only did the women who divorced in their 30s appear to suffer from the marriage and subsequent divorce, they were also more likely than the women who divorced in their 20s and 40s to have children who were dealing with emotional problems, such as suicidal depression, anorexia, or drug abuse (21%, 6%, and 9%, respectively). Previous research on divorce suggests that divorce per se does not necessarily have damaging effects on those involved; it is when there is considerable conflict between the spouses that divorce can be detrimental (see, e.g., Stewart et al., 1997). Our findings suggest that the negative outcomes on the part of the women and their children may not be a result of the personal characteristics of women who divorced in their 30s, but rather the nature of their marriages and subsequent divorces.

Women Who Divorced in Their 40s

Whereas women who divorced in their 20s and 30s focused on self-development and relational concerns, respectively, when describing their divorces, women who divorced in their 40s emphasized how their divorces would allow them to pursue opportunities they had missed. We found that 45% of the women who divorced in their 40s felt that their marriage had hampered their professional or personal development, whereas only 11% of the women who divorced in their 20s and 5% of the women who divorced in their 30s did. For example, one woman who divorced at age 47 stated, "Early on I sacrificed career development and musical development for the traditional homemaker mother community volunteer roles. I was really good at those roles, but eventually came to feel suffocated."

Sacrifices were not just in the professional realm; some of the women who divorced in their 40s felt that their marriages prevented them from realizing dreams they had for their family lives. One woman who divorced at age 44 was disappointed with her life before the divorce because her husband did not wish to have children. Divorcing allowed her the opportunity to pursue her hopes for a family; she proceeded to adopt and provide foster care for several children. When asked at age 53 about the choices she had made about work and family over the course of her life, she stated, "I spent more than the first half of my life trying to please others—my mother, my husband, etc. (I) am now doing (family wise) vaguely what I think I wanted to do 25 years ago."

Women who divorced in their 40s seemed to realize that "time was running out" for them. If they wanted to pursue a lifelong dream, they felt they needed to begin doing so immediately or it would be "too late." For example, one woman who divorced at age 43 stated years later that the least satisfying thing about managing her household when she was married was "the sense that I was treading water, that the best of myself was going into the family. When could I just live for me?" In a similar vein, another woman who also divorced at age 43 stated that the reason why she got divorced from her spouse was "diverging interests; the sexual excitement died; satisfaction at having successfully launched our kids; my desire to live the rest of my life differently than the first half."

One of the reasons that women who divorced in their 40s did not pursue their professional careers earlier might be because they felt they could not undertake a career without considerable expense to the lives of their family members. Whereas 27% of the women who divorced in their 40s perceived negative consequences of combining work and family roles *in principle* (not merely for themselves), none of the women who divorced in their 20s and only 5% of the women who divorced in their 30s did. Commenting on her own experience, one woman who divorced in her mid-40s noted, when asked about attractive opportunities she had not taken, "Mostly getting a Ph.D. and pursuing an academic career of some sort. (Why not pursue?) I got married and had kids and just didn't think it was okay to combine career and wife/mother roles. I really thought you were suppose to do the 50s thing for women. . . ."

The social norms of the 1950s (current when all of the women in the sample were children and young adolescents) weighed more heavily on the women who divorced in their 40s than the women who had divorced earlier. Whereas 18% of the women who divorced in their 40s mentioned the norms of the 1950s, none of the women who had divorced earlier mentioned 1950s norms. As illustrated in the following excerpt from a woman who divorced at age 47, the women's movement eventually played a role in changing these women's expectations:

> The women's movement opened all opportunities for women. When I married, I bought into all the older norms and contracts. I think I was toward the end of a generation of women, but nevertheless got infected by the women's movement—in the middle of my marriage years, when it seemed too late to rewrite the rules and contracts. My husband never "got it."

In addition to perceiving difficulty in combining work and family roles, a second reason that women who divorced in their 40s did not pursue their professional careers was that they felt uncertain about their vocational direction in early adulthood. As with the women who divorced in their 20s, women who divorced in their 40s were more likely to express uncertainty in their 20s about what sort of vocation they wanted to pursue than women who divorced in their 30s (36% versus 9%). For example, one woman who divorced at age 46 expressed the following at age 31:

> The most disappointing thing I did at [college] was choose the wrong major—a field I was not interested in pursuing. [My college is] not a vocational school, but one does spend a lot of time on one's field of concentration. I realized by senior year I'd chosen wrong and I felt I wasted a lot of time and effort. This wrong choice was certainly partly my fault, but I do think the school shared some blame by forcing fairly early decisions on concentration and by lack of counseling. Counseling facilities did exist; but 10 years ago, their use wasn't encouraged. And 10 years ago a lot of us were pretty sheltered and needed a little more external prodding to examine our goals.

The difficulties this woman was experiencing in figuring out her future seem very similar to those expressed by many of the women who divorced in their 20s. Despite the similarities, however, women who divorced in their 40s were different from the women who divorced in their 20s in that they did not feel that they needed to sort through their career objectives right away. Instead, many of the women who divorced in their 40s waited until their 40s to work through uncertainties they had in their 20s regarding their career. For example, the woman who wrote the previous passage returned to graduate school the year following her divorce to pursue one of the career directions that she had contemplated when she was in her 20s. She committed herself to this particular direction after considerable thought about what would be most appropriate for her.

Finally, women who divorced in their 40s also stated that they put their professional and personal development on hold during their marriage because their marriage served a purpose during that earlier period in their lives. Whereas 36% of the women who divorced in their 40s mentioned that their marriage had served a purpose earlier in their lives, none of the women who had divorced in their 20s or 30s did. For example, one woman who divorced at age 43 noted in her mid-30s that she anticipated a divorce in the coming years:

> Both [children] will have completed college, so there will be little family centered on our home, as I imagine the [kids] will be pursuing careers or will have entered graduate school. This would leave my husband and I free. As he enjoys [our lifestyle] less than I, I could envision a breakdown of the parent nucleus at this point into the movement of 2 people into their own particular orbits that overlap less than at earlier times in our marriage.

At age 53, she further emphasized the importance of her marriage, when she expressed this view of paths she had not taken in her life:

I suppose I might have divorced earlier, but I was married to an honorable and loving man and our time as parents together had not ended. (Why not taken?) Some insecurity about my competence alone played a part, but primarily our marriage was still unfinished. I think the 22 years spent married were well spent and reached a natural conclusion.

Although other women who divorced in their 40s did not explicitly state that their marriage had served an earlier purpose, they were more likely than the women who divorced earlier to express satisfaction with aspects of their marriage or family arrangements. For example, one woman who divorced at age 47 stated the following when asked at age 43 how a woman's life is changed by marriage:

> Marriage complicates life. It reduces ability to act spontaneously, autonomously. Marriage enriches life. The wonder of a long-term intimate relationship, the triumphs over adversities together; the survival of bad times in the relationships all provide growth. For me, my husband's career has enabled me to move and travel beyond my wildest dreams.

Although she recognized the drawbacks to marriage, this woman clearly felt that there were benefits that came from her marriage. Like many of the other women who divorced in their 40s, it appears that she was fully cognizant of the decision she made during her marriage to place her personal and professional life on hold. To develop these aspects of herself would mean that she would lose a valued aspect of her family life.

Being willing to place a personal or professional goal on hold for the benefit of family life speaks to the fact that the women who divorced in their 40s were adaptable to the needs of others. As with the women who divorced in their 30s, they were more likely to describe themselves as adaptable or flexible than the women who divorced in their 20s (27% versus none). For example, women who divorced in their 40s often moved for the sake of their husbands' careers or worked as volunteers so they could shape their work hours around their family's needs. This flexibility, however, may have occurred at a cost to their personal well-being. As with the women who divorced in their 30s, women who divorced in their 40s were more likely than the women who divorced in their 20s to express concerns about intimacy (18% versus none) and to describe ongoing depression (18% versus 6%). Although not as prevalent as among the women who divorced in their 30s, women who divorced in their 40s may have been so flexible in responding to the needs of others that they did not recognize or validate their own needs, which in turn may have resulted in their depression.

The fact that women who divorced in their 40s were described as flexible to the needs of others may help us better understand the relationship between divorce and career development for these women. Although women who divorced in their 40s were clearly more likely than women who divorced earlier to perceive negative consequences to combining work and family roles, it is unclear why they continued to feel that the marriage in and of itself stifled their career development, given that these women were less constrained by child-rearing activities at this stage in their lives than earlier. It is possible that women who divorced in their 40s postponed their identity development while their children were young, which fits with their self-descriptions as being adaptable to the needs of others. Once their children had grown, however, women who divorced in their 40s likely had more time to explore their own interests and what they wanted for their lives than when these women were younger. A focus on identity may have resulted in both the pursuit of a new career as well as the dissolution of a relationship that no longer fit with their new sense of self. Thus changes in marriage and career may have occurred at the same time in these women's lives, without one having caused the other. Instead, it may be that both changes in marriage and career were brought about by a third factor—identity exploration—that only emerged at this point in the women's lives because of their willingness to put identity exploration on hold while their children were young.

ADULT DEVELOPMENT AND WOMEN'S ACCOUNTS OF THEIR DIVORCES

Although there were a few similarities among women who divorced in their 20s, 30s, and 40s (e.g., lack of closeness with their spouses), quite distinct stories about their marriages and subsequent divorces emerged from the women's accounts of their lives. Women who divorced in their 20s retrospectively described their divorces in terms of issues of independence, personal goals, and a sense of being true to one's self. They viewed their early marriages as premature attempts to end or resolve an intense process of self-definition, with their divorces permitting them a more satisfactory solution. In short, women's accounts of these early marriages and divorces are quite saturated with themes reminiscent of Erikson's (1968) account of the period of the identity crisis. In that account, Erikson noted that some people, perhaps particularly women, seek their identities through intimate relationships (see also Franz & White, 1985, pp. 147–148). It is, of course, possible that the marriages of women in this group were not different from those of women in the other groups and that women who divorced in their 20s simply recall their divorces as related to background identity issues, because they happened to coincide in time. Even if this were true, that temporal coincidence likely colored not only the memory of the relationship and its meaning but also its meaning at the time.

In contrast, women who divorced in their 30s conceived of their divorces in terms of difficulties they had with their partners and the marital relationship. Whereas women who divorced in their 20s or 40s generally were able to achieve amicable dissolutions of their marriages, women who divorced in their 30s reported conflictual, hostile divorces. Moreover, these women seemed to struggle personally with relationship issues more generally as well as with the balance of their own needs and the needs of others. In terms of education and employment this group was quite similar to the women who divorced in their 20s, and though they married a little later they still married young (the average age was 22). Therefore, their marriages—which mostly included children—were much longer than those of the group that divorced in their 20s and were marked by long-term struggles. Because these women reported strong emotional ties to rather difficult partners, and divorced while their children were relatively young (averaging 9 years old), it seems possible that the strain of parenting, or concern about children, played a role in the divorces. Many of the women complained about unequal responsibilities in the family or about irresponsible or even dangerous behavior on the part of their spouses.

The combination of these contextual factors, these women's commitment to helping professions, and their felt difficulties with articulating their own needs in relationships, suggests that for women who divorced in their 30s intimacy or relationship issues were dominant features of their divorces. According to Erikson (1980), the intimacy crisis follows identity because it is only with the development of identity that the capacity for "fidelity" (to ideas, projects, roles, and persons) emerges. Perhaps these women differ from the women who divorced in their 20s in having left identity issues unresolved in their 20s. Because of this lack of resolution, or different (more accommodating and flexible) personalities, or different (more satisfying?) marriages, they held onto their early marriages much longer. This group's persistent struggles with intimacy issues may be grounded, then, in the fact that their identities that were not as fully defined as were those of women who divorced in their 20s.

Finally, women who divorced in their 40s focused on unmet life goals when discussing their marital dissolution. They had married later than women in the other two groups, but were less highly educated and were not as likely to have full-time employment; moreover, their marriages were very long (averaging 21 years). Often these women expressed the view that the marriage had served an earlier and highly valued purpose—most often parenting or childrearing. At the same time, they felt that the marriage could not accommodate their personal needs for growth. These women often saw themselves as having sacrificed their own personal development for the sake of the family, but felt an urgent need to stop making that kind of sacrifice.

In some ways these women are reminiscent of the women who divorced in their 20s—they both view their divorces as freeing them to pursue their own self-development. However, women who divorced in their 40s left marriages that were longer term commitments, that met earlier developmental needs they acknowledge, and that involved the major project of childrearing. In some important ways both their marriages and their divorces seem marked by the issue of generativity, or the project of caring for and contributing to the next generation. Perhaps they sought new kinds of outlets for generativity—outlets that could not be accommodated in the marriages that had supported childrearing. It is interesting to note that women who divorced in their 40s seem to have pursued the issue of generativity much earlier than Erikson recommended—in early rather than middle adulthood. Moreover, their continued vocational uncertainty in their 40s suggests that they did not build their generativity project on a solid identity foundation. This pattern underscores the contradiction in Erikson's theory that parenting is a natural focus for generativity but that generativity is culturally normative much later and personally may be more feasible only after attainment of a secure identity and a capacity for intimacy (see Stewart & Vandewater, 1998). Erikson understood that cultural norms imposed particular burdens on women's personality development. For example, he commented,

> Women, at least in yesterday's culture, had to keep their identities incomplete until they knew their man. Yet, I would think that a woman's identity develops out of the very way in which she looks around and selects the person with whose budding identity she can polarize her own. Her selection is already an expression of her identity, even if she seems to become totally absorbed in somebody else's life. (quoted in Evans, 1967, p. 49)

Perhaps we are seeing in our data the ways in which women's selections failed—at different points in time—to accommodate their unfinished identity work.

Although we view these data as suggesting that a developmental perspective on the meanings of divorces might be valuable, we are well aware of several important limitations of the data. First, most of the data are retrospective, though this is not a major limitation when the issue at hand is understanding the *meanings* of life experiences. However, they are in some ways differently retrospective. Thus we only have retrospective data about the marriages of women who divorced in their 20s, because these marriages had ended by the first wave of data collection when they were 31. In contrast, we have some data from some of the women in the other two groups both while they were married and after they divorced. Moreover, the groups differ in the psychological distance they can have on their divorces, given the different distance in time from the divorce of the last wave of data collection (which could vary by as much as 20 years). We have seen that in a few ways the women in the three groups are actually similar to each other (e.g., in describing their marriages as emotionally distant); but we have not compared them with their married counterparts. It would be valuable to know whether some of the themes discussed in this chapter differentiate women who married at a particular age, as much as those who divorce by a certain time.

In addition, because little or no research has taken a developmental perspective on women's understandings of their divorces, this study should be seen as both exploratory and as beginning a discussion of how particular developmental periods can affect how women construct an understanding of major life transitions and create the narrative stories of their lives. Finally, the sample includes only women; and the women in this sample are virtually all White, well-educated, and upper middle-class. Their race and class privilege surely shapes their experience of both marriage and divorce, even as their gender exposed them to certain normative pressures. Only data from women and men in other groups will allow us to understand in detail how these larger features of the social context shape women's understandings of their own divorces.

REFERENCES

Ahrons, C. (1980). Divorce: A crisis of family transition and change. *Family Relations, 29*, 533–540.

Ahrons, C. (1995). *The good divorce*. New York: Harper.

Amato, P. R., & Keith, B. (1991). Parental divorce and well-being of children: A meta-analysis. *Psychological Bulletin, 110*, 26–46.

Coontz, S. (1992). *The way we never were: American families and the nostalgia trap*. NY: Basic Books.

Ebaugh, H. R. F. (1988). *Becoming an ex: The process of role exit*. Chicago: University of Chicago Press.

Emery, R. E. (1988). *Marriage, divorce, and children's adjustment*. Newbury Park, CA: Sage.

Erikson, E. H. (1950). *Childhood and society*. New York: W.W. Norton.

Erikson, E. H. (1968). *Identity: Youth and crisis*. New York: W.W. Norton.

Erikson, E. H. (1980). *Identity and the life cycle*. New York: Norton.

Evans, R. (1967). *Dialogue with Erik Erikson*. New York: Harper & Row.

Franz, C. E., & White, K. M. (1985). Individuation and attachment in personality development: Extending Erikson's theory. In A. J. Stewart & M. B. Lykes

(Eds.), *Gender and personality* (pp. 136–168). Durham, NC: Duke University Press.

Gould, R. (1980). Transformation during early and middle adult years. In N. J. Smelser and E. H. Erikson (Eds.), *Themes of work and love in adulthood* (pp. 213–237). Cambridge, MA: Harvard University Press.

Hetherington, E. M. (1979). Divorce: A child's perspective. *American Psychologist, 34,* 851–858.

Hetherington, E. M. (1989). Coping with family transitions: Winners, losers, and survivors. *Child Development, 60,* 1–14.

Josselson, R. (1987). *Finding herself: Pathways to identity development in women.* San Francisco: Jossey-Bass.

Josselson, R. (1992). *The space between us: Exploring the dimensions of human relationships.* San Francisco: Jossey-Bass.

Josselson, R. (1996). *Revising herself: The story of women's identity from college to midlife.* New York: Oxford University Press.

Kurdek, L. (1987). Children's adjustment to divorce: An ecological perspective. In J. P. Vincent (Ed.), *Advances in family intervention, assessment and theory* (Vol. 4, pp. 1–31). Greenwich, CT: JAI Press.

Levinson, D. J. (1978). *The seasons of a man's life.* New York: Ballantine.

Levinson, D. J. (1996). *The seasons of a woman's life.* New York: Knopf.

Marcia, J. E. (1980). Identity in adolescence. In J. Adelson (Ed.), *Handbook of adolescent psychology.* New York: John Wiley.

McAdams, D. P. (1985). *Power, intimacy and the life story.* New York: Guilford Press.

McAdams, D. P., & de St. Aubin, E. (Eds.). (1998). *Generativity and adult development: How and why we care for the next generation.* Washington, DC: American Psychological Association.

Peterson, B. E., & Stewart, A. J. (1990). Using personal and fictional documents to assess psychosocial development: A case study of Vera Brittain's generativity. *Psychology and Aging, 5*(3), 400–411.

Peterson, B. E., & Stewart, A. J. (1993). Generativity and social motives in young adults. *Journal of Personality and Social Psychology, 65,* 186–198.

Peterson, P. E., & Stewart, A. J. (1996). Antecedents and contexts of generativity motivation at midlife. *Psychology and Aging, 11,* 21–33.

Rice, J. K. (1994). Reconsidering research on divorce, family life cycle, and the meaning of family. *Psychology of Women Quarterly, 18,* 559–584.

Riessman, C. K. (1990). *Divorce talk: Women and men make sense of personal relationships.* New Brunswick, NJ: Rutgers University Press.

Skolnick, A. (1991). *Embattled paradise: The American family in an age of uncertainty.* New York: Basic Books.

Stacey, J. (1991). Backward toward the postmodern family: Reflections on gender, kinship and class in the Silicon Valley. In A. Wolfe (Ed.), *America at century's end* (pp. 17–34). Berkeley: University of California Press.

Stewart, A. J. (1994). The women's movement and women's lives: Linking individual development and social events. In A. Lieblich & R. Josselson (Eds.), *Exploring identity and gender: The narrative study of lives* (Vol. 2, pp. 230–250). Thousand Oaks, CA: Sage.

Stewart, A. J., Copeland, A. P., Chester, N. L., Malley, J. E. & Barenbaum, N. B. (1997). *Separating together: How divorce transforms families.* New York: Guilford Press.

Stewart, A. J., Franz, C. E., & Layton, L. (1988). The changing self: Using personal documents to study lives. *Journal of Personality, 56,* 41–74.

Stewart, A. J., & Healy, J. M. (1989). Linking individual development and social changes. *American Psychologist, 44,* 30–42.

Stewart, A. J., & Ostrove, J. M. (1998). Women's personality in middle age: Gender, history and mid-course correction. *American Psychologist, 53,* 1185–1194.

Stewart, A. J., & Vandewater, E. A. (1993). Career and family social clock projects in a transitional cohort: The Radcliffe class of 1964. In K. Hulbert & D. Schuster (Eds.), *Women's lives through time: Educated women of the twentieth century* (pp. 235–258). San Francisco: Jossey-Bass.

Stewart, A. J., & Vandewater, E. A. (1998). The course of generativity. In D. P. McAdams & E. de St. Aubin (Eds.), *Generativity and adult development: How and why we care for the next generation* (pp. 75–100). Washington, DC: American Psychological Association.

Thornton, A. (1989). Changing attitudes toward family issues in the U.S. *Journal of Marriage and the Family, 51,* 873–893.

Wallerstein, J. S., & Blakeslee, S. (1989). *Second chances.* New York: Ticknor & Fields.

Wallerstein, J. S., & Kelly, J. (1980). *Surviving the breakup.* New York: Basic Books.

Weiss, R. (1975). *Marital separation.* New York: Basic Books.

Winter, D. G., McClelland, D. C., & Stewart, A. J. (1981). *A new case for the liberal arts.* San Francisco: Jossey-Bass.

Wrightsman, L. S. (1988). *Personality development in adulthood.* Newbury Park, CA: Sage.

9

ADOLESCENTS' REPRESENTATIONS OF THE PARENT VOICE IN STORIES OF PERSONAL TURNING POINTS

MICHAEL W. PRATT, MARY LOUISE ARNOLD,
AND KATHLEEN MACKEY

My parents work for a church-related organization. They used to work at a little church just down the road, then they grew to a bigger organization so we had to move to where they went, and then we moved again. And everywhere we went I had to change my attitude a little bit. And basically just had to talk to myself and just understand like my personality and what it was. . . . My friends call me like "wacko" because I talk to myself a little bit, and I do a whole bunch of things. I think I've just taken on this scenario of being weird, and so people call me weird. I think it was the adjusting to a different personality like wherever I went. . . . Like my first move I had been in town for eight years, which is longer than I've been anywhere, and I had made a lot of friends and when I had to move away I'm sitting there going "why," and I had no clue. It just never dawned on me. And saying good-bye to a lot of people, that really depressed and bummed me out a lot. I was in like a yo-yo of emotions-type thing. . . .

And I'm sitting there going I don't want to move again, and so my parents talked to me and they said, "OK, *we talked about it with you and we're not gonna be moving.*" And a couple of times we changed that idea and we've found a new place that we really like or that really appealed to our taste and like OK, I like this, but I don't like this because, sort of thing. [And how did things finally turn out?] Things are pretty much OK now. I'm pretty much adapting to my lifestyle here. And I still keep in touch a little bit with my friends. [And how did

This research was supported by a Social Sciences and Humanities Research Council of Canada grant to Michael W. Pratt, Joan E. Norris, and Mary Louise Arnold. The authors thank Susan Alisat and Rebecca Filyer for their help with data collection and transcription. We also thank Dan McAdams, Mark Tappan, and two anonymous reviewers for their thoughtful commentaries on an earlier version of this manuscript.

your parents think about all this?] This was more of a personal thing. *Like to them moving is all in the past and we're not gonna go through it again;* hopefully, it's no big thing, it's nothing to worry about. *So I don't think they'd really give it a second thought. . . .*

For the past several years, we have been visiting a sample of Canadian families in their homes, talking to both adolescents and their parents about the topic of value development, asking them to tell us stories about how this takes place in their families (e.g., Mackey, Arnold, & Pratt, in press; Pratt, Arnold, & Hilbers, 1998; Pratt, Arnold, Pratt, & Diessner, 1999). The narrative opening this chapter is an example of one of these stories, told by a girl whom we will call Sandy. A snapshot of some elements of this 15-year-old's family life emerges from her turning point story, particularly her relationship with her parents. A little background will be helpful in understanding the context of Sandy's feelings. Her family consisted of her two parents and their five children, all girls; three of the daughters now live away from home. Sandy is the youngest child, age 15 at the time of this second interview (the families also had been interviewed two years before, when Sandy was 13). At the time of this second interview, Sandy reported she was interested in becoming a teacher. The parents in this family were both employed by a church organization, and the family seemed quite religious. From Sandy's point of view, as she told us in this second interview, her parents work very long hours; recently, the father had had to take a second job for financial reasons. Sandy's story reflects, though in a somewhat muted way, her ambivalent feelings that her parents do not have time for her, or really seem to understand her when they do. In fact, what struck us most in the stories that Sandy provided was a kind of pointed "absence" of parent voices and perspectives, an absence that Sandy seemed to feel acutely. We will return to the story of Sandy and her parents as they try, like all families, to cope with the sometimes challenging transitions of adolescence.

This chapter draws on a corpus of stories, told by adolescents about events that they have come to see as critical incidents or turning point experiences in their own development. In this study, adolescents from 35 two-parent, mostly Caucasian Canadian families told turning point stories focused on a range of life events, most commonly including deaths, illnesses or serious accidents of friends or family, relationship changes or romantic breakups, family and school relocations, "getting in trouble" with peers, and first jobs and major achievements. Our adolescents' stories about key events in their personal value development thus chronicled many of the commonly cited transitions of this period of the life course (e.g., Simmons, Burgeson,

Carlton-Ford, & Blyth, 1987). The families were visited twice, separated by a two-year period; at the time of the first visit, adolescents were aged 12 to 16. A range of stories, as well as other, more standard data, were collected at each time. There were roughly equal numbers of boys and girls in the sample.

For this discussion we have focused our attention on the particular aspect of these narratives highlighted in the turning point story, the ways in which adolescents depict the "voices" or perspectives of their parents in the context of their descriptions of life events. Stories like this one were interesting to us because of the salience of the parental role, partly as an influence on adolescent experience and value development, partly as a foil for the adolescent's emerging articulation of his or her own "voice" regarding these matters. In some sense, the adolescent stories we collected regarding important turning points that have shaped a sense of values and self for them were often quite directly focused on this construction of the personal voice. But adolescents' perspectives on parental images of their selves are also deeply embedded in this developmental process. Indeed, for Erikson (1968), identity development in adolescence is precisely about constructing a unitary sense of the self for the first time, based in the fragmentary and partial selves of the younger child. Thus adolescence itself becomes the central transition period in the individual's development of the "life story," which comes to define identity (McAdams, 1993). A central root of this emerging personal identity, however, is surely the sense of a parentally mediated ideal and the parental perspective (as seen by the child) that emanates from it.

The present narrative research program is thus meant to investigate how the developing adolescent understands and articulates important value-learning experiences during this central transition period in the life cycle. The theoretical underpinnings for this research program are in the literature on moral and value socialization. We first describe the emerging narrative perspective on this topic. Then we address the sociocultural framework from which we consider these issues. Finally we turn to a discussion of our approach to the narrative data and to case studies exploring adolescents' representation of the parental voice.

A SOCIOCULTURAL PERSPECTIVE ON REPRESENTATIONS OF THE PARENT VOICE IN ADOLESCENT NARRATIVES

Traditionally, approaches to moral and value socialization have regarded cognition, and in particular the development of stages of thinking in this area, as the fundamental criterion of moral growth (Kohlberg, 1976; Piaget, 1965). Recently, however, this approach has been challenged by a range of theorists, who encourage a broadening and perhaps a reformulation of this cognitive paradigm (e.g., Walker & Pitts, 1998). A common thread of these criticisms has been the point that the "particularities" of individual lives are lost in research approaches based in the traditional nomothetic paradigm. One attempt to cast moral and value development in these terms—that is, to see the self as reflected in the construction of a sense of personal "authorship" of moral stances and experiences—has been the work of Tappan and colleagues on moral narrative (e.g., Tappan, 1991; Tappan & Brown, 1989). Colby and Damon's (1992) recent work on commitment to caring is another important example of the use of life histories as a way of describing the integration of the self and morality. McAdams's work (e.g., 1996; McAdams, Diamond, de St. Aubin, & Mansfield, 1997) in the personological tradition also provides a powerful case for considering the role of narrative as central in the construction of the self during the adolescent transition, through the formulation of a life story that becomes the (constantly evolving) core of the individual's emerging sense of identity.

We share with the proponents of narrative analysis (McAdams, 1999; Tappan & Brown, 1989) a view that stories serve as a powerful qualitative lens through which to observe and document human experience and development. Within moral psychology, in particular, stories have been shown to provide rich and meaningful accounts of the formation of moral identity and life history and also are acknowledged for their ability to inspire virtue and imbue others with purpose and mission (e.g., Coles, 1989; Vitz, 1990). Narrative techniques thus can provide a "window" on some of the ways through which children understand and develop an independent, autonomous sense of their own values in the context of parental influence. Narrative also may directly constitute an essential element of the individual's construction of a personal sense of self, as McAdams (1996) has argued.

From the perspective of a broader sociocultural theory of value development, the current research explicitly draws on the notion of voice, borrowing directly from the compelling explication of the ideas of Vygotsky (1978) and Bakhtin (1981) by Wertsch (1991). The term *voice* is used to capture the depiction of the comments and views of influential others—in this instance, parents—as reflected in the narratives told by adolescents about experiences leading to important developments in their personal sense of self and of values. The key feature of this work from the sociocultural perspective is the presumed dialogical basis for all verbal thought, between the voices of others and the self. In this research, as exemplified by Sandy's story, the focus is on parent–adolescent dialogue on family life and on the voices of parents as represented in the child's thinking about these issues. Thus in this perspective, a multiplicity of voices of the mind derives largely from the appropriation onto the inner mental plane of specific historical experiences of interacting with various external influences and agents (such as parents or peers), and these appear in internal conversation in the mind of the adolescent as he or she constructs a personal belief and value system. Bakhtin (1981) graphically described these interpolated voices of others as "ventriloquated" through the individual's own.

Vygotsky's (1978) developmental view was that the attainment of mature thought is a gradual process of appropriation of the social speech of early childhood onto the inner mental plane of verbal self-regulatory thinking (or "inner speech," as he termed this phenomenon). The way station through which this process passes, according to Vygotsky, is the phenomenon of "private speech," the child's use of overt self-directed language to regulate problem solving and behavior (e.g., Duncan & Pratt, 1997). The legacy of this developmental process in the verbal thought of the older individual is the dialogical nature of all such thinking based in the gradual internalization of social interaction (Wertsch, 1991). Thus the mind is always "in conversation" with previous utterances of the self and others as it seeks to ponder and solve problems (Bakhtin, 1981), and these alternatives frequently represent the concrete, historical perspectives of important persons in the individual's past life experiences (Day & Tappan, 1996). Of particular interest in this chapter are parents, who likely play a central role in childhood and adolescence with regard to much of value and moral decision making.

Although the initial expression of the other's "voice" in development is likely to be concretely historical in nature (Ely & McCabe, 1993), it would be expected that such voices might readily come to be anticipatory as well. Thus an adolescent might expect a parent to respond in a certain way as he or she contemplates a choice or action, and thus represent this *anticipated* voice of endorsement or disapproval in inner dialogues of decision making about the issue (e.g., Day & Tappan, 1996; Pratt & Norris, 1999). In turn, these inner voices then would be reflected in the overt narratives that adolescents tell about their experiences of value learning or development, as in the illustration at the outset of the chapter (Sandy's comment that if her parents were asked about her feelings about moving, "This was more of a personal thing. . . . *I don't think they'd even give it a second thought*").

There would appear to be several possible dimensions on which the adolescent's representation of the parent's voice might vary. We have been concerned with two of these in our work so far, including both the clarity of the adolescent's perspective on this voice and the extent to which the adolescent appears responsive to the voice in his or her telling of it. These dimensions are not fully independent of each other. Certainly the parental voice might be clearly "present" in an adolescent's story, but not respected or listened to. However, it is difficult to imagine the converse in narrative—in other words, the voice is uncertain or vague but strongly responded to by the adolescent.

Concerning the issue of the clarity of the parental voice, it seemed to us that this might range from minimal to absent on the one hand, up to the most sophisticated level which would be clearly understood and "appropriated" for the self (e.g., Rogoff, 1990). At these most advanced levels, our operationalization of the voice construct, as described later in the chapter, has also been informed by the distinction Bakhtin (1981) has made between two types of "dialogical discourse," which we believe, with Tappan (1991), may be generally representative of two developmental steps in the internalization process. The first is a form of externalized discourse in which the child's speech reflects an unconditional allegiance to a voice of authority. This is characterized by a more detached "recitation" or parroting of beliefs that have yet to be internalized and fully appropriated as one's own. In the second type, the child engages in what Bakhtin has called "internally persuasive dialogue." Here the voice of others is not only audible in the child's speech, but it has also been assimilated and reconstructed by the child herself. As Tappan (1991, p. 17) described it, the child is now "claiming authority and responsibility . . . and authorizing her own moral perspective."

In our thinking about the meaning of these representations in family narratives, we have also interpreted the adolescent's depiction of the parent's voice as a reflection of the extent to which the adolescent was responsive to parental views. Darling and Steinberg (1993) have suggested that such openness to parental perspectives should be associated with the emotional climate of the family—specifically with the degree to which the family is experienced by the child as "authoritative" in nature. Authoritative parenting is a broad style of parental interaction that is characterized by the provision of both guidance and structure, as well as warmth and responsiveness to the child's individuality (Maccoby & Martin, 1983). Thus we constructed our parent voice measure in the context of such general characterizations of more or less open family emotional climates for adolescent development. Sandy's story shows that issues of family responsiveness may be complex and ambivalent.

To capture these variations in a systematic way, and to be able to relate such qualitative descriptions of the parental voice in narrative to standard quantitative measures of family and personal characteristics, we developed an ordered, five-point index of the degree to which the adolescent represents, and is responsive to, the parent voice (Pratt & Arnold, 1995). We explain and briefly illustrate the construction of this measure next.

DESCRIBING PARENT VOICE IN ADOLESCENT NARRATIVES

Our description of the parental voice in adolescents' stories has been based on a range of narrative elicitations. We first began with a set of stories elicited by asking adolescents to tell how their parents had tried to teach them values that they judged important (e.g., "ambition," "kindness"; Pratt & Arnold, 1995). In other work, we have asked adolescents and young adults to describe a time when their parents had given advice to them about an important issue (Mackey, Arnold, & Pratt, in press). Finally, we have asked adolescents to discuss a "critical incident" in their value development and to comment on how their parents have responded to this issue (adapting a technique from Barnett, Quackenbush, & Sinisi, 1995). This last type of narrative is the focus, although in the case studies that follow, we use narratives of several of these types to try to interpret family issues.

In our analyses of all these types of adolescent stories, we categorize the appropriation of parental voice on a five-point scale. Each level represents the child's responsiveness to the parents' beliefs and values and their integration into his or her own self-regulatory system. The central components of our measure include an acknowledgment of parental voice and the clarity of its representation in the adolescent's thinking and the extent to which this influence has been appropriated and reconstructed in the adolescent's own thinking. As we read the adolescents' stories, we look for possible indicators of parental influence (or voice) that provide evidence of this value acquisition process. Such indicators typically include literal evidence of parents' speech within the adolescents' thought (e.g., "My dad always says. . . ."), statements that explicitly corroborate or contradict parents' beliefs and values (e.g., "I think my parents are on the wrong track when. . . ."), and emotional or affective overtones that imply evidence for responsiveness (or a lack of it) to parental beliefs and values (e.g., "I felt lousy because I knew my parents. . . ."). On the basis of these pieces of evidence, we then classify the child's appropriation of parental voice for that particular narrative in accordance with one of our five levels. We will briefly define each level and illustrate the extreme points of our parental voice scale.

At the lowest level on our scale, level 1, the parents' voice either cannot be heard at all in the adolescent's narrative—perhaps because it is not available to the child or because the child has "tuned it out" of his or her conscious mind—or, it is acknowledged but summarily dismissed or rejected by the child. For example, in one of our more striking cases of the absence of parental voice, a 19-year-old described her parents' reaction to a frightening episode she had recently experienced. She explains that she had been pretty well "sloshed" one night, and narrowly escaped sexual assault after accepting a ride from a stranger:

> What really surprised me was that they [her parents] didn't seem all that shocked. They were like, "Oh really." I felt like I was all alone when that happened, like I was really upset and I really felt like I didn't have anybody to talk to. . . . I told my parents and they said, "Oh, well, if you want to call the cops, that's fine and if you don't, well that's fine

too." I was like . . . , "Are you listening, like didn't you hear what I just said?" So it was really, really weird.

When asked explicitly what her parents thought about the situation and the choices she had made, she struggles to understand their apparent ambivalence: "I don't know. It was kind of like I talked to them a little bit about it, but they wouldn't really talk to me about it at all. So I don't really know if they even really know what was going on." In our interpretation, this adolescent badly needed and wanted her parents' support, and the absence of it has left her with a sense of betrayal (level 1), making her experience all the more difficult to overcome.

At level 2, the parent voice is only minimally present in the adolescent's narrative, and may be passively complied with or perhaps questioned or challenged. The introductory story of this chapter illustrates this level, and is considered in detail later. At level 3, the mid-point on our scale, the parents' voice is clearly audible in the adolescent's narrative but it is "recited" or "parroted" by the adolescent, as opposed to being truly internalized. Typically, the child's responsiveness to his or her parents' influence takes the form of behavioral compliance, rather than a clear formulation of their beliefs and values and acceptance of, or at least respect for, them. At level 4, the parent voice is audible in the child's narrative, and there is clear evidence of his or her responsiveness to it, but it does not appear to be convincingly "owned by" or "internally persuasive" to the child and is not stated in the adolescent's own terms.

In contrast, at level 5, the highest level of our scale, there is clear evidence that the parental voice is not only audible in the adolescent's story, but it has also been appropriated and "authorized" or reconstructed by the adolescent in his or her own terms, in keeping with the notion of "internally persuasive" dialogue described by Bakhtin (1981). One of the stories that conveys this most clearly (and that we enjoy most) comes from an adolescent who tells about his earlier efforts to become accepted by a peer group. He has since come to value his "independence" through the guidance of his parents. He explained,

> Ok, there was a big group of people who were like in my class, and they called themselves the good people, like they were all supposed to be all cool and everything. And I wasn't in that group and I wanted to be, so I did all sorts of like little things for them. I like practically became their slave. And this came to my parents' notice, and they told me not to bother with those people, to like start my own group and stuff like that. At first I didn't listen, because I thought they didn't know what they were talking about. But after a while I began to see that these guys were just using me, and from then on I've never cared what other people think about me—I just do what I think is right. . . . My parents told me I should think for myself; I shouldn't follow what

other people do, and kiss these people on their butts because I want to join the group. . . . I should do what I think is good, no matter what anyone else thinks.

In this narrative, the adolescent illustrates for us a strong example of the constructive appropriation of his parents' beliefs and values. The parents' injunctions about independence of thought are not just echoed or "parroted" by this 14-year-old boy, but also appear to have been gradually "digested" and appropriated ("at first I didn't think they knew what they were talking about") for the child himself in graphic terms ("kiss their butts"). In our view, therefore, this narrative represents a compelling, personally authored "internally persuasive dialogue" on this issue, following the ideas of Bakhtin (1981).

We should note that agreement between raters on parent voice scoring has generally been good (correlations between two independent raters of .80 or better; Mackey et al., in press; Pratt et al., 1999). Furthermore, there was moderate consistency, but also some discrepancy, in parent voice ratings of the turning point and teaching story contexts for parent voice levels in the present family sample ($r = .40$). This finding suggests that the parental voice for adolescents is partly story-specific, as might be expected, but also somewhat generalized across stories, perhaps a reflection of broader family styles.

TWO ADOLESCENTS' REPRESENTATIONS OF PARENT VOICE IN THEIR FAMILY NARRATIVES

We will now compare two families from our parent–adolescent sample in detail. The target adolescent in each of these families was a girl, Sandy, whom we have already met, and Lisa. These particular families were chosen because they represent substantial differences in the level of responsiveness of the two girls to the parental voice in the stories told about family life. By examining these two case studies in detail, we hope to shed some light on ways in which such parental voice differences might be part of wider patterns of adolescent adaptation within the family. The parents and adolescents in these families were interviewed twice, separated by a two-year period; unless otherwise indicated, the material excerpted is drawn from the second round of family interviews (when the turning point or critical incident narratives were elicited). We first discuss each girl's story of a turning point in her value learning. Then we describe other narrative information we obtained from each family and suggest possible interpretations of this material, leading to specific hypotheses about how parental voice in the narratives might be reflective of family and personal dynamics. Finally, we mention briefly some more quantitative analyses of the hypotheses suggested from the two case studies, and discuss issues of the gendered nature of parental voices in our sample (e.g., Pratt et al., 1998).

Sandy

Sandy and her parents have already been introduced in the opening paragraphs of this chapter. In her critical incident story, Sandy expressed her feelings of the difficulties of having to relocate with her family, as well as a sense that her concerns were not especially noteworthy to her parents. This was one of the more negatively toned turning point stories told in our sample of families. Sandy's resolution of the story, which we have not yet described, was also ambivalent:

> **Interviewer:** And how did that experience have an impact on the kind of person you are now?
> **S:** I think it changed my life around so much. It helps me to meet new people, like it helps me to get ready for when I'm changing schools. . . . I don't know. It helps me. It's helped me a little. . . .

The "I don't think they'd really give it a second thought" attribution made by Sandy regarding her parents' perspective, which we noted in the introduction, suggested a sense of little understanding or feeling of support from the parents about what was obviously a deeply felt concern for Sandy. We scored this narrative at level 2 on our scale, representing her somewhat uncertain and conflicted feelings about the parental perspective.

Looking more fully across our narrative material, Sandy's stories were quite consistently expressive of anxieties about parental care. For example, in telling a narrative about a "current issue with her mom," Sandy described the limited amount of time she had to spend with her mother: "I think we should spend more time together because I hardly see her at all, like five minutes in the morning and then she goes off to work and then after work I hibernate in my room and then do homework and then I sleep, so the only time I basically see her is a little bit after work, not very often." As this story about a current problem unfolded, Sandy told about an episode when she had been supposed to go out for dinner with her mother but then had had a reaction to a vaccination and could not go. "So, I was saying like I want to go, I don't want to stay home, there's nothing to do. . . . So she [mother] said, '*Oh well, you better stay home.*' So she took my sister out and since then we've been talking about spending more time together." [How did your mom feel about this situation when you were sick and couldn't go to dinner?] "*I don't think she gave it a second thought.* Like my sister called me once from the restaurant to tape a show for her [on TV], but *I just think my mom was talking to my sister and I don't think she really ever gave it a second thought.*"

Sandy's other stories were quite consistent with this pattern. Sandy's most important personal value for herself was "being open and communicative." In her story about how her parents had taught her about this, she described an experience of going with her family to her father's high school reunion.

I have a lot of trouble communicating with people, like when I get around people I don't know and kind of back off in a corner-type thing. . . . My dad went to his high school reunion, and I didn't really want to go. Well I kind of did, but I kind of didn't. I hardly spoke a word through the entire thing, except maybe to my sister. And my mom and dad could talk to the people openly because they both knew them, and I was, like I don't know anyone and I'm just gonna sit back in a corner and pretend I'm not here type thing, and they [her parents] said, "*Oh, be open, just talk with people*" and so in a way they kind of taught me and they kind of showed me at the same time. They were able to walk around and talk to people even if they didn't know them, and it was just so easy for them to talk to people, and that showed me how easy it was. I still have trouble with it, but it showed me just talking can be easy. I don't think I'm gonna be able to forget it [the experience] for a long time. Just when I have trouble talking to people, I just have to look back on that and say, "OK, my parents can do it, I can do it, it's easy, no problem." [Why do you think your parents responded that way, telling you to communicate more?] I think it was just something that comes natural to them, and it was just easy for them to talk. . . . *I think they want me to be more like them, not stand off in a corner, hiding. . . . They want me to be able to make more friends than I have, instead of being afraid of people*, like I am, unfortunately. [Do you agree?] I think I should try to be more open, yeah. [Did you agree then?] No. I just didn't want to be there. I wanted to hide.

Similarly, Sandy's story about her current problem with her father was about troubles with the family computer, which needed to be fixed but was too expensive to get done at present.

I was typing on the computer and the computer like fritzed and there wasn't really a problem. . . . Just it's been kind of an issue for us because we've been kind of lost without it, so we need a new computer. My dad's been trying to fix it and he doesn't really like computers any more because we keep trying to work it out and it's not connected right. And my dad's got a short fuse. . . . I miss the computer. My dad and I have spent more time working together because we're on the computer and sometimes I feel I'm getting in the way, and *sometimes I feel he thinks I'm getting in the way. . . . I'm not sure how he feels, but that's me. . . . I think he's just frustrated at the computer and he realizes I really need it and it's annoying to him to have me complain all the time. He just sits there going "Please be quiet, we need a new computer but we don't have the money now.*" . . . And I don't want to impose on my parents any more than I already have, and I don't want to bug them saying I really need a computer, because of the money problems. . . .

Despite Sandy's sense of her parents' critical feelings, however, she continues to value her relationship with them. In her discussion of personal influences on her values, she said,

> My mom and dad are really close to me and like they have a huge influence on my life. If I'm doing something wrong, they could talk to me and they could correct it for me or if there's something I don't understand, I could talk to them and they could clear it up. . . . They are really close to me and I love them a lot. My dad keeps me in line and my mom says *"Don't act that way or I'll tell your dad,"* so it's basically they both keep me in line. They're like my role models, like how I want to treat my kids when I get older. They're strict, but not too strict that I want to run away and get a nose ring or something.

Despite this continuing sense of engagement, however, Sandy's narratives seemed to us to illustrate a set of variations on a theme of anxieties around parental support and nurturance. She also appeared to have an accompanying sense that her parents were quite dissatisfied with her shyness and perhaps did not understand her feelings of social anxiety, likely magnified by the repeated experiences of relocation that she has had to cope with during her childhood. In her story about her father's struggles with the cranky household computer, Sandy indicates that she doesn't want to impose on her parents "any more than I already have. . . ." Indeed, Sandy's perceptions of her family on standard questionnaire measures of family support and parenting style were consistently negative over both interview rounds.

Sandy's narratives also show, however, that she has responded to this sense of anxiety with efforts to solicit care from her family, especially from her mother. She certainly has not reacted to her sense of the family situation with alienation, and continues somewhat poignantly to emphasize her parents' importance in her life as role models and disciplinarians. In her turning point story, too, Sandy seemed to demonstrate efforts at identification with her parents, even in the midst of her palpable dissatisfaction. As the initial quotation indicated, Sandy's telling of her family relocations reveals efforts at maintaining family cohesiveness ("*we've* changed that and *we've* found a new place that *we* really like or that really appealed to *our* tastes . . .") This is certainly not the story of someone who has become permanently estranged from the family, but rather of someone who is ambivalent, but striving to stay connected. Again, in her value teaching story, Sandy responds to her family's exhortations to be more sociable in groups both as a criticism and as a positive example of how she might ultimately learn to cope with this anxiety.

Sandy's sense of adaptation in her personal life seemed somewhat fragile, however. As the narratives show, she tends to perceive herself as "somewhat weird" in her friends' eyes, and certainly feels that her parents are critical of her in several ways and really fail to understand her. These feelings were borne out by Sandy's responses on standard adjustment questionnaires we administered, where she was one of the highest scorers in the sample on loneliness and quite low on the measure of self-esteem. In sum, our sense of this adolescent was of someone who was struggling to cope with feelings of relatively low parental responsiveness and ambivalence.

Certainly, we must remember that the narratives described represent the child's views, and that the parents surely have other stories to tell. Undoubtedly, the issues also reflect aspects of the child's distinctive personality and temperament, but it did not seem that the family had so far been able to provide fully for the kind of support that Sandy seemed to need. In their own stories of family socialization in both interview rounds, the parents focused on incidents much earlier in Sandy's childhood, when she had been inclined to "stretch the truth" in the stories that she told, and they had to persistently stress to her that she must be clear about what was truthful and what was not, or (for the father) an episode of stealing which had had to be corrected. The parents reported that they were now satisfied that Sandy had learned these lessons. However, it would be fair to say that there was considerable focus on the control of negative behaviors and little sense of pride in the parents' stories of their efforts toward Sandy's socialization. Elsewhere, we have discussed these same patterns as narrative indicators of parental pessimism regarding the child's development, and noted that these views tend to be associated with parental restriction on autonomy (Pratt, Danso, Arnold, Norris, & Filyer, 2001). Nevertheless, the family clearly continued to make efforts to deal with these problems, and Sandy herself remained ambivalent, but hopeful, that her family, and especially her mother, would find a way to "have more close time" for her. In sum, Sandy's stories seemed to us to reflect well the ongoing dialogical conversation in her thinking between the demanding ideals she perceives from her parents (e.g., to "be open with people") and her own emerging sense of a self, who can only partly cope with these demands. She shows both unhappiness and considerable energy in these narratives in struggling with this critical parent voice.

Lisa

Our second family consisted of two parents, their three adolescent daughters, and a younger adolescent son. The parents had immigrated to Canada from Trinidad, where they had grown up. The target adolescent for our study (whom we will call Lisa) was 18 years old at the second round of the research, from which most material is drawn. She is the middle daughter in this family of six. The mother is a teacher, and the father works as a machinist. The parents both take pride in the children's school achievement, as portrayed in the stories they told about Lisa's socialization at each of our interview sessions. This is a family in which the mother, in particular, was quite involved in a variety of prosocial commitments and volunteer activities, though the father was not.

Lisa expressed much closeness to her family, particularly to her mother. When asked why she had put her mother closest of all in our value influences task, which involved placing chips as markers of important influences on a standard checkerboard, Lisa said, "She is basically my role model in life. She influences everything I do. Everything, it doesn't matter what it is. . . . My mom has more influence when it comes to me than my dad. But he's next in line. . . ." Lisa's plans for the future involved getting lots of volunteer experience at a local hospital, because she hopes to specialize in paediatric medicine.

Lisa's critical incident story was as follows:

Two years ago my friend at school died. He was going off on a Sunday night to buy a chocolate bar. He never got back home. Then, the next day his parents were searching everywhere. At 3:00 p.m. they found him in a lake. His bike was on the other end of the lake, and he had some bruises. . . . But the police never resolved it, they closed the case. We don't know what happened. I still feel the loss because I was head girl at the school, he was head boy, and we were always working together with school events and everything. It's just so sad that he's my age and he's dead. I was so mad when he died because I couldn't believe the police weren't doing anything. . . . But finally the principal said that the parents wanted it to be forgotten, and so we really had no choice. Because I guess it's tradition with the Moslem culture when someone's buried, you stop investigating their death.

Lisa continued about the importance of this event for her:

Like teenagers usually say stupid things, like "just die," and use it so casually. You don't think that it would really happen, but it may. . . . I cried a lot when he died, but then I started to think that crying so much, it's not helping anything. . . . and I tried to keep my emotions in check just for his parents' sake, because I didn't think it would do them any good. . . . We did start a fund for him at school and because I was Head Prefect then, I was involved in it more than anyone else, so we raised the money and now it's a fund at commencement. The person who shows his attributes gets it each year. So it's nice to see that. . . . And his parents were really proud last year at graduation. One of his brothers gave it out, and that was nice. I mean it's hard to sit there in the audience and listen to it, but it's good for you, it's almost like therapy.

[How has this event had an impact on the kind of person you are?] It's helped me not to be so immature. . . . Sometimes you'd make fun of people and you know like I try to be friendlier at school, so that if someone else died, I'd be able to say I was really a friend to them. . . . [And how do you think your parents thought about the situation and the choices you made?] My mom was really supportive, she had to be there for me because I would get so emotional and wouldn't be able to stop crying, and I have an enlarged pulmonary artery, so she has to be able to restrain me so I don't over-react, because when I cry that much, I turn blue. And they [her parents] were really proud that I was gonna do the fund and keep his memory alive. And they tried to lighten things up at home so that I wouldn't get going. . . .

This story seemed to us to be noteworthy for its emphasis on Lisa's active attempts to cope with what was clearly a strong feeling of loss. As we noted in the introduction, several of the adolescents chose to tell stories of death as their value turning points, involving an emerging adolescent awareness of the finality of mortality and loss. Lisa's efforts to provide some sort of memorial to her friend can be seen in the context of her family's orientation to social responsibility as a particularly notable way of dealing with this tragedy. In some ways, this story resembles the redemption themes discussed by McAdams et al. (1997). In such stories, negative events are described, but then are followed by countervailing positive events or out-comes that seem to redeem these problems. Both McAdams et al. (1997) and we (Pratt, Norris, Arnold, & Filyer, 1999) have found these types of sequences more typical of the life stories of generative adults. In this turning point story, this adolescent clearly attempts to turn this tragic event into something more positive and redeeming.

Lisa's sense of the support and pride that her parents (particularly her mother) expressed during this difficult experience seemed to us to warrant scoring this example of the "parent voice" in this narrative at level 5 in our system. The mother's actions and perspective were summarized clearly, and were strongly valued in Lisa's comments. It also seemed to us that the parents' views were phrased in Lisa's own words, and thus warranted categorization as internally persuasive in the sense described by Bakhtin (1981). We should note, however, that Lisa's comments about her parents were directly elicited in this narrative by the interviewer, and were not spontaneous, as were more of the parental comments in Sandy's critical incident story presented. Later we comment on this particular discourse phenomenon in more detail.

In another part of our interview, Lisa discussed an example of how her mother had tried to encourage her to be "kind and caring," her most important value chosen for herself. Lisa's sister had been involved in a volunteer placement helping a handicapped child who needed a lot of physical care. Lisa's sister was in a minor car accident, and so could not help with the child for some months because of the physical demands of the work. So Lisa's mother and sister convinced her that she should help out at this placement for the interim until her sister could return, even though Lisa herself was involved in several such volunteer activities already.

> My mom's a really caring person. She's been a teacher for more than 19 years now and she's always liked by her students because she cares so much for them. And this little kid that my sister was working with . . . my mom has visited her a few times and they have a strong bond, they're really attached. . . . So I think I should help out, because I can afford to do the lifting, and my mother and sister should be able to rely on me. . . .

Later, discussing another child she volunteers with (who is a cousin with severe behavior problems who actually lives at Lisa's grandmother's house), Lisa said,

> I think it's enriched my life, working with her. Because it's made me realize that you have to be patient, and I think I've become more patient dealing with that, because I have no choice really. If I'm not patient with her, I'm gonna end up hurting her and I don't want to do that. . . . I think I've helped her [the child] as well, because I'm nice to her, she's nice to me. . . .

Lisa explained how her grandmother had also encouraged "kindness and caring" in this situation:

> Well, she played on my love for my cousin and the family connection thing to get me to work with her, but I was willing to do it because even though she's very violent and bad most of the time, she's funny and I like her, she's a really unique person. And she really likes me. We have a bond. . . .

Certainly this is an adolescent with a broad range of prosocial influences in her family.

Lisa's narratives about particular current problems with each of her parents focused on difficulties in meeting her many commitments and responsibilities. For example, her "problem" with her father involved the fact that she wanted to do her high school co-op placement at a downtown hospital, where she could get better opportunities for working with children, whereas her father was concerned about her traveling alone and wanted her to work at a closer hospital where she would have less traveling but might not get such a strong experience. Most noteworthy was Lisa's tendency to treat this as a sort of collaborative issue with her parents:

I don't think it's really an issue of right and wrong. I think it's just his [father's] concern for me. He's a little over-protective with that and I think most parents are with the safety of the kids, but he's going to be dropping me right to the station and back and picking me up afterwards. . . . So, he's not that strong against it. Because he knows it would be better for me to go downtown. He knows my goals.

For us, Lisa's narratives illustrate several points. She clearly has a strong sense of support from her parents, especially her mother, as well as a great deal of respect for both of them. Her mother is a role model of a caring person for her, an aspect of her developing sense of identity that is obviously quite central. Lisa already seems mature in her interpersonal commitments and in her level of reflectiveness about these volunteering experiences ("I think it's enriched my life. . . ."). In her discussions of family issues, there was an attitude of mutual problem solving with both parents in the stories she described, and optimism that these matters would be worked out. It was our sense from these narratives that she was quite mature and adaptive in a number of ways. Her profile on our adjustment measures (standard questionnaire indexes of loneliness and self-esteem) bore this out, as she was one of the most positively adjusted in this adolescent sample on these measures. Noteworthy too was the fact that Lisa seemed to emphasize especially the importance of her mother's voice and presence as a model throughout these stories.

As noted, Lisa's parents' stories of the family emphasized their pride in her scholastic accomplishments, her independence, and her responsibility. For example, her mother, a teacher herself, discussed how she had tried to encourage Lisa to be more independent in working on her school assignments: "So she did her senior project on a very difficult author . . . and I even offered to help in some parts, and when I did she didn't need it. She said, 'It's OK, I have my own way of putting that!' So I'm happy that now she can stand on her own. . . ." The optimistic tone of these stories stood in strong contrast to those of Sandy's parents.

LESSONS FROM SANDY AND LISA

These two case studies of adolescents' family stories have provided us with a snapshot of the family context of our adolescents' stories of their development. We were interested specifically in the parental voice, partly as a marker of the extent to which the adolescent is responsive to parental influences. The contrasts between Sandy's and Lisa's perceptions of their families also provided suggestions about some of the characteristics that might help to define differences in the ways in which parent voices are represented in the thinking of adolescents. Before we begin to discuss these contrasts, however, it is necessary to comment briefly on issues of the different story contexts we elicited and the discourse markers of the parental perspective associated with them.

An important question was the extent to which the parental voice was spontaneously represented within the various stories (as in Sandy's turning point story that opened the chapter), versus elicited by the interviewer through probing (as in the case of Lisa's turning point narrative). In fact, these patterns varied considerably by story context. In the turning point or critical incident stories, only about 40% of the adolescents provided a spontaneous quotation from parents as part of their narrative. In contrast, about 75% of the parent value teaching stories contained such direct quotations. Why might this be the case? In fact, the turning point stories were more likely, especially among the older teenagers, to involve events outside of the family realm. As a consequence, the parent voice was more often elicited for these older adolescents' turning point stories and was more in the nature of a commentary on these older children's personal experiences (as in Lisa's example). In contrast, the value teaching story focused more directly on the parent voice itself, as construed by the child, and it was much more often spontaneously present (as in Sandy's story of the high school reunion). Despite these differences in discourse form among the contexts, however, we found that the parental perspective was typically available to our adolescents and readily elicited by our probing. This is certainly consistent with the idea that voices of significant others are often anticipated in thinking and come to function as important sounding boards in consideration of personal decisions (Day & Tappan, 1996).

Returning now to Sandy and Lisa, what were some of the most interesting patterns suggested by these two case studies? First, the extent of support and mutual responsiveness within the parent–child relationships of the family are likely to be closely reflected in the adolescent's stories of specific experiences. Sandy's ambivalence about parental support and engagement, as reflected in her representations of the parental voice, contrasts with the sense of care and pride that Lisa's representations of her parents' voices marked for her. Overall, then, we expected that measures of family climate and parenting from the adolescents would be linked to the adolescent's narrative construction of the parent voice as assessed on our scale.

Second, the adolescent's feelings about the parent voice in the stories also appeared likely to be linked to their general sense of personal adjustment and optimism. Lisa's engagement with her family, particularly her mother, seemed to be reflected in a confidence about her own capacities and a sense of good social adaptation. In contrast, Sandy's social anxieties seemed at least partly tied to the discomfort she had around her sense of her parents' more critical views of her personality and behavior, and this was portrayed in her depiction of the parental voices in her family. Consistent with this pattern then, we anticipate that adolescent adjustment should be positively linked to our narrative parent-voice measure, given the substantial role that the parents likely play in children's feelings of self-worth and adjustment.

Third, we also feel, based on these two case studies, that representation of the parental voice might be linked to the developing sense of personal identity, a central task of the adolescent life transition (e.g., Erikson, 1968). Lisa, 18 at the time of the second interviews, was the older of the two girls in these studies, and she also seemed much the more mature in her sense of independent personhood. We believe that a more mature sense of one's *own* voice should make it possible for the adolescent to also represent the parental perspective in a more tolerant and responsive way in his or her thinking (Mackey et al., in press). There may also be important gender-linked components in the role of the parental voice for these adolescents. Clearly, the maternal perspective had a special place in both Sandy's and Lisa's stories. Likely this reflects basic processes in construction of a sense of personal identity.

The results of some quantitative analyses of this family data set provided support for the first two hypotheses. The 35 adolescents in our study at the second round of interviews reported their perceptions of authoritativeness of parenting style in their families on a standardized questionnaire (adapted from Dornbusch, Ritter, Leiderman, Roberts, & Fraleigh, 1987). Families in which the adolescents were more responsive to the parent voice in their turning point stories were more likely to be seen as authoritative in their parenting styles by the adolescents, following the framework of Baumrind (1991). The correlation in our sample between these measures was moderately positive ($r = .42$), as predicted (see Mackey et al., in press, for further evidence).

Adolescents' feelings of personal adjustment were also measured in our study by use of standard questionnaires focusing on feelings of loneliness (the UCLA Loneliness Scale; Russel, Peplau, & Cutrona, 1980) and on self-esteem (the Rosenberg Self-Esteem Scale; Rosenberg, 1979). In families where the adolescent represented the parent voice at a more sophisticated level in the critical incident narrative, the child's self-esteem was likely to be higher ($r = .65$), and reported levels of loneliness were lower ($r = -.41$). Overall, then, these quantitative data were consistent with the first and second hypotheses suggested from the case studies. It was not possible to examine the third hypothesis in such a quantitative fashion, because we did not have indexes of identity development in this data set (however, see Mackey et al., in press, for some evidence on this hypothesis). Nevertheless, it was possible to examine the question of gender patterns in the adolescents' representation of parental perspectives.

GENDER PATTERNS IN THE REPRESENTATION
OF PARENT VOICES

It was evident that both girls in our cases focused somewhat more clearly on their mothers' perspectives or voices in their narratives of family life, while representing the father's views somewhat less fully. Lisa, for example, seemed particularly explicit in valuing her mother's support in her turning point narrative, saying nothing about her father at all. Similarly, though Sandy was less likely to distinguish her parents in her narratives, her sense of deprivation was especially acute with respect to maternal attention. Given these observations, we felt it would be important to try to understand potential gender patterns in the representation of parental voices in our data set more fully, especially because of their likely role in the construction of personal identity during this developmental period. As a contrast with the two girls discussed earlier, we provide a critical incident story from one of our male participants.

> We went over to this guy's place, and we started drinking. . . . I guess we passed out, I don't even remember. When I got up in the morning, I was like really sick. . . . So that's given me the mentality that drinking too much is just dumb. . . . It was an instant decision, never doing this again. That was a strong decision because I'm not changing my mind about it. . . . My dad was cool, he's like *"It was your choice, you got drunk and now how do you feel?"* I told him horrible, I'm never doing that again. So he said *"Yeah, that's how I felt when I used to go overboard."* But he told me he thought it was good that I made a choice never to do it again. And he just says, *"You know, try everything, so you're a better all-around person, but if it's bad, do it once, that's it, don't get into it."* But my mom, if she knew, she would freak out. . . . I'd probably be grounded, *blah, blah, blah,* all that stuff.

In this story of a 17-year-old male, both parents' own (quite divergent) voices are clearly audible. In the turning point stories, adolescents sometimes spontaneously distinguished the voices of mother and father, though none more clearly than in this instance. In this quotation, the son's sense of closeness and identification with his father comes through very strongly ("My dad was cool. . . ."). The father's voice is explicitly and approvingly quoted as a guide and support for the son's perspective on his value learning from experience, in the future as well as for the particular instance described. In contrast, the mother's voice is abbreviated and dismissed, almost caricatured. For this 17-year-old male, the mother's perspective on such risky, "testing-the-limits" behaviors is not even worthy of consideration.

In contrast to this story by a son, a critical incident story by a 14-year-old girl about her turning point episode exclusively highlighted the role of mother's voice:

I didn't have a very good year in Grade 7 and when we were gonna be moving to Grade 8 in the new school, I wanted to make more friends than I had before because I didn't like how it was before. And so it took awhile to figure out what it was, except my mom and I talked it through and we just figured out together what I wanted it to be. . . . Well, *my mom she agreed with me changing completely, and we both talked together and decided what I wanted to be like.* . . . [Why did she feel that way?] Well, she moved to Canada from England when she was eleven. And *she didn't have a very good Grade 8 and 9 because she was a year younger than everybody and had an accent and she would have liked to start over again,* and I was starting over again, so she wanted to help. . . . And I made a big effort to talk to people a lot more and so I made a few really good friends which I still have.

This girl's construction of her own personal turning point thus interestingly reflects a strong sense of identification with her mother's personal history. The mother's voice as represented conveys both support and understanding of these difficulties at the intimate level of shared experiences. In fact, the father is nowhere to be found in this story.

Many of the adolescents in our sample did not distinguish clearly between mother's and father's perspectives in their critical incident stories, as noted. However, an examination of only those who *did* showed that daughters were more likely to spontaneously represent the voices of mothers in their turning point stories, whereas sons were more likely to depict the perspectives of fathers. This pattern of differences by gender was even more pronounced in the adolescents' narratives of parent value teaching, for which about 60% of the stories highlighted one of the two parental voices more clearly. Although mothers' voices were generally more salient overall (15 of 21 cases where any distinction was made), 5 of the 6 stories for which fathers' voices were clearer than mothers' were told by sons. For mothers' voices, meanwhile, 12 of the 15 stories with mother's voice more salient were told by daughters ($p < .05$ by Fisher Exact Test for these gender differences). Thus these narrative differences in adolescents' stories reflected the typical pattern of same-sex identification observed across many domains of sex-role development (e.g., Ruble & Martin, 1998).

But why should gender-typing be as important in these stories as it apparently was? At least in the cases exemplified, the same-sex parent was important as a role model and resource particularly because of the shared past experiences that each of these parents provided for the child. The 17-year-old male quoted went on to describe his father's influence on him in our personal influences interview:

Right now, I just talk to him way more than I talk to my mom. I do things with him more than I do things with my mom. He's just. . . . I realize that he's done everything that I have, so he sort of tells me everything he did, like he doesn't hide anything. And I go out and try it and stuff, so that's why [he's so important to me].

Thus gender appears to be one highly salient category in the minds of these adolescents as they grapple with issues of values in constructing a sense of self. The corresponding devaluation of the mother's voice by this boy in the story may also reflect this difficult process of identity development in adolescence, perhaps particularly among males, as has been noted previously (e.g., Ruble & Martin, 1998). At any rate, the heightened salience of the same-sex parent's voice in our adolescents' stories surely indicates that the voice construct as investigated does reflect important underlying developmental processes in a meaningful and interesting way.

CONCLUSIONS

This research arose from an interest in applying a sociocultural, narrative framework to the phenomena of adolescents' value and autonomy development during personal life transitions. Listening to the stories that adolescents told about parents' views and advice regarding important value learning experiences, we developed a categorization system, based in sociocultural theory, to describe the ways in which this parent voice of influence could be heard in different families. The cases we have reviewed have provided a context for developing hypotheses about the meaning and representation of this parent voice within different family contexts. Sandy and Lisa differed notably in their feelings of family parenting and support, as well as in their own sense of personal adjustment. These differences appeared consistent with our sense that the parental voice in adolescents' stories tapped important aspects of the family's organization from the child's point of view. These cases in turn provided ideas about the interpretation of parent voice, specifically as a reflection of aspects of both family climate and personal adjustment and development. We also believe that these cases illustrate well the richness of this conception of voice in stories and the advantages of a narrative approach, both to eliciting data and to understanding and contextualizing these family phenomena in development.

As we noted, we have found that our narrative voice measure does seem to be consistently associated with more standard quantitative measures of family climate. Given this, we have recently been thinking about ways in which the voice construct may be effectively differentiated from more global quantitative measures, such as indexes of parenting style or family cohesion. In general, of course, we would expect that this narrative measure would be more concrete and specific to the particularities of context than standard summary rating indexes of parent–child climate. Consistent with this, we noted that the parent voice measure was only moderately correlated across different stories told by the same child. We have also found that this voice index is specific by topic in ways that parenting style measures are not. For example, fathers' voices in stories of late adolescents told about advice on the topic of relationship issues are substantially less salient than are those in stories about advice on the topic of future educational and vocational plans. In contrast, mothers' voices are relatively strong in young adults' narratives on both of these topics. These findings using our narrative methodology are consistent with previous interview and questionnaire results that show fathers are viewed as less knowledgeable by adolescents on relationship issues (e.g., Youniss & Smollar, 1985).

Adolescents did often spontaneously distinguish between the voices of mother and father in their narratives. These patterns were associated with child gender, with the voice of the same-sex parent generally more salient in these stories. Although such a gender-based pattern is predictable, differentiation of the parents' perspectives also must reflect other relationship distinctions within the family, with children at all ages feeling closer to one parent than the other for a variety of reasons. Beyond trying to understand these differences between the two parental voices more fully, we would also like to study the role of other voices of influence in adolescents' stories— for example, those of peers, grandparents, and teachers.

Some limitations of the material as presented should be noted. First, this chapter has focused on the adolescents' views of the family, and has not developed the parents' perspectives in any detail (see Pratt et al., 1999, for more description of parental narratives in this sample). Second, our sample, as in all research, is restricted in certain respects. In particular, it is Canadian, generally Caucasian, and drawn entirely from intact, two-parent families. In the future, it would be of interest to study the parental voice in a more diverse range of family structures and ethnicities. Third, although this research program is longitudinal in nature, discussion of the adolescent's representation of the parent voice over time, and the factors it may be associated with, is beyond the scope of this chapter. Such longitudinal analysis could help to unravel the complex and certainly bidirectional nature of adolescent–parent interaction and development within the family context.

This research points to interesting distinctions in the ways in which the concrete voices of others may be represented by adolescents in the stories they tell about life events that they perceive as turning points in their personal development. Parents' voices, in particular, echo through their children's stories in diverse ways. Our examination of cases from a family interview sample suggests that these differences are not random but reflect important distinctions in the adolescent's feelings about the family and its contexts of growth and development. Focusing on the adolescent's construction of his or her personal experiences in narrative, and, in particular, the parents' role in these life stories, allows the researcher to obtain a rich set of data from which to understand the nature of the family context during this central transition period of the life cycle.

REFERENCES

Bakhtin, M. (1981). *The dialogic imagination*. Austin: University of Texas Press.

Barnett, M., Quackenbush, S., & Sinisi, C. (1995). The role of critical experiences in moral development. *Basic and Applied Social Psychology, 17,* 137–152.

Baumrind, D. (1991). Effective parenting of adolescents. In P. Cowan & E. M. Hetherington (Eds.), *The effects of transitions on families* (pp. 111–163). Hillsdale, NJ: Erlbaum.

Colby, A., & Damon, W. (1992). *Some do care: Contemporary lives of moral commitment*. New York: Free Press.

Coles, R. (1989). *The call of stories: Teaching and the moral imagination*. Boston: Houghton-Mifflin.

Darling, N., & Steinberg, L. (1993). Parenting style as context: An integrative model. *Psychological Bulletin, 113,* 487–496.

Day, J., & Tappan, M. (1996). The narrative approach to moral development: From the epistemic subject to dialogical selves. *Human Development, 39,* 67–82.

Dornbusch, S., Ritter, P., Leiderman, P., Roberts, D., & Fraleigh, M. (1987). The relation of parenting style to adolescent school performance. *Child Development, 58,* 1244–1257.

Duncan, R., & Pratt, M. (1997). Microgenetic change in preschoolers' private speech: Effects of task difficulty, task novelty, and task repetition. *International Journal of Behavioral Development, 20,* 367–383.

Ely, R., & McCabe, A. (1993). Remembered voices. *Journal of Child Language, 20,* 671–696.

Erikson, E. (1968). *Identity, youth and crisis*. New York: Norton.

Kohlberg, L. (1976). Moral stages and moralization: The cognitive-developmental approach. In T. Lickona (Ed.), *Moral development and behavior* (pp. 31–53). New York: Holt, Rinehart, & Winston.

Maccoby, E., & Martin, J. (1983). Socialization in the context of the family. In E. M. Hetherington (Ed.), *Handbook of child psychology* (Vol. 4, pp. 1–101). New York: Wiley.

Mackey, K., Arnold, M. L., & Pratt, M. (in press). Adolescents' stories of decision-making in more or less authoritative families: Representing the voices of parents in narrative. *Journal of Adolescent Research*.

McAdams, D. P. (1993). *The stories we live by: Personal myths and the making of the self*. New York: William Morrow.

McAdams, D. P. (1996). Personality, modernity, and the storied self: A contemporary framework for studying persons. *Psychological Inquiry, 7,* 295–321.

McAdams, D. P. (1999). Personal narratives and the life story. In L. Pervin & O. John (Eds.), *Handbook of personality* (2nd ed., pp. 478–500). New York: Guilford Press.

McAdams, D. P., Diamond, A., de St. Aubin, E., & Mansfield, E. (1997). Stories of commitment: The psychosocial construction of generative lives. *Journal of Personality and Social Psychology, 72,* 678–694.

Piaget, J. (1965). *The moral development of the child.* Glencoe, IL: Free Press.

Pratt, M. W., & Arnold, M. L. (1995). Narrative approaches to moral socialization across the lifespan. *Moral Education Forum, 20,* 13–22.

Pratt, M. W., Arnold, M. L., & Hilbers, S. (1998). A narrative approach to the study of moral orientation in the family: Tales of kindness and care. In E. E. Skoe & A. von der Lippe (Eds.), *Personality development in adolescence: A cross-national and life span perspective* (pp. 61–78). London: Routledge.

Pratt, M. W., Arnold, M. L., Pratt, A., & Diessner, R. (1999). Predicting adolescent moral reasoning from family climate: A longitudinal study using narrative and observational techniques. *Journal of Early Adolescence, 19,* 148–175.

Pratt, M. W., Danso, H., Arnold, M. L., Norris, J., & Filyer, R. (2001). Adult generativity and the socialization of adolescents: Relations to mothers' and fathers' parenting beliefs, styles and practices. *Journal of Personality, 69,* 89–120.

Pratt, M. W., & Norris, J. (1999). Moral development in maturity: Lifespan perspectives on the processes of successful aging. In T. Hess & F. Blanchard-Fields (Eds.), *Social cognition and aging* (pp. 291–317). New York: Academic Press.

Pratt, M. W., Norris, J., Arnold, M. L., & Filyer, R. (1999). Generativity and moral development as predictors of value socialization narratives for the young across the adult lifespan: From lessons learned to stories shared. *Psychology and Aging, 14,* 414–426.

Rogoff, B. (1990). *Apprenticeship in thinking: Cognitive development in sociocultural activity.* New York: Oxford University Press.

Rosenberg, M. (1979). *Conceiving the self.* New York: Basic Books.

Ruble, D., & Martin, C. L. (1998). Gender development. In N. Eisenberg (Ed.), *Social, emotional, and personality development* (pp. 933–1016). New York: Wiley.

Russel, D., Peplau, L. A., & Cutrona, C. (1980). The revised UCLA loneliness scale: Concurrent and discriminant validity evidence. *Journal of Personality and Social Psychology, 39,* 472–480.

Simmons, R. G., Burgeson, R., Carlton-Ford, S., & Blyth, D. (1987). The impact of cumulative change in early adolescence. *Child Development, 58,* 1220–1234.

Tappan, M. (1991). Narrative, authorship, and the development of moral authority. *New Directions for Child Development, 54,* 5–25.

Tappan, M., & Brown, L. (1989). Stories told and lessons learned: Toward a narrative approach to moral development. *Harvard Educational Review, 59,* 182–205.

Vitz, P. (1990). The use of stories in moral development: New psychological reasons for an old educational method. *American Psychologist, 45,* 709–720.

Vygotsky, L. S. (1978). *Mind in society*. Cambridge, MA: Harvard University Press.

Walker, L., & Pitts, R. (1998). Naturalistic conceptions of moral maturity. *Developmental Psychology, 34*, 403–419.

Wertsch, J. V. (1991). *Voices of the mind: A sociocultural approach to mediated action*. Cambridge, MA: Harvard University Press.

Youniss, J., & Smollar, J. (1985). *Adolescents' relations with mothers, fathers, and friends*. Chicago: University of Chicago Press.

10

LIVING IN THE AMBER CLOUD:
A LIFE STORY ANALYSIS
OF A HEROIN ADDICT

JEFFERSON A. SINGER

The commitment to living sober after years of addiction can come at any stage of adulthood, but for many men and women the late 30s and early 40s are critical junctures for this life transition. Confronted with an aging process accelerated by the physical and emotional toll exacted by alcohol and drug abuse, addicted individuals entering middle-age often have an acute sense of what they have already lost and may never regain unless radical change occurs.

In the following life story analysis, I examine a man in his early 40s addicted to heroin and struggling to realign his life with certain positive sober ideals he holds for himself. What makes his story particularly useful in a volume on narratives of transition is in fact his inability to make a successful transition to recovery. His story informs us about what may be the deficits and conflicts within an internalized narrative that stymie individuals and leave them poised at thresholds of change, unable to embrace a healthier and more coherent narrative identity.

The vocabulary and theoretical structure that I use in this life story analysis draws on McAdams's life story theory of identity (1988, 1990, 1993) and my own work on self-defining memories (Singer, 1995; Singer & Salovey, 1993). This research focuses on how individuals' narrative structures influence the ongoing thoughts, feelings, and behaviors that constitute personality. One of the driving ideas in this work is that the narratives individuals recount of their lives serve a functional purpose (Habermas & Bluck, 2000; Pillemer, 1992; Singer, 1995). Individuals do not simply possess life stories, but they use them for interpersonal persuasion, psychological regulation of self-concept and mood, and motivational guidance in life pursuits (Pillemer,

1992). Analysis of individuals' life stories uncovers not only the themes of a given life, but also the dynamic properties of that story in a given personality. McAdams (1996) has proposed that this form of inquiry exists at a third level of personality organization (identity) along with level 2 studies of personal concerns (e.g., coping mechanisms, defenses, strivings, personal projects, life tasks) and level 1 study of personality traits.

In general, life story analyses of identity have focused on well-functioning individuals in the normal range of development. The goal of this chapter, along with previous recent work (Singer, 1997), is to examine the consequences for an individual of an internalized narrative that contains irreconcilable fragments—prominent subtexts and characters that are in opposition to each other and cannot be integrated by an overarching narrative. An implicit premise of this exploration is that life transitions inevitably require choices; we ultimately construct and adhere to a particular narrative version of ourselves that will guide our movement into a new phase of our lives. Tragically, the man described in this chapter, Richard Markham (not his actual name), is unable to trust in a self-narrative that incorporates his recovery. During his sober periods, it is almost as if he tries on this more healthy and idealized version of himself, but before too long he slips back to the familiar trappings of his self-destructive addicted identity. Equally dissatisfied with this negative self-construction, he swings back and forth between stories of himself, lacking a coherence that would give unity and purpose to his actions and sense of self.

In offering this story of a failed transition from a life of addiction, let me add one proviso. This life story analysis of an addicted individual should not be construed as a replacement for more traditional approaches to the study or treatment of addiction, such as the biomedical, psychological, social-learning, and family systems perspectives (see Thombs, 1999). As Vaillant (1995) has aptly demonstrated, the etiology and persistence of addiction can best be understood from an integrated, multifactorial perspective. Though I have at times applied a narrative perspective in my addiction treatment work with meaningful results, it would be premature to make claims about a "life story therapy" for addiction. The value of the narrative approach for addiction research and treatment is that it highlights what additional concerns need to be addressed as individuals attempt to maintain lasting sobriety and adopt new identities in their sober lives (see Singer, 1997).

In the sections that follow, I describe the basic tenets of the life story theory of identity and then apply them to Markham's narrative. In the final section, I discuss what this life story analysis has suggested about the importance of a coherent life story for the healthy functioning of personality, especially at critical junctures of life transitions, such as the movement from addiction to recovery.

McADAMS'S LIFE STORY THEORY OF IDENTITY

McAdams (1988, 1990, 1993) has argued that individuals are engaged from adolescence onward in an effort to fashion a meaningful life narrative that will infuse their lives with a sense of unity and purpose. This life story consists of archetypal characters that express idealized aspects of the self (*imagoes*), ongoing assumptions about the fairness and security of their surroundings (*ideological settings*), significant self-defining memories (*nuclear episodes*; see Singer, 1995; Singer & Salovey, 1993), and expectations about the story's end (*the generativity script*). Each of these components contributes to an ever-evolving answer in narrative form to the question of, "Who am I?" and "Who might I become?"

These life story components are woven together by two basic dimensions of theme and structure. *Thematic lines* are the motivational currents that run through any given narrative, organizing and directing the flow of the story to a desired endpoint. Though there are many potential themes, our culture is centrally focused around the dual pursuits of agency and communion. These terms are borrowed from Bakan (1966), and date back to Freud's conceptualization of "love and work" as the primary motivators of healthy individuals. *Agency* refers to a striving for autonomy, independence, competence, and self-definition. Agentic individuals seek individuation and separation. *Communion* encompasses connection to others—intimacy, nurturance, and interdependence. The life story emerges as each theme rises and falls in prominence for the individual—the ideal actualized life in our society strikes a balance between the two.

The structure of the life story depends on its *narrative complexity*. How much nuance, contradiction, and ambiguity does the narrator build into the story? Stories that are straightforward, lacking digression and complexity, reflect a less integrative and multilayered ego development. Individuals with unnuanced life stories may be less open to novelty, growth, or challenge to their current self-understanding; they may be less able to accept conflicting visions of themselves or others in their lives.

Each component—imagoes, ideological settings, nuclear episodes, and generativity scripts—expresses thematic and structural influences as it takes its place in the developing life narrative. *Imagoes*, recurring characters in the narrative, reflect the individual's personal idealizations that combine different blends of agency and communion. The capacity of imagoes to transcend unidimensional caricatures and allow for contradictory elements within the same character would indicate evidence of complexity in the life story.

Ideological settings express the background values or belief systems individuals use in their moral choices and actions. The accounts of incidents in their lives convey opinions about how just or unjust the world is, whether people are loving or self-serving, how inevitable love or loneliness might be.

Nuclear episodes take the life story and encapsulate it in specific memories from our lives. Nuclear episodes are particularly heightened examples of self-defining memories, which are narrative memories that play a conscious role in determining individuals' life choices and goals (Singer & Salovey, 1993). Nuclear episodes, distinctive peak experiences or low points that express themes of agency and communion, are the most significant and life-altering of self-defining memories.

Finally, the *generativity script*, or the outline of the story's ending, addresses the question of how our stories will turn out—what we will ultimately contribute or leave as our life's legacy—by what acts or products of our actions will we be known by those who follow after us? The generativity script comes in the form of stories about both agentic products (e.g., accomplishments, artistic works, material goods, donations), and also communal acts (e.g., raising of offspring, community service, religious faith). As we look back over the course of our life story, how we describe its meaning and interpret its various divergences and disappointments will again express the sense of wisdom and narrative complexity we bring to our own self-understanding and sense of identity.

In the following life story analysis, Markham's narrative helps to clarify the importance to optimal well-being and identity of each element—a balanced sense of agency and communion, a narrative that tolerates ambiguity and contradiction, an overall positive and tolerant image of the self, an optimistic view of the world and its vagaries, a memory that incorporates positive turning points in one's life, and a conviction that one can offer something of value to the world. The healthiest of us may have all of these in place; the majority of us, some. What happens when few or none of these elements can be found in the life story we construct to depict our sense of identity? The answer lies in the story I now present.

INTRODUCING RICHARD MARKHAM

In *Message in a Bottle: Stories of Men and Addiction* (Singer, 1997), I described my work as a staff psychologist for Lebanon Pines, a residential treatment facility that serves indigent and chronically addicted individuals. One of my familiar experiences during my years with the "Pines" was to discover ex-clients' names in the police logs of the local newspaper. When I would see Richard Markham's name in the logs, it would hit me particularly hard, and memories of my work with him would quickly overtake me. Of all the men from the Pines with whom I worked, I knew Richard the best, serving as a therapist to him during his stays at the Pines and later on working with him when he lived in 3/4 houses (aftercare homes for people in recovery that are less restrictive than halfway houses) and his own apartments.

The narrative that follows is based on a variety of sources—biographical material gained through therapy sessions, focused life history interviews, autobiographical writings, letters, and prison visits (all of this material is reviewed with the participant's informed consent).

CHILDHOOD AND EARLY YEARS

Born in 1954 to well-off parents in one of the elite towns of Connecticut, Richard felt early on the acute contradictions of his family life. His father, educated at Harvard, and his mother at the Eastman School of Music, carried the perfect paper credentials. Originally involved in banking, his father took his place among the "gray-flannel" men of the 1950s, building a suburban castle with colonial columns and lush green lawns. Rich recalled little domestic happiness, however. From his earliest memories, he retained flashes of his father's drinking and fights with his mother. He wrote me once in a letter about that period in his life between ages 5 and 9:

> The problems at home were starting to get extreme, with the alcoholic behavior influencing both the family and the whole neighborhood. The nightly events at our house must have been the talk of the town for those neighbors and they probably told their children to stay away from the house. The end result of this—I didn't make friends easily.

In this nuclear episode from his earliest years, Rich identified the fundamental themes of his future struggles with achieving intimacy in his life. First and foremost, his primary models for intimacy, his mother and father, were depicted as engaging in violent arguments loud enough to wake the neighbors. Already the influence of a mind-altering substance played a decisive role in upsetting the household and escalating the friction between his parents. The stigma of his parents' conflicts and his father's drinking undermined his efforts at making friends and corrupted his sense of community. This incipient suspicion that others would reject him would later blossom into near paranoid states of distrust and accusation; these fears would plague all of his adolescence and adulthood. By highlighting this memory from his childhood, he revealed a fundamental ideological setting (or expectation about the world) that he brought to all encounters with both authorities and intimates.

Rich's stay in this elevated world of Connecticut society unraveled by the time he reached 10 years of age. His parents divorced in 1964 and Rich was sent to live with his grandmother in Florida, while his younger brother and older sister remained behind with his mother. Years later in therapy, he would question numerous times why he was the one sent away, as if he deserved the punishment for the divorce. He also developed a confusing and conflicted understanding of how to be agentic in the world. He imagined his father as high in agency because of his Harvard education and business success, but at the same time he saw his father as abandoning his family and incapable of self-mastery over his alcoholism. In terms of communion, his father was always cold and distant from him, critical of his mother and of all the children's behavior. From early on, Rich had little sense of how to find a balance between agentic ambitions and a desire for communion and intimacy.

Struggling with confusing messages from his father's behavior, he developed early doubts about his worth as a person, about his "goodness." These doubts were compounded by his difficulty making new friends in Florida, and his rejection by old friends when he returned to Connecticut at the age of 11. He felt that his Connecticut friends avoided him on the advice of their parents, who said he came from a "bad home." At this same point in time, he had become extremely self-conscious about his two top front teeth that had come in crooked and slightly overlapping. In a particularly revealing moment in therapy with me, Rich revealed the cause of his crooked teeth. He had heard from his brother that he would receive silver dollars when each of his baby top front teeth came out. Excited by the prospect of the money, he wiggled and pulled his two front teeth out prematurely and the position of the permanent teeth was subsequently affected. In telling this story, Rich said to me, "I was a dope fiend even then, always looking for a quick fix."

Growing more convinced of his negative attributes and his inability to be liked, Rich withdrew into himself, more and more adopting the attitude of a resentful loner. He dated the origin of a central self-image or "imago" to this period—the birth of "Jack." This "Jack" persona could be traced to the destructive aspects of his father's agency. Rich described Jack as an amoral, sneering manipulator who scammed to win advantages for Rich.

Before the reader begins to speculate about Rich suffering from a dissociative personality disorder, an important qualification should be addressed. "Jack" is a narrative device that Rich used to describe aspects of himself at certain points of his story. It is a name he created to aid the two of us in identifying moments in which a certain aspect of his personality or "narrative identity" dominated his story. I never received from him any sense that he saw himself in a literal sense as a person named Jack, as opposed to Richard Markham. Unlike the dissociated individual who experiences "alters" that may have no awareness of each other, Richard knew painfully when he was allowing the "Jack-like" side of him to take over.

In moments of loneliness or social rejection, Rich could draw on Jack to show contempt toward others or exact revenge on them. Later on, Jack would become a major ally in Rich's relapses. Jack is clearly linked to Rich's adult tendency toward a destructive agency—an expression of autonomy through hurtful separation and the infliction of pain on others and one's self (see Singer, 1997, for an extensive discussion of this inverted form of agency).

Rich's social frustrations continued when his mother moved the family from their original home to a smaller apartment in a nearby city. Anonymous in a more urban neighborhood, Rich gave up any hope of friendships and spent entire afternoons and evenings reading or walking alone. Reading books had become a great comfort, and he harbored ambitions of doing something with his mind, eventually becoming a scientist or a physician. In these more pleasant afternoons, we can locate the beginning of a personal myth for Rich (see McAdams, 1993, for a discussion of how individuals' investment in a personal myth can come to guide the evolving life story). He imagined himself as a scientist or physician, someone with mastery over the world and great agentic power (Rich called this image of himself the Wizard). This Wizard imago was also a link back to his father's aloof intelligence and Harvard education. Rich's intellect, like his father's, could both win him status and protect him from further rebuffs in his efforts at intimacy.

As Rich started high school, his mother, brother, and he moved once again, to a less fashionable part of the city. Taking up with a classmate who was similarly lonely, he first tried pot and LSD. He quickly found that they offered the escape from pain and loneliness he had long desired. Now in addition to the protection of his books, drugs offered another way to buffer him against social rejection.

Even with all this disruption in Rich's adolescence, the greatest blow came when his mother developed a malignant cancer and died in his 17th year. The same letter quoted earlier talked about this time.

> I was a ship sailing away from the fleet of humanity, others didn't know me and I didn't know them, even my siblings were strangers. My mother had died during this time and I was really alone then. The next years were filled with various people, who probably didn't know anything more about relationships than I did, or they didn't care much more than I because they were as high as I was. The saying in those days was "I got stoned and I missed it." I missed a lot. I have been alone all my life, by the course of events and my choice.

As McAdams has suggested, the ideological setting of our life story is first tentatively forged in adolescence. For Rich, his mother's death confirmed his view of the world as essentially untrustworthy and dangerous. He saw his own place in the world as fundamentally isolated (even his siblings were strangers). Now to his loneliness he added the imagery of running, of sailing away, especially through the medium of drugs.

At this point, it would be helpful to step back and examine how the fundamental elements of Rich's life story narrative had fallen into place as he moved into adulthood. Richard presented his childhood in narrative terms as a "bad" story of familial strife and personal loneliness. He emerged from childhood with little understanding of positive agency. Introduced into an environment of privilege, he developed no understanding of how individuals achieve such success or mastery in their lives. From an early age, he portrayed himself as looking for magical transformations that would bring him a sense of power and success (the story of his twisted teeth is a dominant metaphor). Far from associating agency with values of industry, responsibility, and self-discipline, he had begun to incorporate the imago of Jack into his identity; this idealized image of negative agency willing to take destructive action to achieve ends of pleasure and material benefit.

Contrasted with Jack is a second idealized imago—the Wizard—a figure who has achieved scientific and spiritual wisdom and through this knowledge is able to rise above the material demands and hurts of the world. What both Jack and the Wizard share is a lack of insight into the daily application of one's labors toward a desired end. The immediate attraction of drugs for Rich fits nicely—they are not only pain-killers but also vehicles of magical transformation to a sense of mastery and aloof distance from the world.

After his mother's death, he took flight, hitchhiking and traveling around the country. He tried a semester at college while living with his father and stepmother, but did not finish the term. He made his way back to Connecticut and even lived in upstate New York in an apartment with his brother for a time. His brother was also swept along into the 1970s youth movement of drifters and hitchhikers; he became a sexual hustler and fell deep into drugs as well. Years later, Rich would get word from his father that his brother had hung himself; they had never had a chance to share any part of their adult lives together.

Rich's 20s were a blur of drinking and drug use. Even during this period, he continued reading, most often books related to psychology and spiritual journeys. As he withdrew from close relationships, he increasingly became fascinated with agentic themes of self-mastery and spiritual empowerment, all of which reinforced his Wizard imago.

He then took a job as a technician in a medical laboratory. Though he still had not finished even a semester of college, he soon began to lie about having a college degree. He was immensely proud of this job and, being an autodidact, taught himself a great deal about chemistry and physiology. The other aspect of the job he loved was that it gave him access to a number of controlled narcotics. Along with his studies, these drugs became his greatest friends. After many forays into Demerol and Dilaudid, he ended up mainlining heroin and began his career as a full-blown junkie. He once described for me what he loved about heroin: "When I shoot up, it is like a cloud of amber descends around me. I am inside it and the rest of the world is out there and can't come in. I'm safe and warm, like in my mother's arms. If it's good dope, that feeling can last for a whole day, eight hours, and nothing can touch me or worry me. It's a blissful, liberating place to be."[1]

Here then began a second complementary theme in Rich's personal myth—the safety of the amber cloud. Similar to the protection offered by his Wizard imago, the amber cloud could buffer Rich from the pain of human relationships. It could preserve him, womb-like, in a peaceful world that loss or rejection could not enter. It is interesting to note that once Rich developed his heroin habit, any efforts at meaningful relationships with women were placed on hold.

In his late teens, he had been deeply in love with one girl and had discovered in himself a willingness to be vulnerable to females that he would not allow himself with friends. He wrote to me,

> My defense against the possibility of being hurt by people is strong and maybe it should be, for the pain of being hurt by people when I think they care about me, is hard to deal with. . . . The AA program is people-based and the reason I have so much trouble with it is because I am self-based. My little system is remarkable except for when it comes to women, I am wide open for their emotional evils and I have many wounds to prove it. In the associations I have had with women I tend to be very passive, possessive, and mistrustful.

His desire for an ideal woman represented his third wished-for "magical transformation." In addition to Jack's reliance on drugs, and the Wizard's wish for sudden enlightenment, Rich held out the vision that the ideal woman would change his chronic loneliness and self-contempt. Yet once engaged in a relationship with an actual woman, his possessive behavior would ultimately alienate her and undermine the relationship. The rigidity of his narrative and its lack of nuance in tolerating the complexity of others ultimately sowed the seeds for its painful repetition.

Heroin soon became Rich's main transformative vehicle for the escape from daily life and its demands of love and work. Once high, all needs for

---

[1] See Fiddle (1967). The author connects this love of heroin to the anger at the world that many addicts feel. "Paradoxically, the person who is enraged with the world around him may often be trying in some way to restore some lost period of innocence, of joy now denied him. The memory of this period may be one of the themes of his life. Hence we would expect that some people who live this life may react to a drug such as heroin as though they were children suckling at the breasts of their mothers" (p. 27).

agency or communion could be relinquished in the pleasure of the "nod," the barely conscious dream-like state induced by the infusion of heroin into the blood and brain.[2] The nod could supply a womb-like substitute for his idealized mother and protect him from any risk of actual engagement with others.

In the early 1980s, when Rich was approaching 30 years of age, he began to develop legal difficulties and financial problems. He had lost his medical lab position because of his pilfering drugs from the facility; he had also had various scrapes with police over shoplifting and disorderly conduct. All of these illegal behaviors suggest how he would not hesitate to call on Jack when the need to hide behind his amber cloud overwhelmed him.

He initiated his first treatment programs in this period, and went on Methadone for a stretch of 4 to 5 years. During long months in treatment, he studied the Bible and religious texts, as well as more philosophy and psychology. He made several efforts to connect with AA and to build periods of sober time. Developing skills as a house painter, he was able to sustain himself for stretches of a year or so without using drugs. Inevitably, he would relapse, first by using pain pills or alcohol and then finding his way back to heroin. Finally, after multiple treatment programs, he made his way to the long-term rehabilitation facility of Lebanon Pines.

MY FIRST ENCOUNTERS WITH RICH

Rich came to speak with me after several conflicts with the counselors and staff at Lebanon Pines, complaining that the staff would not allow him more time off grounds to attend the church of his choice. He was also lecturing the other men about God and encouraging them to take up his spiritual path. He was conveying a general attitude of disdain toward both the counselors and the residents of the Pines, as if it were a strange mistake or cruel joke that he found himself among this "illiterate," substance-addicted crowd. Hearing this report about Rich and his mixture of religion and aggression, I prepared myself to determine if he might be suffering from religious delusions or an underlying psychosis.

Rich appeared before me wearing a white linen collarless shirt and a large black crucifix around his neck. He was extremely blond, with blue eyes and a fair complexion. He wore his straight fine-textured hair parted and in a sloping bang across his forehead. There was something anachronistic about his hairstyle; he looked a bit like a California "beach boy" from the

---

[2]Fiddle (1967) described the meaning of the nod, "It represents the end of striving, the cessation in varying degrees of all troubled reflection as well as the abandonment of all other projects except that of the quest for apparent euphoria and homeostasis" (p. 36).

1960s. Roughly 5'8", he had a strong, compact frame with large arms and hands that signaled sustained outdoor work—painting, carpentry, or possibly roofing. If you did not look closely at his hands and if he did not open his mouth to reveal his tobacco-stained and oddly angled front teeth, he could have passed for younger than his 35 years. The other physical feature that contrasted with his clean-cut good looks was an odd habit he had of licking his lips with a wide circular swipe of his tongue. Because he had no history of psychiatric medication, this intermittent act had almost a gluttonous or lascivious aspect to it.

He was not at all happy that he had been referred to see me. Many men saw a referral to the "shrink" as a punishment or a first step toward discharge from the Pines to an emergency room or a psychiatric unit. He refused to sit down, and paced the carpet of my office. He complained of the ignorance of the counselors and how they could not appreciate the books he was reading, including Plato's *Republic*.

In an effort to form an alliance with him, I asked him questions about his reading. He soon calmed down and took a seat beside my desk. Displaying the characteristic splitting behavior used by an individual with a borderline personality organization (and Rich, as I repeatedly learned, met virtually all of the criteria for both a borderline personality disorder and a narcissistic personality disorder),[3] he proceeded to cultivate me as the one intelligent and sane voice in the desolate wilderness of the Pines. Though I could see this gambit for what it was, I could not help take a liking to this philosophy-quoting book-worshipping wise guy. I decided to see him in biweekly sessions for a few months, with the goal of redirecting him back to the work of building his recovery.[4]

Once we began our meetings I found this refocusing harder than I expected. He often turned the talk to religion and would speak with passionate contempt for his recent despoiling of his body with drugs and alcohol. In addressing how he had become so deeply interested in religion, he spoke with great reverence of a young nun whom he had met in a doctor's office.

---

[3] The criteria for a borderline personality disorder include frantic efforts to avoid abandonment; a pattern of unstable and intense interpersonal relationships characterized by extremes of idealization and devaluation; identity disturbance: markedly and persistently unstable self-image or sense of self; impulsivity in at least two self-damaging areas (including spending money and substance abuse); recurrent suicidal behavior; affective instability as a result of marked reactivity of mood; inappropriate intense anger or difficulty controlling anger; transient stress-related paranoid ideation or severe dissociative symptoms (American Psychiatric Association, 1994). Rich also corresponds to a narcissistic personality disorder profile as well. In particular, he displayed grandiosity, fantasies of power, a sense of "specialness," a need for admiration, a sense of entitlement or expectation of special treatment, a tendency to manipulate or exploit others, envy, and arrogance (American Psychiatric Association, 1994).

[4] Because I only spent two afternoons a week at the Pines, the agency preferred that I not see men in weekly psychotherapy. My main duties were not direct treatment, but instead evaluations and crisis referrals.

She had given him some religious material and he had struck up a friendship with her. When he relapsed and entered inpatient treatment, he began a fervent correspondence with her, expressing all his hopes for recovery and redemption. His efforts at intimacy remained limited to his capacity to form intense attachments with idealized women. In terms of an idealized mother, who could fit the bill better than a woman sworn to chastity?

Rich and the nun continued to communicate by telephone from Lebanon Pines. As I heard more about this relationship over the months, I came to feel that Rich was of two minds about "sister" (as he referred to her). He maintained her on an elevated plane, seeing their relationship as "clean" and of a spiritual essence; he called it the pure light that exists behind those "mere shades" of most daily existence. On the other hand, he seemed to harbor a romantic fantasy of having a life together with her. She had expressed doubt at times about her own calling in her letters to him, and he had perhaps seized on these questions to build a daydream of a different life for both of them.[5] Passing mentions of this fantasy were interspersed with a possibility that he would go to work at a monastery as a handyman, while slowly acquiring the necessary religious knowledge to join the brotherhood. Continually, Rich's story would express these unreconcilable contradictions—on one hand, the holy man (Wizard), and on the other, the slick Jack, who might seduce the "sister" to leave her habit. It is a critical dimension of his sense of identity that his narrative does not have the sufficient complexity to integrate or make sense of these divergent features of his story.

Rich's day to day behavior toward the staff and other men stood in stark contrast to the spiritual divagations he shared with me in our sessions. His counselor found it a source of sardonic amusement that he would talk spirituality to me and run card games and betting pools for money and cigarettes when outside my office. He would dismiss the other residents as ignorant and spiritually empty, but did not hesitate to milk them out of small amounts of money. Just as Rich could not reconcile the lofty agentic accomplishments of his father with his father's aggressive and addictive behavior, Rich presented the same contradictions of integrating the Wizard imago of spiritual and intellectual purity with the antisocial behavior of Jack.

In several sessions, Rich would refer to an "old tape" in his head about other people, that they could not be trusted, especially figures of authority. In some rare moments, he would allow himself to mention his childhood, how his father's drinking had left him feeling deserted, and how this desertion was followed by his mother's marriage to an "asshole" stepfather, and ulti-

---

[5] Yalom (1980) talked about how patients in a defense against their death anxiety can develop an "ultimate rescuer" fantasy that portrays significant figures in their lives as their potential deliverers from all harm and suffering. At times, Rich may have cast the sister, and later myself, in this light.

mately her bitter death. He talked about the wall he had built and how when anyone at the Pines made him feel criticized or judged, his defenses would go up and Jack would go on the attack. Despite this considerable intellectual insight about the central problem of relationships in his life, Rich showed little ability to stop or change the tape.

Near the end of Rich's stay at the Pines, his twisted front teeth had gone bad and needed to be pulled and replaced with a bridge. He struggled with the staff over which dentist he might use. This struggle reflected in part his desire to go to a dentist who might be more inclined to give him narcotic pain medication. In common with many heroin addicts, Rich had a tremendous dislike and fear of any physical discomfort. He was adept at invoking the rationalization that even though he was an addict, he still "needed" something to make the pain bearable, and this "need" had nothing to do with his habit.

Rich managed to stay long enough at the Pines to have his bridge made and thus achieve an almost life-long wish to show a full smile without self-consciousness. His religious fervor had begun to fade, as a result in part of less contact with the sister but also perhaps his increased fascination with psychology, after having undergone his first sustained psychotherapy. As Rich readied to leave the Pines, we agreed that as part of his treatment plan, he could continue to see me in my private practice.

In another repetition of his ideal mother imagery, Rich called himself my "newborn," claiming he needed all the help he could get in learning how to function in a sober world. I hoped that the consistent relationship we had developed during his time at the Pines might be the beginning of a corrective emotional experience (Alexander & French, 1946), which could help him overcome his early disruptions in developing a genuine communal relationship. Lurking behind all this hope, of course, was the threat of the amber cloud; at any moment he could retreat back into a world of drugs and alcohol. With this in mind, I extracted a promise from him that he would attend AA meetings several times a week in addition to his meetings with me.

He moved to a ¾ house in a town next to New London and began to look for work. We had our first therapy session in my office in early 1992. From the beginning of this new work together, I realized that Rich would do everything he could to avoid talking about the daily work of building sobriety. In uncanny fashion, he quickly found fault with both the house manager and his fellow residents. He steered the therapy sessions into critiques of the self-interested motives of the manager or into criticisms of fellow residents who were secretly using drugs. He feuded with house members about cleaning and cooking chores.

His other preoccupation was money. He had found some painting jobs and was working all hours to pull together cash. With this demanding work, he also began to complain of an old knee injury that throbbed with pain (a warning bell for "med-seeking"). As the weeks continued, his work pace escalated markedly and his attendance in therapy became more sporadic.

A symbolic hint that his recovery was collapsing occurred when Rich's bridge cracked around the sixth week after he left the Pines. In his frenetic state of working all hours, struggling with other residents of his house, and generally not taking care of himself, he made no time to fix the bridge. In both a literal and metaphoric way, his teeth, which had always been a source of shame with regard to relations with others, were now being disregarded.

Crucially, his familiar narrative of magical transformation was now in conflict with a fragile new life vision of day-to-day agency, represented by his work efforts, his sobriety, and his repaired teeth. Not prepared internally to accept this new narrative, and overwhelmed by daily life, Rich resumed Jack's familiar "twisted" narrative that relied on a magical out from these demands. The biological urgings of his addiction, which were omnipresent and which could only be subdued by subscription to a more powerful competing vision, now began to dominate.

A couple of days later, as I arrived at work, the charge nurse handed me a clipping from the newspaper, describing how Rich had knocked down an elderly lady and taken her purse. The nurse told me that Rich was in the county jail and would stay there until he could post bail or come to trial. Rich had relapsed on heroin and alcohol, and now in jail, was detoxing cold turkey from both. There was no possibility of raising sufficient money to bail him out, and he was looking at as much as 90 days before his case could come to trial. He wrote to me after a few weeks from jail,

> This letter I write is from a 6 x 10 foot cell in the med unit, for fate has it that I was beaten up and can see out of one eye and have a broken nose. The reason for this situation is because I asked if anyone knew a certain guy who, according to my sponsor, was supposed to be in the jail. This may require more explanation, but I will just say that the laws of sane or reasonable behavior don't apply here. I write you for a few reasons. One is to touch home with what I know as reality, which is slipping from me. . . . I understand more than ever why my brother did what he did. Maybe this is the good of the experience. Somehow I don't think I will ever be who I was. I have lost something, the mouse runs in the wheel of adversity and tragedy; he fights to keep up with the treadmill course; he is aware that sometimes he adds to its pace in a self-defeating way, finally he gives up and flops over, flopping over and over.

Rich's letter conveys an additional dimension to his life narrative of destructive agency. Despite Jack's attempts to make immediate magical transformations in his life, these efforts ultimately lead to Rich's depression and adversity. Though Rich may gain the short-term benefit of the coins he accrued for twisting out his teeth, he is left with a crooked mouth and a resultant despair.

Concerned for his welfare, I visited Rich at the Montville jail. When Rich emerged from the steel door in the side of the visitors' hall, I quickly saw that his letter had not exaggerated. One eye was completely red around the iris and pupil, which were both a murky, clouded blue. The skin below the eye was as black as boot polish, marbled by blue swollen veins. His nose was splinted, but I could see how red and swollen it was from the sides, literally the color of raw hamburger. He had great difficulty sitting down, and it was clear he had been punched or kicked in the ribs as well. Whatever harm he had caused in his latest relapse had been repaid in this physical toll, as well as the psychological humiliation of presenting himself in this light to me. The thought passed through me, "How can a man who enjoyed philosophy, who sought spiritual understanding and release, reconcile those aspects of himself with the beaten up, broken down junkie self seated before me?"

I visited Rich one more time at the Montville jail, and when I entered the visitors' hall, I learned that he was on additional security. As a consequence, the guard led me through the bank vault-like steel door to a row of cubicles with Plexiglas windows. Soon Rich's face appeared from shadows on the other side of the Plexiglas and we waved to each other. There was a circular concave indentation in the Plexiglas with perforations that served as a speaking hole. He told me he had been caught drinking smuggled alcohol with some other inmates and had been placed on a week's restriction. He just hoped that this setback would not screw up his chances with the judge in the coming month. Before I could comment on his words, he told me that life was such hell in the jail that he could not think about sobriety right now; he would take anything to get him through the misery and bottomless depression he felt. He also went on to describe the excruciating pain he had from his broken ribs and how the doctors refused to give him anything stronger than aspirin for it. As I listened, I thought how pale he looked in the yellow light behind the window of the cubicle. The muffled sound of his voice through the pinprick holes in the Plexiglas was detached from his body. He looked almost like a figure in the display case of a wax museum, his voice more like a recording played from a speaker than his own live words. I thought in that moment of the amber cloud and the odd irony that he now seemed similarly encased, once again removed from the embrace of human intimacy or any step toward constructive action.

Rich did make it back to the Pines—a nine-month commitment, with any violation resulting in a full three-year prison sentence. Of course the director of the Pines and I hoped he would be humbled and grateful for this reprieve and that he would bring a new appreciative attitude to his sojourn at the Pines. Unfortunately, Rich's own defense against his sense of inadequacy kicked in again and he soon began to take exception to his treatment at the Pines. He complained about his counselor, his work duties, medical treatment, and the Pines's handling of his probation conditions. Most of all, he felt humiliated, returning to the Pines after having left it sober and prideful the previous spring.

Rich used his nine months there to reapply for and receive a disability status under both physical and psychological conditions. After his seventh month at the Pines, Rich received a check for approximately $13,000. Several thousand dollars of this sum went to cover costs he had incurred from a variety of social services and some of the money went to Lebanon Pines, but he was still left with close to $8000. For someone who owned no more than a duffel bag of clothes, this represented a staggering windfall. In his more hopeful moments, Rich saw these funds as a new chance in life, the first time in his adult life that he could start out with a nest egg to establish a decent living situation, purchase a car, and resume his ambition of a college education. He genuinely cried about these possibilities, especially when contrasting them with his recent time in jail. Here indeed was the wave of the magic wand—a chance to live the Wizard's life and not revert to Jack's destructive and painful pillages.

By the time Rich left the Pines in late spring, with the legal system's blessing, he seemed focused on making a new life for himself, based in sobriety and his hunger for a college education. He had once again avoided any genuine commitment to AA, while simultaneously alienating most of the staff of the Pines and many of the residents. Still, he left the Pines confident and optimistic about his future as a college student.

THE COLLEGE MAN AT LAST

After a few rough patches of transition to his life outside the Pines (including a loss of a considerable amount of his nest egg at the local Foxwoods casino), Rich settled into a sober existence at a ¾ house. As summer ended, he began three courses at the local community college.

The resumption of his college career was also the rekindling of his personal myth of becoming a scientist–healer. In therapy he explained to me with great emotion what it meant for him to be back at college given his parents' success with school. He told me how he had promised his mother before she died how he would go to college. He would come to sessions in button-down shirts, a blue crewneck sweater, and khaki pants. His hair was carefully cut and combed to a blond sheen. If you did not look closely at the small blotches of drinking damage and age under his eyes or subtle scars from fights or drunken falls that were woven into his face, you might have mistaken him for a well-scrubbed and shiny college boy from a wealthy

Connecticut suburb. Rich referred to this side of himself as his new "preppie" image; and indeed this positive student-intellectual role became an important relative to his Wizard imago, both of them aligned against the darker one of Jack. Knowing that I held a position as a professor, Rich relished a chance to show off his new learning to me and to share his successes at school. In my idealized role as therapist–mother, I could serve as a model and affirmation of his new college status.

Despite the positive trends of these first two months of school, he could not escape the central problems of isolation and loneliness in his life. He felt far too old to consider dating any of the female students. Even so, he began to attend student parties and became part of a study group of older students like himself. He found himself incredibly sensitive to rejection and the possibility of ridicule by his fellow students. In one instance he was invited to a party and then uninvited when some of the cohosts of the party heard him make a bigoted remark. He was able to patch up this situation, but felt humiliation and self-hatred. He wanted to shoot a bag of dope to hide from the sense that he could never fit in with real educated people, that he would always be a junkie and nothing more.

With excitement at his achievement in school and continued attendance at AA meetings, Rich made it through the entire first semester, maintaining sobriety and enhancing his life. He had opened a bank account, purchased a car, and bought a word processor. He had also discovered another way to generate money for himself. As a full-time student, he was eligible for a variety of student loans to help his living expenses. Having a large influx of cash continued to be a dangerous trigger for him. It fed his sense of grandiosity, that he could magically transform himself from a recovering drug addict to a sophisticated, well-heeled intellectual–professional. With this new money, he decided to move out from the 3/4 house and take his own place. In his familiar pattern, he had created friction and animosity among the men at this new house and was now fleeing from further rejection.

His student loan also gave him a war chest to gamble again. He was increasingly finding his way back to Foxwoods, winning some big stakes but inevitably suffering big losses as well. Despite achieving a full semester of college credit at the local community college with grades of As and Bs, he seemed to have already begun the spiral downward into relapse. By the end of January, he had been ostensibly sober for six months, attending AA meetings and therapy, but he still lacked a genuine connection with another person outside his therapy.

In a particularly painful session with me, he confessed he had begun to use some pain medication that he conned a doctor into giving him for his knee injury. Soon after that session, Rich called me in a suicidal state, threatening to stab himself. Alternately yelling and crying, he told me he had screwed up again, that there was no point to anything, that he was crashing from going off his antidepressant, that he would be better off killing himself like his brother did. I was finally able to calm him down and to reach a neighbor of his, who helped Rich to settle down and put him to sleep. After that incident, I had one more meeting with Rich, and then I did not see him again for another two and a half years.

When I look over my notes from that meeting, it strikes me that he spoke very honestly and humbly with me that day. He told me that he had started to give up a few months earlier as he went deeper into debt because of his gambling and failure to manage his money. He had felt the pressure mounting at school and the ever-present sense of loneliness. Abusing the pain killers, he had quickly built up an addiction to them. He started to overdraw his bank account, floating checks and making false deposits at the casino. When the gravity of all this hit him, he gave up and went out and bought a bottle of vodka. In my notes, I recorded his words to me,

> **RM:** It's like I can only go between two realities. I'm either the preppie student, which is what I should have been, or a total despairing junkie bent on destruction. There's no middle.
> **JS:** What would the middle be?
> **RM:** What I am. A recovering drug addict who must stop dancing, who needs to do an honest day's work and accept where I am in life.

Rich had articulated the two unsatisfactory ways in which he protected himself from engagement with genuine relationships and constructive sustained agency. Neither the Wizard ideal nor the amber cloud of drugs could sustain him against his loneliness and the emptiness he felt in his life. His gambling was simply another quick way to patch over his feelings of emptiness and inadequacy. As he clearly understood, only an honest acceptance of the loss in his life and then a determination to move forward with the daily business of living would close the deep hole inside him. From a narrative standpoint, such an acceptance would require a refashioning of his story to include his contradictory elements—to weave together both intimacy and pain, both intellectual success and moral weakness. His narrative contained all these diverse elements, but they had yet to be integrated into a complex but coherent life story. Even more, his narrative lacked an ideological setting of optimism that might give him the requisite hope to endure daily setbacks or frustrations.

Rich left therapy that night, hoping to stay out of trouble, but I sensed his resignation to disaster. Within a few days he was arrested for drunk driving when his car ended up on a grass median. While being held for this arrest, the array of other charges regarding his fraudulent money dealings began to come home. A judge ended up committing him to another treatment center in a different part of the state. He eventually left this treatment center some months before his commitment ended and went on the run. He was subsequently picked up and sent to prison. He often contemplated killing himself while there and wrote some of the following stanzas about death in a poem for an inmate creative writing class:

A peace so calmly awaited,
A freedom from the gross noise of life
An end that is sweet, a freedom
From the distress of life that abounds
To sit and wait for it to come, not in fear
But with an excitement that says only
It is over, there is no more, never more.

I received this poem in a letter written in the middle of 1995, about 16 months after our last therapy session. The letter was much more positive and dated the poem to an earlier period of his imprisonment. He claimed that he had discovered Zen in prison and was virtually a new person (once more, the Wizard imago that substitutes self-mastery for intimacy and sudden insight for mundane agentic pursuits). He felt more optimistic and hoped that he would move to a half-way house soon.

LAST CONTACT

After several months in that house, Rich called me in June of 1996 and suggested we resume therapy. He felt ready to tackle some of the family issues he had left unfinished and he also looked forward to having my support. He added that he was committed to continuing his attendance at AA meetings and placing sobriety before all other concerns.

He was in the middle of a Zen Buddhism course at a college near his home. He spoke of his determination to be fully honest with me and not run from the therapy. Above all, he stated that he finally understood that sobriety must come before all else. Agreeing to see him, I set certain preconditions on our work. He would not use drugs or alcohol; he would continue to go to AA meetings; he would not go to the casino; he would not steal; he would make every effort possible to be honest in therapy.

A week later he was already lost. Rich had met a woman at a meeting and they had begun an intense relationship. This was a dream come true to him, especially after absolutely minimal contact with women in the past six or seven years. He knew all about AA's dictum that someone new to recovery should not engage in a relationship until at least a year of sobriety. He knew about this dictum, but did not care. As the weeks unfolded, he lavished presents on her, alternated between feeling ecstasy and total despair, depending on how she responded to him. He soon realized that she had a complex life of her own, including an ex-boyfriend who was not completely out of the scene and several financial problems that she hoped Rich would help to solve. As she placed financial demands on him, Rich found his way back to the casino with the idea that he could win big and continue to afford the presents and high lifestyle he was sharing with her. As usual, he followed big wins with equal or bigger losses. In tears, he confessed this violation of our preconditions and swore he would not go back.

Within a few weeks, he simply stopped showing up for sessions and we lost all contact. A month later, I received a final telephone call from him, detailing a new round of crimes, hospital visits, and drug use. He told me he had wanted to please me the way he had wanted to please his mother, but he had also felt he could never do it; he would always be a "fuck-up." He knew he needed to reconcile Jack with the Wizard/Preppie, but he knew no other way to be, except to hide behind the amber cloud. He spoke vaguely about returning to the Pines, but was unclear about his plans. I have not heard from him since, but learned from another client that he did indeed return to prison.

DISCUSSION OF RICHARD MARKHAM'S LIFE STORY

In presenting Richard Markham's life narrative, I have chosen to look at it through the lens of McAdams's life story theory of identity. What does this type of narrative analysis add to other analytic frameworks, such as an object relations or ego-psychological perspective? One might also ask how this type of analysis contributes to our understanding of individuals' struggles with the transition from addiction to recovery.

In the parlance of traditional psychiatry and psychology, Rich clearly suffers from both addiction and a severe personality disorder. The disruptions in his early relationships through childhood and adolescence have left him with a profound problem with intimacy and self-image. To compensate for his acute fear of loss and social rejection, he relies on a number of self-defeating ego defenses, including externalizing blame, intellectualizaton, splitting, grandiosity, idealization, and denial. Behaviorally, he defends against emotional pain through withdrawal, flight, rage, and most important, substance abuse. Though these character defenses were most likely set into place before he developed a full-blown addiction, his years of drug and alcohol dependency have only aggravated them and prevented him from developing more adaptive ways of handling pain in his life.

His object relations are poorly developed. He possesses unintegrated object representations of paternal figures that have led to a dissociated set of internalized self-representations. He swings between the extremes of these representations, lacking a unified sense of identity that might tolerate their contradictions and ambiguities.

In the language of addiction treatment, Rich was biologically vulnerable to addiction, given his father's alcoholism. Through his years of substance abuse, he has altered his brain chemistry. His brain's low tolerance for pain and its need for chemicals that institute states of pleasure threaten to overwhelm him at any point. He suffers from a chronic illness that must be treated with a combination of abstinence, medication, support groups, and counseling.

It is interesting that although all of these views of Richard Markham are accurate and certainly helpful as potential treatment conceptualizations and strategies, they tell us very little about what it is like to *be* Richard Markham. As I have attempted to show, the life story approach comes the closest to giving us the phenomenological texture of how Rich experiences himself. The narrative structures Rich has selected—his repeated mention of his crooked teeth, his referral to himself as Jack or the Wizard/Preppie, his invocation of the amber cloud, his pursuit of the ideal woman—these images, characters, and themes make up the story he himself tells of his life.

Why should the surface story by which one knows one's self matter to the psychologist? Is the story only the window dressing for the underlying dynamic or biological structures that explain and propel personality? I am offering a metapsychological assertion that life stories are more than this. As McAdams (1988, 1990, 1993, 1996) has repeatedly argued over the years, we rely on our life stories to provide unity and purpose to our sense of identity. The stories we tell of our lives define whom and how we love, for what and why we work, and where all that we have done in our lives should ultimately lead us. They tell us how we see ourselves, how we want to be seen by others, and what we hope to become. The life story is the distillation into consciousness of the various affective, cognitive, and motivational components of personality (Singer, 1995).

It follows from this statement that the healthy functioning of personality depends, in part, on a "healthy" life story. What is a healthy life story in Western society? In the initial section of this chapter, I laid out what aspects of life stories might signal optimal health: Individuals' narratives would reflect a blend of loving relationships and meaningful independent activity. They would be infused with an overall setting of hope and possibility. They would possess enough complexity to tolerate the inevitable contradictions and reversals that adhere to any lived life. They would contain specific memories of positive turning points that reflect communal or agentic successes in life. Finally, they would link their stories to a generative contribution or legacy that would outlive the self.

Individuals who combine each of these aspects in the story they tell to themselves and others feel a rich sense of meaning and satisfaction in their lives. Self-actualization may in fact be the capacity to tell such a coherent and purposeful story of one's life. In contrast, what do individuals lose when they cannot tell a coherent story of the self? What do they suffer when their narrative contains fragmented sections, a fatalistic vision of life, limited accounts of successful communal or agentic experiences, and no sense of what contribution they might make beyond themselves?

My work with individuals suffering from chronic addiction suggests that they lack the ability at critical life transitions to draw on positive aspects of their life stories to guide them toward change. The serious flaws in how they have constructed their narrative identity often undermine their attempts to forge more positive sober identities. Unable to sustain a more hopeful or healthy narrative identity, they repeatedly allow the destructive and disintegrative aspects of their stories to overwhelm them. They give in to a sense of fragmentation that allows impulse and acts of meaninglessness to prevail. At such times, when attempts at more purposeful stories have once again failed them, they raise the cry of "fuck it," which is the antistory, the ultimate expression of nihilistic exhaustion.

Often when individuals chronically relapse, especially after another round of intensive treatment, the statements, "He clearly wasn't ready" or "She didn't want it badly enough," will be raised. "Readiness" or "desire for sobriety" may actually be a function of the quality of the story individuals can tell themselves. For example, individuals who can accept the life-affirming and generativity-rich story of AA recovery have a capacity to see the AA narrative as compatible, at least minimally, with their own personal stories. To make this shift, individuals' stories must possess elements of communion and hope, but also of self-discipline (a constant refrain used in AA is that individuals must "work" their program).

A crucial point is that what ultimately matters is not the sheer number of bad events or examples of destructive parenting to which individuals have been exposed in their lives. Virtually every individual with whom I worked over the years in an inner-city detox facility had had negative and traumatic experiences in their lives. What differentiated individuals who sustained recovery from those who did not was often how they configured the events of their lives into a narrative that supplied meaning and hope. Those individuals who could extract a sense of wisdom and moral lesson from even the most painful and cruel past experiences were the ones most likely to maintain a sober path.

At those critical existential moments of decision in any of our lives, when we choose to leave a marriage or change a career, when we abstain from or give in to a destructive course of behavior, we recruit and examine what we know of ourselves. We ask, "What has been my story up to this point, and do I want it to continue this way or to change?" If we want to change, what preexisting elements are there in the story that might give us assurance that we will be able to sustain the new path we have chosen? The study of life narratives allows psychologists to approximate most closely how individuals phenomenologically wrestle with decisions at crucial transition points in their lives. At such moments, individuals do not consult their genes or evaluate their object representations. They ask, "Who am I?" and find the answer in memories, stories, and images from the life they have lived. Richard Markham's difficulties with sobriety were clearly a function of his biology and his personality disorder, but they were also complicated by the jagged and disillusioning narrative he examined when he looked inside himself.

One additional point should be raised about Rich's dilemma at this life transition. He might also have elected to throw out his story in entirety, to reject its contradictory elements that pit the bestial Jack against the ethereal Wizard, but to do so would have left him in the terrifying position of being storyless. Better to oscillate back and forth between these two incompatible ways of being than to feel he had no past at all. Some individuals do take this plunge and radically remake themselves, but this reinvention of the self smacks of the cult-like "conversions" that healthy recovering individuals who have benefited from AA often disdain. Such sobriety, they say, replaces one addiction with another.

Unwilling to give up both the Jack and Wizard aspects of himself, Rich remained committed to a vision of agency that was grounded in either impulsive destructive acts or passive magical transformations. His narrative held no place for a picture of himself as enduring or even learning to enjoy the day to day activities of sober living. When he veered too closely to his Wizard ideal, as he did in his Preppie period, the fragility of this ideal led him to seek the protection of the hardened and cynical Jack.

Yet he could not be both the Wizard and Jack at the same time; this was a fundamental flaw in his life story as currently constructed. Its narrative complexity fell short—it did not allow for the integration of personality that would give his identity coherence and help to make him whole. Despite the Preppie's best of intentions, Rich's story still portrayed the twisted crooked teeth behind the blond good looks, a symbol of a self-perceived internal corruption. When overwhelmed by this conflicted self, he retreated into the amber cloud of drugs that removed him, albeit temporarily, from his story. And last, his retreat away from relationships and meaningful agency left him no possibility of fulfilling a generative script. He saw no obvious way either through offspring or accomplishment that would allow him to leave a lasting contribution or legacy to the world he inhabited (see Maruna, 2000, for the importance of generativity to sustained recovery).

If I have offered Richard Markham's story as an example of how a problematic life narrative can have devastating effects at critical life transitions, does this also mean that his life narrative is unlikely ever to change?

Will the same destructive understandings of agency and communion, the same fragmentary self-images haunt him the rest of his life?

The best answer I can provide is that in my experience stories of this kind do sometimes change, but only slowly and in almost imperceptible degrees (despite his frequent attestations of spiritual discoveries and rebirths). Rich's understanding that he should learn to see himself as "a recovering drug addict who must stop dancing, who needs to do an honest day's work and accept where I am in life" was a critical insight. In one of our last sessions, he also told me that he had to stop hating Jack and accept that Jack had helped him through periods of intense loneliness. If he could fully acknowledge this, he might feel less self-hatred and shame. If this self-hatred could diminish, he might have less trouble accepting his Preppie self-image as genuine.

Rich's honest moments in therapy and the productive months he spent in college are now part of his life story, or at least they have the potential to become part of the narrative he weaves. If he draws on this modified story at times of decisions, it may begin to give him more positive and constructive answers about the direction he should take.

CONCLUSION

I have argued that the life stories we tell to portray our lives to others and ourselves serve a functional purpose. They provide a conscious record to us at critical junctures in our lives about our capacity for relationships and constructive action in the world. They express our most salient self-images, and help us to reconcile these images into a coherent sense of identity. They let us see how our story connects to larger familial and societal stories, clarifying the legacy we might offer to others.

Richard Markham's difficult story provides a cautionary tale about the efforts we must make in our own life stories to accept the disparate aspects of ourselves and others, as well as to overcome our flights from intimacy or our impulses to turn agentic powers toward destructive ends. At the transition points in our lives, those of us unburdened by addiction still face this same challenge of story-making, albeit with a greater sense of possibility and hope. This hope is based in an underlying trust that by striving to construct and tell our stories, we might ultimately get things more or less right, and find our way to an ending that gives meaning to our lives.

REFERENCES

Alexander, F., & French, T. M. (Eds.). (1946). *Psychoanalytic therapy*. New York: Ronald Press.

American Psychiatric Association. (1994). *Diagnostic and statistical manual of mental disorders* (4th ed.). Washington, DC: Author.

Bakan, D. (1966). *The duality of human existence: Isolation and communion in western man.* Boston: Beacon Press.

Fiddle, S. (1967). *Portraits from a shooting gallery: Life styles from the drug addict world.* New York: Harper & Row.

Habermas, T., & Bluck, S. (2000). Getting a life: The emergence of the life story in adolescence. *Psychological Bulletin 126,* 748–769.

Maruna, S. (2001). *Making good: How ex-convicts reform and rebuild their lives.* Washington, DC: American Psychological Association.

McAdams, D. P. (1988). *Power, intimacy and the life story: Personological inquiries into identity.* New York: Guilford Press.

McAdams, D. P. (1990). Unity and purpose in human lives: The emergence of identity as the life story. In A. I. Rabin, R. A. Zucker, R. A. Emmons, & S. Frank (Eds.), *Studying persons and lives* (pp. 148–200). New York: Springer.

McAdams, D. P. (1993). *Stories we live by.* New York: William Morrow.

McAdams, D. P. (1996). Personality, modernity, and the storied self: A contemporary framework for studying persons. *Psychological Inquiry, 7,* 295–321.

Pillemer, D. B. (1992). Remembering personal circumstances: A functional analysis. In E. Winograd & U. Neisser (Eds.), *Affect and accuracy in recall* (pp. 236–265). New York: Cambridge University Press.

Singer, J. A. (1995). Seeing oneself: A framework for the study of autobiographical memory in personality. *Journal of Personality, 63,* 429–457.

Singer, J. A. (1997). *Message in a bottle: Stories of men and addiction.* New York: Free Press.

Singer, J. A., & Salovey, P. (1993). *The remembered self: Emotion, memory, & personality.* New York: Free Press.

Thombs, D. (1999). *Introduction to addictive behavior* (2nd ed.). New York: Guilford Press.

Vaillant, G. (1995). *Natural history of alcoholism revisited.* Cambridge, MA: Harvard University Press.

Yalom, I. D. (1980). *Existential psychotherapy.* New York: Basic Books.

11

SENSE OF PLACE AND ITS IMPORT FOR LIFE TRANSITIONS: THE CASE OF HIV-POSITIVE INDIVIDUALS

MICHELE L. CROSSLEY

In previous research I have demonstrated that being diagnosed HIV-positive, as with any other life-threatening illness, represents a traumatic life transition (Crossley, 1997b, 1998a, 1998b, 1998c, 1999a, 1999b, 2000a, 2000b; Davies, 1997; Schwartzberg, 1993; Taylor, 1989). The underlying basis of this trauma stems from the individual's confrontation with the threat of imminent or early death, a confrontation that can serve to shatter a whole range of taken-for-granted assumptions about self, world, reality and meaning (Janoff-Bulman, 1992).[1] In some cases the shattering of these assumptions can lead the HIV-positive individual to experience a sense of total alienation, helplessness, and meaninglessness, a mental state that is not conducive to the recovery or maintenance of good physical health (Crossley, 1997a, 1997b). On the other hand, as my research with people living relatively long-term with an HIV-positive diagnosis has shown, many people *do* manage to adjust constructively to a life in which their previous taken-for-granted assumptions have been shattered. One of the main ways in which they do this is by implicitly rebuilding images of self and world, which enables them to make sense of their trauma and helps explain the meaning and purpose of events to themselves. This process of rebuilding enables traumatized individuals to restore some sense of order (however rudimentary) to their lives. It is a process through which people use sociocul-turally available resources in the pursuit of psychological coherence and moral justification.

---

[1] This also could be described as the shattering of the "natural attitude" (Schutz, 1962) toward everyday life.

The data in this chapter derive from in-depth, semistructured interviews I conducted with 38 HIV-positive individuals who had been living with an HIV-positive diagnosis for at least five years. These people were selected from a larger sample of HIV-positive individuals who were surveyed as part of a European Community-commissioned study exploring the psychological, emotional, and service delivery needs of people living with an HIV-positive diagnosis (Davies, 1995). At the time of the interviews all of the sample were largely asymptomatic; none was diagnosed with AIDS-related conditions. The average length of HIV-positive diagnosis was nine years. The majority ($n = 31$) of interviewees were gay men, four were women, and three were hemophiliacs. The median age of the sample was 38.5 years.

In the process of analyzing this material in terms of how an HIV-positive diagnosis affects a person's conception of him- or herself and how he or she accommodates to such changes, it became apparent that "space" and "place" played an important role in the creation and maintenance of identity. For instance, when I asked HIV-positive individuals to reconstruct the story of their diagnosis and the impact it had had on their lives, many of them conjured up strong images of place. These images contained personal and cultural associations that were often double-edged. They sometimes appeared as both positive and negative idealizations that symbolized safety or danger, liberation or repression, morality or immorality (Douglas, 1966; Falk, 1974; Volkan, 1988). This led me to a more specific exploration of the role played by place in the HIV-positive individual's construction of his or her identity. I found that the process of creating "healthy" and "unhealthy" images of self involved the delineation of psychogeographical spaces that were "safe" and "unsafe," "open" and "prohibited," "included" and "excluded." These spaces were fashioned in opposition to one another and represented different moral values, contrasting images of "right" and "wrong," alternative visions of the world. It is in this sense that space can be characterized in Lefebvre's terms (1991, p. 79) as being experienced as a "representation of the interplay between 'good' and 'evil' forces at war within the world."

The role played by place was obviously more dominant in the lives of some individuals than in others. I therefore decided to select a number of case studies that best highlight some of the interconnections between experience of place, emotion, morality, and culture. The qualitative case-study approach method seemed to be the most valid way of approaching this material, because it enabled a more holistic, detailed, descriptive approach characteristic of narrative types of investigation (Crossley, 2000b; McAdams, 1993). Although this chapter is specifically on HIV-positive individuals, it is hypothesised that place may play a similarly important role in other life transitions. Before proceeding to look at these case histories, it is necessary to present a more detailed overview of theoretical issues pertaining to the relationship between place and identity.

PLACE AND IDENTITY: SOME THEORETICAL CONSIDERATIONS

Studies examining the role played by place in processes of identity construction and regulation (e.g., Korpela, 1989) build on theoretical approaches appreciative of the emotionally and subjectively infused nature of the human experience of place. Lowenthal, for instance, claimed that "geographical epistemology is founded on personal geographies composed of direct experiences, memory, fantasy, present circumstances and future purposes" (1961, cited in Relph, 1980, p. 23). Such recognition contrasted with earlier geographical approaches that failed to acknowledge the subjective nature of spatial experience. In the 1950s, for example, Dardel argued that although geography could not avoid being stretched between *knowledge* and *existence*, there was a real possibility that it would solve such a tension by abandoning itself to a narrow vision of "objective" science and thus lose contact with its existential sources of meaning (Dardel, 1952, cited in Relph, 1980, p. 31). Phenomenological approaches to the study of human behavior, such as the work of Merleau-Ponty (1962), Schutz (1962), and Heidegger (1962), were important in placing individual experience as central to an understanding of space and perception. The concept of "lived-in-the-world" existential space that emerged from these works served as a means by which this understanding could be empirically operationalized (Relph, 1980, p. 318). In his more recent existential–phenomenological study of place, Relph broke down the concept of space into many different forms, and concluded that two forms of space were of particular relevance to the development of an understanding of the role played by subjectivity in spatial experience: perceptual and existential space.

Human beings are unique in their ability to reflect systematically on space and thus to experience it self-consciously. Precisely because the center of perceptual space is the perceiving human, it is finite, heterogeneous, and subjectively defined and perceived. Not surprisingly, then, it is undesirable and invalid to study perceptual space without recourse to individually defined and perceived aspects of space; thus perceptual space is not amenable to the "objective" measuring instruments used in traditional scientific or positivistic geographical approaches, because these fail to capture the unique quality and idiosyncratic ramifications of each individual's spatial experience (see also Korpela, 1989; Sarbin, 1983). In addition, an important previously disregarded dimension of this perceptual experience of space is its emotional contours. This is what is meant by the idea that space is not just perceived—rather it is "lived" (Matore, 1962). Space is richly differentiated into places or centers of special or personal significance—for example, for children places constitute the basis for the discovery of self and a source of stability and meaning (Relph, 1980; Sebba, 1991).

This notion that the physical environment can be used as a source of stability and meaning has been further examined by Korpela (1989), who concluded that people use certain places (either by identification or avoidance) as a means of regulating and maintaining basic processes of identity functioning such as the psychic balance of pain and pleasure, coherence of self and self-esteem. Korpela also pointed to Swann's (1983) work, which examines the processes whereby people work to ensure the stability of their self-conceptions. Just as people may choose certain interaction partners and strategies as a means of supporting and affirming their conception of themselves, they may also choose certain environments.

Assuming that cognitive clarity or the maintenance of a coherent concept of self is an important factor in human motivation, Kaplan (1983) argued that reflection or contemplative processes permitting one to organize thoughts and feelings are important. He concluded that people have an intuitive sense of "restorative environments," which permit this kind of contemplation. Restorative environments are intrinsically enjoyable and give a sense of being away from the constraints of the everyday environment; they provide a sense of fascination and self-coherence, a place for the "rediscovery of self" and the reestablishing of order and meaning. Common examples include vacations, country cottages, and "natural" environments.[2]

Babineau (1972) also conducted a study that suggested the existence of an intrinsic relationship between the experience of place and psychological functioning. As a psychiatrist working for the U.S. army in West Berlin from 1967 to 1970, Babineau witnessed many border crossings from West to East Berlin. He was convinced that some people actually crossed the border as a means of resolving personal conflicts and identified a number of emotional themes characteristic of border crossers. Babineau concluded that "Crossing an international border is a complicated psychological experience" (Babineau, 1972, p. 290).

---

[2] As an article in *The Guardian* (Bartlett, 1997, p. 11) made clear, the idea that nature or natural environments can serve as a cure for the stresses of everyday life is not new (see also Schama, 1995). However, there is a new interest within the field of psychology about how nature can affect mental health, which is partly fueled by the expansion of environmentalism. Ecopsychology was a term first used by Theodore Roszak, director of the Ecopsychology Institute in America. Roszak claimed that, "It's a revolution in modern psychology. . . . It represents an attempt to find ecology within the context of human psychology, and, in turn, to find human psychology within the context of ecology." In Britain the field of ecopsychology has led to the creation of a Centre for Creation Spirituality, which is a network of 40 local groups that explore the "relationship between the human spirit and the planet."

All of these studies, although founded on very different theoretical orientations, share the conception that the experience of place incorporates important emotional and psychological dimensions and that place can therefore be used as a means of adapting to various life transitions. The main difference between these studies, however, rests with the degree of consciousness attributed to the individual with regard to these regulatory psychological mechanisms. For instance, the studies by Korpela, Kaplan, and Swann all seem to imply that the use of physical environment as a strategy in creating and maintaining self is the product of active and conscious self-regulation. Babineau's work, on the other hand, implies that the psychological dimension of spatial experience is less explicit, less conscious, and to some degree unconscious.

This brings me on to a consideration of the second form of space previously alluded to: existential space. The concept of existential space (Relph, 1980) embodies a realization that although the individual's experience of place is saturated with meaning and intention, the source of such meaning is not entirely isolated within the individual but is *intersubjectively* linked to culture (N. Crossley, 1996). The meaning of spaces and places is one that derives not simply from individual subjectivity but from our experience as members of particular social and cultural groupings. Such meanings may not be available directly to consciousness insofar as they may be tacit and taken for granted, existing simply as part of our natural way of making sense of the world (Schutz, 1962). Examples are our concepts of "sacred" and "profane" places (Relph, 1980, p. 13), what Lefebevre (1991, p. 294) called "holy or damned heterotopias." These places tacitly correspond to a whole variety of implicitly accepted social beliefs, conventions, taboos, and practices, thus serving as a perfect illustration of the intersubjective dimension of place experience.

TRAUMA, LIFE TRANSITION, AND THE ROLE OF PLACE: THE CASE OF HIV-POSITIVE INDIVIDUALS' TRAUMA AND THE SEARCH FOR "HOME"

> I went into an identity crisis . . . absolutely everything, everything you have had in life just breaks down, becomes dust, powder . . . and you become completely naked and utterly lost. You do not know what to do, *where* did you come from, *where* do you go and *where* are you standing at that moment. This is something indescribable and nobody can help you. . . .

This quote from Simon, an HIV-positive gay man, sums up the shattering degree of insecurity an HIV-positive diagnosis can introduce into a person's life (see also Davies, 1997; Crossley, 1998a; 1998b). As with other traumatic situations and problematic stages of the life cycle like adolescence, such turbulence frequently compels the individual to face eternally profound questions such as, "who am I?"; "Where do I belong?"; "To whom do I belong?" The individual's extreme and frightening feeling of being utterly alone, "naked and lost" in this man's words, leads him or her to the search for some form of belongingness, some form of connection. Frequently, this sense of connection and disconnection is strongly related to particular places that represent vast oases of intersubjective emotions and feelings.

That certain places are experienced with positive and negative valences can be illustrated in relation to the experience of John, a 38-year-old gay man who had been living in San Francisco with an HIV-positive diagnosis for 10 years. John had recently moved back to England, where he originally came from. He had experienced multiple bereavements during his time in the states, including the death of four partners over a period of five years. On his return to England he was no longer involved in an intimate relationship and lived alone. Spontaneously, he portrayed a very negative image of his time spent in the states, especially the few years preceding his decision to return to England. His portrayal illustrates the way in which the emotional valences shrouding our memory of places are associated with the people and events that took place there and the individual and cultural meanings bestowed on them.

John described how life in San Francisco was very "extreme and exceptional." It was the epicenter of the AIDS crisis during the mid- to late 1980s, and "there were so many thousands of people dying. . . . I had four partners in five years and they have all died." John found life in this "death-infused" climate extremely distressing and mentally destabilizing. As he stated clearly,

> It was the whole environment I was living in over there. People were dying on a daily basis so you didn't get time to say good-bye. It just became a fact of life that people were going to die. It was really sad when I got to the point of picking up my telephone book and looking through the pages and thinking "I haven't called him for a long time" and then remembering he was dead. Then you would turn another page and "he's dead" and then "these two on this page are dead" and I mean, you deal with it. I don't know if it is really frightening, or if it hurts, it's just a weird feeling because you build up a kind of wall . . . in one sense you're dealing with it but in another sense you're not dealing with it. . . .

The "weird" feeling and the "building up of a kind of wall" refer to the way in which John tried to maintain some degree of security for himself to protect against the continuous threat of impermanence and transitoriness imposed on him by the repeated death of partners, friends, and acquaintances. John's experience of radical insecurity was exacerbated by strong feelings of guilt relating to his past behavior and again, the "whole environment" he had lived in over the past 10 years. The fact that his partners had all died created a kind of paranoia in which he was plagued by the thought that he was "a carrier," spreading the disease to people. He said that if he was really honest with himself he felt "unclean and dirty." This, perhaps not surprisingly given the predominantly negative stereotypes of homosexuality in Western culture, was a feeling expressed in differing degrees of frankness by many gay men. For example Gary, who was also diagnosed in the states, claimed that he felt "horrible and dirty and a menace to society. . . . It was almost like a retribution for all my sins." And Craig offered further insight into these internalized negative feelings when he explained that

> [My father] has always said to me over the years, all queers do is just spread disease and especially when I was younger, he said, "what kind of a life are you going to have, sleeping around with men, you are never going to be happy, you are going to grow old and you are going to be alone." . . . And I remember at the time thinking, maybe this is going to be the case . . . and with all this at the moment I sometimes think, my God, it is happening . . . it is coming true.

For the purposes of this chapter it is important to note that for John, all of these feelings of instability, worthlessness, and immorality became connected with a particular place, San Francisco. His experience and memory of the place was so charged with negative emotional investment that he felt he had to escape San Francisco before he could even begin to rebuild his life.

The positive counterpart to John's negatively contoured memory of San Francisco was England, more specifically an Arcadia-like village called Wycliffe "in the middle of nowhere . . . two miles to the nearest shop . . . no buses" and inhabited by only 20 people. He felt far more "comfortable" in this environment and his life had "totally changed" since leaving a "whole environment of stresses" behind him. He characterized his existence in his new environment as "natural." It was a place in which everyone knew about his HIV-positive status and yet a place where he was treated "as John as opposed to a person with HIV infection." That, he claimed, was the most important thing to him. Wycliffe had totally transformed his life from a "dirty" life full of stresses, instability, and rejection, to one where he experienced a "clean" life full of calmness, serenity, peace, and acceptance.

This attempt to "purify" physical and mental health by a change in environment is a classic example of Kaplan's (1983) "restorative environment" in which the individual creates for him- or herself a space to feel coherent and integrated in the face of everyday and (in this case) more life-threatening traumas. Another example of such an attempt was evident in the case of Simon, the man who characterized his experience as an "identity crisis" that left him with a feeling of existential isolation and loneliness. His attempted "solution" to this crisis was to return to the place where "my roots are, Spain." He described himself as having to do this because of his "need to find a greater understanding in life." It was only when he had returned that "it was like God came into my world suddenly or suddenly I went to God, it is difficult to explain." After a period of meditation he entered a monastery and devoted his time to reading St. Augustine.

Most people's change of environment was not quite so dramatic as this, but the "need" or "desire" to experience a renewed sense of rootedness in the face of enhanced rootlessness was a familiar theme among HIV-positive individuals. Most commonly, this manifested itself in the desire to return "home," as was very clearly shown in Gary's comments:

> I felt quite devastated, like I had been given a life sentence. . . . I felt there was no point in staying here in America, I wanted to get home, back to England. Which is exactly what I did. . . . I wanted to live the rest of my days out in my home area with familiar things and not feel like a foreigner. . . . I wanted some security around men whereas before I was always in a state of transition. I wasn't able to put down roots and this is the first time I have been able to put down roots. . . . I was very keen to get my own place and have as stable environment as possible, something to call my own because I don't know what the future will hold. . . .

In this quote Gary lucidly illustrates the deeply felt need of humans to form close attachments with particular places, to experience a profound tie with place, to live in a place that is familiar to them (Relph, 1980, p. 37). The cases discussed corroborate Weil's comment that "to be rooted is perhaps the most important and least recognised need of the human soul" (cited in Relph, 1980, p. 53). This sense of being rooted serves as a vital aid in the search for meaning, which seems to be of crucial importance for some HIV-positive individuals: "To have roots in a place is to have a secure point from which to look out on the world, a firm grasp of one's position in the order of things" (Relph, 1980, p. 37).

Although the places to which we are most attached can take on a myriad of different forms, they tend to be the settings in which we have had a multiplicity of experiences, places that harbor a whole range of emotional associations. For many of us, this place is the place we call home, a place where we feel we most belong and are most secure, the "profound centre of human existence" (Relph, 1980, p. 39). Home is a place where we feel a sense of "existential insideness": "It is the difference between safety and danger, cosmos and chaos, enclosure and exposure" (Relph, 1980, p. 49). It is in direct contrast to the sense of "existential outsideness," an experience in which we are "aware of meaning withheld," of "alienation from people and places, homelessness, a sense of the unreality of the world and of not belonging" (Relph, 1980, p. 51). Hence the desire expressed by some HIV-positive individuals to return home to (sometimes mythical) safety and "roots" was understandable in terms of their need to counterbalance the extreme sense of danger and instability introduced into their lives by an HIV-positive diagnosis.

THE "DRUDGERY" OF PLACE

The positive valence associated with the dream of home or roots is, however, double-edged. The return home is often not an easy return to stability, tradition, and order. Home is often a place consisting of once familiar people, (families, especially parents), traditions, rules, norms, morals, and lifestyles (Schutz, 1962). The cost of the increased sense of safety and order of home is compliance and conformity with those accepted, taken-for-granted rules and traditions. Of course, for many gay men such acceptance is tantamount to the highest degree of hypocrisy, because they are themselves aware that their lifestyle "goes against" all the accepted rules of the parental home. One man expressed this succinctly when he said that to his mother he epitomized "everything she loathes. I am a sexual deviant, I have got this dirty thing and I have obviously been having anal intercourse." Gary, who said that HIV infection felt "like a retribution for all his sins" and had returned to his parental home in the search for a sense of security and rootedness, had not informed his parents of his HIV-positive status or even of the fact that he was gay. He was totally afraid of "being found out" because his parents were very "anti-gay . . . any mention of taboo subjects and 'Oh god that is revolting,' dreadful people and all that kind of thing. . . ." Tom, a gay man originally from the Caribbean, also expressed similar fears with regard to his own family, who, he said, would think HIV infection was a "retribution for my lifestyle, that is your reward, that is your payment." Thus although the memory of home may be haloed by positive connotations of safety and order, for many it also induced a sense of anxiety, fear, and sometimes anger with regard to the knowledge that they would never be able to "live up" to the required standards of life at home. The oppression of living within the rules of a "small town mentality" where, as one man from Cleethorpes commented, "my mother would never have come across anybody that was gay if the guy who called the numbers out at the bingo hadn't have been," served to mar the positive feelings of order and security associated with home. Tom expressed his ambivalent feelings toward returning home very clearly. Throughout his interview he referred to going back "down there," returning home to the Caribbean. When I asked him to describe his dream for the future he said it was to go back and live and work in the Caribbean. But simultaneously he was also very aware of the dangers associated with such a life. One had to "think very carefully of going back to the Caribbean with HIV status," he said. "People are very narrow minded ... they gossip a great deal." As an example when he described his lack of faith in God and his belief that when he died "that is the end of me, I am just like an element in a lamp," he said that he would never be able to express such beliefs in "the environment I was brought up in." "In a small island you can't go around saying these things, you will be stoned." People would look at you as "evil, as if something is wrong with you." Thus although on the one hand Tom had a kind of utopian image of the Caribbean that he longed to return to, this coexisted with his image of the stark reality of the place. He would only return, for instance, if medications improved and if he was rich enough to pay for expensive doctors and clinics, "Because they love money, they want to help humanity but they still want to line their pockets. I shouldn't say this on tape but that is the way it is."

The notion of a "small town mentality" was not just restricted to perceptions of the parental home or place of origin. For instance, Sean conjured up the very same image of his own life before he received his HIV-positive diagnosis. He characterized his previous life as a very "settled and in many respects very exclusive life." Sean lived with his gay partner in an "expensive house" with two cars, two dogs, and two annual holidays in Europe. It was "domesticated bliss really." Life was very comfortable. But then with the advent of the HIV-positive diagnosis, "suddenly all my values changed" because

> Suddenly you discover things which you have been led to believe were certainties can't be taken for granted any more, not just issues around health or your relationships or your career or your economic position. Suddenly they all become uncertainties and that is the nearest I have come to feeling that all the supposed rules, set in stone, no longer apply to you. And somehow you feel that it is legitimate for the rest of population to claim it is true for them but suddenly it isn't for you.

This resulted in him not valuing "property or possessions any more"; "investing in insurance policies and having a pension . . . all suddenly became entirely meaningless." The diagnosis forced him to discover that his "horizon wasn't real . . . it was self-imposed . . . and the world was actually a bigger place." The same relativity of perception was experienced by other gay men who had left home, traveled and traversed other climes, and then contemplated a return home. They anticipated a lack of perceptual and moral relativity at home that led to an image of pettiness, triviality, small-mindedness, oppression, and imprisonment. In Lefebevre's (1991) words, they remembered the "misery of everyday life" and in Relph's (1980, p. 42) terms "the drudgery of place," the tedious tasks, humiliation, meanness, and pettiness of the safely ordered life. Hence these cases clearly demonstrated that "our experience of place, especially of home, is a dialectical one, balancing a need to stay with a desire to escape" (Relph, 1980, p. 42).

PLACES AND REBELLION

It is clear from the cases discussed that the positive emotional valence associated with the stable, safe image of home and roots also has negative fringes related to the claustrophobic taken-for-granted rules and conventions often experienced as repressive and restrictive of self-expression. This perception and experience of repression adds an important dimension to the negative emotional valence associated with particular places discussed earlier. These negative emotions, such as John's memories of San Francisco, are often related to feelings of insecurity, worthlessness, immorality, and associations with death and danger. However, just like the positive images of "home," this is not the whole story. The predominantly negative images of these places are also tinged with "positive" feelings of excitement and pleasure, manifestations of a libertarian desire to rebel against the accepted, humdrum order of things. This desire can express itself in a multitude of ways, which vary in terms of social acceptability.

For example, as has already been shown, John's overwhelmingly negative emotional associations with San Francisco were instrumental in forcing him to leave the states and set up "home" in his utopian Wycliffe village, where he was "cleansed," stability ruled, and he was accepted as a person in his own right. This move to establish a sense of order and safety made up an explicit attempt to reconvene a balance in his life after the death-infused environment of San Francisco had tipped the scales too far in the direction of disorder and danger. But even then John was not satisfied, because although he had stationed himself in his paradise-like village of Wycliffe he actually found it very difficult to adjust because he felt he had lost "any sense of direction." "Maybe it's just the thing of moving back here from the States and re-establishing," he suggested but "I don't know, I have found it difficult to know what direction to go in." John's response to this lack of direction, his way of getting "back into my skin" as he characterized it, was to travel to India. He described his experience as follows:

> I have just come back from India, Tangiers, one of the dirtiest cities in the world, and I did everything. Everything I am told I shouldn't do. I don't know, probably I'm rebelling. Being in India, you know, it's filthy, the plague was going on, there were loads of other infections and there I was, up to my knees in sewage taking photos of water lilies.

And I fell off my bike a couple of times, and *that* is what is important to me, falling off my bike, it's so stupid, but normal everyday stuff.

In these comments John makes abundantly clear that his attempt to create a safe, ordered life in Wycliffe had once more tipped the scales too far in one direction to such an extent that he felt compelled to "rebel" against the safety he had created for himself. In stark contrast to the "clean," "good," "moral," and "neighborly" life of Wycliffe, he threw himself into "dirty" plague-ridden India and engaged in "bad" "immoral" acts, "everything" he had been told (by doctors) not to do. Thus for John, although India, like San Francisco, symbolized emotional associations with danger, death, and immorality, those associations took on an overwhelmingly positive valence because of their link to rebellion and libertarianism, manifestations of John's need for self-assertion at that particular point in his life.

The same was true of Mark, the man who described himself as epitomizing for his mother "everything she loathes" because he was "a sexual deviant" and had been having anal sex. Mark believed strongly that his dreams were "inner sources of guidance." On a number of occasions during his interview he expressed his solipsistic philosophy that "one's outer circumstances are just a mirror of your own inner state."

One of his dreams was instrumental of convincing him of this fact. His understanding of the message of this particular dream was that it told him that "it wasn't anything I *had* done which would cause my demise . . . that would kill me . . . it is not a fuck on the Heath or anything like that, but an inner process. . . ." In relating the message of this dream to me Mark inadvertently provided an image of one the places that had strong negative emotional valences for him—the Heath. Hampstead Heath figured strongly in his account of his life as an HIV-positive individual. It became clear that for Mark, the Heath figured analogously to John's memories of San Francisco, as a place connected with insecurity, worthlessness, immorality, and associations with death and danger. The Heath was the place where, in his words, he went to get "fucked rotten" and thus enacted the guilty, internalized image of himself that his mother supplied for him—the sexual deviant having anal sex. That he *did* feel guilty about such actions is apparent in the fact that his dream was trying to convince him otherwise. He also talked at later stages in the interview about HIV-positive gay mens' problems of "self-worth and self-hate . . . which I am not yet free of."

The important point to note, however, is that for Mark the emotional connotations associated with the Heath were in no way wholly negative. For instance, the associations with anal sex and guilt were also simultaneously charged with feelings of exhilaration and pleasure, once again manifestations of a libertarian desire to rebel against societal, especially parental conventions. This was apparent in an episode recounted by Mark when he felt totally oppressed by the "guilt and associated fear" imposed by "doctors" and "other people" who were saying HIV-positive gay men should abstain from having sex. He suddenly said to a friend, "I must take back my sexuality." Thus, "I borrowed someone's leather jacket and I went up to the Heath and I stood by a tree and I would not leave that tree until I got fucked rotten, to put it bluntly. I had to take it back, take the power back for me. . . . through that I have become much stronger. . . . It is not a negative thing, it is very positive, this is *me*, who *I* am." Mark makes clear in this episode that his image of the Heath is positively associated with his rebellion against accepted social values and intrinsically connected with his attempt to assert his own unique identity ("this is me, who I am"). Indeed, his interview narrative revealed that on other occasions when he experienced problems he explicitly went to the Heath to demonstrate to himself his own independence. For instance, Mark described "falling in love" with a man and being totally "committed" to him. During this period of time Mark abstained from sex completely. However, this man "ended up in prison" for reasons that Mark would not reveal, although he did say that he could "crucify him at times for what he has done." When the police came to arrest this guy Mark was "so angry" that he hired a car and thought "I am going to that bloody Heath and I went and I still go." From this story it was clear that, for Mark, the Heath had become a place where he could act in such a way to moderate his unstable sense of self and maintain his own sense of independence. In this way, he used his physical environment to classically maintain the psychic balance of pain and pleasure (Korpela, 1989).

The same was also true of Alicia, a 38-year-old HIV-positive woman. Alicia had established a "safe," orderly, and stable environment for herself over the course of the 12 years in which she had been diagnosed as HIV-positive. She lived a very busy and socially "responsible" life in which she was heavily engaged in volunteer work as well as working full-time in social work. She talked about her HIV-positive diagnosis as having had a very "positive rebound" on her life insofar as it had enabled her to realize the importance of "nurturing" her relationships with family and close friends. She conjured up a positively tinged image of her life "at home" among her "big family" and "my dogs. I talk to them a lot. They are very important to me." Coexisting alongside this positive identification with the safety of home, however, was also a dream of place that revealed a "darker" desire for disorder, irresponsibility, immorality, and freedom from the conventions of her "very privileged environment." This manifested itself in her positive emotional associations with Africa, the place where she was infected with HIV. As she said,

> I have a very positive connection about Africa. I don't know why because I was born in Sweden and it is so different from my own culture

and background. But the first time I went to Africa. . . . the moment I got there I felt good and despite the fact that I was infected there . . . despite the fact that the African man I was infected by has now died . . . despite all the pain of that . . . I have been back to Africa a few times since then . . . and the moment I get off the plane it feels like that is the place I feel most healthy and vibrant and alive, it is quite odd really. A lot of my partners during my lifetime have been black, most of my partners have been black. . . ."

In this quote Alicia describes the feeling of "existential insideness," the "profound centre of human existence" (Relph, 1980) normally associated with home; Africa is the place where she feels most "healthy," "vibrant," and "alive." She proceeded to say that she did not know why she experienced such a positive connection with Africa. She was sure, however, that "it was significant that I was infected there and I still have a black partner" and that she was brought up in a "privileged environment so different to a developing country." Her further emotional associations with Africa also provided a clue to this sense of positive identification. For Alicia, Africa and her Black partner symbolized the "struggle against racism and all the racism around HIV/AIDS and homophobia. . . ." It felt, she said, "like genocide again of black people in Africa, equivalent to slavery and stuff. All of these issues touch me a lot." Alicia's comments made clear that the positive emotional valency attached to her image of Africa and her associated commitment to the struggle against racism served as a necessary disorderly counterbalance to her ordered and privileged lifestyle; they introduced danger, unpredictability, and rebellion into a life that she had self-consciously fashioned along safe lines because of the threat imposed by HIV infection. At the same time it was interesting to note that she protected herself from disconfirmation of her dream of Africa by refusing to move there. Although, for instance, her African partner was keen to move back to Jamaica, Alicia said that "it doesn't feel to me that that is the best place for me to move to."

The final place to be discussed in this chapter is "the City" and the emotional connotations associated with it. John's narrative, in which he experienced and remembered San Francisco in a predominantly negative manner, is one way in which the City is often experienced in contemporary society. This trades on cultural conceptions of the city as a source of harmful psychological and social influences: a site of tension, stress, physical disease, distrust of others, and so forth. In the city "primary" groups and traditions are weakened and states of normlessness, anomie, immorality, and crime persist—thus fostering the worst in human behavior and the social organization of human groups (Proshansky, 1978, p. 148). Operating with such an implicit conception, in their search for "restorative environments" people in contemporary society often turn to what they perceive as a more "natural" environment, a place where they are able to connect more meaningfully with nature, with other people, with themselves—hence the search for a place like Wycliffe, a monastery, or a place signifying greater permanence, a place like "home." However, this negative conception of the City is certainly not universal. A direct counterpart to this image is one of the City, and more specifically of London, as a place of liberation, where the shackles of tradition and convention can be overthrown, leaving the individual free to express him- or herself as she or he sees fit. This was apparent in the case of Sean, whose life of "domesticated bliss" suddenly became "entirely meaningless" to him after he was diagnosed HIV positive. His conception of "home in the middle of the Pennines" became totally negative as he felt the need to share his HIV-positive status with other people, to talk with other people who were in the same situation: "Suddenly I found all the things I wanted to do required me to be near a city center . . . being the only person willing to own (my status) in Yorkshire was a very pressurized experience because I was having to travel 220 miles to London to find somebody else who would share their status with me."

Another gay man, Andrew, expressed the same positive associations with London after receiving his HIV-positive diagnosis when he was in South America. His "first instinct" he said, was to "get back to England, back to London where I had never been before because I thought, well, if there is any hope of dealing with it would be in London. It is right because as soon as you leave London you might as well be on the moon. I have discovered that as far as the kind of knowledge that you can get hold of in London."

These comments corroborate Proshansky's (1978) observations that the City does not necessarily exercise a wholly negative confusing, destabilizing influence on its citizens; rather, it is a place that may actually provide a greater measure of security in times of natural threat and disaster. These HIV-positive individuals certainly characterized the City as a site of safety because it facilitated access to knowledge and information that was unavailable in less "developed" places. Such knowledge also came about through contact with other HIV-positive people, who were willing, in the "safe" context of a large city, to "come out" and talk about their diagnosis, something they were unable to do in the more "restricted," "closed," "prejudiced" context of their "home" environment. This notion of the safety of the City is largely related to the sheer volume of people living there, which in turn gives rise to high degrees of plural and diverse lifestyles and thus a relativity of morals and values not typically found in other places. Sean's appreciation of this diversity was apparent in the following quote:

> Suddenly I discovered there was a whole new range of people whose
> attention and involvement I did need, and it was so surprising at the

time, they weren't all gay middle class men, they were black as well as white, and they were people who were lesbians etc. I suddenly discovered that my horizon wasn't real, it was self-imposed . . . as a matter of gay culture . . . it wasn't real . . . the world was a much bigger place.

The anonymity associated with large cities also, for some people, made them an attractive and "safe" place to live. For instance, Tom, who dreamed of his return to the Caribbean, also realized that life was probably "safer" in Manchester, where "I could lose myself for months." In contrast, "The population of the Caribbean is very small . . . people are very narrow minded and gossip a great deal." These positive associations with the City connect with more recent theorizing in postmodernist circles, which celebrates the "unoppressive city" as "a model of living with diversity" and an emblem of pluralism and freedom (Young, 1990; see also Pratt & Hanson, 1994).

CONCLUSION

This chapter has attempted to explore the "complicated psychological" dimension of place experience (Babineau, 1972.). It has demonstrated the way in which individual experience of place is intertwined with feelings of safety and danger, repression and liberation, "self" and "nonself," "goodness" and "badness." The experiences of place manifest in the biographies of these HIV-positive individuals and the implicit psychological, emotional, and moral dimensions they represent are commonly but implicitly used by all of us in the course of our everyday lives and in our adaptation to various life transitions. We all live with culturally saturated images of places of Paradise and places of Hell. Although to the individual it may seem that his or her place of freedom and authenticity is totally exclusive and personal, the place for such experiences is heavily socially circumscribed (Cohen & Taylor, 1992). The "rebellious" search for authentic selves leads us into various morally dubious "escapades": Travel and sex in "risky" places; "risky" liaisons with the heterogeneous populace of The City. The "backlash" route home is similarly culturally inscribed. When things go wrong or become too much, restorative places and lifestyles abound; abstinence, "the good life," parental home . . . perhaps even a monastery?

REFERENCES

Babineau, G. R. (1972). The compulsive border crosser. *Psychiatry, 35,* 281–290.

Bartlett, J. (1997). The peak of health. *The Guardian,* April 15, p. 11.

Cohen, S., & Taylor, L. (1992). *Escape attempts: The theory and practice of resistance to everyday life.* Routledge: London.

Crossley, M. L. (1997a). "Survivors" and "victims": Long-term HIV positive individuals and the ethos of self-empowerment. *Social Science and Medicine, 45,* 1863–1873.

Crossley, M. L. (1997b). The divided self: The destructive potential of a HIV positive diagnosis. *Journal of Existential Analysis, 8,* 72–94.

Crossley, M. L. (1998a). Sick role or empowerment: The ambiguities of life with a HIV positive diagnosis. *Sociology of Health and Illness, 20,* 507–531.

Crossley, M. L. (1998b). Women living with a long-term HIV positive diagnosis: Problems, concerns and ways of ascribing meaning. *Women's Studies International Forum, 21,* 521–533.

Crossley, M. L. (1998c). A man dying with AIDS: Psychoanalysis or Existentialism? *Journal of Existential Analysis, 9,* 35–57.

Crossley, M. L. (1999a). Making sense of HIV infection: Discourse and adaptation to life with a HIV positive diagnosis. *Health, 3,* 95–119.

Crossley, M. L. (1999b). Stories of illness and trauma survival: Liberation or repression? *Social Science and Medicine, 48,* 1685–1695.

Crossley, M. L. (2000a). *Introducing narrative psychology: The self and the construction of meaning.* Milton Keynes, UK: Open University Press.

Crossley, M. L. (2000b). *Rethinking health psychology.* Buckingham, UK: Open University Press.

Crossley, N. (1996). *Intersubjectivity: The fabric of social becoming.* London: Sage.

Davies, M. (1997). Shattered assumptions: Time and the experience of long-term HIV positivity. *Social Science and Medicine, 44,* 561–571.

Davies, M. L. (1995, March & November). *Interim and final reports to the Health Directorate DGIV of the European Community: An exploration of the emotional, psychological and service delivery needs of people who have been living with a HIV positive diagnosis for five years or more.* Brussels: European Community.

Douglas, M. (1966). *Purity and danger: An analysis of the concepts of pollution and taboo.* Routledge: London.

Falk, A. (1974). Border symbolism. *Psychoanalytic Quarterly, 43,* 650–666.

Heidegger, M. (1962). *Being and time.* Oxford: Blackwell.

Janoff-Bulman, R. (1992). *Shattered assumptions: Towards a new psychology of trauma.* New York: Free Press.

Kaplan, S. (1983). A model of person-environment compatibility. *Environment and Behaviour, 15,* 311–332.

Korpela, K. M. (1989). Place identity as a product of environmental self-regulation. *Journal of Environmental Psychology, 9,* 241–256.

Lefebevre, M. (1991). *The production of space.* Oxford: Blackwell.

Merleau-Ponty, M. (1962). *The phenomenology of perception.* London: Routledge.

Matore, G. (1962). *L'Espace humain.* Paris: La Columbe.

McAdams, D. (1993). *The stories we live by: Personal myths and the making of the self.* New York: Morrow.

Pratt, G., & Hanson, S. (1994). Geography and the construction of difference. *Gender, Place and Culture, 1,* 5–27.

Proshansky, H. M. (1978). The city and self-identity. *Environment and Behaviour, 10,* 147–169.

Relph, E. (1980). *Place and placelessness.* London: Pion.

Sarbin, T. R. (1983). Place identity as a component of self: an addendum. *Journal of Environmental Psychology, 3,* 337–342.

Schama, S. (1995). *Landscape and memory.* London: Harper Collins.

Schutz, A. (1962). *Collected papers. Volumes I and II.* The Hague: Martinus Nijhoff.

Schwartzberg, S. (1993). Struggling for meaning: How HIV positive gay men make sense of AIDS. *Professional Psychology: Research and Practice, 24,* 483–490.

Sebba, R. (1991). The landscapes of childhood: The reflection of childhood's environment in adult memories and in children's attitudes. *Environment and Behaviour, 23,* 395–422.

Swann, W. B. Jr. (1983). Self-verification: Bringing social reality into harmony with the self. In J. Suls & A. G. Greenwald (Eds.), *Psychological perspectives on the self.* Hillsdale, NJ: Erlbaum.

Taylor, S. E. (1989). *Positive illusions. Creative self-deception and the healthy mind.* New York: Basic Books.

Volkan, V. D. (1988). *The need to have enemies and allies: From clinical practice to international relationships.* London: Jason Aronson.

Young, I. M. (1990). The ideal of community and the politics of difference. In L. Nicholson (Ed.), *Feminism/postmodernism* (pp. 300–323) New York: Routledge.

AUTHOR INDEX

Numbers in italics refer to listings in reference sections.

297

Perry, W., 123, *148*
Pervin, L., *31, 251*
Peters, R. S., 55, 66
Petersen, B. E., 11, *32*, 204, *225*
Phillips, S., 151, 153, *172, 174*
Piaget, J., 229, *251*
Pillemer, D. B., 253, *277*
Piorkowski, G. K., 95, *119*
Pitts, R., *252*
Plunkett, M., 152, 161, *174*
Podhoretz, N., 113, *119*
Pratt, A., 228, *251*
Pratt, G., 294, *296*
Pratt, M., 11, *32*, 28, 231, 232, 233, 235,
        236, 239, 241, 249, *250, 251*
Proshansky, H. M., 292, 293, *296*

Quackenbush, S., 233, *250*

Rabin, A. I., *33, 277*
Rahv, P., 55, 66
Rainwater, L., 123, *147*
Randall, J., 11, *33*
Relph, E., 281, 282, 283, 286, 287, 288,
        289, 292, *296*
Reuman, D., *118*
Reynolds, J., 26, *32*
Rice, J. K., 206, *225*
Rice, K. G., 111, *119*, 126, *148*
Ricoeur, P., 39, 66, *202*
Rieff, P., 37, 66
Riessman, C. K., *225*
Ritter, P., 245, *250*
Roberts, D., 245, *250*
Roberts, R., 152, 154, *174*
Robinson, J. A., 39, 47, 52, 66
Rodriguez, R., 113, *119*
Roemer, L., 37, 66
Roese, N. J., 65
Rogoff, B., 232, *251*
Rosenberg, M., 245, *251*
Rosenwald, G. C., 11, 29, *33*, 54, 64, 66,
        98, 117, *119, 149*
Ross, L., 63, 66
Ross, R., 85
Rosselson, R., *33*
Rothbaum, F., 25, *33*
Ruble, D., 247, 248, *251*
Runyan, W., 98, *119*

Russell, D., 111, *118*, 245, *251*
Ruth, J-E, *31*
Ryan, J., 113, *119*, 123, *148*
Ryff, C. D., 11, 27, 28, *31, 33*

Sackrey, C., 113, *119*, 123, *148*
Salovey, P., 11, *33*, 87, 253, 255, 256,
        277
Sampson, E. E., *202*
Sarbin, T. R., 66, 281, *296*
Savage, M., 92, 97, *119*
Savio, M., 43, 66
Schama, S., 282, *296*
Schmidgall, G., 67, 88
Schneider, D. J., 37, 66
Schneidman, E. S., *32*
Schroots, J. J. F., *31*
Schultz, W. T., 74, 88
Schuster, D., 152, *174, 226*
Schutz, A., 281, 283, 287, *296*
Schwartz, M. B., 22, *31*
Sebba, R., 282, *296*
Sennett, R., 93, 111, *119*
Sewell, W., 124, *148*
Shah, V., 124, *148*
Sheed, W., 52, 66
Shotter, J., *202*
Simmons, R. G., 228, *251*
Singer, J. A., 11, *33*, 87, 253, 254, 255,
        256, 259, 273, *277*
Sinisi, C., 233, *250*
Skoe, E. E., *251*
Skolnick, A., 206, *225*
Smelser, N. J., *225*
Smirles, K. A., 11, *32*
Smollar, J., 249, *252*
Snyder, S. S., 25, *33*
Solomon, M., 152, *173*
Sorokin, P. A., 92, *119*
Stacey, J., 206, *225*
Staszkiewicz, M., 156, *174*
Steinberg, L., 232, *250*
Stein, J. A., 96, *119*
Sternberg, R., 88
Stevens, G., 126, *149*
Stevens, E., *147*
Stewart, A., 95, *119*, 158, *174*
Stewart, A. J., 11, 30, *119*, 175, 203, 204,
        205, 217, 223, 224, *225, 226*
Stickel, S., 151, 152, *175*

SUBJECT INDEX

Depression, 29–30, 210, 216–217, 266–267
De Profundis (Wilde), 69–73, 75, 76, 77–78, 83, 85
Divorce, 203–224
Dostoevsky Fyodor, 38, 40, 41, 53. See also Crime and Punishment
Douglas, Lord Alfred, 68–69, 76, 77, 85. See also Wilde, Oscar
Drug use, 253–276

Education. See also Schools, colleges, and universities
    completion and time-out, 159, 163, 165, 169
    generativity and, 11
    liberal education, 123
    parent and student views of education, 121–125, 127–130, 132–140, 145–147
    social mobility, 91–117, 121–147
    women, 152
Emotions. See also Psychology
    anger, 58–59
    international border crossings, 282
    love, 55–56
    morality and, 653
    overruling of, 55
    place and space, 281–282, 284, 286–287
    upward mobility and, 101
Employment, 93–94
Epiphanies and key episodes, 178–180, 256, 257
Epistemology, 154–155, 281
Erikson, E., 94, 142–143, 151–152, 159–160, 221, 229
Ethnic issues. See Racial and ethnic issues

Fairy tales, 17
Family and family system, 95–96, 99, 113–115, 203, 219–220. See also Home and hometown; Parents and parenting; Siblings
Feminism and feminists. See Women's issues
Fitzgerald, F. Scott, 121

Folklore, 17
Freud, Sigmund, 255

Gambling, 269–270, 272
Gender issues, 128. See also Women's issues
Generativity
    contamination sequences and, 19, 22–23, 25
    definition and meaning, 10
    divorce and, 223
    in life stories, 10–18, 255
    parenting and, 223
    redemption sequences and, 16–17, 27
    script, 256
Great Depression, 6–7
Gross Indecency (film), 68

Health issues, 25–26, 279–294
Heath, 290–291
Hemingway, Ernest, 121
Hinduism, 18
HIV. See Human immunodeficiency virus
Holocaust, 43
Home and hometown, 104–106, 112, 286–289, 292
Hoover, J. Edgar, 4–5
Human immunodeficiency virus (HIV), 279–294

Icarus Complex, 22, 67
Identity. See also Psychology; Self
    of addicts, 274
    adolescents, 245
    college students, 91–117
    development of, 96
    ego identity, 94–96
    embeddedness, 112
    HIV-positive diagnosis, 283–284
    life stories and, 38, 41, 62, 230, 253–254, 255–256, 273, 275
    marriage and divorce and, 221, 222
    novice phase of development, 152, 159, 160, 170
    place and space in, 280, 281–283
    redemption and contamination sequences, 28

self-questioning, 210
serendipity and, 167
toleration of uncertainty, 160, 172
upward mobility and, 111–114
women's issues of, 223–224
Importance of Being Earnest, The (Wilde), 67
Improvisation, 158
Intimacy. *See* Relationships
Islam, 18
Isolation, 46

James, Henry, 82
James, William, 17–18, 79, 80, 81, 85, 87
Job, 74
Judas Kiss, The (film), 68

King, Martin Luther, Jr., 1–2, 5

"Legacies of Loss" (Power), 60, 61
LGS. *See* Loyola Generativity Scale
Life cycles and periods, 10, 152
Life stories. *See also* Narratives
    of adolescents, 229
    benefit-finding stories, 25–26
    choice in, 29
    commitment stories, 14–16
    compensatory, 49
    contamination sequences, 18–24
    context of, 63–64
    of highly generative adults, 10–18, 27
    of a heroin addict, 253–276
    identity and, 38, 41, 62, 230, 253–254, 255–256, 273, 275
    interpretation of, 28–29, 62, 273
    life-story interview, 12–13
    life-story therapy, 254
    limitation–remediation script, 17
    narrative form and elements, 24–30, 39–45
    personal fables/myths, 42, 259
    psychological well-being and, 26–28, 254, 273–274
    redemption sequences, 6–18, 27, 241
    self-absolutory narrative, 49–50
    setting and context, 39

Limitation–remediation script. *See* Life stories
Locus of control. *See* Psychology
Loyola Generativity Scale (LGS), 10–11

Marquess of Queensberry, 68, 69, 77
Marx, Karl, 39
Meir, Golda, 152
Men's issues, 153, 157, 246–248, 256–276
Mental health, 11, 213, 282
Mentors and mentoring, 10–11, 111, 121–140, 153, 160
Message in a Bottle: Stories of Men and Addiction (Singer), 256
Michigan Study of Adolescent Life Transitions, 97
Morals and values
    of children and adolescents, 232–233, 247–248
    culture and, 123
    emotion and, 37
    narrative perspective of, 60, 255–256
    in nihilism, 40–41
    personal punishment, 50
    in recovery from addiction, 274
    socialization, 229–230
    space and, 280
    upward mobility and success, 105, 113–114, 116–117
Motivation, 61, 255, 282
Mythology, 22

Napoleon, 41
Narratives. *See also* Life stories
    of adolescents, 227–250
    classification of, 61
    coherence and, 39, 199–200
    complexity of, 255
    conflict, 43–44, 77
    a doctor's career, 177–200
    epiphanies and key episodes, 178–180, 190–193, 256, 257
    ideological setting, 39, 255–256, 270
    integration of, 270
    internalization and, 96–97
    listeners, 199–200
    outcome/denouement, 52–53

Narratives, *continued*
  parental voice, 227–250
  protagonists, 39–45, 77
  quest narrative, 153
  self and, 49–50, 82, 230
  speech and voices in, 179–180,
    181–200
  transmutations of, 60–61
  of turning points, 74–75, 81–83, 86–
    87, 178–180, 190–193, 228–229
  upward mobility, 93
  young women and their careers,
    151–72
  Wilde's crash narrative, 68–73, 82
Narratology, 37–38
Nature and natural environments, 282
Nihilism. *See* Social theory
Nirvana, 18
Nixon, Richard, 43

Occupations, 93–94. *See also* Careers

Paradigms and paradigm shift, 78, 155
Parents and parenting. *See also* Family
    and family system
  adolescents and, 98, 99–102
  authoritative parenting, 232, 245
  of college students, 99–102, 109–11,
    121–122
  of gay men, 287
  generativity and, 11
  parental voice, 227–250
  view of children's development,
    239
Pasteur, Louis, 155
Persephone and Demeter, 17
Personality. *See* Psychology
Picture of Dorian Gray, The (Wilde), 67
Place and space. *See* Identity; Psychology
Plato, 141
Play writing, 76–77
Poetics (Aristotle), 76
Political issues. *See also* Social theory
  60s radicals, 37
  antiwar movement, 36, 40, 42, 43,
    44–45
  generativity and, 11

Power, Katherine Ann
  antiwar movement, 42, 43, 44–45,
    62
  approach to regret, 37, 49, 56–57,
    62–63
  background, 35–36, 38, 39, 40, 42–43
  Catholicism of, 41–42, 45, 53, 56,
    60
  conflicts of, 43–44
  the crime and consequences, 45–52,
    62
  epilogue, 38–39, 55–64
  life story of, 38, 54, 55, 60–63, 64
  love and anger, 57–59
  outcome/denouement, 52–54
  Raskolnikov, Rodion Romanych
    and, 36, 44, 45, 63
  Schroeder, Walter and family 46,
    48, 51, 53, 59–60
  self-concept of, 61–62
  view of killing, 44, 45
Prison, 75. *See also* Wilde, Oscar
Psychology. *See also* Identity; Relation-
    ships; Self
  analysis, 272–276
  borderline personality disorder, 263
  development, 94, 158–160, 203–
    224, 228, 231, 244–245
  dissociative personality disorder,
    258–259
  divorce and, 203
  drug use, 261–262, 272
  ecopsychology, 282*n*
  expectations, 178–179, 180–181,
    184, 187–189, 193–194
  identity, 94–96, 104
  locus of control, 156
  loneliness, 245, 259, 261
  narrative, 37–38
  nature in, 282
  passivity, 156
  personality, 227, 253–254
  place and space, 279–294
  rebellion, 289–294
  serendipity and agency, 153–158,
    164–166, 170–172
  sibling rivalry, 103–104
  thinking and thought, 231
  upward mobility, 91–117
  women's career development, 157–
    158, 165–167

Siblings, *continued*
    cultural capital, 122–123
    education, 123
    marginality thesis, 92
    nihilism, 35, 40–41
    status attainment, 92
    upward mobility, 111–114
    utilitarianism, 35, 40, 41
Sociocultural issues, 229–232
Socioeconomic issues, 121–124, 91–117
"Soul of Man Under Socialism, The"
    (Wilde), 67
Space. *See* Psychology
Stages. *See* Adulthood
Suffering
    and deliverance, 17–18
    effects of, 56–57, 73–75
    pathos of Aristotle, 76
    Wilde, Oscar and, 70, 71–72, 73
Suicide, 49, 58

Terman Genetic Studies, 157, 158
Thinking and thought. *See* Psychology
Transatlantic Blues (Sheed), 52
Transitions
    choices in, 254
    definition and meaning, 73
    divorce, 203
    durability of, 82–85, 87, 254
    "fresh starts," 74
    HIV-positive diagnosis, 279–294
    place and space, 280
    qualia of, 81
    redemption and contamination, 5,
        13
    research and theories of, 73
    to sobriety, 253
    suddenness of, 80–83, 87
    Wilde, Oscar and, 70–87
Trouble and jeopardy. *See* Suffering
Turning points. *See* Transitions

Universities. *See* Schools, colleges, and
    universities

Upward mobility, 91–117, 121–147. *See
    also* Class issues
Utilitarianism. *See* Social theory

Vaillant, G., 254
Values. *See* Morals and values
Varieties of Religious Experience, The
    (James), 17–18, 79
Vietnam War, 36, 40, 42, 43, 44–45

Wilde (film), 68
Wilde, Oscar
    background, 67–68
    De Profundis, 69–73, 75, 76, 77–78,
        83, 85
    Douglas, Lord Alfred and, 68–69,
        76, 77, 85
    epiphany, 78–86
    as playwright, 76
    prison and its effects, 68–69, 75–76,
        83–85
    transition of, 70–85, 86–87
Women's issues
    age differences, 210–221
    career and work, 151–72, 211–213,
        217, 218–219, 220–221
    developmental context, 158–160,
        165, 208–209, 217
    feminism and women's movement,
        154, 156–157, 205, 218
    expectations and roles of women,
        152, 153, 211, 218, 223–224
    relationship considerations, 153,
        164, 172
    serendipity and agency, 153–158,
        164–166, 170–172
    social change and, 205–206
    upward mobility, 93
Wycliffe (England), 285, 289, 290

Zen, 79, 80, 81

ABOUT THE EDITORS

Dan P. McAdams is the Charles Deering McCormick Professor of Teaching Excellence, professor of human development and psychology, and director of the Foley Center for the Study of Lives at Northwestern University. A Fellow of the American Psychological Association (APA) and recipient of the 1989 Henry A. Murray Award, he has published widely on the topics of identity and the self, intimacy, generativity and adult development, and the role of narrative and life stories in personality and developmental psychology. He is author of *The Stories We Live By* (William Morrow, 1993) and *The Person: An Integrated Introduction to Personality Psychology* (3rd ed., Harcourt, 2001) and editor (with Ed de St. Aubin) of *Generativity and Adult Development: How and Why We Care for the Next Generation* (APA, 1998).

Ruthellen Josselson is professor of psychology at The Hebrew University, Jerusalem, on the faculty of the Fielding Institute, and professor emerita from Towson University. Recipient of the 1994 Henry A. Murray Award from the APA and a Fulbright Research Fellowship for 1989 to 1990, she has also been visiting professor at the Harvard Graduate School of Education. She is the author of *Revising Herself: The Story of Women's Identity From College to Midlife* (Oxford University Press, 1996), which received the Delta Kappa Gamma International Educators' Award, and *The Space Between Us: Exploring Dimensions of Human Relationships* (Jossey-Bass, 1992). With Terri Apter, she coauthored *Best Friends: The Pleasures and Perils of Girls' and Women's Friendships* (Crown, 1998). She has also published many scholarly articles on narrative and life-history research.

Amia Lieblich is professor of psychology at The Hebrew University, Jerusalem, where she served as chair from 1982 to 1985. Her books have presented an oral history of Israeli society, dealing with war, military service, prisoners of war, and the kibbutz. Recently she published two psychobiographies of female writers: *Conversations About Dvora* (University of California Press, 1998) and *Towards Lea* (Kibbutz Ha-Meuchad Press, 1995). She has taught graduate courses on life stories and their use in research, and she recently coedited with Rivka Tuval-Mashiach and Tamar Zilber a book that presents her approach to narrative research, focusing on different readings of a life story: *Narrative Research: Reading, Analysis, and Interpretation* (Sage, 1998).